LGBTQ Clients in Therapy

"This beautifully written, accessible book is not just for the straight therapist, every one of whom should purchase a copy. Therapists who identify as LGBTQ also will want Dr. Kort's book because it updates theoretical approaches to thinking about and treating the younger generation who think about sexual orientation differently than their elders. Plus, as an AASECT-certified sex therapist, Dr. Kort includes straightforward information on understanding LGBTQ sexuality that other authors shy away from."

—Stephanie Buehler, PsyD, CST-S, Author, *What Every Mental Health Professional Needs to Know about Sex, 2nd Edition*, Director, The Buehler Institute

"Joe Kort has done his 'Homo-Work.' This updated and informed clinical manual crafts a compassionate narrative for the trauma, drama, and shifting diorama of gender and sexual relationship diversity in America. By naming historical and contemporary psychotherapy ignorance Kort opens the reader's mind to essential psychotherapy skills and practices for today's LGBTQ clients. Thank you for the privilege of reading this book and providing a comment that may interest in the reader in wanting more."

—Douglas Braun-Harvey, MFT, CST, CSTS, The Harvey Institute

A NORTON PROFESSIONAL BOOK

LGBTQ Clients in Therapy

Clinical Issues and Treatment Strategies

Joe Kort

W.W. Norton & Company
Independent Publishers Since 1923
New York • London

Copyright © 2018, 2008 by Joe Kort

Portions of the book were previously published in hardcover as
Gay Affirmative Therapy for the Straight Clinician: The Essential Guide.

All rights reserved
Printed in the United States of America

For information about permission to reproduce selections from this book, write to
Permissions, W. W. Norton & Company, Inc., 500 Fifth Avenue, New York, NY 10110

For information about special discounts for bulk purchases, please contact
W. W. Norton Special Sales at specialsales@wwnorton.com or 800-233-4830

Manufacturing by LSC Harrisonburg
Production manager: Christine Critelli

ISBN: 978-1-324-00048-8 (pbk.)

W. W. Norton & Company, Inc., 500 Fifth Avenue, New York, N.Y. 10110
www.wwnorton.com

W. W. Norton & Company Ltd., 15 Carlisle Street, London W1D 3BS

3 4 5 6 7 8 9 0

This book is dedicated to all the LGBTQ people who have come through my life, professionally and personally. This includes those who abused me and betrayed me for being a gay man, as that gave me the strength to write this book and teach LGBTQ individuals how to be strong. I especially want to thank every straight ally who came to my talks and trainings. This book was influenced by your questions and comments.

Contents

Acknowledgments

First and foremost, I want to thank my partner of 24 years, Mike Cramer. You are my good-luck charm. Ever since we met, my life has totally changed for the better, and has continued to get better ever since. You encouraged me to write and follow my dreams. I cannot imagine any other partner being as supportive as you have been of a partner like me who is so driven to get the words and message out about the lives of LGBTQ individuals and couples. I appreciate your encouragement, support, and love for my dreams—without them, I am not sure I could have done as much. I love you.

Next, I don't know where I would be without the mutual love and respect of my niece and nephews Jacob, Zack, Noah, and Zoe. I never knew how much better the world looks through the eyes of a child. You're growing into mature and beautiful teenagers and young adults. You make me smile.

- Lynn Grodzki, MSW, my private practice and business coach, who has believed in me and in my words and helped me maintain my private practice and write at the same time. You have been very meaningful to me as a coach and a human being.
- Deborah Malmud and the W. W. Norton staff for accepting the idea of a book like this for clinicians and seeing the need for them to have this as a reference when working with lesbians, gays, bisexuals, transgender individuals, and those who are questioning and sexually fluid.
- To Terry Ulch, who is my physical trainer and coach. You are so much more than that to me. You are a mentor and a friend. Thanks for making me stronger and for believing in me.
- To all the clients I have worked with, who have touched my life professionally and

personally. You have made me a better therapist, as I have learned from each and every one of you.

- Every therapist who took my trainings and classes and encouraged me to write a book for them. Your support and encouragement of my work is invaluable.
- I especially want to thank those who helped me with the chapter on being transgender, including Neil Cannon, Nick Zielke, Lucie Fielding, and Kelly Wise. You all helped this chapter be stronger, updated, and informative.
- To Alexander Morgan, my writer and editor, who has helped keep me focused. I could never have revised this book without you. You are brilliant at keeping my voice and making my words more powerful and succinct.

For more information about my workshops, therapy, trainings, supervision, and coaching services, go to www.joekort.com, which provides regular updates and online newsletters.

LGBTQ Clients in Therapy: Clinical Issues and Treatment Strategies

My book *Gay Affirmative Therapy for the Straight Clinician* (*GATSC*) was published in 2008. Only 10 years have passed. Why do we need another book on essentially the same topic? The reason is that so much has changed in the LGBTQ universe in the last decade. This book extends the scope of *GATSC* to give more attention to gay teens and to consider the transgender, bisexual, and sexually fluid clients that *GATSC* hardly discusses at all. This book also acknowledges major shifts in mainstream society's understanding of LGBTQ issues. Gay marriage was not legal in many states in 2008. Now it is the law of the land.

How This Book Is Different From *GATSC*

I regularly give trainings for clinicians on LGBTQ issues in therapy. Ten years ago, my set of PowerPoint slides for these trainings had hardly changed for a decade. Then, suddenly, I found myself changing them on the airplane as I flew from talk to talk to keep them up-to-date.

In fact, there has been a renewed interest in my gay-affirmative trainings over the last 10 years. But now therapists want to know more than the basics about gay and lesbian clients. They also ask me about sexual fluidity and bisexuality, about the special needs of gay teens, and about all the complex issues associated with treating transgender individuals. These are enormously challenging areas, and their associated social, scientific, political, and clinical frameworks are constantly being scrutinized, criticized, and revised.

Therefore, this book—although modeled on *GATSC*—contains completely new chapters on these rapidly evolving areas. In addition, a number of topics in the book have been updated and revised. I now see gay affirmative therapy in terms of the whole LGBTQ spectrum, and the language of this new book reflects that.

On certain topics, I have a radically changed perspective in keeping with new findings in sexual health. I wrote about sexual addiction in the last book, but I have changed my paradigm around working with people with out-of-control sexual behaviors. I no longer see sexual addiction as a useful framework for treatment. In fact, I think it's mostly abusive to gay and bisexual men. I discuss this further in Chapter 9.

I am shocked when I reread *GATSC* at my apparent heterosexist, heteronormative, monoganormative mindset. We in the LGBTQ community have opportunities that straight people don't have. I don't think I honored that reality or recognized it enough in *GATSC*. In this book, I am less afraid to bring up various sexualities, various fluidities, various sexual preferences as healthy possibilities for LGBTQ individuals.

Changes in the LGBTQ Community Since *GATSC* Was Written

I have been noticing a generation gap. For the older generation, there is still an orthodoxy around preferred sexual roles and preferred sexual practices. And there's still a split between the communities. Lesbians keep to themselves and don't want "outsiders." Gays are an island that really doesn't feel connected to the bisexuals. Older-generation gays and lesbians and bisexuals are often not comfortable with transgender individuals.

On the other hand, LGBTQ people who are under 40 are coming together more as a community. Lesbians and gays, for instance, are starting to care about each other and work toward each other's causes. I've even had younger gay people say that they're not bothered by the term "homosexual." They don't have the history of hatred and discrimination that taints the word for those of us who remember how bad things used to be. (The term is generally still considered derogatory by mainstream LGBTQ organizations.)

Several issues for the LGBTQ community have not progressed very much over the last 10 years. Transgender individuals are still not accepted or given support in many gay and lesbian circles (see Chapter 14). Suicide is still a big problem, especially for LGBTQ adolescents (see Chapter 13).

Changes in Mainstream Society

In keeping with the generation gap, younger straight allies of LGBTQ people have become much more active and visible and supportive. School groups like gay-straight alliances are common now, whereas in the past they were rare. It's now cool to have an LGBTQ friend. While many older people have not changed their prejudices, younger people do not seem to be that concerned if someone is LGBTQ.

In fact, the distinction between straight and nonstraight is not maintained with the same rigidity as in the past. Younger adults and teens of all orientations are experimenting with sexual fluidity and gender fluidity. That's a huge change and a fairly recent one.

The Internet, of course, has changed our society in many ways. One is to facilitate communication between the straight world and the LGBTQ world. People are talking about their own lives on the Internet, and it is uncensored and raw. Through Facebook and Twitter and Instagram, people are seeing LGBTQ lives and feeling empathy. The vilification of LGBTQ people has given way to the reality that they are no different from straight people.

One result, I believe, is the legalization of gay marriage, which I didn't expect to happen in my lifetime. I wept when I saw President Obama's White House lit up by spotlights in gay pride colors on the day of the Supreme Court decision.

Another significant change has come through social apps like Grindr, Scruff, and Tinder. We didn't have such ease of connecting when I wrote *GATSC*. These apps certainly challenge conventional therapeutic wisdom about what is "healthy connecting" and what is not. Therapists used to think that if you're online, you're not really connecting in a healthy way. I don't believe that anymore. I think a person can have meaningful friendships that are just online. You can develop a deep connection with people you never meet face-to-face.

A therapist who treats LGBTQ clients needs to be more than just "gay friendly." Gay, lesbian, bisexual, and transgender clients have their own specific issues and needs. Clinical experience and scientific research are advancing rapidly, and the task of being "gay aware" is ongoing in this fast-changing environment.

There's a culture war going on around sexual orientation and identity, both within the LGBTQ communities and between those communities and the straight dominant culture. People are arguing about what it means (and should mean) to be gay, lesbian, bisexual, and queer. So you're going to have clients coming in bashed and confused and disoriented by the cultural controversies and mass shootings and prejudicial laws, and your job will be to help them find their own sexual selves through their own lens, not through a political lens, and not through your lens, either.

This book offers up-to-date information for clinicians treating LGBTQ clients. It is a starting point to understand what your LGBTQ clients will need.

LGBTQ Clients in Therapy

CHAPTER 1

Psychotherapy for LGBTQ People: Setting the Record—Straight!

> Q: *How many therapists does*
> *it take to change a light bulb?*
> A: *Only one. But the light bulb*
> *has to want to change!*

Historically, LGBTQ people were told that their only salvation was to seek good psychotherapy and that they really had to *want* to change. If they weren't highly motivated, they were told, psychotherapy would fail, condemning them to a life plagued by depression that would ultimately end in suicide.

Modern attitudes toward homosexuality, including those in psychotherapy, have religious, legal, and medical underpinnings, and prejudice and misinformation have prevailed over accurate information (Ritter & Terndrup, 2002). The past offers a sad litany of ineffective, wrongheaded treatments for homosexuality, right up to the present-day reparative therapy and sexual reorientation camps. Every such "cure" is based on some faulty etiology, yet the debate of nature versus nurture still rages with regard to the "origins" of homosexuality.

I will generally use *homosexuality* as an umbrella term to include all LGBTQ people. I will often use *gay* as an umbrella term to include all LGBTQ people. The context will be clear when I intend the more restricted meanings of these words. In particular, *gay affirmative* always means "LGBTQ affirmative." *Homophobia* is used to mean "LGBTQ-phobia."

Given this history of pathologizing homosexuality, LGBTQ clients are often understandably wary of psychotherapy and fear hiring a therapist who won't be objective about their gayness. Many seek out LGBTQ therapists, but this isn't necessarily the best step. It's no guarantee that they won't still receive doses of homophobia and heterosexism, as LGBTQ therapists can harbor negative thoughts about gay culture in general, even when they are comfortable with being LGBTQ themselves. It is therefore crucial that clinicians know and understand the history of psychotherapy for LGBTQ people. It is also important to remember that, like other clients, most LGBTQ clients seek therapy for help in dealing with their presenting problems—they don't want to be bothered with what you might do or feel about their sexual orientation.

Even young LGBTQ clients who have not been directly exposed to the harmful effects of psychotherapeutic treatment for homosexuality are still well aware of the historical record. Furthermore, because of societal homophobia, straight therapists may receive negative transference just for being straight. It was, after all, heterosexist straight therapists who pathologized homosexuality as an alternative negative lifestyle.

Although the psychotherapy field has changed dramatically in its attitudes toward homosexuality over the past 60 years, homophobic therapists are still around, often treating patients while keeping their homophobia closeted and hidden—from their clients and even from themselves. Many of these therapists are involved in "reparative" therapy—also known as *sexual reorientation therapy* or *conversion therapy*. While today reparative therapy is judged by most mental health organizations as unethical, and some states are making it illegal, some therapists are still using it to help people "change" from gay to straight. Many of these therapists are religious and call it something other than reparative therapy. This chapter is geared toward helping clinicians treat clients who have directly experienced homophobia from psychotherapists who still use outdated modes of psychotherapy. The more you know and can show you know about LGBTQ history and gay affirmative therapy (GAT), as well as gay affirmative living, the more you will gain the trust of your LGBTQ clients and be able to help them effectively.

Nature or Nurture?

To date, there is no scientific evidence suggesting that homosexuality is either innate or learned. However, science seems to be on the side of biology, where it is probable that hormones and genes play a large role.

Research has indicated that sexual orientation may be related to maternal stress during pregnancy, to high or low prenatal sex hormone levels (either estrogen or testosterone), to an extra gene, to a smaller or larger hypothalamus, and even to different sizes of various sections of the brain (Wilson & Rahman, 2005). There is also growing evidence that the more male children a woman has, the higher the likelihood she will have a gay son. This is attributed to hormones. The best books on this topic are *Born Gay: The Psychobiology of Sex Orientation* (Wilson & Rahman, 2005) and *Gay, Straight, and In-Between* (Money, 1988). Clearly, more research is needed if we are to fully understand the impact of biology on sexual orientation.

Traditionally, psychology viewed homosexuality as a "stage" toward the natural, eventual goal of heterosexuality. There is still a belief among psychologists, social workers, and counselors that homosexuality is just "straight gone bad," and that it is a behavior rather than a true orientation. The belief is that LGBTQ individuals didn't make it out of childhood or adolescence successfully. They are developmentally stalled and somehow damaged, like a moth whose wings did not open fully when it emerged from its cocoon. This theory leads many psychotherapists to believe that in adolescence, young men and women get a second chance to "repair" their homosexuality. But trying to repair something that is not broken does an untold amount of damage to these young people's lives.

During one's teen years, experimenting with homosexual (and heterosexual) behavior is commonplace. Boys may engage in "circle jerks" or perform fellatio on one another, and girls may digitally masturbate each other or kiss to teach each other how to kiss boys. LGBTQ teens experiment both homosexually and heterosexually as well. This is where some of the controversy lies.

The heterosexist perspective viewed homosexual behavior as simply experimentation, because heterosexuality was seen as the natural ending for everyone. Thus, LGBTQ people were viewed as being developmentally stunted at the experimental stage and were accused of being confused, misguided heterosexuals acting out homosexually. Gay affirmative therapy, on the other hand, views homosexuality as the *natural culmination* of a sexual identity—a sexual and romantic development—not as experimentation only.

Psychologists also used to believe that overprotective mothers and absent, distant fathers "made" their sons gay. Sadly, too many parents still believe this and come into therapy thinking they made their child LGBTQ. But these parental attitudes are a reaction rather than a cause. If a mother senses that her infant is "different," she might react by being more protective of him, whereas a father may distance himself from his gay son. A similar impulse to blame the parents occurred with early hypotheses about the causes of schizophrenia. Mothers of schizophrenic adolescents and young adults typically showed little or no signs of attachment, leading psychologists to assume that these "refrigerator moms" were the root of the problem. Subsequent neurobiological research, of course, vindicated these mothers, who were simply reacting to their children's inability to bond with them.

Now that we are more than certain that family constellations do not make a child LGBTQ, we must begin the task of cleaning up the mess that therapy has left. The psychotherapy ghosts of the past still haunt the therapy sessions of today, and clients can be equally vulnerable to archaic thinking and outdated myths that may keep them closeted.

The Case of Ellen

When 16-year-old Ellen came out to her parents, they made an appointment with a straight therapist, Sarah, to discuss ways of helping Ellen be heterosexual. Ellen's parents did not believe that their daughter could know that she was a lesbian at such a young age, and they felt guilty that their parenting had somehow made her think she was a lesbian. Ellen's parents were in their late 40s and had heard that it was the parents who caused a child to be homosexual. Their church had reaffirmed this belief and had told them to pray for their daughter and try to persuade her to seek reparative therapy.

Sarah explained to the parents that current information showed that family constellations do not make a child gay or lesbian, but the parents were not convinced. They still believed it was something they had done, and they insisted that Ellen was too young to know whether she was a lesbian.

Sarah could see the problem. If Ellen's mother and father believed that homosexuality was caused by parenting, accepting Ellen's sexual orientation would automatically make them bad parents. Sarah suggested that if their daughter said she was lesbian, it was to their advantage to take her word for it. She explained that their feelings of accountability made sense given what they had been told throughout their lives, but she also gently told them that the problem was not with Sarah but rather with *them* and their unwillingness to accept their daughter. She followed this by giving them the titles of several current books and referred them to organizations where families of LGBTQ people meet and support one another. Sarah also cautioned them about adding to any suicidal ideation Ellen may have had. She cited the research that lack of parental support is the leading cause of the 30% suicide rate of LGBTQ teens (Massachusetts Youth Risk Behavior Survey Results, 1999; more on this in Chapter 13 on LGBTQ teens).

My Own Therapy

As a 15-year-old in 1978, I met with a psychoanalytic therapist who strongly believed that "homosexual tendencies" resulted from a dominant, smothering mother and a distant, mostly absent father. His theory (shared by most others at the time) was that poor parenting structure could vandalize a young heterosexual toddler and that if homosexuality was not corrected there, it could be corrected during adolescence.

We always argued about whether I was gay. He believed it wasn't my true orientation; I knew it was—and that I could not change, try as I might. To me, however, he was a doctor, an authority figure. So I tried dating a girl named Laurie. While she taught me to French-kiss, I fantasized that she was Billy, a boy in my class whom I was in love with.

I did everything my therapist asked. I tried to establish a stronger relationship with my father. I made efforts to distance myself from my mother. The truth was that my mother had already been doing this for me throughout my life by putting me in situations with other males—mostly through sports—to make a "man" out of me. However, I hated it all. It was not the type of male I knew I was.

Although my therapist's efforts did not make me heterosexual, his encouragement of my being open and frank about my homosexuality helped me grow more comfortable talking about it—and for that I'm grateful. He'd ask me for details of my sexual and romantic interest in boys, and I'd talk to him about it—twice a week, for 3 years. Without his insistence that I talk candidly about my homosexuality and my persistence in getting what I want out of life, I couldn't have come out at as young an age as I did.

Pathologizing Homosexuality: An Overview

The pathologizing of homosexuality in psychiatry and psychology can be traced back to religious edicts and beliefs, which were eventually incorporated into legal sanctions, including stiff criminal penalties for sodomy (Silverstein, 1991). Before the 19th century, neither medicine nor psychiatry universally viewed homosexuality as pathology, but by the end of the 1800s, these disciplines were effectively competing with religion and the law for jurisdiction over sexuality (Herek, 2006a). As a consequence, discourse about homosexuality expanded from the realms of sin and crime to include that of pathology.

Many people believe that it was Freud who related homosexuality with psychopathology. This is not true. It was Freud's followers who interpreted his studies of homosexuality as indicating pathology. I first learned about this in Kenneth Lewes's *The Psychoanalytic Theory of Male Homosexuality*. Lewes wrote that Freud seemed to have been undecided on the relationship between homosexuality and psychopathology and that much of what is attributed to Freud's thinking is taken out of context. Lewes found in his research that "Freud's own attitude toward homosexuality included a profound respect for the achievements of homosexuals as well as an interest in the way homosexuality threw a new light on more usual behaviors and orientations taken for granted" (1988, p. 34).

Dr. Gregory Herek, a professor of psychology at the University of California at Davis and an authority on prejudice against lesbians and gay men, hate crimes and antigay violence, and AIDS-related stigma, wrote that Freud's basic theory of human sexuality was that all human beings are innately bisexual, and that they become heterosexual or homosexual as a result of their experiences with parents and others (Herek, 2006a). Unlike many who tout the "nurture" explanation of homosexuality, however, Freud believed that a homosexual orientation should not be viewed as a form of pathology. In a now-famous letter to an American mother in 1935, Freud wrote:

> Homosexuality is assuredly no advantage, but it is nothing to be ashamed of, no vice, no degradation, it cannot be classified as an illness; we consider it to be a variation of the sexual function produced by a certain arrest of sexual development. Many highly respectable individuals of ancient and modern times have been homosexuals, several of the greatest men among them (Plato, Michelangelo, Leonardo da Vinci, etc.). It is a great injustice to persecute homosexuality as a crime, and cruelty too. . . .
>
> If [your son] is unhappy, neurotic, torn by conflicts, inhibited in his social life, analysis may bring him harmony, peace of mind, full efficiency whether he remains a homosexual or gets changed. (Jones, 1957, pp. 208–209)

"Advances" in Psychotherapy

It was Freud's psychoanalytic followers, not Freud himself, who expounded on the homonegativity they interpreted from his writings (Lewes, 1988). Some analysts argued that homosexuality resulted from pathological family relationships during the oedipal period (around 4 to 5 years of age) and claimed that they observed these patterns in their homosexual patients. Dr. Bieber is known for contributing to the myth that male homosexuals are a result of "close-binding intimate mothers and detached fathers." In a 1962 research study, he gave a 500-item questionnaire to

106 male homosexuals, with a comparison group of 100 male heterosexuals (Bieber et al., 1962). He believed the outcome proved that family constellation caused homosexuality.

In the documentary film *One Nation Under God* (Maniaci & Rzeznik, 2004), there is a black-and-white clip of the antigay Dr. Bieber talking to a class of psychiatry students in the 1960s. A student asks him if there is such a thing as a "happy homosexual." The good doctor responds by saying, "An *obligatory* homosexual can never be happy, so there is no such thing as a 'happy homosexual.'"

Another analyst practicing during the 1960s, Charles Socarides, speculated that the etiology of homosexuality was preoedipal and, therefore, even more pathological than had been supposed by earlier analysts (Drescher, 1996). Socarides also espoused the notion that family-of-origin dynamics produced homosexuality, as he noted in his 1968 book, *The Overt Homosexual*: "The family of the homosexual is usually a female-dominated environment wherein the father was absent, weak, detached or sadistic. This furthers feminine identification. The father's inaccessibility to the boy contributed to the difficulty in making a masculine identification" (quoted in Drescher, 1996, pp. 158–159; Socarides, 1968, p. 38). (In an interesting, later turn of events, Charles Socarides's son became an openly gay activist in LGBTQ rights. I wonder what kind of father Socarides would now portray himself as!)

Another contributing factor to the pathologizing of homosexuality was that psychological studies only examined homosexuals who were *already* under psychiatric care. Patients, however, are not necessarily representative of well-adjusted individuals in the general population. Just as it would be inappropriate to draw conclusions about all heterosexuals based only on data from heterosexual psychiatric patients, we cannot generalize from observations of homosexual patients to the entire population of LGBTQ people.

It is also important to note that although psychoanalytic theories of homosexuality have had considerable influence in psychiatry and in the larger culture, they have not been subjected to rigorous empirical testing (Herek, 2006a). Instead, they have been based on analysts' clinical observations of patients they already knew to be homosexual. Overall, it seems that the negative framing of homosexuality by the mental health field has been the result of theoretical orientations, expectations, and personal attitudes that biased clinicians' observations of LGBTQ clients (Gould, 1995).

Given the homophobia and prejudice throughout the 20th century, it is not surprising that LGBTQ professionals in social work, psychology, psychiatry, and other mental health fields worried about exposure and losing their jobs. Many who were closeted stayed away from out LGBTQ professionals, who were growing in numbers by the late 1960s. As Silverstein (1991) noted in *Gays, Lesbians, and Their Therapists*, a handful of brave gay and lesbian psychotherapists were essentially banned from employment and psychoanalytic training. Many of these clinicians applied to and were accepted by programs in Gestalt training, which was a more radical approach for therapy at the time and more liberal in admitting therapists.

Historic Treatment of Homosexuality

Historically, the most common treatments for homosexuality were aversion therapies such as electroshock treatments, castration, hysterectomy, clitoridectomy, lobotomy, and various drug and hormone therapies (especially on women). Sometimes drugs were used to induce vomiting while patients were shown images of members of the same sex in various states of undress. Other treatments involved showing pictures of partly unclothed individuals of both sexes and applying shock therapy when the patient chose the "wrong" picture (i.e., that of the individual of the same gender as the patient). The aim was to achieve asexual or heterosexual orientation as a means to relieve the homosexual orientation.

These "treatments" for homosexuality (except lobotomies) are still being used today in treatment centers and inpatient hospitals (often religious) around the country by those who are practicing reparative therapy.

These are just a few examples of the brutality of the various treatments employed to cure homosexuality. For a more in-depth look at these treatments, see Martin Duberman's (1991) *Cures: A Gay Man's Odyssey*, and the previously mentioned documentary *One Nation Under God.*

Changing Views

A few people and events have been responsible for the changing views in the field of mental health as it relates to homosexuality. Those individuals who made the most change did not have a bias but more of a heuristic approach to understanding homosexuality. Perhaps the biggest force for change toward viewing homosexuality as a healthy lifestyle came from LGBTQ individuals themselves, who broke the silence and began sharing their lives and pointing out that most were not in therapy and had developed happy, healthy lives, adjusting well to their sexual and romantic orientations.

Today, the media, including social media, and the Internet seem to be the biggest contributors to changing views overall. LGBTQ teens and adults are using social media for coming out before seeking support from their friends and family. LGBTQ individuals are using Facebook, Instagram, and other social media outlets to talk about their lives openly and honestly, which helps non-LGBTQ individuals become educated and empathic toward the issues facing the LGBTQ community.

Alfred Kinsey

Dr. Alfred C. Kinsey, a pioneering researcher on sexual orientation, originator of the Kinsey scale and subject of the 2004 film *Kinsey*, suggested that most people's sexual behavior exists on a continuum from heterosexuality to homosexuality. Up to the time of his research in the late 1940s, much of the antigay prejudice and misinformation was specifically about gay men. Kinsey's books, by contrast, included information about women as well, and attempted to clear up some harmful misconceptions (Kinsey, Pomeroy, Martin, & Gebhard, 1953). Kinsey and his colleagues reported that 10% of the males in their sample and 2%–6% of the females (depending on marital status) had been more or less exclusively homosexual in their behavior for at least 3 years between the ages of 16 and 55 (Kinsey, Pomeroy, & Martin, 1948). This research situated sexuality on a more normative level and helped pave the way for dismantling myths about homosexuality.

In the field of psychotherapy, this continuum from straight to gay (known as the Kinsey scale) has been largely ignored until more recently as bisexuality and sexual fluidity have become better understood. More on the Kinsey scale in Chapter 15.

Evelyn Hooker

Evelyn Hooker's well-known 1957 study suggested that homosexuality as a clinical entity does not exist and that homosexuality is not inherently associated with psychopathology. Rather than simply accepting the predominant view of homosexuality as pathology, Hooker posed the question of whether homosexuals and heterosexuals differed in their psychological adjustment. She recruited a sample of homosexual men who were functioning normally in society, rather than studying psychiatric patients, and she employed a procedure that asked experts to rate the adjustment of men without prior knowledge of their sexual orientation.

This method addressed an important source of bias that had vitiated many previous studies of homosexuality. Hooker ultimately found that, in terms of psychological adjustment, you could not tell the difference between men who were homosexual and men who were heterosexual.

Stonewall

Another important development contributing to the depathologizing of homosexuality was the event known as Stonewall. Stonewall was a gay bar in New York City's Greenwich Village. Like many other gay bars across the United States, Stonewall was frequently raided by police, who arrested and accused patrons of lewd conduct. These bars would be shut down for serving alcohol without a liquor license. But one night in 1969 during a routine raid, the patrons of Stonewall rioted against the police, protesting being arrested for doing nothing wrong. There are many stories and fables about what happened that night at Stonewall, and it has continued as an enduring marker of advances in gay and lesbian civil rights. (The best overview and compilation of accounts from sources who were there is the 1993 book *Stonewall* by Martin Duberman.) Much of gay and lesbian life is talked about in terms of "before Stonewall" and "after Stonewall." It remains a landmark symbolizing the point at which LGBTQ people declared, "We are not going to take it anymore!"

The *DSM* and Homosexuality

In 1973, the weight of empirical data, coupled with changing social norms, led the board of directors of the American Psychiatric Association to remove homosexuality from the *Diagnostic and Statistical Manual of Mental Disorders* (*DSM*). In 1980, in the third edition of the *DSM*, the term *ego-dystonic homosexual* was created to describe clients who are uncomfortable or in conflict with their homosexuality and want to change their orientation. Typically, clients would report that homosexual urges were interfering with their lives and that a lack of heterosexual arousal interfered with the clients' desired lifestyles. The opposite term, *ego-syntonic homosexuality*, was used to acknowledge the significant numbers of gays and lesbians who were quite satisfied with their sexual and romantic orientation and showed no signs of psychopathology.

Ego-dystonic homosexuality remained in the *DSM-III* until 1987, when the manual was revised as *DSM III-R*. The board concluded that *all* gays and lesbians start out as ego-dystonic (that is, uncomfortable with their orientation), but upon fully coming out, they become ego-syntonic.

The *DSM-IV* (1994) didn't include homosexuality as a disorder but still permitted a diagnosis of "Sexual Disorder, Not Otherwise Specified" for anyone with "persistent and marked distress about sexual orientation"—the same diagnosis used for sexual addiction and compulsivity. The *DSM-V* has completely eliminated both.

As a social worker and a gay man I knew that in 1973 homosexuality was removed as a disorder from the *DSM*. What I did not know was that gay political pressure did *not* play a role in the APA's decision to have it removed, a myth that was popularized by the antigay therapists Irving Bieber and Charles Socarides. In reality, the decision was "influenced by the weight of scientific studies" and put into effect by a vote by the APA board of trustees with two abstentions (Drescher & Merlino, 2007).

Today's Psychoanalysts

Psychoanalysts today have changed a great deal. Author and psychiatrist Richard Isay helped make it possible in 1991 for openly gay men and women to be accepted into analytic institutes (Drescher & Merlino, 2007). Isay's books *Becoming Gay* (1994) and *Being Homosexual* (1996) had a profound effect in advancing analytic circles to embrace LGBTQ analysts and clients.

The approach to treating LGBTQ clients has changed as well. The psychoanalytic community has shown LGBTQ clients that it no longer considers homosexuality a disorder. The message is getting out, but much suffering and anger persist from the damage done to victims of past misguided psychoanalytic views. Many who felt abused by psychoanalysis went to other, more accepting therapeutic approaches such as Gestalt and humanistic therapies. Some, however, did not, as in the case of Rob who ultimately goes to a humanistic therapist.

The Case of Rob

Rob, a heterosexually married, 55-year-old schoolteacher with four children, spent 20 years with an orthodox psychoanalyst. During sessions, Rob laid on a couch behind his analyst, who worked to help him not give in to his "pathological" homosexual tendencies. Rob was closeted to everyone but himself—and his analyst.

Rob terminated his psychoanalysis and met with a new, humanistic therapist, Sally, shortly after a session in which the psychoanalyst made a startling comment. "After 20 years," Rob told Sally, "my analyst turns around and we face each other. With grief in his eyes and sadness on his face, my analyst has the nerve to say to me, 'I am sorry, Rob. I have been wrong. You are gay and I have done you a disservice trying to make you straight. You are not heterosexual. I believe you are gay.' What was I supposed to do with that?!" Rob asked Sally, with anger in his voice. "I knew he couldn't change me—I told him that the day we met! But I wanted to believe him and I wanted to be changed."

The following few months of therapy with Sally were difficult for Rob. He missed the language and free-associating of psychoanalysis, and he was not used to being directed or coached by a therapist. When Rob began criticizing Sally, she responded by defending her approach and trying to educate him on humanistic psychotherapy, but this just made him even angrier.

Rob then began criticizing Sally about not being lesbian. "I think I need a gay therapist, but are they any good?" he asked. "How are they trained? Are there any analysts who can help me come out and not fight me on who I am?" Clearly Rob was angry, grieving, and placing negative transference onto Sally.

Sally contacted me for a referral and told me Rob had been difficult. She thought he might have borderline personality disorder because of his continuous anger and criticism of her and her work. I agreed to evaluate the client to see if I could work with him, but when Sally presented this option to Rob, he said he did not want to leave Sally completely. Instead, he agreed to attend my gay men's group therapy and continue to see Sally for individual therapy.

I set up an initial evaluation with Rob to make an assessment about a possible borderline diagnosis, as I do not place personality-disordered individuals in group therapy. Immediately upon sitting down in my office, Rob said to me, "You are 20 years younger than I am, and look at you! You are an out gay man, you have a partner, a successful practice, and pride in who you are. I am older, closeted, and spent the best parts of my life—and a lot of money—trying to change who I am." He said he was not mad at Sally or me—he was mad at his analyst and angry about his lost years. He talked about his analyst's trying to be the "good father" but letting him down just like his birth father had done. He wondered now if I was going to let him down too.

It was obvious that Rob had a tremendous amount of negative and positive transference toward me, but he did not seem to have any characterological disorders. We all agreed it was a good move to put him in the gay men's group and continue seeing Sally. Sally and I both knew that his decision to continue seeing her was a way of keeping his foot in the door to heterosexuality, but neither of us acknowledged that to him, as we wanted to allow him to have that insight for himself.

Rob: Clinical Interpretation and Treatment

I quickly normalized Rob's anger about the lost years spent in analysis regarding his homosexuality. He was right that he could have been an out gay man much earlier had he not been in psychoanalysis. Although he was close to his four children and was grateful for them, he was not particularly fond of his wife.

He talked for months about nothing else but his past therapy and how he felt betrayed, misled, and manipulated. I helped the group relate to the homophobia and the trust they put in the hands of other professionals—and family—who wanted them to be gay. It took Rob a year before he felt that he could trust anyone in the group or even me. It took another year before he felt like he finally belonged.

Group therapy for Rob was about calling into question everything he'd learned in psychoanalysis and identifying what parts were good and helpful and what parts were not. This questioning caused much stress and duress for him. Rob also role-played talking to his former therapist and telling him how angry he was. This took a while to get him to do; he minimized the efficacy of role-playing, as he had never done this before in therapy and saw it as contrary to therapy norms. Although the group and I encouraged him to go back to his former therapist to talk to him face-to-face, Rob saw this as too tall a task. His anger and depression worsened as he thought about how he should come out and what it would do to his wife and now-adult children.

I encouraged Rob to talk about how his family of origin had let him down as well. He talked about how his father had made fun of him for being a "sissy" and a "mama's boy." For years, he had thought that this was what had made him gay, but he was beginning to realize that this was not true.

Rob began stating his jealousy, envy, and anger toward other group members, saying things like, "At least you have someone and a supportive family," and "Why are you complaining? You are young and have all this time to change your life!" I interpreted these comments for Rob as negative transference and helped him reflect back to himself what the comments meant. I created a safe place for the group to hear him and for him to be able to speak openly and honestly about the loss of time, opportunities, and experiences that he could have had as a younger gay man. His projections were that everyone's lives were better than his, and he spent much of the time staying in the victim role.

Over time, however, Rob was able to get past his victimhood. He came to realize that he could come out and move forward in the time he had left. It was not easy, but he eventually told his wife he was gay and started his coming-out process socially.

Today's Antigay Therapists and Therapies

There are still therapists today who view being gay as a disorder that needs to be changed or cured via so-called reparative therapy. Even though *all* the major mental health professions—the American Counseling Association, the American Psychiatric Association, the American Psychological Association, and the National Association of Social Workers—have gone on record to say that reparative therapy is unethical and should never be implemented, it is still being done.

Too many LGBTQ people find themselves drawn to "reparative" therapies (especially in the early stages of coming out; see Chapter 7) that supposedly will "return" them to heterosexuality, with all its privileges and status. Reparative therapies assume that LGBTQ people aren't fully developed, that there's some inherent flaw in being gay. In my judgment, this is abuse—specifically, covert cultural sexual abuse, a subject I address in Chapter 4.

Reparative therapy, also known as conversion therapy, was developed in 1991 by Dr. Joseph Nicolosi, who until his death in 2017 sought to help clients change their sexual orientation. His website's tagline is "If gay doesn't define you, you don't have to be gay" www.josephnicolosi.com). Nicolosi and his followers theorized that a "failure to fully gender-identify" with members of the same gender leads to a "deficit in sense of personal power," causing a homosexual identity (Nicolosi, 1997, p. 212). Because reparative therapy views homosexuals as "sexually broken," Nicolosi purposefully avoided using affirmative words like *gay*, *bisexual*, and *lesbian*, which don't reflect the negative connotation that *homosexual* does. Dr. Nicolosi appeared on *Dr. Phil* (2009), where he shamed the mother of a transgender child, accusing her of being overly smothering and attached to her child, contributing to the child's transgender identity.

Nicolosi formed the National Association for Research and Therapy of Homosexuality in 1992. In 2016, it was revamped with a new website, a new campaign, and a new name—the NARTH Institute. NARTH claims considerable success in changing homosexual clients' orientation and pathologizing transgender identity. NARTH's primary goal is to provide psychological therapy to all LGBTQ men and women who seek to change (www.narth.com). Furthermore, the institute wishes to open for public discussion all issues relating to homosexuality and those who are transgender. It serves as a division of the brand-new Alliance for Therapeutic Choice and Scientific Integrity (ATCSI; therapeuticchoice.com).

Those who go through these types of therapies and programs call themselves "ex-gays." In his book *Anything But Straight*, author Wayne Besen explains the histories of—and differences between—ex-gay groups like Exodus, Courage, and Homosexuals Anonymous (Besen, 2003). Exodus closed its doors in 2013, and one of its board members, Alan Chambers, posted the following announcement:

> I am sorry for the pain and hurt many of you have experienced. I am sorry that some of you spent years working through the shame and guilt you felt when your attractions didn't change. I am sorry we promoted sexual orientation change efforts and reparative theories about sexual orientation that stigmatized parents. (Snow, 2013, para. 4)

Each of these groups, along with reparative therapy, use religion as a primary form of healing. Exodus professed to "cure" homosexuals' broken sexuality and to help them become more male or female. Courage gives "the gift of chastity," according to Besen, and was founded by the Catholic Church. Homosexuals Anonymous (HA) was begun by a man named Colin Cook.

Reparative therapies hinge on several basic concepts, among them "same-sex ambivalence" and "gender rejection." Coined by reparative therapists, this terminology is "a veil that thinly disguises their contempt for same-sex relationships" (Drescher, 1998, p. 170). "Same-sex ambivalence" is based on the erroneous belief that two people of the same gender are "looking for parenting through each other, yet they cannot provide parenting to each other, as they are both damaged" (Besen, 2003, p. 102). "Gender rejection" is about "defensive detachment" from one's gender, where "boys will avoid sports and girls will shun their femininity and embrace more masculine endeavors, such as fixing cars" (pp. 101–102).

Today's reparative therapists are getting savvier about what they call their work and the words they use to describe it. They are aware that the public is catching on to the fact that their work is disrespectful toward LGBTQ individuals. They now use terms like *unwanted same-sex attractions* rather than *ex-gays*.

Sadly, some individuals who identify themselves as having unwanted same-sex attractions enter into therapy for "sex addiction," their same-sex attractions being classified as addiction, and find sex-addiction therapists willing to treat them. They learn to attribute their same-sex attractions to trauma, and they follow a 12-step treatment model to fight it. This is nothing more than a new form of reparative therapy. I will speak more about this in the part of Chapter 7 where I discuss the early stages of coming out.

I actually don't totally disagree with the concept of people recognizing that they are LGBTQ but deciding not to embrace the identity. You will read about cases in this book where LGBTQ clients cannot adopt an affirmative lesbian, gay, or bisexual identity (or express their trans identity or queerness) and do not choose or wish to do so. I have helped many men and women who have a "homosexual" orientation—but do not wish to adopt a gay, lesbian, or bisexual identity or lifestyle—live a heterosexual or celibate lifestyle. For them, coming out as lesbian, gay, or bisexual would mean more trauma. Similarly, the way individuals express their trans identity will vary with how they choose to live. However, these individuals cannot change their innate sexual and gender orientations. Therefore, putting them at odds with their sexual orientations by using reparative therapy or "sex addiction" therapy only makes things worse for them. You can't choose your orientation, but you can choose how you will live and whom you will love.

This is, of course, a complex and hotly debated issue, with people at one extreme declaring that there is no such thing as a "happy homosexual" and people at the other extreme insisting that homosexuality is the *only* right choice for LGBTQ people. I believe, however, that there are many shades of gray between these polarized views, which I hope this book illuminates.

Top 10 Myths About LGBTQ People

It is important for this book to debunk the myths about LGBTQ people, so that you are aware of them and do not allow them to get in the way of your work with the LGBTQ population. Being overtly aware of the myths can help clinicians challenge personal beliefs that stem from what they learned early in their careers and even from childhood.

Myth 1: Being LGBTQ results from stunted, immature sexuality. Any stunting that occurs in relation to being LGBTQ results from a lack of permission to explore and express one's true orientation or gender. Beginning in childhood, the sexual development of LGBTQ individuals is neglected, and LGBTQ children (and adults) receive numerous developmental insults (see Chapter 6). They are shamed for being what they are. GAT asks, What is *wrong* with a boy being effeminate or a girl being tomboyish? Certain actions or appearances do not define masculinity or femininity. Also, this concept fails to take into account the fact that there are many *heterosexuals* who are sexually immature or stunted in their gender development.

Myth 2: Homosexuality is caused by a smothering, overprotective mother and an absent, emotionally distant father. As I noted earlier, a mother can tell very early on that there's something different about her child. She may become more protective of him or her to prevent any teasing and playground abuse. The father, sensing that his son or daughter might be nonstraight, will distance himself, seldom knowing exactly how to react. Children are born with their sexual and gender identities, and parents can only react to those identities, not create them.

Myth 3: Acquainting children with LGBTQ individuals and teaching them about homosexuality can change their gender or sexual orientation. Perhaps one of the biggest myths is that a child can be swayed by a homosexual role model. This myth is the main argument behind the claim that LGBTQ individuals should not raise children, who will perhaps be influenced by their parents to "choose" a gay lifestyle.

Research confirms that heterosexuality is not that fragile and children can handle knowledge and exposure to nonstraight people. In fact, studies show that children of openly LGBTQ parents grow up more tolerant and accepting of differences. These children do experiment more with gender-nonconforming behaviors than children raised by heterosexual parents, but their orientation remains stable in terms of what they are innately. The truth is that all children should be able to grow up exploring their own sexuality and learn for themselves what their sexual and gender orientation is.

Myth 4: Being sexually abused in childhood can turn a person LGBTQ. This is not true. I always say, "Sexual abuse can disorient you, but it will not orient you." Early sexual abuse can't shape sexual orientation, but it can shape sexual *behavior* and confuse individuals as to their real orientation. If a boy is sexually abused by an adult male, when the boy grows up, he may unconsciously respond to his own abuse by seeking sex with other men. We call this *trauma reenactment.* This is not innate homosexuality, as it is based only on behavior. I will talk more about it in Chapter 16.

Women sexually abused at an early age by male perpetrators might seek out women for romantic and sexual relationships to avoid reexperiencing the trauma that was originally perpetrated onto them by men. For lesbians, this can spark an earlier awareness of an innate lesbian orientation, but it does not *create* that orientation: These women would be lesbian even if they had not been abused. Innately heterosexual women who were abused and later partner with women might eventually return to relationships with men. There is a link between early sexual trauma and later sexual acting out, which can include same-sex behavior, but it has nothing to do with orientation. After psychotherapy helps clear away the trauma, the imprinted sexual behavior often subsides and the client's true orientation—gay, lesbian, bisexual, or straight—can surface.

Myth 5: LGBTQ orientation can be prevented or cured. No matter how gentle or loving a parent may be, trying to prevent or forestall homosexuality inevitably ends up harming a child, causing gender dysphoria, depression, or low self-esteem. In my office, countless LGBTQ individuals have shed tears as they recalled how a parent took away their "inappropriate" toys or imposed stereotypical gender behaviors. As adults, LGBTQ people who engage in "reparative therapies" experience high rates of relapse and suffer a considerable amount of trauma due to these therapeutic approaches.

Religious fundamentalists and reparative therapists assert that no one is born homosexual. Heterosexism teaches that everyone is or should be heterosexual. GAT, on the other hand, assumes that we are all born with a certain sexual and gender orientation, just as we are born with a given temperament.

Myth 6: People can choose to change their orientation. People *can* choose to live as they wish, but orientation, like temperament, is stable. Children are born with a temperament and personality traits that can shift somewhat as they grow into adulthood. They can learn to modify and adapt to their environments, but their core temperament and personality stays largely within the same range.

The same is true of sexuality. People can mimic a heterosexual lifestyle, but they cannot change their true orientation. Study after study shows that for those who do try to change, the relapse rate is very high. Those who "succeeded" at changing were *not* essentially homosexual to begin with but rather were either acting out past sexual abuse or were bisexual, tending more toward heterosexuality than homosexuality. Their basic orientation did not change.

This myth arises because of the seeming suddenness of an LGBTQ individual's coming out of the closet. For the LGBTQ person, of course, making the decision to come out can take months or years, but to those who are hearing about their friend or family member's homosexuality for the first time, it seems like the person was straight one day and LGBTQ the next. People then assume that one can change one's orientation consciously. But if young people felt free to explore sexual and romantic orientations (which today's teenagers and young adults in college are doing increasingly), they would not need to suppress their innate sexuality and could come out earlier rather than later.

However, there really is a phenomenon of "sexual fluidity," which is also not about changing sexual orientation. A person might at one time or another experience sexual interest in a person who is not the gender expected from their natural orientation. This variation in desire is not intentional and does not reflect an ability to change sexual orientation. It represents a person's evolving sexuality, often depending on specific individuals and circumstances. This will be discussed further in Chapter 16.

Myth 7: Adolescence offers a "second chance" at heterosexuality. Many teens experiment during adolescence: Straight kids try out same-sex relationships, and LGBTQ kids try out the opposite sex. This is a normal part of the developmental process. But this investigation doesn't prove that teens are interested in converting to a new orientation. Each teenager ultimately discovers his or her true orientation if allowed to do so, no matter how much experimenting and exploring is done. Again, orientation is predetermined.

Myth 8: LGBTQ refers merely sexual behavior. Being LGBTQ is not limited simply to sexual behaviors. It is also about attraction, attachment, and identity—psychological, emotional, mental, and spiritual. Behavior follows from all aspects of a person's humanity.

Myth 9: LGBTQ is an "alternative lifestyle." Calling LGBTQ an "alternative" implies that being straight is standard for everyone. Since childhood, we are taught the negative belief that being LGBTQ is a more difficult way to live. But for an LGBTQ person, pretending to be heterosexual or pretending to be the wrong gender is actually more difficult and can lead to depression and self-defeating, or even self-destructive, behaviors.

Myth 10: Nonstraight relationships don't last. LGBTQ relationships do last and can endure—just like their heterosexual counterparts. There is less support for these relationships in terms of the law, religion, and sometimes family, which puts the relationships at risk. But just like healthy heterosexual relationships, healthy LGBTQ relationships that are based on good communication, validation of one's partner, and respect for each other's differences can and do survive.

CHAPTER 2

What Is Gay Affirmative Therapy?

It is prejudice to be only gay friendly. You must be gay informed.
—Joe Kort

Many straight therapists who say they are "gay affirmative" mean that they are gay positive or gay friendly. They tell LGBTQ clients things like, "I'm open-minded," and "People are people." These well-intentioned therapists are, indeed, accepting and pro-gay—but they're also uninformed. Even LGBTQ therapists may be uninformed (Kort, 2004). Over the years, I've known well-meaning LGBTQ colleagues and students who were unaware of the specific issues that LGBTQ individuals face. They've said they didn't realize there were stages to coming out, or that there were differences between gay, lesbian, bisexual, and straight couples. Often, they confused issues of sexual identity and issues of gender identity—for example, confusing the needs of transgender clients with those of gender-nonconforming clients who are not transgender.

To be uninformed is a form of prejudice and a microaggression by omission. Having a healing, affirmative stance in the therapy room does help relieve some of the distorted thinking that most clients bring in, but having an affirmative stance *without* being informed about the specific issues of LGBTQ individuals limits your clinical effectiveness.

The first time the term *gay affirmative* was used was in an article by Alan Malyon (1982) in which he described the most complete definition of gay affirmative therapy:

Gay affirmative psychotherapy is not an independent system of psychotherapy. Rather, it represents a special range of psychological knowledge which challenges the traditional view that homosexual desire and fixed homosexual orientations are pathological. . . . This approach regards homophobia, as opposed to homosexuality, as a major pathological variable in the development of certain symptomatic conditions. (pp. 68–69)

In essence, Malyon coined the term by giving a name to a concept already used in journals and books when explaining how to use psychotherapy techniques with lesbians and gays without stigmatizing these clients. (And we have since extended these insights to all LGBTQ clients.) The two books that were already published at the time were *Loving Someone Gay* by Donald Clark (2004) and Betty Berzon's *Positively Gay* (2001). These books advocated improving the lives of lesbians and gay men without regarding homosexuality as pathological. These two books were the first to advocate GAT for gays and lesbians without actually using the term.

GAT takes the position that there is nothing inherently wrong with being LGBTQ. What's wrong is what is *done* to LGBTQ individuals by a homophobic, homo-ignorant society and heterosexist therapy. Living in a shame-based culture creates a variety of behavioral and psychological disorders. GAT focuses on repairing the harm done to these clients, helping them move from shame to pride. GAT does not in itself constitute a specific system of psychotherapy but rather is meant to provide a framework that informs psychotherapeutic work with LGBTQ clients (Friedman & Downey, 2002).

In and of itself, an LGBTQ orientation does not *create* disorders. Religions condemn LGBTQ individuals as having no hope for salvation. Imagine believing your higher power is against you simply for being who you are at your core. This leaves LGBTQ children, teenagers, and adults not even having a higher power or god to talk to. Although it doesn't attack homosexuality overtly, the educational system remains silent on the topic, doing little to help LGBTQ students who are picked on, bullied, and ignored. It is only by looking at the trauma done to them and by addressing the specific problems and post-traumatic stress they face that individuals can fully achieve a healthy self-esteem.

LGBTQ individuals themselves often do not know the issues and facts, and you, as a therapist, need to inform them of the issues related to their being LGBTQ. Begin by dispelling the top 10 most common myths about homosexuality outlined in Chapter 1.

The Fundamentals of Gay Affirmative Therapy

Providing clients with a corrective emotional experience is of utmost importance while examining the roots of issues that arise for LGBTQ individuals. Specifically, in many cases, their sexual identity development has been suppressed, and therapists need to know the negative psychological consequences of this.

As you do GAT, some fundamental principles operate. Many of the terms used here have political connotations, but the psychological consequences of these politics affect the work of the gay affirmative therapist.

Understanding and Combating Heterosexism

The concept of heterosexism is usually explored from political, social, and legal perspectives. It is the assumption that all people are (or should be) heterosexual—the belief that heterosexual is superior and homosexuality is inferior. Rights and privileges automatically granted to heterosexuals are denied to lesbians, bisexuals, and gays. The most egregious examples of heterosexism are that LGBTQ individuals can be evicted from housing and legally terminated from their jobs. Most people in the general population, including therapists, are not aware of this.

The bias that everyone is heterosexual does psychological harm to the development of an LGBTQ child (Rich, 1980). This book will not be looking at the politics of heterosexism as much as at the psychological consequences of heterosexism on lesbians and gays. This is explored further in Chapters 3 through 6.

Understanding Heterosexual Privilege

Heterosexism breeds heterosexual privilege, which—like any other unearned privilege—seems to operate largely unconsciously, with no malice. With heterosexual privilege come institutional, legal, and societal freedoms that are granted automatically.

- *Institutional freedoms.* Heterosexuals can be employed and housed without fearing termination or eviction because of their orientation. They are able to adopt children andare accepted in religious practices.
- *Legal freedoms.* Heterosexuals have the right to adopt children without having to prove they are good parents simply for being heterosexual. Their heterosexuality is not in question, as is the case for an LGBTQ potential parent.
- *Societal freedoms.* Heterosexuals can hold hands and kiss the ones they love without concerns for their physical safety or fear of harassment or negative judgments.

Heterosexual privilege teaches LGBTQ individuals that misleading others into thinking they are straight is the standard—indeed, the only—way to live. Honesty brings the threat of rejection, isolation, and even punishment. Your clients may experience some degree of grief from losing heterosexual privilege, and their expression of this grief can range from adjustment disorders to dysthymia to major depression.

There is also the issue of cisgender privilege, which includes rights and privileges granted to natal males and females and denied to transgender individuals. I will talk more about this in Chapter 14.

The Case of Vicky

Vicky, a 35-year-old school counselor, entered therapy after she discovered she was lesbian, 6 months after having sexual feelings for—and then sex with—another woman. Vicky and her husband had three children under the age of 10, and prior to meeting this woman at her job, she had no idea that she was anything but straight, although her husband's "aggressive sexual urges" had always turned her off. She was married to her high school sweetheart, whom she loved with all her heart, and lived a mainstream life in a Detroit suburb. She considered her husband her best friend and enjoyed being a wife and a mother, loved coaching her son and daughters in sports, and enjoyed the company of her neighbors. Devastated by the thought of losing all this, she entered therapy to fight her "urges" and return to the life that she'd enjoyed.

Vicky's first therapist could not understand why Vicky's depression kept worsening. She affirmed Vicky's sexuality and applauded her for coming out and finally grasping the true nature of her sexuality. Her husband was supportive, as were her family and friends. The therapist told Vicky that all the literature suggested that her staying closeted was the root of her depression. But this did not help Vicky's affect, and she continued spiraling down into an ever-deeper depression. The therapist put Vicky on antidepressant medication and sent her to support groups for coming out, but neither approach helped.

When the therapist came to me for supervision, I told her that Vicky was grieving the loss of the heterosexual privilege she had worked hard to establish. Vicky had achieved the straight woman's ideal—staying married to the first man she fell in love with. She still loved her husband, and everything was good except for the fact that she now knew she wasn't heterosexual.

Because Vicky didn't want to change anything in her life, she viewed her lesbianism as more of a problem than a positive discovery. She did not want to leave her family and lose everything. But Vicky was no longer able to be sexual with her husband, who had decided he couldn't stay married to a woman who was not able to be there for him "a hundred percent." Vicky also was worried about how she would be judged as a mother, and that the courts might not let her keep her children. Her husband reassured her that he would not do anything to stop the children from seeing her. But the worries kept piling up: Would she be fired from her job if the school discovered her sexual orientation? What would it be like to live with another woman? How would she be perceived by the other parents with whom she'd grown so close?

Her grieving process triggered depression and high levels of anxiety. It also activated post-traumatic stress disorder (PTSD) caused by Vicky's suppressing the conflict of growing up lesbian and hiding her same-sex attraction from everyone, including herself—a subject I address in Chapter 5.

Vicky's therapeutic work was to grieve the loss of what she and most everyone else take for granted—heterosexual privilege. Embracing her lesbianism was bittersweet, as it was a welcome piece of integrity to align who she was on the inside with who she was becoming on the outside. However, she loved her life and everything and everyone in it, and having to end the very things she had worked so hard to nurture and love made her feel threatened and anxious.

Vicky's emotional response was realistic, and she needed to be supported. Coming out of the closet was not enough for Vicky to feel better. Inside that closet were other closet doors that still needed to be opened.

Affirmation Versus Alienation

Marcia, a clinical therapist, received a phone call from Pam, a potential client, who identified herself as a lesbian. Pam wanted to come in concerning problems with her partner, Susan. But before she agreed to make an initial appointment, Pam asked Marcia about her own sexual orientation.

Marcia replied that she saw Pam's question as "a treatment issue," and that her own "sexual preferences" should not affect the sessions. She told Pam that if she came in, they could discuss it during the session. "I've worked with many homosexuals in the past," Marcia added. "To me, a couple is a couple." Pam reluctantly agreed to meet with her.

During the initial individual intake, Marcia referred to Pam as "gay" and asked her how long she and Susan had been "lovers." Pam replied, "For 20 years—much longer than most gay and lesbian relationships." Marcia commended her, agreeing. When Marcia inquired about Pam's sex life with Susan, she asked how often they had "intercourse." When Pam replied, "Never—I think we have lesbian bed death," Marcia didn't know what the phrase meant, but she did feel that their lack of intercourse indicated a stunted and immature form of sexually relating to each other.

Later in the session, Pam asked if Marcia knew of any lesbian support groups for couples. Marcia responded that she did not provide resources to her clients and urged the two to seek out what they felt they needed. Most of her responses to Pam were deliberately reflective and mirroring, not offering much in an attempt to let Pam come to her own conclusions. This was Marcia's therapeutic style.

Over the next two sessions, while taking Pam's history from childhood, Marcia asked when Pam came out to her parents, but did not ask about Pam's childhood as a lesbian little girl. Pam recalled having crushes on other girls in first grade, but Marcia dismissed this as normal and natural, saying, "Children that young cannot know. They were most likely just feelings of closeness."

Pam had questions for Marcia as well: How long had she been in practice? How much of her caseload had been working with the LGBTQ population? What was her approach in working with clients? Marcia did not respond to any of these questions, considering them in terms of therapeutic transference. She again placed the emphasis back on Pam: "What does it mean to you to know this?"

Pam thought that Marcia was being homophobic and heterosexist and experienced multiple microaggressions in her questions about her sexuality, and she confronted Marcia with this. "I am not antigay," Marcia responded. "I feel comfortable with the LGBTQ population and am very gay friendly." She added that for Pam, this was a transference issue.

After four sessions, Pam terminated therapy without explaining why. Marcia followed up with phone calls and a letter, but Pam did not respond.

As you can see, much is wrong with this scenario. Marcia meant well and was using much of psychodynamic theory and practice, but she made many of the following 10 common errors in her therapeutic responses and orientation. These errors effectively alienated her client.

Error 1: Not disclosing your own sexual orientation when asked. An LGBTQ client calling for an initial appointment may ask about your sexual and romantic orientation as well as how you gender identify. Many therapists do not answer, believing that's a therapeutic question best left to the consulting room. It's true that this may be a therapeutic issue, but clients "shopping" with initial calls still want to know whom they're entering treatment with. Most LGBTQ individuals are well aware of the history of psychotherapeutic treatment for their sexual orientation, and they're sensitive not just to homophobia and microaggressions but also to ignorance and insensitivity. If you're not open about your own orientation, you may lose the referral.

Error 2: Denying your own homophobia and heterosexism. Marcia wasn't even willing to consider that she harbored any level of heterosexism, even covert, and dismissed Pam's concern as transference. Many therapists who genuinely like working with LGBTQ individuals still do not see their own homophobic countertransference, simply because they feel so accepting of the population.

From childhood, we are all imprinted to be heterosexist, and denying this is a form of covert homophobia. If you don't check your countertransference when working with the LGBTQ population, you will inadvertently collude with *their* internalized homophobia. For example, when Pam said that the number of years she and Susan had been together was uncommon within the gay community, Marcia agreed, inadvertently supporting Pam's internalized homophobic belief that gay and lesbian partnerships do not last.

Asking if the women had "intercourse" as the only sign of whether or not Pam was sexually active with her partner was also a form of heterosexism. As I explain later, many gay and lesbian couples do not have intercourse, yet still consider themselves sexual and satisfied. Penetration is a gold standard set by a heterosexist, patriarchal construct to which many couples—lesbians, particularly—do not always aspire. On the other hand, to assume that two women only snuggle and never engage in intercourse is erroneous as well.

Error 3: Not offering resources for clients. Marcia admitted she did not know of any resources, locally or otherwise. Some therapists believe in keeping the therapy room completely neutral by not suggesting resources to clients. However, clients who have suffered prejudice and discrimination are at the mercy of what the popular media says about them. Often they have been isolated and need good, correct information and resources about the challenges they need to face.

For these clients, one of the most important tasks is what I call homosocialization. The job of any gay affirmative therapist is to inform clients of the kinds of resources that heterosexuals automatically know about through churches, schools, families, and the media. You might need to contact the local LGBTQ community center or go online to research what newsletters and gay newspapers are available in your area. And why not subscribe to a couple of them to offer to your clients?

Error 4: Using the wrong terminology. Terms like *sexual preference* and *alternative lifestyle* are not considered appropriate. *Preference* implies that sexuality is a choice—which it's not—and for gays and lesbians, heterosexuality is the "alternative" lifestyle. The correct term is *sexual and romantic orientation.*

Although the term *homosexuality* is still used, describing gays and lesbians as "homosexuals" is as offensive today as the words *Negro, colored,* or *crippled.* The correct words are *gays* and *lesbians* or the *LGBTQIA* (lesbian, gay, bisexual, transgender, queer/questioning, intersex, and asexual) *community.*

It's also vital that you ask how clients self-identify. Marcia referred to the couple as "gay," but some lesbians do not like to be referred to as gay—they prefer lesbian. As a therapist you can ask, "How do you self-identity sexually?" and "How do you gender identify?" which we will talk more about in Chapter 14 on transgender clients.

Error 5: Using heterosexist and heteronormative paperwork and intake forms. Your intake form should ask about sexual and romantic identity, and include *partner* and *significant other* in addition to *married* and *spouse.* Your new-client paperwork should ask, "How do you self-identify?" for sexual and romantic orientation. Options should let the client self-identify as *heterosexual, bisexual, gay, lesbian,* "queer," *transgender, questioning,* and *other.* In place of *marital status,* ask whether the client has a partner and if so, ask the partner's first name. (This is also a good measure for being inclusive of straight couples living together.) If you are concerned that some straight clients might have a negative reaction to this, check out your own heterosexist attitudes and homophobia.

Error 6: Adopting a blank screen as a therapeutic style. In an attempt to stay neutral and not self-disclose, many therapists do not share personal information about themselves, but this is not helpful to gay and lesbian clients. In their daily life, these clients feel disconnected and are treated as outsiders. Being a neutral mirror to these clients can make them feel even more excluded and disenfranchised. In therapy, lesbian and gay clients who feel shut out by others need relational models. Appropriate self-disclosure by the therapist is not just therapeutic—it is essential.

Marcia could have easily revealed her sexual and romantic orientation and then explored whether there was a therapeutic issue behind the question, keeping in mind that there might not have been. She could have confirmed information about herself that her client had already gathered. These kinds of disclosures do not need to involve divulging extremely personal issues but rather can be limited to sharing understandings she might have arrived at as a woman and as a marriage partner. Such sharing would have helped Pam view her own relationship to Marcia in a more useful, authentic way.

A therapist's self-disclosure helps clients connect to the therapist. (Zur, 2007). Citing research, Zur stated: "Self-disclosure that is in tune with clients' needs and personalities also reduces clients' sense of alienation" (Zur, 2007, p. 158). He reinforced that it is therapeutic to self-disclose with members of minority groups as well as those who are trauma survivors and suffering PTSD—all of which applies to gays and lesbians (see Chapters 4 and 5). This is why it is essential to offer some elements of self-disclosure to your gay and lesbian clients.

Error 7: Neglecting to recognize that your gay and lesbian clients were gay and lesbian since childhood. Your lesbian and gay clients were once gay and lesbian children. This insight makes most people (including clinicians)—uncomfortable: They do not like to think of children as being sexual. However, being gay does not relate to sexual behavior alone. Heterosexual adults were once heterosexual children. Although most gays and lesbians did not self-identify as such as children, they will tell you as adults that they knew they were different. How did they know? What made them feel different? Their answers are important in helping them in the consulting room.

Error 8: Having a waiting room devoid of gay and lesbian literature. Your waiting room says a lot about you as a therapist and how you treat clients. I have had therapists tell me that they want to keep their waiting rooms "neutral" and still keep magazines such as *Time* and *Newsweek* around. But the absence of gay-oriented magazines mirrors the neglect that your gay and lesbian clients have felt before walking in your door. Having literature, magazines, and newspapers aimed only at heterosexuals communicates the impression that you don't acknowledge—or at least don't welcome—any other clients. *The Advocate*, which is the *Time* and *Newsweek* for the gay culture, is a good publication to include in the waiting room. At the very least, have flyers for local gay community and health-oriented services on your waiting room bulletin board to offer an immediate welcome.

Error 9: Believing that "a couple is a couple." I often hear well-intended therapists say that "a couple is a couple" in an effort to show that they are nonjudgmental. But gay and lesbian couples are very different from straight couples, with very different dynamics. The "doubling" factor—which you will read about in Chapter 10—intensifies the traditional gender role conditioning of both partners. Male couples are often disengaged, magnifying conflicts around restricted emotional expression, achievement, competitiveness, and sexual expression. Female couples are typically too engaged: They struggle with enmeshment, lack of differentiation, and sexual expression.

Error 10: Failing to assess your clients' stage of coming out and failing to ask about their coming-out process. Without knowing the stages of gay and lesbian identity development (see Chapter 7), clinicians can misunderstand certain thoughts and behaviors. For example, Stage 5 (identity pride) resembles an adolescent stage of development—meaning that short-term relationships with some sexual promiscuity are to be expected and are developmentally appropriate. In Stages 1 and 2, clients prefer to be identified as "homosexual," not as gay or lesbian. In GAT, the Cass model of coming out is the most widely used (Cass, 1979). Asking clients how their coming-out process went or is currently going will tell you where their strengths and weaknesses are developmentally. This is discussed further in Chapter 7.

Homophobia: The Client's and Yours

In the late 1960s, George Weinberg coined the term *homophobia* for "the feeling(s) of fear, hatred, disgust about attraction or love for members of one's own sex and therefore the hatred of those feelings in others" (Lorde, 1984, p. 45). The word first appeared in print in 1969 (Weinberg, 1983). Then, as now, many people, especially straight men, fear associating with lesbians and gays—physically, mentally, and emotionally—lest they be perceived as "one of them." Fears of venturing beyond accepted gender roles can afflict even lesbians and gays.

Today, *homophobia* does not apply as it was originally defined, as it does not fit the definition of a true phobia: an uncontrollable, irrational, persistent fear of a specific object, situation, or activity. Use of the term is more important today as a way to track, in your clients and yourself, attitudes that are homonegative, homoprejudiced, and homo-ignorant (Morrow, 2000). Ignorance is usually the most common of the three.

Homophobia can manifest, for example, in a straight therapist in the form of worry that potential and existing straight clients might perceive you as gay or lesbian yourself simply because you have gay clients or keep gay resource materials in your office.

I've seen such reactions firsthand. Several years ago, I decided to advertise my group therapy and weekend workshops for gay men by doing an unsolicited mailing. Scanning phone books and newsletters, I compiled a list of about 500 local listings of gay and likely gay-friendly businesses. I printed up a batch of one-page flyers, tri-folded them, and affixed a sticker to make sure they'd stay shut after I mailed them. I figured that if recipients were not interested, they would simply toss the flyer or, at best, pass it along to a friend. Having been open and out for 12 years myself, I'd grown quite distant from the kind of reactions I was about to encounter.

I received several heartening calls from men in the Detroit area, eager to join a gay men's group. To their knowledge, if anything like this existed, it hadn't been advertised—until now. But other callers were outraged! "How dare you send me this mailing about a gay group with no envelope?" Some feared that a family member or someone they lived with—to whom they were not out—would notice my flyer and connect the dots. Still others were annoyed at my presuming that they were gay.

My next mailing was in a sealed, opaque envelope, but even these provoked outrage. One man called me to heatedly demand that I take him off my mailing list. "I ain't gay!" he insisted. "Never been gay! Just because I slept with a guy once, that don't make me gay!" A woman left a voice message saying that she was "not gay" but "a *good* Christian woman" and how dare I send her a piece of mail regarding homosexuality? She then swore at me, before leaving her name so that I could take it off my list.

For most of those who overreact this way, my mailings simply rekindle their own inner conflicts. I could stop my mailings, but I won't let homophobic reactions keep me from advertising effective, supportive therapy for my gay brothers and sisters.

Homo-Avoidance

The vast majority of people—clients and therapists alike—are *homo-avoidant*, not knowing how to react to someone's being gay. Many therapists tell me they suspect a client might be gay, but fear to ask. Conversely, some lesbians and gays get upset because their therapists, after learning that they're gay, never ask follow-up questions or initiate any discussion.

The homo-avoidant often fear assigning "negative" labels, lest they be wrong in thinking the client is gay. For instance, many therapists avoid asking clients—particularly adolescents—if they are gay or lesbian. "I don't want them to think I assumed they were." "What if they get offended or self-conscious?" "What if they think my question is homophobic or ignorant?"

My answer is that the client's reaction then becomes diagnostic and therapeutic. Either way, it can be of help to the client. If they are struggling with homosexuality, the door is open. If they are not gay and have a strong reaction to your question, that can become part of their work in therapy.

Still other therapists are gay and lesbian themselves but avoid telling their gay and lesbian clients, believing that it would be inappropriate. "If the client were to ask, I would tell, but otherwise I let them transfer onto me whatever comes from them." Although this can be a very effective form of helping someone through transference, it can also be a way for the gay therapist to avoid being out. Ultimately, such a decision serves the therapist's needs rather than those of the clients, who need to have a role model and ally during the times they feel alone and isolated. It also further discourages clients from revealing their concerns to you.

Gay and lesbian clients often express their own homo-avoidance by claiming that if someone else doesn't broach the issue of their being gay, the individual doesn't want to talk about it, is homophobic, or simply is not interested. After clients come out, you'll hear these types of remarks:

"I told my family, but they never brought it up again."

"My friend asked, and I told her, but she never asked me any further questions."

"My children know. But they never ask, so I can tell they don't want to talk about it."

These excuses and reasons may—or may not—be true. But the only way for clients to discover whether their own beliefs are accurate is to *keep* talking about it themselves. After clients announce themselves as gay, I encourage them not to wait for others to keep the conversation going, but rather to bring up the subject whenever appropriate and to keep informing friends and family about their lives. I remind them that other people may not want to seem *too* interested—or disinterested. With any troubling issue, most people's default solution is avoidance: "Don't ask, don't tell."

Clients should be coached on how to ask others how they are dealing with the information. Encourage them to stop "editing" and to keep bringing up subjects in their lives that involve being gay. Have them tell friends, coworkers, and family members, "If you have any questions, go ahead and ask."

If others complain that clients are "talking too much about being gay," encourage clients to ask them what they mean by that. Remind them that they have a right to talk about their relational lives, just as straight people do.

Microaggressions

I once gave a talk at a church on LGBTQ affirmative issues, including homophobia and the harm it does. After the talk, a woman came up to me and put her arm around me and told me she was not homophobic. "If I were homophobic, I couldn't hug you, I couldn't tell you I love you and see you as a child of God." She then looked at me and said, "I just don't think your people should be allowed to marry." I took her arm off me and told her that what she had just said was homophobic, to which her response was shock and disbelief. I have since learned to call such subtle digs "microaggressions."

Microaggression is a term coined by psychiatrist and Harvard University professor Chester M. Pierce in 1970 to describe insults and dismissals he regularly witnessed nonblack Americans inflict on African Americans (Sue, 2010, p. xvi).

It is now also used to describe insults and dismissals to women and LGBTQ individuals.

Examples of microaggressions toward African Americans include assuming they are criminals. I have had black clients tell me they are followed in stores, or see people clutch their wallets and purses in elevators as they get on, or lock their car doors as they walk across the street at a traffic light. These are subtle yet hurtful messages people of color receive every day.

The best book on this topic for LGBTQ individuals is *That's So Gay!: Microaggressions and the Lesbian, Gay, Bisexual and Transgender Community* (Nadal, 2013). In this book, Nadal gave examples of microaggressions toward LGBTQ individuals, including:

- Use of heterosexist or transphobic terminology
- Endorsement of heteronormative or gender-normative culture and behaviors
- Assumption of a universal LGBTQ experience
- Exoticization (dehumanizing, comic relief, gay BFF, fetishizing trans women)
- Discomfort with or disapproval of LGBTQ experience
- Denial of the reality of heterosexism and transphobia
- Assumption of sexual pathology or abnormality
- Denial of individual heterosexism (heterosexuals deny their own heterosexist and transgender bias)

The idea behind microaggressions is that the aggressors mean well, but they don't see that the outcome of their good intentions has caused harm to the person to which it was directed. Nadal used examples such as:

- "Have you ever had real sex?"
- "I'm not being homophobic. You're being too sensitive."
- "Why don't you ever wear dresses?"
- "So . . . who's the man in the relationship?" (spoken to a gay male couple)
- "That's totally cool with me as long as I can watch."
- "You are so Jack on *Will & Grace* or Cam on *Modern Family*."

While someone may think these are innocent and funny to an LGBTQ person, they are often experienced as hurtful.

Intersectional Identities
This is a term used today regarding the unique combination of an individual's multiple social groups (race, ethnicity, gender, sexual identity, gender identity, age, religion) and the identifications, experiences, and worldviews that come with them.

For example, I am a white, Jewish, 54-year-old, cisgender, Detroit male. All of those identities make up who I am and are separate but connected.

Intersectional identities often are significant for clients when they are religious, people of color, or people of another minority group, and those identities conflict with their sexual or gender identities.

In the 1990s, African American, Asian American, and Arab American males would come to my office telling me they were homosexual but would never come out as gay because of their other identities in their families and communities. For them, being Arab, Asian, or African American was their main identity and subordinated their other identities. They would tell me that they would never come out, for fear of being rejected by their families, which they could not tolerate. At the time, I didn't understand this and told them that research showed that staying in the closet would lead to a life of depression. But they would tell me that for them, coming out gay would lead to a life of depression. I pressured them to come out, and many stopped treatment with me. Today, I understand. I didn't appreciate their intersectional identities.

Today, when someone comes to my office and tells me that their religion or any other part of their identity prevents them from coming out as gay, I support them in finding ways to live that allow them to keep their sexuality separate. I realize today that it is not the job of a therapist to impose "what should be" on a client. I will work with them to reduce any internalized homophobia or gay shame they may be experiencing, and let them self-determine how they will go forward with their own sexual orientation.

Internalized Homophobia

All clients, gay or straight, have experienced some form of oppression related to their sexuality—directly or indirectly. You as a gay affirmative therapist must bring a client's subjective reaction into consciousness so that you both can work with it and remove it. For lesbians and gays, this subjective reaction is called *internalized homophobia*.

Gays and lesbians don't normally walk in stating, "I have internalized homophobia," or "I'm grieving the loss of heterosexual privileges." Typically, clients are depressed, anxious, and troubled about issues that don't *seem* to arise from being gay or lesbian. It's your job to rule out any problems resulting from internalized homophobia and poor self-esteem due to being lesbian and gay.

Internalized homophobia is a national, if not international, experience among gay men and lesbians. I especially realized this after writing my first book. I'd written the book because I felt confident that I had something to tell gay men locally and in Midwestern states about the internalized homophobia that comes from living in these more repressed regions. But I never imagined that gay men in San Francisco, New York, Chicago, and Los Angeles would benefit as much as they did. At a book reading and signing in San Francisco, I asked the men attending why they thought my book was so well received there. One said, "Joe, you have to remember, we are not from here originally. We fled here from places like where you grew up." They said that reading my book reminded them of the unfinished work on internalized homophobia they had yet to do. It still haunted them, even while living on the West Coast.

Internalized homophobia is really internalized shame about being gay or lesbian— an internalization of the very thing you have been taught to despise and consider evil. Buloff and Osterman (1995) explain it eloquently:

> In her search to find mirrors that reflect her emerging self, a lesbian enters a veritable Coney Island Hall of Mirrors. She sees queer reflections. Mirrored back to her are grotesque and distorted image [sic] reflected back in words like: perverse, sinful, immoral, infantile, arrested, inadequate, or she sees no reflection at all—a peculiar silence—invisibility. (p. 95)

Unconscious internalized homophobia manifests in negative imagery that becomes the lens through which gays and lesbians see each other and themselves. Learning to recognize subtle forms of unconscious internalized homophobia—even in gay and lesbian clients who are out and open—takes experience and skill. This is why it's vital to be aware of your own covert homophobia, or you might collude with your clients' internalized version, with your countertransference adding to their problems.

Signs of internalized homophobia include lesbians who put down "chapstick lesbians" and gay men who look for "straight-acting" gays. They are just as biased as Jewish males looking for gentile females or African American women seeking "white-acting" men. Other symptoms of internalized homophobia include:

- Discomfort with obvious "fags" or "dykes"
- Denigration of gay ghettos by asking, "Why do gays and lesbians all have to live in the same area?"
- Fear of being found out, even when there is no danger
- Romantic attractions to only unavailable targets—particularly heterosexuals

- Passing as straight even when it is safe to be openly gay or lesbian
- Making comments like, "I don't have to tell others what I do in bed; I don't want to know what they do!"
- Commenting that a person or establishment is "too gay"
- Looking for straight-acting boyfriends or girlfriends

Shame

Our American culture does not have the ability to admit that shame even exists, let alone have a language for how to talk about the experience of it (Kaufman & Raphael, 1996). This silence is deafening and creates toxic shame for gay and lesbian individuals. In *Coming Out of Shame: Transforming Gay and Lesbian Lives*, authors Kaufman and Raphael wrote:

> How does that silence originate? Shame itself is the source. What cannot be openly expressed is perceived as too shameful to speak about. It is shame that bars the tongue from speaking. When parents either fail or refuse to speak openly about some subject, whether sexuality or a family secret, shame forges the chains of their silence. When a culture's media, churches and synagogues, as well as its schools all fail to engage in frank discourse about homosexuality, that deafening silence only strengthens and validates shame. (p. 10)

Tracking the manifestations of shame and internalized homophobia in your clients is imperative. As a gay affirmative therapist, you must know what to look for and how to help clients understand that it exists within them.

What Gay Affirmative Therapy Is Not

In general, GAT explores the trauma, shame, alienation, isolation, and neglect that occur to lesbians and gays as children. Although this is important, it has the potential of going too far and eclipsing other issues that your clients face. Because of the historical pattern of pathologizing homosexuality (discussed in Chapter 1), GAT has tended to deemphasize emotional disorders and not examine *any* pathology. GAT is not supposed to explain all the problems facing gays and lesbians—rather, it is supposed to be an essential inclusion.

In an effort to avoid pathologizing the gay or lesbian client, therapists may blame homophobia for too much and overlook mental and emotional problems. As a gay affirmative therapist, being affirming and supportive is only part of your work. The other part is looking for other issues that could—or might not—result from the client's homophobia and heterosexism. Some emotional and personality disorders, I believe, result from a lifetime of closeted dissociation, adapting to the sexual and romantic orientation that others expect.

Historically, gay-negative therapists jumped to conclusions and applied homophobic and heterosexist trauma models and theories, when in fact gay clients exhibit *other* individual problems. For example, a gay male who has multiple hookups and is in Stage 5 of the coming-out process could actually be a suffering from bipolar disorder or out-of-control sexual behaviors (OCSB). The closeted lesbian complaining of low libido may not be repressed but rather have suffered sexual abuse in her childhood. That said, don't be afraid to diagnose and pathologize gay-specific problems, if need be, just because homosexuality itself has been overdiagnosed and pathologized.

If this seems confusing, you're on the right track! As therapists, our responsibility is to be armed with all the up-to-date information. If you know all the ways problems *can* arise, you can then assess—with the client's help—what applies and what doesn't.

"Homo-Work" for the Straight Therapist

Just as you strive to have clients do their "homo-work," so should you examine your own imprinted heterosexism and heteronormative values and develop comfortable, appreciative feelings about homosexuality, bisexuality, transgenderism, and sexual fluidity. As a clinician, it is important to examine yourself for any covert and overt bias that hampers your effectiveness. It can also be helpful to explore any homosexual impulses, homoerotic interests, or tendencies that you may have.

Targeting Your Countertransference

Imagine yourself going to your local bookstore, choosing gay and lesbian books and magazines like Signorile's *Outing Yourself,* Tracey and Pokorny's *So You Want to Be a Lesbian,* Isay's *Becoming Gay,* or *The Advocate,* and letting customers and cashiers clearly see what you're buying, believing the books are for you and that you are lesbian or gay. Or imagine yourself reading these books openly on a plane, at the park, or at the beach. Consider putting McNaught's *Now That I'm Out, What Do I Do?* (1997) on your coffee table at home where visitors can see it. Although these examples may seem extreme, they can be a good litmus test to see what level of shame and homophobia lives in you.

To check yourself for heterosexist and homophobic countertransference, ask yourself the following questions:

- Do I question the origins of how my clients became LGBTQ—if not aloud, then to myself?
- Do I assume that same-sex attractions have a pathological origin? Do I infer etiology rather than healthy developmental identity formation?
- Do I align with my client's reluctance to admit being LGBTQ?
- Do I think LGBTQ individuals should not tell others they are LGBTQ unless they are asked?
- How do I really feel about legal and religious marriage for gays and lesbians?
- How do I feel about LGBTQ individuals parenting children?
- Do I agree with complaints from LGBTQ clients that the LGBTQ community is immature and too focused on sex and politics?
- How comfortable am I talking to 5- to 15-year-olds about the possibility that they are LGBTQ? Do I assume they can't really know their sexual orientation and gender identity at that age?

Having screened yourself for covert homophobia and microaggressions, you can more easily spot it in your clients—and especially in other therapists who believe that placing heteronormative expectations on their LGBTQ clients is helpful. Actually, the longer I am a therapist and the more training I receive on sexual health, the more I realize putting heteronormative and heterosexist standards even on straight people is inappropriate.

CHAPTER 3

Growing Up Lesbian, Gay, or Bisexual

When I told my parents I was gay, they said,
"Let's see how the second grade goes first, dear."
—Carson Kressley, of the TV show
Queer Eye for the Straight Guy, to Oprah Winfrey

This epigraph—although funny—is based on the reality that LGBTQ children know from a very young age that they are different. They may not know exactly *how* they're different or what to call themselves, because there is little to no permission to explore anything other than heterosexuality, but they still know they aren't like most other children. GAT acknowledges that children are gay, lesbian, bisexual, or transgender—from birth. To deny this would be to believe that sexual and gender orientation come from life experiences that change an innate heterosexual or cisgender orientation.

Many LGBTQ individuals aren't able to identify what makes them different until adolescence. As children, they received messages—verbal and nonverbal—about how to sit, walk, dress, talk, and so on. One client told me he hadn't danced for 30 years because he thought being a good dancer would out him as gay. Another man told me that since his teens, he'd been careful about how he dressed because the clothes he felt drawn to were ones his peers saw as "gay." A lesbian client said that she wore dresses, grew her nails long, and used nail polish even though she felt uncomfortable doing so—just to pass as heterosexual.

Clients also talk about the playground prejudice they encountered and how it was typically discounted by teachers and parents. Adults assume that if heterosexual children hurl "That is so gay!" slurs and chortle over homophobic jokes, no harm is being done. But LGBTQ children pay attention to what other kids are saying and doing—and to what the teachers are allowing. They pay very close attention. They get the message: It's okay to demean others by calling them "fags" or "dykes."

I don't mean to imply that there is only one type of LGBTQ boy or girl, or one way of growing up LGBTQ. However, there is little discussion, let alone research, that focuses on the traumatic experience and shame of growing up LGBTQ. One excellent book that does tackle this subject is Jean M. Baker's *How Homophobia Hurts Children* (2002). In it, she talks about how not anticipating or knowing your child might be or is gay can have a negative effect on the child.

Given all of this, it doesn't matter how functional one's family of origin is—an LGBTQ child can experience trauma both within the family and outside of it. Remembering that your clients were once LGBTQ children who endured trauma while growing up will help you better understand them and how to work with them.

From the Beginning: LGBTQ Children

When I talk about LGBTQ children, the one question I'm commonly asked is, "How can you tell if a child or teenager is LGBTQ?" I don't have an answer for that, and I haven't found any scientific literature that claims to, either. There are anecdotal writings from mothers and fathers who, looking back, recall signs that their children might have been LGBTQ. One thing I *do* stress is that, as I mentioned earlier, every LGBTQ adult was once an LGBTQ child.

However, many people—including too many psychotherapists—do not believe this. They cannot imagine that a child before the age of 12 (or even an adolescent) can be born with and have a fixed LGBTQ sexual, romantic, and gender identity. They can imagine the child being born with and having a fixed *heterosexual* identity, however, as all children (and adults, for that matter) must be heterosexual unless proven otherwise. When I ask therapists about this, they often say they don't even think of children and teenagers as LGBTQ or straight. However, they will ask their young clients if they have a romantic interest in the opposite sex and assume they are heterosexual. This is their covert homophobia in their countertransference. When I teach and lecture about GAT to therapists, usually half the audience believes that one is born LGBTQ and the other half believes that one becomes LGBTQ through learning and from environmental factors. It makes straight individuals, even therapists, uncomfortable and anxious to consider a child to be LGBTQ. Their anxiety results from their belief that homosexuality is an adult condition, primarily sexual.

However, being LGBTQ is about having an identity, just as being straight is. In other words, sex and sexuality are present in both orientations. But homosexuality is overly sexualized by others, an important point that is discussed in more depth in Chapter 4.

Children and teenagers *can* handle their own LGBTQ orientation. What they cannot handle is the trauma of concealing it, of not being able to express it or talk about it, and the negativity by others around them about it.

The Case of Jake

Jake, 13 years old, told his mother he was gay. Surprised and concerned, she offered to take him to therapy. He agreed to go, but not for the reasons she assumed.

Jake's mother believed that no boy could know what his orientation was at such a young age—but Jake did. His Unitarian church had offered a human sexuality course, and when they reached homosexuality and bisexuality, Jake recognized himself as a gay male on the cusp of becoming a teenager.

He'd thought he could handle hearing other kids saying, "That's so gay"; in fact, he had even said it himself. But now that he was accepting himself as gay, hearing it was making him feel isolated from his peers. Being self-aware at such an early age, he figured he needed therapy.

My work with Jake was to build up his confidence enough that he could tell his peers that he didn't appreciate their "humor." We worked together on ways he could invite the teachers he felt safe with to help him, as well as his mother, who wanted to help him feel secure in school.

Jake is an excellent example of how young teens and even children can—if given permission to explore their own sexuality—have some awareness of their sexual and romantic orientation. His case also illustrates the fact that young people can handle the development of their core identity—gay or straight and everything in between.

Fortunately, Jake was spared the severity of trauma that you will see in many of your gay and lesbian clients.

The Oedipus and Electra Complexes

Homosexuality was long considered as "Oedipus gone wrong" or "Electra gone badly," wherein children failed to achieve an alternative, "healthy" heterosexual identity. Heterosexuality was seen as nature's default. Therapists typically misunderstood, underreported, dismissed, or ignored the messages found in the developmental narratives of gay men and lesbians. And, of course, their theories reflected the values of the culture in which they practiced.

More contemporary psychotherapists and gay theorists, including Lewes (1988), Drescher (1998), and Isay (1994), have added to this oedipal discussion of how gay boys develop. All agree that oedipal feelings exist, but they add that from these oedipal feelings arise other issues that are *not* about homosexuality but instead revolve around the lack of acknowledgment of *normal* homosexual development. They surmise that gay boys naturally yearn to get physically close to their fathers, and so fall in love with them—which usually leads to rejection and a source of wounding that never gets resolved.

Working psychodynamically involves understanding the developmental Oedipus or Electra complex (as described by Freud), and how our clients negotiate this as small children in their families. In thinking of children as being gay or lesbian, it makes sense to consider *both* complexes. When a young boy announces that he plans to grow up and marry his mother, he'll probably be told that he cannot marry his mother, but he may be told that when he grows up he can marry a woman *like* her. Likewise, when a young girl announces that she plans to grow up and marry her father, she'll probably be told that she when she grows up, she can marry a man just like him. This is the positive resolution of the Oedipus and the Electra complex and is seen as the standard of a healthy heterosexual male and female identity.

But what of the girl who wants to marry her mother, or the boy who expresses a desire to marry his father? Gay boys learn that they not only can't marry their fathers, but also can't marry other boys. Little lesbian girls learn there is no hope for them either, and they must face the loss of their mothers and any other women for their future. So these little gay children not only get rejected by their parents, but also never receive a promise that someday they will meet someone to care for.

I spend a great deal of time with my sister's four children. They understand that I am married to my partner, Mike; when they were toddlers, the oldest two attended our wedding. When one of my nephews was 6, he asked me why I'm not married to a woman. I told him that I love Mike, so I married him.

"Boys can't marry other boys," he told me.

"You can marry anyone you fall in love with," I said, "as long as you're both adults."

My nephew then said, "Then when I grow up, I want to marry you!"

My answer to my nephew—"You can marry anyone you fall in love with"—kept the door open for him, as he probably did not know his sexuality, nor did we. This is why I recommend that parents and caretakers keep their responses gender-neutral. This is the best way not to harm a gay or lesbian child.

Neglect of LGBTQ Children

Therapists know that clients coming from neglectful families are harder to treat and often remain in therapy longer because of what *didn't* happen or what *wasn't* said. Overt abuse is often easier to treat, even when clients are in denial, because what *was* done or said to the client can be pinpointed and addressed. Passive forms of abuse are harder to spot. For example, if a client says she was loved and attended to, and you ask, "How so?" she may tell you how well-fed, clothed, and housed she was. You would then ask, "But how did they show their affection for you?" Clients who say, "It wasn't shown, I just knew I was loved," have a harder time understanding that what *didn't* occur was itself neglect and, therefore, a form of abuse. Custodial care is what foster care can offer. Providing love by overt forms of affection—mirroring children and highlighting the special talents they bring to the family—honors children as individuals and gives them a sense of belonging.

LGBTQ children have an additional element of "lack of attunement" from their early primary caretakers—no one was tracking or attending to the LGBTQ side of their core selves. No matter how attuned these children may be, they may still feel lost because of the neglect and silence surrounding their sexual and gender orientations.

LGBTQ children are not offered the same sense of belonging as straight kids by their families, schools, or religious institutions. Media and books offer few, if any, LGBTQ characters that are out and proud. Parents who hope that their children are not LGBTQ simply do not talk about it. Schools, for the most part, hardly acknowledge the presence of LGBTQ students. Churches, synagogues, and other religious institutions condemn not being straight by denying the existence of the LGBTQ members of their audiences. Essentially, GAT examines the negative psychological effects on LGBTQ individuals of having to split their sexual and gender identities from the rest of their authentic selves, beginning in early childhood. This early repression dishonors and ignores the reality that LGBTQ adults were once LGBTQ children and teenagers.

Looking at how our society handles cartoon characters created for children sheds light on what is done *to* children. Bert and Ernie from *Sesame Street* minded their own business for years, singing show tunes together, taking baths together, and sleeping next to each other in twin beds. But in 1990, a North Carolina minister, Joseph Chambers, pronounced Bert and Ernie a gay couple. "They're two grown men sharing a house—and a bedroom!" bellowed Chambers, whose radio ministry is broadcast in four Southern states. "They share clothes. They eat and cook together. They vacation together and have effeminate characteristics. In one show Bert teaches Ernie how to sew. In another, they tend plants together. If this isn't meant to represent a homosexual union, I can't imagine what it's supposed to represent."

Although the Children's Television Workshop and *Sesame Street* both issued statements defending the characters, the pair's behavior changed. They no longer took baths together, for example. Clearly, the message was sent and received that it's bad and wrong for children to be exposed to a couple who might or could be LGBTQ.

An equally ridiculous outing of a cartoon character occurred in 1999, when Reverend Jerry Falwell outed the Teletubby Tinky Winky, pointing out that he is purple (the gay pride color), has a triangle on his head (the gay pride symbol), carries a purse (though it is really a magic bag), and speaks in a high voice. While the Tinky Winky controversy was unfolding, I spoke to a class at a nursing school. One of the nurses told me that on the children's ward where she worked, Tinky Winky had been banished. What a cruel metaphor it was, because this is what happens to gay boys. They are made to feel that they are not wanted and that they certainly shouldn't be around other children. The Itsy Bitsy Entertainment Company, which created the Teletubbies, did a press conference saying that Tinky Winky is not gay; the gay pride symbol is the Lambda, not a triangle; and the gay pride color is pink, not purple. One gay commentator noted at the time, jokingly, that Tinky Winky cannot be gay because gay men would never be caught dead in a purple outfit with a red bag and flats!

A few years later, James Dobson, the founder of Focus on the Family, accused SpongeBob SquarePants and his creators of "promoting the gay agenda." The creators of SpongeBob did their own press conference and said that SpongeBob was a cartoon and a sponge and didn't have a sexual orientation. Those who thought he did should increase their psychotropic medications and move on with their lives!

Interestingly, female cartoon characters are never outed. Peppermint Patty's friend March from the *Peanuts* comic strip, clearly a lesbian, is obviously in romantic love with Peppermint Patty—always following her around, and she even calls Patty "sir"! Some lesbians say that Velma from *Scooby-Doo* is a lesbian because her hairstyle is very butch and she always wears sensible clothes and shoes.

Author and psychotherapist Terrance Real (1997) accurately summarized why males are punished for engaging in nontraditional male behavior:

> Boys and men are granted privilege and special status, but only on the condition that they turn their backs on vulnerability and connection to join in the fray. Those who resist, like unconventional men or gay men, are punished for it. Those who lose or cannot compete, like boys and men with disabilities, or of the wrong class or color, are marginalized and rendered all but invisible. . . . The exclusion, isolation, of a failed winner is so great, it is as if he never existed at all. (p. 180)

Not standing up to denounce homophobic slurs is another form of neglect. To an LGBTQ child, or to any abused child, the fact that he or she wasn't protected is sometimes more of an insult and an assault than the initial abuse itself. These children internalize the message that they are not worthy of being protected and that no one will come to their defense. This neglect manifests in LGBTQ children's feeling invisible, as if they have no right to exist.

Trauma

All LGBTQ children are touched to one degree or another by neglect stemming from the invisibility of their sexual and gender orientation. This can be traumatic. How they are affected and how it manifests depends on the individual, his or her personality, and the family of origin. When working with LGBTQ individuals, it is important to assess and treat them through the lens of the effects of the trauma of homophobia, heterosexism, and microaggressions.

My working definition of trauma is an event or episode, acute or chronic, that causes overstimulation without an outlet or release for that overstimulation. This leaves individuals feeling helpless and overwhelmed. According to this definition, any seemingly harmless event or situation can be *subjectively* traumatic when it leaves an individual feeling unable to cope, or fearing some ongoing threat.

You've heard many clients recount traumatic experiences—typically abrupt, dramatic, and therefore memorable. You've also probably seen victims of long-term verbal abuse from a spouse or parent. These clients grow accustomed to chronic insults and habitual belittling that, if it were to come all at once from a stranger, would feel intolerable and would spark a normal fight-or-flight reaction.

Growing up LGBTQ is similarly incrementally traumatic. Slights happen over a period of many years, and children learn to internalize them, all the while struggling to cope with being alone and in secrecy. For those for whom heterosexuality is the "alternative lifestyle," trying to develop an identity while role-playing (or, as one of my clients calls it, "doing straight drag") is chronically painful. And it sets the stage for awkward identity development and difficult future functioning.

As Bessel A. van der Kolk (1996) warned in his book *Traumatic Stress: The Effects of Overwhelming Experience on Mind, Body, and Society*:

> If clinicians fail to pay attention to the contribution of past trauma to the current problems in patients with these diagnoses, they may fail to see that

they seem to organize much of their lives around repetitive patterns of reliving and warding off traumatic memories, reminders, and affects. (p. 183)

According to van der Kolk, a therapist's attitude toward traumatic symptoms will determine his or her approach to treating clients. This is why it's crucial to understand the trauma that has overwhelmed your LGBTQ clients, whether or not they report it. Most won't view it as trauma at all, and if they do, they believe it is all "done and gone" in the past. But if left unresolved, the effects of trauma repeat themselves. Keeping a discerning eye out for this likelihood is the best way to help your LGBTQ clients.

Religious and Spiritual Abuse

Another place—and perhaps the worst—where there is a break in a sense of belonging is religion. Because of the damage so many religions have done to the developing self of LGBTQ people, these individuals cannot seek spiritual counseling and guidance. They not only are isolated from others but also feel isolated from their higher power and from anyone in a religious or spiritual capacity. So they turn to psychotherapy and often ask the therapist to give them spiritual guidance and counseling.

In my practice, I've had LGBTQ individuals who called themselves "recovering Catholics." They'd spent years in therapy trying to undo the damage of hearing, throughout their lives, that gay sex is an "abomination" and that they'd go to hell if they "practiced" it.

Joe Amico, an ordained minister, licensed substance abuse counselor, and president of the National Association of Lesbian and Gay Addiction Professionals, wrote "Healing From 'Spiritual Abuse': Assisting Gay and Lesbian Clients" (2003). In it, he addressed the difference between religion and spirituality. At his talks, for example, he asks people to shout out what comes to their minds about religion. They say things like rituals, money, rules, the Pope, priests, nuns, ministers, rabbis, confirmation, confession, abuse, obligation, and homophobia. When he asks them about spirituality, they yell out things such as peace, serenity, nature, hope, trust, acceptance, unconditional love, and individual and personal fulfillment. Amico wrote that at his talks, "everyone agrees that the words on the spirituality side are more positive than those on the religion side" (p. 18). Many lesbians and gays agree that religion does not feel accepting for them and that spirituality does. They wish to stay with their own religion but feel rejected and out of place. Amico has said: "To ignore spiritual abuse is the same as ignoring sexual, physical or emotional abuse as a part of the healing process" (p. 18).

One book of interest is *What The Bible Really Says About Homosexuality* (Helminiak, 2000). I also have an up-to-date resource page on my website (www.joekort.com) with a list of LGBTQ-friendly religious groups. These are alternative groups within religious organizations that are LGBTQ friendly, allowing members to can hang on to their intersectional identities of being LGBTQ and religious at the same time. The case of Cindy is one instance of these intersectional identities.

The Case of Cindy

Cindy was a 53-year-old woman who came to treatment after her diagnosis of breast cancer. She needed guidance as to whether to undergo a recommended double mastectomy or to begin a different treatment. She wanted to receive spiritual guidance, but she hadn't attended her Catholic church in a decade—she'd vowed to never return after she came out at the age of 42. Although she had turned to other religious institutions for spiritual direction, she never connected successfully to any of them. Seriously depressed and estranged from her religion, she entered therapy.

Like with many gay and lesbian individuals, Cindy's self-awareness and eventual coming-out were delayed by her strict Catholic upbringing. Her religious family was rigid when it came to rules and gender roles. Determined to please her devout family, Cindy became rule-oriented and believed—as they taught her—that the Church's teachings were law.

When Cindy turned 18, the Church changed its stance on a number of teachings. Eating meat on Fridays was now acceptable. Mass was done in English, a change that disillusioned Cindy, but she still subscribed to the Church's teachings and remained a good Catholic girl in terms of sexuality.

In her 20s and 30s, Cindy completely repressed her awareness that she was a lesbian. She married and had two children. She prided herself on living out her childhood mission of being a "good little Catholic girl" and felt that if it were not for her homosexuality, she could have maintained the life she "was meant to have with [her] husband and children."

At the age of 42, when her children reached adolescence, Cindy became a teacher and fell in love with the principal of her school. She divorced her husband and began a relationship with the woman, with whom she had stayed ever since.

In therapy Cindy expressed anger at herself and worried that she was being punished for having come out and not "doing God's work"—that is, staying closeted as a lesbian. She cried often, remembering the comfort the Church teachings had once offered her.

In Cindy's 6 months of treatment with me, she became angry about minor inconsistencies she noticed in my therapeutic interventions. She remembered details of things I had said and would directly confront me if she witnessed anything that resembled a contradiction. She became exquisitely sensitive to the words I chose. But the issue she had the most trouble with was when she was charged for an appointment she missed without giving me sufficient notice. This upset her greatly. She acknowledged that she'd signed consent forms agreeing to my rules about missed appointments, and she knew that this was standard practice in the mental health field. When I became ill, however, and had to cancel her appointment with less than 24 hours notice, she claimed that this was unfair. She felt that because I did not give her enough notice, she should get a free session. This became such a central issue for her that she almost terminated, claiming that therapy was no different than the Church: Both had unfair rules. She accused me of "changing the rules" at my own whim.

Cindy: Clinical Interpretation and Treatment

Cindy could easily be characterized as difficult; some might assess her as borderline. She could also have been diagnosed as having an adjustment disorder with depressed mood over the news of her breast cancer. However, knowing her feelings about the Church and listening to how she suppressed her anger toward it and directed it toward herself, I interpreted her anger as negative transference.

Cindy's negative transference toward me arose from the feelings she had repressed about the Catholic Church. She focused on perceived inconsistent "rules"—like the inconsistent Church rules—which allowed her to express her anger in a "safe" way that didn't contradict her childhood imprint to stay neutral toward the Church. I taught Cindy about negative transference and pointed out to her that it was positive that she finally was directing her anger away from herself. I assured her that I could handle her anger. She struggled with this for 3 months and ultimately was able to see that her anger was, in fact, motivated by the hypocrisy of the Catholic Church. Over time she was able to retrieve her anger toward the Church. As she said, "changing rigid rules at their own whim" conflicted with their teachings that once God spoke, His words could not be changed. After this realization, she began conversations with prominent people in her church about why they did not change their "archaic" beliefs about homosexuality.

During therapy, she expressed her sadness that the Church's teachings had affected her to the point of suppressing her true lesbian orientation for all the years she lived heterosexually. In adapting to her religious and rigid family, she had put her own needs last.

Week after week, we reviewed Cindy's memories of being best in school, perfect in church attendance, best employee, top athlete, and ideal wife. The goal had been to distract everyone, including herself, from seeing that inside, she was an ashamed, self-loathing, anxious young girl—mostly because of what she'd learned in church.

Now our work was uncovering the trauma that was preventing her from finding spiritual direction. She knew about Dignity—the unauthorized version of Catholicism for gay and lesbian Catholics. She had stayed away from this organization, believing that because the Catholic Church did not recognize it, it was like "playing house" and not real. However, now that she was aware of the trauma she had suffered, she was freed to make a decision for herself. Attending Dignity, she found it to be of great help to her as she decided what direction to take to fight her cancer.

Applying the model of abuse to what gay and lesbian children and teenagers learn at church and calling it "spiritual abuse" helps clinicians understand the trauma their clients have experienced. Giving a name to what they are going through helps them get in touch with their anger and direct it where it belongs—at the religious institution and not at themselves.

Sometimes, people who have felt shamed by religion compare their experiences to growing up LGBTQ. I have had people say that their religion shamed them for having sex outside of marriage and for masturbation. But this is different from being shamed for being LGBTQ. Sex outside of marriage and masturbation are behaviors. Being LGBTQ is an identity. Comparing the two diminishes the fact that LGBTQ individuals are literally being told that *who they are* is wrong, not just what they do.

Integrity and the Divided Self

Integrity is a lifestyle of congruency; it means outwardly being who you are on the inside. LGBTQ children quickly learn that being out and open means ridicule, negative judgments, and lack of emotional and physical safety. So the most formative years are spent learning to live out of integrity—in relation to themselves and others.

Of course, LGBTQ individuals don't corner the market on living out of integrity. Heterosexuals get through childhood by burying and disowning parts of themselves that are not acceptable to their families or cultures. LGBTQ and straight alike, we must all come back into integrity—which is often what a midlife crisis is all about. This is why most of our clients enter therapy—they are out of integrity with themselves or someone else. They arrive in our offices in order to find out who they really are and move toward it.

For children of any orientation, integrating all the parts of themselves is impossible. Family rules as well as socialization norms call for children to disown aspects of who they are. For LGBTQ children, an additional part gets disowned—their sexual and gender orientation—and this corruption happens very early. The cost is a lost self and a damaged core that leaves its victims with many mental health problems, addictions, and characterological profiles. The process of coming out—which is about integration, or becoming congruent with oneself and with others—can be a very difficult task, prompting its own set of maladaptive behaviors. LGBTQ clients may present as personality disordered or mentally ill, when the real cause of their symptoms is the difficulty of growing up LGBTQ and the suppression of the coming-out process.

Restrictive Socialization Messages

All kids get *some* social limitations from their families, schools, and communities. Many of these messages are important; they teach children how to behave appropriately in order to be accepted. But the problem with restrictive messages like "don't think," "don't act," "don't feel," and "don't touch" is that they limit children and cause their core selves to remain underground. If, for example, an innately playful child is taught to curtail her playfulness, she is being forced to deny that part of herself.

And so the false self begins. LGBTQ children learn to split off important parts of their core identities. This causes them to lose their sense of self early on. We therapists can help clients resurrect their "buried treasures," as I call these lost parts of the self, to discover their authentic identity.

Disowning Aspects of the Self

Cutting off romantic and sexual urges becomes habitual for LGBTQ individuals. The individual's sense of identity becomes fugitive, and she tends to misinterpret who she really is—not only in relation to sexuality but also in relation to her social sense of self in terms of how to act, feel, think, and experience body sensations. Straight children may disown *parts* of themselves that shape their identity, but LGBTQ children suppress much more of their identities.

When LGBTQ children cut off and disown parts of themselves, they go underground. They still, however, repeatedly seek conscious expression, if only in excessive denial. But such an attempt at camouflage—being the *exact opposite* of what the individual hopes to hide—is often recognizable.

Pretending That Nothing's Wrong

Early on in life, almost everyone learns to present his best face to his peers and classmates—and, conversely, to minimize or deny anything that might subject him to judgments and ridicule. Many LGBTQ children and teenagers hope that someone will see through their pretending to be straight and cisgender. They long for someone to say, "I can see that something is wrong; let me help you." The "something wrong" is not their homosexuality, bisexuality, or gender identity. It is that they are pretending to be someone whom they are not. Unfortunately, this longed-for offer of sympathy and help rarely if ever happens.

Becoming a Master of Pretense

Just because a client comes out and seeks to integrate his sexual and romantic orientation doesn't mean he's vowed to embrace integrity in every other aspect of life. Becoming a master of pretense and living out of integrity is the consequence of suppressing homosexuality, bisexuality, and gender identity. Displaying a false self as a heterosexual and cisgender person to others—and oneself—becomes a way of life. This may explain why many LGBTQ individuals don't stop pretending and hiding even after they come out. Pretending has become a way of life, manifesting in other ways that need to be addressed. They often do not even realize they are continuing with this defense in relationships.

For example, I spent over a year with a client in group therapy helping him come out as gay to his family and friends. During the second year he revealed he'd had a boyfriend for the last 6 months and they were planning their first vacation. He had not told me or the group about this. When group members became angry with him about this, he was stunned and innocently replied, "It didn't even occur to me to talk about it." This client had learned to compartmentalize his life through hiding to the extent that he wasn't even able to allow himself to enjoy the positive accolades he would have received from the beginning of his relationship.

Helping Clients Overcome Humiliation, Shame, and Victimization

Overall, clinicians can see from this chapter that it is humiliating and victimizing to be treated as inferior or invisible simply for being different. As I have already emphasized, most LGBTQ adults knew as children that something was different about them. Feeling different often gets worse as adolescence approaches.

Freud envisioned trauma as "a breach in the protective barrier against stimuli leading to feelings of overwhelming helplessness" (Levine, 1997, p. 197). It is this sense of helplessness children experience that is humiliating and victimizing. LGBTQ children are overwhelmed with heterosexuality, knowing that something inside is not aligned with the way the world wants them to be.

Being held in contempt by others for being different and being taught that you are not okay is shaming, as your difference is out of your control as an LGBTQ child. In addition, the type of gender bashing that occurs toward male, female, and nonbinary children who do not conform to rigid, stereotypical gender behaviors or expressions further degrades and humiliates these children.

LGBTQ children often grow up to be codependent—that is, they subordinate their needs to others and conform to what is expected of them. LGBTQ children often seek to win approval by following the rules "religiously." This is a way of compensating for their own diminished self-worth. Ultimately, of course, it is exactly their self-worth that ends up taking the greatest hit.

Therapeutic Tools for Psychosocial Information Gathering and Treatment Planning

As a clinician it is important to know the right questions to ask and terminology to use to obtain the best possible assessment and decide what direction to head in for treatment. As a straight clinician you need to watch for the negative transference of your clients, who, as you ask these questions, may feel that you are coming from a pathological stance about homosexuality, bisexuality, and gender identity.

I would suggest that as you do the initial intake, you tell your clients that the questions you ask are those you ask in most every session about growing up in a minority status. Assure LGBTQ clients that you do not believe in the pathogenic models of sexual orientation and gender identity. Reassure them that you want to obtain the best information to help them and that knowing about their LGBTQ childhoods—even if they did not know they were LGBTQ as children—is important to helping them understand the type of adult they have become.

You can tell clients that you do not want to contribute to a victim mentality by asking these questions, but that you *do* need to understand their experiences in order to be able to know who and what is accountable for their not having permission to explore their sexuality and gender identity. Explain that this is an important part of understanding their adult functioning as LGBTQ individuals.

Following are some suggestions of what to ask your clients:

- When do you recall knowing that something about you was different from other children of the same gender—even if you did not call it LGBTQ?
- When and how did you discover your gayness, lesbianism, bisexuality, or gender identity?
- Did you feel different from your peers—particularly those of the same gender?
- Did others—adults or peers—notice you were different and shame or bully you for it? If so, how?
- Were you consciously making decisions to hide or pretend to be like everyone else?
- Even if you don't recall overt forms of abuse for being LGBTQ as a child, what do you feel about covert abuse—that is, the absence of permission to explore your true sexual and gender identity or the lack of role models?
- Do you think that not being acknowledged by yourself or others as an LGBTQ child affects your life today in terms of self-esteem and relationships? If so, how?
- Why do you think you did not tell anyone when you were young?
- What were your family of origin's messages on being LGBTQ? Your messages from religion? From your community? From your school?

As a psychotherapist, your goal is to teach LGBTQ individuals that they're not responsible for any of the abuse they received as children and teenagers. Accountability rests on the guilty shoulders of those who did the abuse. Having strong and healthy therapeutic attachments helps LGBTQ individuals recover the birthright of their sexuality and heal the effects of covert cultural sexual abuse.

CHAPTER 4

Covert Cultural Sexual Abuse

Only by dealing with Gay Shame will we
ever get to a definition of Gay Pride.
—Andrew Holleran

As I described in Chapter 3, the trauma LGBTQ children experience growing up is pervasive. However, this trauma goes even deeper than that described in the previous chapter, and it often falls under the radar of therapists and even LGBTQ individuals themselves. The trauma I'm referring to is a *sexual* trauma.

My second book, *10 Smart Things Gay Men Can Do To Find Real Love*, addresses the shame of growing up gay. Another book that is very popular that came out that year was titled, *The Velvet Rage*, by Alan Downs who talked about the shame and trauma of growing up gay as well but his book doesn't address the sexualized nature of the trauma as I did in my book.

The assault on an LGBTQ person's sexuality and gender identity is profound and becomes worse as he or she enters adolescence and adulthood. The trauma not only affects psychological identity but also negatively influences psychosexual formation and identity. The psychological consequences of microaggressions, homophobia, and heterosexism parallel those of sexual abuse.

The fact is that most children—straight and nonstraight—learn they have to hide and change sexual parts of themselves that are discouraged. This hiding modifies, vandalizes, and compromises their identities. The sexual oppression and terrorism experienced by those who grow up LGBTQ—particularly during the adolescent years when sexuality and intimacy development is at a crucial stage—is profound.

For years, psychological researchers and clinicians believed that those with a homosexual orientation were unable to form close attachments, maintain relationships, and have healthy self-esteem. In other words, it was thought that these negative characteristics were innate to homosexuality. The truth is that they are the *result* of what is done to LGBTQ people. The effects of covert cultural sexual abuse persist into adulthood and are just as pernicious as those of sexual abuse.

This chapter will demonstrate how the trauma is sexualized, how it manifests, how to identify it for your clients, and how to help them heal from it.

Defining Covert Cultural Sexual Abuse

Covert cultural sexual abuse is the foundation for many (if not most) problems for LGBTQ individuals. And most therapists working with LGBTQ individuals miss this phenomenon. It's not enough to simply say that these people were permanently scarred by the microaggressions, homophobia, and heterosexism they experienced growing up. Microaggressions, homophobia, and heterosexism are *inherent* to covert cultural sexual abuse and have devastating, complicated psychological and psychosexual consequences, causing guilt and shame to run as deep as in those who have been sexually abused (Kort, 2005b).

I define covert cultural sexual abuse as chronic verbal, emotional, psychological, and sometimes sexual assaults against an individual's gender expression, sexual feelings, and behaviors. Conceptually, it is similar to sexual harassment in that it interferes with a person's ability to function socially, psychologically, romantically, affectionally, and sexually. Its effects persist into adulthood and wreak havoc in people's lives—as does sexual harassment.

My working definition of sexual abuse (both covert and overt) comes from Wendy Maltz's *The Sexual Healing Journey: A Guide for Survivors of Sexual Abuse*. She stated: "Sexual abuse occurs whenever one person dominates and exploits another using sexual feelings and behavior to hurt, misuse, degrade, humiliate, or control another. The abuse comes from a person who violates a position of trust, power, and protection of the child" (2001, p. 31). In other words, sex is simply a tool with which to exert power, dominance, and influence—just as in rape.

Overt sexual abuse involves direct touching, fondling, and intercourse with another person against that person's will. *Covert* sexual abuse is subtle and indirect. It includes inappropriate behaviors such as sexual hugs, sexual stares, or inappropriate comments about one's buttocks or genitals, as well as verbal assaults and denigration, such as punishing a child for not being the "right type" of male or female and homophobic name-calling.

Covert *cultural* sexual abuse involves bullying through humiliation, offensive language, sexual jokes (of antigay nature), and obscenities. These attacks can be directed at the LGBTQ person directly or indirectly. In other words, what I define as covert cultural sexual abuse is the expression of heterosexism, a belief in mainstream society that demands that all people be—or pretend to be—heterosexual. Heterosexism uses homophobia and microaggressions to exploit the sexual feelings and behaviors of those who are not heterosexual. In other words, heterosexism perpetrates and violates the trust that LGBTQ children have in those in who are in positions of power over, and protection of them.

To be clear, I am *not* saying that all LGBTQ people are sexually abused. Nor am I diminishing the profound negative effects of overt sexual abuse. I, myself, am a sexual abuse survivor and believe this helps inform my ability to see the parallels of sexual abuse and growing up LGBTQ. What I am trying to help clinicians understand is that many of the deep-seated problems of their LGBTQ clients have come from covert cultural sexual abuse.

Others have also noticed that the results of sexual abuse parallel the experience of growing up LGBTQ. In 1993, Joseph H. Neisen wrote an article in which he explored the parallels of heterosexism and sexual abuse. He wrote of heterosexism as being "a form of cultural victimization that oppresses gay/lesbian/bisexual persons" (p. 55). Niesen's article pointed to the cultural victimization as an abuse that causes painful effects similar to those of sexual or physical abuse. The cultural victimization of heterosexism, he added, stymies individual growth and development just as it does in individuals who have been sexually or physically abused. I don't believe Neisen took this far enough. What he called "cultural victimization" I would call "covert cultural sexual abuse."

Don Wright has also compared the effects of homophobia to those of sexual abuse. He talked about homophobia as a "sexuality abuse" with "deep lasting effects on a bisexual or gay male, undermining his sense of self as a male, and tainting what for him is a natural attraction to his own gender" (2000, p. 122). He noted the parallels between the resulting shame and guilt and the shame and guilt experienced by those who have been sexually abused.

Children (and adults) are bombarded with messages—from church, from politicians, from their schools, from their peers and their families—that being LGBTQ is morally wrong, sinful, and forbidden, and they internalize these messages on some level. The shame and guilt they feel are profound and become a part of their identity.

Here are some other examples of covert cultural sexual abuse:

When I was in sixth grade, I had a best friend named Max. We'd go everywhere together; looking back, I can see that I was in love with him. But I did not know that at the time. One day we were late for gym class, and when we entered the gym at the same time, everyone—including the physical education teacher—laughed at us. Later we learned that the teacher had predicted out loud to the class that Max and I would arrive late together because we were "fags together." Of course, the implication was that we were sexual with each other. This became a running joke not only for the rest of the school year but also for the remainder of middle school. Imagine how humiliated we felt, especially because we had no one to talk to about how we were being treated. And imagine how other gay and lesbian children in my school felt, hearing my gym teacher call us "fags" and worrying that they'd be next.

Another example: When I was 12, my mother told me I was going to be showering with other boys in gym class. My sexuality had already surfaced and my fantasies were of other boys, so this information left me very stimulated and titillated. I fantasized about it for weeks, thinking how much fun it would be to see my classmates naked. Soon, however, I realized the negative consequences of staring too long—showing an obvious erection.

These memories are quite vivid for me. Many of my LGBTQ clients recall similar types of things happening to them. Gay men often remember how much they hated gym class and how they did anything they could to avoid participating. Some LGBTQ teenagers dissociated more than I did and were not conscious of why certain environments were difficult and provocative for them. They were not aware of their homoerotic impulses other than being uncomfortable.

How Covert Cultural Sexual Abuse Operates

Heterosexism is the umbrella for the cultural victimization that LGBTQ individuals suffer. Most people understand heterosexism in terms of politics and how it denies rights to LGBTQ individuals on a social level. The sexual abuse is overshadowed by the politics and the inhumanity that most people focus on when seeing the effects of heterosexism on LGBTQ people.

As clinicians, it is your job to help your clients see that what happened to them during their growing-up years was a covert form of sexual abuse. But you can do this only by being convinced and educated yourself that this is a phenomenon for LGBTQ children. Not all will suffer the negative consequences of covert cultural sexual abuse. We know that even some children of overt sexual abuse do not have the symptomology that most survivors have. However, it is imperative that the clinician rule covert cultural sexual abuse out in assessing clients and their presenting problems.

Believing that Lesbianism and Gayness Equal Adult Sex

Because people typically associate LGBTQ *identity* with adult sexual behavior, thinking that children might be gay superimposes adult sexuality onto them—which is certainly inappropriate. But considering a child to be LGBTQ is not more (or less) sexually suggestive than assuming he is straight.

Savin-Williams (2005) stated that the reluctance to perceive children as gay is rooted in the belief that children are asexual. Few are willing to identify prepubertal gay children, assuming that gayness "arrives" only with adolescence or the onset of puberty.

Some (perhaps to avoid accusations of pedophilia) argue that they don't think of children as sexual at all. But as the popularity of Hummel figurines attests, we do think of children as romantic—holding hands, even kissing. We don't sexualize grade school crushes, but justify them as healthy "practice" for teenage dating and adult marriage. We often ask little girls if they have crushes on their male teachers, or a little boy if he "has a girlfriend yet." As early as kindergarten, teachers have students send each other valentines—albeit on a round-robin basis. Later on, we tolerate little girls having crushes on other girls without labeling them lesbians. No one flinches if first- and second-grade boys hold hands. None of this is considered sexualization, because we insist that children can't be sexual.

But the underlying assumption in all of these cases is that the child will grow up to be straight, and encouraging or allowing these childhood behaviors is considered acceptable because everyone recognizes that heterosexuality involves more than just adult sexual behavior—it also involves romance. Homosexuality and bisexuality, on the other hand, are typically seen in terms of purely adult sexual behaviors rather than as a multifaceted *identity* that involves affection, romance, and sex, just like heterosexuality. So if a child or adolescent *does* express romantic feelings toward someone of the same gender or actually embraces an LGBTQ identity, we immediately react by sexualizing him or her.

Sexualizing same-sex attraction among children does the same damage that would occur to any child who is oversexualized. These children are not developmentally ready to handle adult sexual overtones of any kind. We know as clinicians that early imprinting is most profound, and that the earlier the abuse, the more severe the consequences suffered will be.

The negative effects on the child exposed to this early sexual abuse—whether overt or covert—will be feelings of shame, a belief that it is their fault, self-destructive behavior, depression, low self-esteem, anger directed at the self or others, and an inability to trust others.

The Case of John

John, a 43-year-old executive, was experiencing depression, not sleeping well, and becoming easily agitated after his partner of 11 years left him. John had strong negative feelings about the gay community and repeatedly said that no one would want him as a partner because he was monogamous and didn't enjoy "kinky gay sex."

John confided that in all the 11 years he and his partner were together, he never told anyone except his close friends that they were a couple. He was not officially out to coworkers or friends outside his social circle. At family events, he referred to his partner as "my friend." His partner finally grew frustrated at not being included and ultimately left. Though upset by the breakup, John blamed it on his partner and didn't see how his refusal to publicly recognize the relationship negatively affected it. He repeatedly said in sessions, "I don't want to flaunt my sex life," which he felt being out to friends, coworkers, and family meant.

John stated that he knew it was safe to be out to his family and they would have embraced his partner, but he just felt it would have been inappropriate to announce that "this is my sex partner." "Straight people don't have to do this, and nor should I!" he said.

This comment was a big red flag for me. I recognized that John was buying into the concept that gayness equals adult sex, and that being an out gay man was like telling people about his sex life. This had already cost him his relationship. When I questioned him about this, he became defensive: "Why should I have to tell them? They don't tell me what they do in bed, nor do I want to know."

"Telling them you are gay isn't telling them what you do sexually in bed," I quickly replied. "It is about honoring the love you had for your partner and ensuring that your family and friends honored and treated you as a couple." He strongly disagreed and told me how ridiculous I sounded. He had normalized his way of living and accused me of being an "activist gay therapist" who wanted him to wave a rainbow flag. This, of course, was negative transference, and it revealed more about him and his internalized homophobia. John said he purposely stayed away from the gay community because it was too "sexual and immature."

"Why tell them, only to have them think of me and my partner being sexual? It is better they not have that image or discomfort," he replied.

I responded to John by telling him that his concern about how people react is also a form of internalized homophobia and that his decision not to tell had more to do with what other people thought than what he actually thought.

"Do you think that your relationship with your partner is solely based on sex?"

"No," he responded.

"Then I am saying it is your opportunity and responsibility to educate your family for your benefit, your relationship's benefit, and your family's benefit. You lost your relationship over this. Imagine the detriment of a heterosexual man not telling his family and friends that his significant other was his wife?"

"This is different—when you tell someone that you are gay, they immediately think of sex!" he argued.

"But your job to heal and grow as a gay male and have successful relationships is to get past this yourself," I responded. "I don't even think about what others think any longer. If they imagine my partner and me being sexual, or even just me, that is their issue, not mine. It does not dictate who I tell. As a Jewish man, I don't refrain from sharing I am Jewish just because others might stereotype me. The same needs to hold true about your being gay."

This was the place where John needed to do his work in therapy. He was suffering from covert cultural sexual abuse.

John: Clinical Interpretation and Treatment

Protecting his family was another form of internalized homophobia, as was John's denial that he equated homosexuality with adult sex. LGBTQ individuals must detach from the reactions of others, unless they are in danger of physical violence, losing their job or housing, or being rejected by their family when they are dependent on the family financially or otherwise. For John, none of these factors applied: It was safe to tell others. The trouble was that he did not feel safe inside himself. He wanted to protect his family, and I interpreted him as saying unconsciously, "I see my gayness as sexual given that I have reduced myself to only that—not only in the eyes of others but also in my own." To me, John was struggling with the effects of covert cultural sexual abuse, which manifested in internalized homophobia. Recovery would be intolerance of not letting others know his authentic self. Moreover, recovery would entail being out everywhere it was safe to be out. Ultimately, John's work was detaching from others' false assumptions that his gayness was purely sexual, "sick," or negative in any other way.

Uninformed therapists may overlook signs of internalized homophobia and unintentionally align with a client's reasoning that, for example, the gay culture is "overly sexual" and that it isn't important to come out to people you speak to or exchange cards with once a year. Even if therapists do catch the internalized homophobia, they may treat *it* and not address the covert cultural sexual abuse. The informed gay affirmative therapist, however, will catch these forms of internalized homophobia and covert cultural sexual abuse and help clients identify and heal from them.

Gender Bashing

Gender bashing is one of the predominant forms of covert cultural sexual abuse imposed on all children, but especially LGBTQ children—and particularly transgender children. As I have already mentioned, many of my LGBTQ clients—males more than females—recall being "different" in a negative way from an early age but didn't know exactly what that difference was. The reason males notice their difference earlier than females is often because of their desire to play with opposite-gender toys—such as Barbie dolls rather than G.I. Joes—which they were shamed for. Many admit that if others had granted them permission, they could have discovered why they were different. Instead, they compartmentalized, or even demonized, this major part of their identity.

For example, one of my male clients played mostly with girls as a child—they dressed up and played house. He was gentle, soft-spoken, and poor at sports. He was teased in school and bullied by being pushed, slapped, spit at, and verbally abused. He still experiences the effects of this trauma. The shame he felt for being the "wrong" kind of boy penetrated his core identity.

A lesbian client of mine was a tomboy as a little girl, excelling at sports and dressing in male-identified clothing. She was then forced to wear dresses by her mother and to "act more like a lady." She was shamed for being the type of female her mother did not want her to be.

Children and adolescents may be overly stimulated by the opposite-gender behaviors they wish to engage in. They may even notice something about the same sex that is attractive in a romantic or sexual way but have no one with whom to share this. If they do share, they are often met with contempt or denial. They are titillated by the overwhelming feelings of romance and sexuality and have no positive outlet for these powerful feelings. For these individuals, PTSD symptoms result from having to keep such important and highly emotionally charged information inside. In addition, our patriarchal society punishes LGBTQ individuals from the start for not complying with rigid gender roles that mandate that only the opposite sex can be your object of passion and desire sexually and romantically. While we are seeing incredible pushback from teenagers challenging the binary prejudices that narrowly define male and female, there is still punishment for nonconformity.

Overall, little boys tend to be shamed and degraded more often than girls for not being gender conforming. Being male is a privileged status, and anything else is viewed as inferior. Little girls are even rewarded for engaging in opposite-gender behaviors and interests. For example, it's okay for girls to be tomboys for a period of time, but there is no acceptable time frame for boys to be sissies.

However, this isn't always the case, as the film *Fried Green Tomatoes* (1991) illustrates. Although the theme of lesbianism is played down in this movie, it is apparent that the lead character, Idgie, is lesbian. One flashback recalling her younger life shows Idgie as a little girl—a tomboy with scorn for wearing dresses—being coerced to wear one to her sister's wedding. For Idgie, this is humiliating and out of sync with who she naturally is. When her younger brother makes fun of her discomfort, she climbs up to her tree house and flings the dress down to the ground.

But the next scene portrays something that most gay and lesbian children lack—a family member who validates who she is. Idgie's older brother Buddy accepts her being "different." While she's still half-naked and humiliated, he climbs up to the tree house and tells her about "all the millions of oysters . . . at the bottom of the ocean. And then one day God comes along and sees one and says, 'I'm going to make that one different.' . . . He puts a little piece of sand in it [so that particular oyster] can make a beautiful pearl."

"What if God made a mistake?" Idgie asks.

"The way I figure it, He doesn't make mistakes."

The next scene shows her in church wearing a suit and tie—and looking proud, in integrity with herself once again.

As this film shows, the extent of the trauma from growing up LGBTQ would be reduced tremendously—or even avoided altogether—if all nonstraight children had someone like Buddy in their lives.

Forced Gender Identity Confusion

Research is showing that many gay and lesbian children, as well as transgender children, experience gender dysphoria. It isn't until adolescence, when puberty kicks in and hormones are released, that gay and lesbian children recognize they are attracted to the same gender and their dysphoria goes away. However, adolescence is when transgender children experience an increase in gender dysphoria to the point of being suicidal (more on this in Chapter 14). Gay and lesbian children have no innate confusion regarding their maleness or femaleness, whereas transgender children do. Little girls such as Idgie are *not* confused. They know the type of female they are. It is *others* who are uncomfortable, not them. The confusion and problems come from outside themselves, as others try to mold them into the type of male or female they are "supposed to be." This is counter to the idea that gender confusion causes homosexuality—a belief espoused by the reparative therapies discussed in Chapter 1. This is also true of transgender children. They are not confused but rather do not have permission to explore their true gender identity.

Reparative therapy asserts that gay men weren't adequately taught how to behave as boys, and lesbians weren't taught how to be girls. It holds that gay individuals can be "changed" to become straight by eliminating homosexual desires. The male and female ideals touted by these therapies are sexist and outdated. Making people with homosexual desires ashamed for being the "kind" of male or female they are is a form of covert sexual abuse. Your LGBTQ clients may be suspicious of any therapy at all, thanks to the harmful practices of reparative therapy. Watching for this transference is imperative, and assuring clients that you are not in favor of reparative therapy in any form is important.

Probably the most abusive book toward gays and lesbians is *A Parent's Guide to Preventing Homosexuality* by Joseph Nicolosi and his wife, Linda Ames Nicolosi (2002). In a veiled way, this book evaded the American Psychological Association's warning that trying to "help" gay people suppress their sexual and romantic desires may lead to a lifetime of depression. Nicolosi's book on preventing "homosexual" orientation in the first place is nothing more than child abuse.

Nicolosi and others in his "extreme makeover" camp have gotten wise to the criticism of their approach and thus have disguised it. They softened their terminology, telling parents to correct children but not shame them for playing with opposite-gender toys. If your son plays with a doll, they advised taking it away and telling him you're giving it to a little girl who needs it. To me, this is abominable. They want men to be good fathers but stop their children from playing with dolls—which is one way to learn how to parent. Removing toys, whether you do it nicely or in a shaming way, will only wound a child's self-esteem.

Furthermore, playing with dolls does not *make* a boy homosexual or lead to orientation problems. In *The "Sissy Boy Syndrome" and the Development of Homosexuality*, Richard Green reported a study in which 75% of the boys who played with girls' toys and identified with girls grew up to be gay (1987). Green speculated that playing with feminine toys won't *make* a boy gay, but that it is one possible indicator that he *already is*.

A Parent's Guide to Preventing Homosexuality tells mothers to "back off" and turn away from their sons, giving the example of a mother who was "disgusted" by her son's asking to use her makeup. The only good advice they give is for fathers to get more involved. I couldn't agree more: Fathers abandoning their sons, gay and straight alike, has caused much of the anxiety and depression in gay men today. More involved fathers can help their sons grow into more mature men, but they cannot make them straight or gay.

Although most of the literature on this subject tends to focus on male homosexuality, this isn't a phenomenon specific only to males. Females also experience coercion to act like traditional girls.

The Case of Kim

Kim, age 40, came to see me after the loss of a third relationship with a woman whom she had been with for 5 years. Kim was starting to wonder whether or not she was a lesbian. She'd already consulted a therapist who convinced her that her childhood had contributed to her lesbian identity and that her relationships failed because she was living the wrong sexual identity.

Kim was the younger of two siblings; her brother, Tom, was 2 years older. Kim recalled having a distant relationship with her mother early on. Her mother wanted her to wear nail polish and dresses and keep her hair long. However, Kim did not like that from a very young age. If her mother put her in dresses she would change into pants and get punished by her mother. If her mother polished her fingernails she would chew the polish off by the end of the day. Kim's mother even forced her to get her ears pierced, trying to bribe her with diamond earrings. When Kim "lost" the earrings, her mother became very angry.

Kim's mother repeatedly shamed her, asking her why she "did not want to be a girl." But Kim recalled wanting to be a girl even from a very young age—just not the type of girl her mother thought she should be. Kim was labeled a tomboy and her mother ultimately distanced herself from her in frustration.

As a child, Kim was jealous of her brother, who went to baseball games with her father—trips on which she was not included. Her father had been a star athlete in high school and hoped for Tom to follow in his footsteps. Although Kim played baseball in second grade and hoped her father would attend and possibly coach, he was coaching Tom's team instead.

When Kim complained to her father, he would side with her mother, telling Kim to go along with what her mother wanted. "Little girls must be pretty and soft for their boyfriends," he would say to her. She felt rejected and alone.

By fifth grade, however, Kim began to excel at baseball, and by sixth grade, she was the star jock of her school baseball team. Her father began taking a stronger interest in her baseball events and began coaching her. Eventually her father mostly abandoned Tom, as his playing was below average and paled in comparison to Kim's. Kim recalled hearing her mother fighting with her father over this, and over time her mother distanced herself from Kim and became closer to Tom.

In high school, Tom complained that he was referred to as the "brother of the best baseball player in their school" and was unhappy about being in Kim's shadow. Kim grew closer and closer to her father, and although she enjoyed her relationship with him, she felt badly for her brother.

Kim also felt responsible for her parents' fighting and for how her father treated

Tom. She would hear her mother expressing contempt for Kim and wondering if she was the type of girl who really wanted to be a boy. Her father finally stood up to his wife, stating that all that mattered was that she was good at something and he was proud. The truth of the matter, according to Kim, was that he was invested in a child who could play baseball well, and it happened to be her. She knew both her parents would have preferred her to be more feminine.

By the time she came to see me, Kim was a physical therapist for sport injuries and a coach for several girls' baseball teams; she'd built her entire identity around sports. She had a distant relationship with both her mother and brother and had difficulties in her relationships with women as well. All three of her partners told her she was emotionally distant and did not offer enough closeness and dependency. After seeing the last therapist, Kim wondered now if she might have been attracted to women because of her distant relationship with her mother. She worried that the therapist was correct—that perhaps she turned away from men out of fear of being "smothered" and engulfed by her mother and her attempts to make Kim more feminine.

Perhaps, she wondered, she was looking toward women in an effort to meet her "mother hunger" needs.

Kim: Clinical Interpretation and Treatment

Staying in the model of GAT, I told Kim that how one is raised cannot create sexual orientation. Kim did not have any attraction to men in any way and knew inside that she was romantically and sexually attracted to other women and always had been. She acknowledged that this was true, and admitted that this realization had led her to change therapists.

I explained to her that she had taken on the problems in her family, making them her "fault" for how things turned out. I normalized how children blame themselves and have magical thinking about controlling the way things occur in their families. We worked together on understanding that her father was playing out his dream of having a star athlete for a child. That she was naturally athletic, unlike her brother, was not something she made happen.

In terms of her relationships with women, it made more sense that her distant mother created a childhood imprint and that this was why Kim distanced herself from her partners, which led to failed relationships. I explained to her that her mother's discomfort with the kind of female Kim was as a child was her mother's issue, not hers. This had caused a distance between Kim and her mother, which became her love map in terms of keeping a distance from the women with whom she had relationships. In other words, her relationship with her mother caused problems in her relationships; it did not *create* her sexual orientation. This helped Kim direct her attention away from "what made her gay" to the real question of what was causing her relationships to fail.

Linking Homosexuality With Pedophilia

One of the most damaging myths is that homosexuality and pedophilia are linked. This is by far one of the worst forms of covert cultural sexual abuse that children (particularly boys) are taught—to beware of homosexuals who might prey on them. Many of the people who link pedophilia with homosexuality are those who equate gay men with members of NAMBLA, the North American Man-Boy Love Association—which has everything to do with pedophilia and nothing to do with homosexuality.

Many of my male clients were warned as children that there were male sexual predators that they should recognize and avoid. These predators were usually described as homosexual men. (Generally, we distinguish three categories: A pedophile is an adult with primary or exclusive sexual attraction to prepubescent children under the age of 11, a hebophile is an adult with primary or exclusive sexual attraction to pubescent children ages 11–14, and an ephebophile is an adult with primary or exclusive sexual interest in adolescents between the ages of 15–19.) This link between sexual predators and gay sex obviously scares young gay boys, but it can also make a boy curious about the men whose sexual interests are like their own. (This is illustrated in the following story.) Many of my gay male clients have talked to me about being intrigued, when they were boys themselves, hearing about men who were interested in boys. They didn't understand that it was about abuse. Instead, because of their isolation and interest in meeting someone also attracted to other males, they would find themselves seeking these pedophiles out.

When I train therapists, I tell them to ask about childhood sex with adults when getting histories of both gay and bisexual men. Some clients will tell you that the sex they had as children with an older man did not traumatize them, and for many this seems to be true. I've been told by many gay and bisexual male clients that they enjoyed their childhood sexual experiences with adult perpetrators; many romanticize it as their first sex. This is something I've had to get accustomed to as a therapist. It can be difficult to hear stories of sexual abuse described in the warm tones of first love.

The Case of Mike

Mike was a 54-year-old teacher, still closeted, never married, who paid male prostitutes for sex. When he was a child his parents taught him that he needed to stay away from the man at the end of the block because he was dangerous. The entire neighborhood knew this man was a "homosexual" and tried to be sexual with little boys.

At the age of 13, Mike became titillated by this information. He did not know where to find other males like him interested in being sexual with one another. He reported in therapy that approaching another boy in school would never have been acceptable and he was isolated and alone, wanting connection with someone like him.

Over the summer he began going over to the man's house and they became "friends." Nothing sexual happened initially, and Mike believed the man really liked him. Then, one summer night at dusk, he went over to the man's house and, sure enough, the man began a sexual relationship with him. The man was in his 30s and although Mike knew it was wrong and shameful, he felt compelled to continue seeing this man, whom he described as loving and nurturing.

One day while Mike was at the man's house, another 12-year-old boy came over, and the man forced the two boys to be sexual. The other boy did not want to, but the man forced him, telling both boys that if they told anyone he would kill their families. The man took pictures of the boys masturbating and fellating one another.

Horrified, Mike went home afterward trembling and frightened. When he returned the next week, the man told him to never come back. Mike never saw the man again. He felt betrayed and abandoned—but most importantly, he felt that this man had loved him and then rejected him.

Mike: Clinical Interpretation and Treatment

Mike lived with this secret all of his life until stepping into my office. He had equated homosexuality with pedophilia. Even though as an adult he knew this wasn't true, he could not break the link. He blamed himself for what had happened, as all sexual abuse survivors do.

My first step in Mike's treatment was to educate him about sexual abuse. I told him that a sexual advance from an adult to a child is always sexual abuse. The adult is in a position of power and the child is not. Sexual abuse confuses individuals in terms of understanding their true sexual and romantic orientation and causes them to sexually act out promiscuously.

"But I asked for it. He was my first love," Mike told me vehemently. "Sexual abuse is something that happens involuntarily, without love—I signed up for what happened!"

I told him that was not possible as a child. He was a gay teenage boy looking for love and attention and a sexual experience. Not knowing where else to go, he sought out the pedophile in the neighborhood, whom he was told was a "homosexual." I explained that as a gay adolescent not knowing of any other resources, it made sense that he sought out this man. I also emphasized that this experience should *not* have happened, as the man took advantage of him.

"But I loved this man, too, and thought he loved me," Mike told me. I told him this relationship was not about love but about power and abuse, and that it had nothing to do with homosexuality and everything to do with trauma and rape.

This made sense to Mike. Weeping, he told me that he felt he was dangerous and had worried throughout his life that he, too, would become a child molester. As an adult, he had compulsive sexual behaviors; he was driven to meet male hustlers and pay them for sexual connection. I interpreted this as his PTSD: Mike felt that he was "a danger" to others the same way the man down the street was identified as dangerous. Paying male hustlers for sex was his way of avoiding feeling dangerous. However, I pointed out, and he agreed, that he often put himself at risk again by finding these male hustlers in dangerous ways and not knowing them very well. Indeed, Mike had been not only robbed by some of these men but also blackmailed—they had threatened to out him if he did not pay them off.

Mike's work in therapy was to understand that he was not at fault for what happened to him or for being a gay little boy who was overstimulated by being told that the molester down the street was a homosexual. It made sense that he went to meet this man, as he had felt so alone and isolated.

With today's access to the Internet, gay children can even more easily make contact with pedophiles and other dangerous characters. If children are overstimulated by having to suppress their innate sexual and romantic feelings as well as their core identity, they will absolutely find places to express themselves that could prove dangerous or even deadly.

In her book *Predators, Pedophiles, Rapists and Other Sex Offenders*, Anna C. Salter (2004), a leader in the field of pedophilia, pointed out that when a man molests little girls, we call him a "pedophile," not a "heterosexual." Research psychologist Gregory Herek (2006b) defined pedophilia as "a psychosexual disorder characterized by a preference for prepubescent children as sexual partners, which may or may not be acted upon." He added that because of our society's aversion to male homosexuality, and the attempts made by some to represent gay men as a danger to "family values," many in our society immediately think of male-male molestation as homosexuality. He compares this with the time when African Americans were falsely accused of raping white women, and when medieval Jews were accused of murdering Christian babies in ritual sacrifices. Both are examples of how mainstream society eagerly jumped to conclusions that justified discrimination and violence against these minorities. Today, gays face the same kind of prejudice.

Of importance here is that pedophilia should be viewed as a kind of sexual fetish, wherein the person requires a child or the mental image of a child to achieve sexual gratification. Rarely does a pedophile experience sexual desire for adults of either gender. They usually don't identify as homosexual—the majority identify as heterosexual, even those who abuse children of the same gender. They are sexually aroused by youth, not by gender.

In fact, some research shows that for pedophiles, the gender of the child is immaterial. Accessibility is the more important factor. This may explain the high incidence of children molested in church communities and fraternal organizations; in these venues, pedophiles easily have access to children. In such situations, an adult male is trusted by those around him, including children and their families. Males are often given access to boys to mentor, teach, coach, and advise.

In recent years, pedophilia, ephebophilia, and hebophilia are being seen as their own sexual orientation. Some newer research on nonoffending adults with this sexual orientation (attraction to children) divides these men into two categories: those who offend and those who don't. Those who don't offend often see their sexual interest as unfortunate and a handicap and know they will never act on it with children in any way, including viewing child porn. Some of these men identify as straight or LGBTQ, and some do not. For more information on this topic, see Salon (2015) and Pedophiles About Pedophilia (2015). I am not trained to work with pedophilia, ephebophilia, or hebophilia, and I refer these clients to therapists who are.

Your LGBTQ clients have had to live with this false link from childhood. If they have children, want to have children, or want to work with children, it is important that you explore with them whether or not they hold this erroneous belief.

Covert Cultural Sexual Abuse: The Perfect Crime

Covert cultural sexual abuse is the perfect crime because the perpetrator offends, the victim forgets, and the offender gets away scot-free. By the time LGBTQ children become adults, they may repress the abuse, deny that it ever happened, and blame themselves for whatever they do recall. Having been warned that homosexuality is evil, they grow up thinking that the evil lies within them. Then, blaming themselves, they believe they deserve to be treated poorly. Out of envy, they may even identify with their homophobic oppressors. Your job as a therapist is to help these people realize, after they come out, that their problem lies mainly in what's been *done* to them and is not a result of *who* they are.

Sexual Abuse Will Disorient You, Not Orient You

Many of my clients insist that some long-ago incident of sexual abuse made them LGBTQ—even if they have no memory of such an event and have no evidence that it could have happened. Some of this is because of the myth that sexual abuse causes a nonheterosexual orientation, which is completely false. But it also may be due to the fact that these clients harbor unconscious feelings about the effects of covert cultural sexual abuse on them—without knowing what to call it—which they sometimes misidentify as covert sexual abuse.

Those who *were* sexually abused believe that that's precisely why they're now LGBTQ. They buy into the old assumption that sexual abuse turns a bewildered child away from his inborn heterosexuality and "makes" him LGBTQ. As discussed earlier, sexual abuse may lead to sexual acting-out behaviors, but there is no evidence that it can shape one's sexual orientation, much less create it. The only thing it does do is cloud and confuse people about what their sexual orientation truly is. Again, sexual abuse can influence *behavior*, not basic orientation. And covert cultural sexual abuse can create a barrier to achieving any sense of belonging with others who are LGBTQ.

Confusion About Sexual Orientation

An enduring aspect of sexual abuse, assault, or harassment is the confusion it creates. Sexual abuse leaves victims—gay or straight—dissociated from their true sexual orientation. Covert cultural sexual abuse forces gays and lesbians into a daze and rewards them for playing straight.

One of the dynamics of sexual abuse is that the perpetrator's sexuality overlays that of the victim. In other words, during and after the abuse, the victim's needs are secondary, if involved at all. For lesbians and gays, the perpetration of heterosexism leaves them wondering whether they truly have heterosexual feelings and desires or if those heterosexual desires are a result of imprinting from the dominant culture.

Because gay males and lesbians typically surrender their innate sexuality to heterosexual standards—heterosexism being the "perpetrator"—it's no wonder that, like sexual abuse survivors, they often remain confused about their orientation once homosexual or homoerotic thoughts and feelings begin to surface. Only when they finally get the courage to rebel and reclaim their own identity does their confusion and indecision dissipate.

By the time such clients arrive in your office, they've become adept at dissociating in ways that are profound and chronic, reflexive and automatic—even about matters that aren't sexual at all.

The Case of Eric

Eric, age 30, was a medical student studying to be an ophthalmologist. He admitted that most of his life was spent "in [his] head" and said he was more cognitive than emotive in nature. He was about to graduate and wanted to move into the next part of his life, but he was confused about whether he was gay, straight, or bisexual.

This dilemma had prompted him to seek therapy 2 years earlier. Eric was cautious about being in therapy with me. To assure himself that I would not "force [him] to be gay," he continued to see the straight therapist he still saw weekly. The other therapist believed that he was bisexual and could go either way. Eric was looking for someone more pro-gay to help him.

Eric had been in several relationships with women, and he said he had felt romance and love with these past girlfriends. But he was not attracted to women sexually, and he often took erectile dysfunction medications. With men it was different—he was sexually attracted to them instantly, but he never felt an emotional attraction. In fact, as soon as something turned emotional he would become uninterested, which made him think his homoerotic feelings were not about identity and only about sex. Eric had never been among gay men other than those he met online or at bathhouses. His lack of homosocialization was perhaps the problem—he couldn't discover a sense of belonging as a gay man.

Eric: Clinical Interpretation and Treatment

Eric took my suggestions and began attending gay community functions—he went to bars and community, political, and sporting events—but he felt that he didn't fit in at all. He spent 3 years seeing me and his other therapist, which I interpreted as a metaphor for not committing to an identity for himself. He agreed with my interpretation and thought about dating women and committing to that side of himself. I told him that if he did so, he needed to tell them that he had homoerotic feelings and interests. He did not wish to do this.

Eric said he could not imagine life with another man in terms of living together and waking up each morning facing each other. He worried what the neighbors would think and how it would affect his professional life as a physician. He was stuck in an ego-dystonic place about how he wanted to live his life, which arose from his being heteroemotional and homosexual. Eric had internalized the condemnation and hostility toward homosexuality from the homophobic culture.

My work with Eric was to help him explore his inner world of emotions, feelings, and values, as well as his core identity, which was very difficult for him. Ultimately, he met a man online whom he felt romantically attracted to. As I discuss in Chapter 7 on coming out, many gay men do not connect to their homosexual orientation until they fall in romantic love with another man, which is exactly what happened with Eric. He never did find an outlet within the gay community where he felt comfortable, but over time he created a relationship with this new love, came out of the closet, accepted his gayness, and made a life with his partner and with friends outside the gay community.

Brian McNaught (1997) put what I call covert cultural sexual abuse into perspective in terms of what happens to a young gay or lesbian child's development:

> Most gay people have been enormously, if not consciously, traumatized by the social pressure they felt to identify and behave as a heterosexual, even though such pressure is not classified as sexual abuse by experts in the field.
>
> Imagine how today's society would respond if heterosexual thirteen- to nineteen-year-olds were forced to date someone of the same sex. What would the reaction be if they were expected to hold the hand of, slow dance with, hug, kiss and say "I love you" to someone to whom they were not and could not be sexually attracted?
>
> The public would be outraged! Adult supervisors would be sent to prison. Youthful "perpetrators" would be expelled from school. Years of therapy would be prescribed for the innocent victims of such abuse. Volumes would be written about the long-term effect of such abhorrent socialization (as today we lament the ill-conceived efforts to turn left-handed people into right-handed ones).
>
> Yet, that's part of the everyday life of gay teenagers. And there's no comparable public concern, much less outcry, about the traumatizing effects on *their* sexuality. (p. 48)

McNaught's perspective offers excellent insight into the sexual trauma gays and lesbians experience growing up. By imagining heterosexual children and teenagers under the same circumstances that gay and lesbian children suffer, the covert cultural sexual abuse is highlighted and obvious.

Children can be vulnerable to sexual abuse, whether covert or overt—especially in homes where there is physical and emotional abuse and neglect. Children who do not have a sense of belonging or identity and who have troubled relationships with their parents are especially vulnerable to sexual abuse. LGBTQ children, even those who come from the best of families, can suffer the effects of covert cultural sexual abuse, internally knowing they don't belong and that their identity is something that could be met with contempt and rejection.

Lacking emotional and intellectual maturity, children automatically trust their caretakers and authority figures and incorporate their beliefs. LGBTQ children, then, are particularly vulnerable to covert cultural sexual abuse because they automatically trust their "perpetrators"—caretakers, doctors, teachers, coaches—none of whom necessarily mean any harm, but who are simply expressing the "wisdom" they have learned about homosexuality.

Comparing Covert Cultural Sexual Abuse to Sexual Abuse

If you view LGBTQ clients as the victims of a cultural rape that unfolded over the course of years, you may well find you can adapt many of the standard techniques used to counsel sexual abuse survivors with surprising effectiveness. In my experience, LGBTQ individuals who experience the shame of covert cultural sexual abuse as they grow up tend to exhibit PTSD symptoms similar to those of survivors of sexual abuse, as is illustrated in Table 4.2.

Table 4.2
PTSD Symptoms of Sexual Abuse and Covert Cultural Sexual Abuse

Sexual Abuse Survivor	Covert Cultural Sexual Abuse Survivor
Sexual secret about abuse	Sexual secret about being LGBTQ
Pretend nothing is wrong and abuse is not happening	Pretend nothing is wrong and pretend not to be LGBTQ by role-playing heterosexuality

Self-perception is hopelessly flawed	Self-perception as LGBTQ is that you are hopelessly flawed
Confusion about your sexual orientation	Confusion about whether you are LGBTQ or straight
Self-hate and blame for what was done to you	Self-hate and blame for being LGBTQ, resulting in internalized homophobia or transphobia
Believing you are to blame for the abuse	Believing you are to blame for not being able to suppress same-sex desires
Belief that people who care for you may kill you, abandon you, or be harmed themselves	Belief that people who care for you may abandon you, shame you, or harm themselves upon learning about your LGBTQ identity
Isolation from others out of fear and distrust of intimacy	Isolation from others (especially LGBTQ people) out of fear of betrayal and distrust of intimacy
Deadening of all feelings to avoid sexual arousal	Deadening of all feelings to avoid same-sex arousal (staying closeted)
Self-abuse or injury through drugs and alcohol	Self-abuse through drugs and alcohol and unsafe sex
Suicidal thoughts, gestures, and attempts	Suicidal thoughts, gestures, and attempts
Fear and avoidance of sexual arousal	Fear and avoidance of same-sex arousal
Displays of affection are inappropriately sexualized	Displays of affection are inappropriately sexualized (more so for gay men)
Becoming master of pretense and living out of integrity	Becoming master of pretense and living out of integrity, role-playing heterosexuality
Settling for too little	Settling for too little and not expecting much as an LGBTQ person
Short-lived and volatile relationships	Short-lived and volatile relationships before fully coming out of the closet

Since childhood, your LGBTQ clients have been taught—if only implicitly—that they're largely responsible for whatever abuse and neglect they've suffered. Thus, they're often wary of demonstrating affection or warmth for anyone of the same gender. Especially if they've sought to "pass" in straight society, LGBTQ individuals feel lonely and alienated, which only contributes to their emotional isolation and repression.

CHAPTER 5

Trauma From Growing Up LGBTQ

It is not difference which immobilizes us, but silence.
—Audre Lorde, writer, poet, and activist

Post-Traumatic Stress Disorder, Complex Trauma, and Simple Trauma

As a clinician, you know that the effects of trauma surface at different times—sometimes not for years. For LGBTQ individuals, trauma symptoms reveal themselves most dramatically when clients are repressing their sexual orientation and gender identity or attempting to come out. The more they push themselves or are pressured toward staying in or coming out, the more they'll have to struggle with trauma symptoms. Staying in the closet is prolonged trauma. The coming-out process reactivates all the trauma that was suppressed—which is one of the things that makes coming out so difficult. Once an individual comes out and is fully self-actualized as an LGBTQ person, the symptoms of trauma abate.

Judith Lewis Herman (1992) eloquently described the effects of chronic trauma:

The features of post-traumatic stress disorder that become most exaggerated in chronically traumatized people are avoidance or constriction. When the victim has been reduced to a goal of simple survival, psychological constriction becomes an essential form of adaptation. This narrowing applies to every aspect of life—to relationships, activities, thoughts, memories, emotions, and even sensations. And while this constriction is adaptive in captivity, it also leads to a kind of atrophy in the psychological capacities that have been suppressed and to the over-development of a solitary inner life. (p. 87)

This explanation of PTSD applies to the experience of growing up gay and lesbian better than any other I've read. It points to why so many gays and lesbians struggle with problems in their inner lives and interpersonal lives.

According to the *DSM-IV*, post-traumatic stress disorder results from exposure to an overwhelmingly stressful event or series of events. The *DSM-IV* talks about how the stressor can be a threat or perceived threat to one's physical integrity. It also addresses the victim's response to the event, involving intense fear, helplessness, or horror. PTSD prompts symptoms of hypervigilance, hyperarousal, and the perception of threat to one's emotional and physical self.

The Case of Patricia

Jane, a therapist I was supervising, was working with Patricia, a 37-year-old hairstylist. Patricia had begun the coming-out process and was grieving over the years she'd lost having not come out earlier. Jane did a thorough history on Patricia, learning that she felt she came from a functional family where she was loved and cared for by both her parents but particularly by her father. There was not any alcohol or drug abuse. Jane began helping Patricia through the coming-out process, which progressed slowly. Patricia would frequently get angry and upset about not having come out earlier. She knew her family would take the news of her being a lesbian well. She recalled that her father had enjoyed playing ball with her and came to all of her soccer games and coached. He often told her she was the "son he never had." She couldn't understand why she didn't feel comfortable, when she discovered she was lesbian at the age of 20, telling them about her homosexuality.

Jane became impatient with Patricia's reticence about coming out, and the more she pushed her, the more Patricia's anxiety symptoms surfaced. This only further agitated Jane, which stimulated countertransference, prompting her to see me for some supervision.

Jane told me that Patricia's father was a police officer whom Patricia described as conscientious, rule-oriented, and full of integrity. Her paternal grandfather had been a police officer as well.

I coached Jane to ask Patricia about her mother's—and particularly her father's—values and beliefs about homosexuality. Sure enough, Patricia had plenty to say that she hadn't said before. Although she maintained that her father was loving and accepting, she also said that her dad was an "Archie Bunker type"—that is, he did not have nice things to say about anyone who wasn't Caucasian, Catholic, and middle-to upper-class. He frequently made fun of Arabic men, calling them "towel heads," and was very verbal about his negative feelings toward homosexuality, using words like "faggot" and "sissy queer" toward gay males. Although these verbal assaults were never directed at her or at lesbians, Patricia recalled them vividly.

Both her father and grandfather were involved in raiding rest areas where gay men would sexually cruise and hook up. Patricia watched the contempt and disgust both her father and grandfather had toward those "homos." Early in life, Patricia learned that her family's loving and unconditionally accepting attitudes didn't extend to gays. Recalling this was Patricia's "aha" moment. To come out entailed telling her homophobic father that she was one of those "queers" he had always talked about.

At age 37, when Patricia realized it was time for her to tell her father, she started exhibiting what she called OCD symptoms: She didn't sleep, became irritable, and found herself anxiously locking and relocking her house and car as she had done when she was a child. Jane had agreed that it was OCD as well.

But this wasn't a case of OCD. These were PTSD symptoms. Understanding this, Jane began addressing Patricia's internalized homophobia, which came from growing up in a homophobic house and society that supports negative feelings toward homosexuality. She was also able to help Patricia with her PTSD symptoms. Without this understanding, Jane would have treated Patricia's supposed OCD, wasting time on an ineffective treatment for a misdiagnosis.

Ultimately Patricia did tell her father, who accepted her instantly, as did her entire family, including her grandfather. They cried together upon learning how hurtful they were to Patricia as a young lesbian girl and apologized for their lack of care around that issue. But now Patricia was left with unresolved feelings of anger and sadness that as a young girl and young woman she did not allow herself the opportunity to come out and actuate her inner identity. She was able to let Jane help her be angry toward her father for the homophobic slurs and at the same time understand she was loved and cared for in every other way. I also coached Jane to help Patricia look at her mother and grandmother's role—they never said anything to her father about his homophobic and ethnic slurs. Their silence, and the implied acceptance of these slurs, contributed to Patricia's trauma.

As you can see, it is crucial for the therapist to identify and understand the trauma of growing up gay. There are many clients who will come to you describing terribly dysfunctional childhoods with parents who were addicted, sexually promiscuous, or abusive. It's easy for clinicians to focus on these issues and ignore the trauma of growing up gay. But it's vital to consider trauma with every lesbian or gay client you see. Of course, not *all* gays and lesbians suffer from PTSD. It depends on the client's temperament, how severe the abuse was, and how rigid and strict the client's upbringing was.

Vicarious Trauma

LGBTQ clients can be suffering from "vicarious trauma" from news reports and other media sources. Research has shown that even though no LGBTQ individuals were involved in hate crimes directly, nor even present, nor even knew the victim, they felt unsafe (Noelle, 2002).

Silence Is Not Golden

Many parents—even therapists—will argue that children grow up without hearing any homophobic comments directed at them. Usually, they are correct. But direct insults do not always contribute to covert cultural sexual abuse as much as hearing and witnessing negative statements and acts directed toward other gays and lesbians as a group or individually. Another silent assault is perpetrated by the absence of lesbian and gay role models and discussions about homosexuality. Invisibility communicates the message that you don't exist, you don't belong, and that if you do express yourself, you will be alone.

It's difficult to understand the scope and nature of the trauma gays and lesbians experience growing up. To help, I use the following guided imagery exercise, which I've adapted from one written by Brian McNaught (1993).

GUIDED IMAGERY

Think back in your own life to when you were 13 years old. For the sake of this exercise, pretend that regardless of your sexual orientation, you have always been attracted to a different gender from yourself. Now pretend that when you were a baby, you were adopted by a gay male or lesbian couple. Without trying to figure it out, just go with your feelings of what it would feel like to have been raised by either two men or two women who love you very much, are proud of you, and want you to be happy.

In this fantasy family you have an openly gay 17-year-old brother (or sister) who brings home a boyfriend (or girlfriend) who is always welcome at the dinner table. Your parents wait up when your sibling comes home from dances to find out what a great time he or she had, and you notice that they are expecting that of you, too. You realize that if you want to be cherished in this family you, too, need to bring home someone of the same gender to make them proud.

At 14 years old, you are on your way to your first day of high school. The bus driver has a song on the radio and everyone on the bus, including the bus driver (and you), is singing along, and what you are singing is "I'm gay, I'm gay, I'm gay." What would that feel like? What would it feel like if every billboard you passed featured two people of the same gender? If every comic book hero were gay? If every television program and movie featured mostly or only gay people?

What would it feel like if your homeroom teacher were gay? And the librarian? And the principal? And the guidance counselor? What would it feel like if everyone in school thought you were gay, too?

But not *everybody* in this fantasy is gay. There are people sexually attracted to and interested in people of the other gender—they're called "heterosexuals." Most people—mean people, particularly—call them "breeders," and you've seen bumper stickers that read *Kill a breeder for Christ* and *Make love, not breeder babies*. A boy in your seventh-grade class was hit in the head with a dodgeball because the other students thought he was a breeder. You read newspaper articles about and see on television small groups of heterosexuals trying to get legislation passed so that they won't lose their housing or employment for being heterosexual. People preach that these people want "special rights" for what they do in the bedroom. In your religious institution, you hear that heterosexuality is an abomination and that those who act on it are sinners. You see yourself as a sinner because you know you are a breeder, so you don't even have God to talk to.

Do you have the nerve to get on the family computer and look up heterosexual issues? And do you risk doing it on your phone and risk your family discovering that you are looking up sexual orientation issues and they may ask you why and out you?

It is a Tuesday night, a school night, you are at home, and your parents say, "Come to the phone and talk to somebody." If you are a man, talk to Bob. Bob is 16 and is on the wrestling team and is president of the student government, and Bob wants to take you to your first high school dance. Bob and his friends have seen you walking in the hall, and they think you are cute. If you are a woman, it is Susan on the phone. Susan sits next to you in homeroom and she has been smiling at you every week, and she wants to take you to the dance.

Now it is Friday night and the gymnasium is filled with same-gendered couples. You are 14 years old, and you are in the arms of a person of the same gender. Slow dance after slow dance, you are in the arms of a person of the same gender, who keeps nuzzling your neck and whispering in your ear, "Are you having fun?" At the end of the evening, you two walk to your front door and have your first goodnight kiss. You walk inside your house and your gay family says to you, "Honey, you look so cute! Tell us all about it . . . did you have fun?"

So you get a boyfriend if you are a boy and a girlfriend if you are a girl, and you go to gay movies together and hold hands and learn how to French-kiss and bring them home to meet your family and you say to them, "I love you."

When you go to college, you hope things will be different, but everyone there is dating people of the same gender, too—except a small group of heterosexual students who gather at the student union periodically. Every time they put up a notice of meetings someone rips it down or writes breeder across it.

As a junior you finally have your first gay sexual experience. How do you feel about that? Later in the year, you look up a bar online frequented by people attracted to the other gender, and you want to go because you think you might make a new friend who understands you there. At the bar, an attractive person of the other gender smiles at you, introduces themselves, and asks you to dance. The next day, your gay friends comment on what a good mood you're in and ask where you went the night before. What do you tell them?

After dating this person for a long time, you decide to live together. How are you going to do that? How are you going to have your gay family and gay friends over? The answer is you get a two-bedroom apartment, and you put your belongings in one bedroom and theirs in the other. You always pull the shades at night. You get a secret cell phone, and you don't put your partner in your regular cell phone as a significant other. You don't put his or her picture on your desk at work, and you don't call him or her from the office because someone might overhear you. You even bring a gay date to office functions.

One evening you arrive home late from work to find your neighbor asking about your partner, "Did they make it? How are they doing?" And you find out the most important person in the whole world, your significant other, was taken to the hospital hours earlier, but you didn't know. No one called you because there was no ID or indication to contact you in case of emergency. You were afraid that if your wallet was stolen, you would be found out. When you arrive at the hospital, you stand behind the plate glass window looking at your partner fighting for his or her life all alone, and you must decide whether to tell the gay doctors and gay nurses that this person is your significant other, the person you love most in the whole world. You also have to decide whether to tell your coworkers who you really are and why you won't be coming to work for the rest of the week.

This exercise helps people understand what it would be like to grow up straight in a homocentric world. Once the concept of this kind of trauma is understood, people are often able to accept and understand gays and lesbians more effectively.

The trauma of growing up LGBTQ can be acute, but for the most part it is chronic and insidious. LGBTQ children grow into teenagers and young adults feeling devalued; they have low self-esteem, high levels of anxiety, and are hypervigilant. The result can be traumatic stress disorder symptoms like those Patricia suffered. Trauma complicates and compromises almost all areas of the lives of LGBTQ individuals, including the coming-out process, relationships, sexual expression, and mental health, along with addictions.

Bessel van der Kolk, a leading authority on the neurophysiology of trauma, wrote that "the younger the age at which the trauma occurred, and the longer its duration, the more likely people were to have long-term problems with regulation of anger, anxiety and sexual impulses" (1996, p. 187). Most overt as well as covert abuse occurs within the context of pseudo-cooperation, manipulation, and coercion rather than outright force. That agreement is part of the problem. The internalization of this trauma can manifest in symptoms such as impairment of basic trust, negative effects on identity, negative impact on play and relationships with others, and excessive interpersonal sensitivity.

How Trauma Manifests in Sexual Secret Keeping

To restore LGBTQ individuals to intact functioning requires that clinicians learn to discern how the trauma is acted out, as it can be very subtle. In fact, clients themselves may not even know about it. Referring to Table 4.2 in the previous chapter, I will outline how to look for each of the ways the trauma manifests.

A look at the existing literature (Maltz, 2001; Lew, 2004; Gartner, 1999) shows that those who have been sexually abused develop in ways that parallel the development of LGBTQ adults in terms of their thoughts and behaviors: Both carry the effects of the trauma into adulthood. The most profound trauma similarity between LGBTQ individuals and sexual abuse survivors is sexual secret keeping. Like sexual abuse survivors, LGBTQ people are taught that their sexuality is their fault and that if they tell someone about it, they will be harmed in some way, whether psychologically, physically, verbally, or emotionally. Silence is rewarded by the dominant mainstream culture, and hiding becomes a way of life. Keeping these sexual secrets can also lead to withholding sexual information from others. LGBTQ individuals may find, like sexual abuse survivors, that they are keeping sexual secrets even from themselves. This explains why so many people do not know they are LGBTQ before they come out. They are in complete denial.

Like with survivors of sexual trauma, the feelings of fear, shame, and secrecy that LGBTQs experience lead to loneliness and isolation, helplessness and hopelessness. The intense fear of being "outed" is similar to the fear of others' learning that you were sexually abused. Survivors think there must be something wrong with them; that it's somehow *their* fault for causing the abuse in the first place.

The Case of Jerry

Jerry, 28, was leading a comfortable life as a stagehand at a local theater. He fit the widely held stereotype of the effeminate gay man who couldn't pass as straight. He felt good about being gay and was out to his friends and family.

During one of his sessions with me, Jerry recounted a terrible story: One evening, when he was 21 and not yet out or comfortable with his homosexuality, he was approached by two men as he was leaving his fitness club. Claiming to be lost and in need of directions, the men lured Jerry into a rusting red van and promptly raped him anally.

While this was going on, Jerry dissociated—as most rape and abuse victims do. As he described it to me, he felt as if he had left his body and drifted out of the van, into a nearby billboard. The two men called him "faggot" and "queer," kicked and punched him, and then threw him out of their van, naked, before flinging out his clothes and gym bag and speeding away.

The next morning, Jerry dutifully went to rehearsal, worried that if he mentioned the incident, the world would discover he was gay. He feared both his family's rejection and being fired for "bringing [his] problems to work." As many gays do, he internalized the aggression of the men who had raped him and blamed himself for the attack. By thinking of the abuse as "justified," a victim unconsciously identifies with his attacker—thus empowering himself.

Jerry acted as if the whole incident had never happened—until 2 months later, when he was diagnosed with a deadly form of hepatitis. The doctor asked if he had contracted the disease through sexual contact. Rather than admit he'd been raped by two men, which in Jerry's mind would call attention to the fact that he might be gay, Jerry said nothing.

Most male victims of rape—whether gay, bisexual, trans, or straight—fear that telling will make others question their sexual orientation or gender identity. Research shows these rape victims worry about being asked questions like "Why didn't you make him stop?" It's even worse for a closeted GBT male who, like Jerry, is invested in keeping his sexuality a secret. He will be afraid that if people find out he's GBT, he will be accused of baiting the men or "asking for it" because of his sexual orientation or gender identity.

Jerry's health grew worse. Finally the doctor told him he would probably die if he didn't provide accurate information so the doctor could make the appropriate diagnosis and determine the best treatment. But for Jerry, fear of death was secondary to fear of his family's rejection if they discovered he was gay. Ultimately, he did admit that he must have contracted hepatitis from another man, but he didn't disclose having been raped and made the doctor promise not to tell his family.

Over the next few months, as Jerry was treated successfully, he recovered. Some years later, Jerry finally came out to his family, and they didn't reject him.

Although Jerry's story is an extreme example, it illustrates the sexual secrecy that manifests from the trauma and covert cultural sexual abuse that gays and lesbians suffer, as well as the lengths they'll go to—and even die for—to avoid further abuse and rejection.

How Trauma Manifests as Cognitive Distortions

The negative and shaming messages of covert cultural sexual abuse are learned early in life and develop into cognitive distortions similar to those exhibited by sexual abuse survivors. These cognitive distortions are:

- Pretending that nothing is wrong
- A self-perception that they are hopelessly flawed
- Confusion about their sexual orientation
- Self-hate and self-blame for what is done to them
- The belief that people who care for them may abandon them, harm them, or kill themselves

Pretending That Nothing Is Wrong

Early in life, LGBTQ children learn to cover up anything that suggests in any way that they might be homosexual, bisexual, or transgender. This is when LGBTQs begin living "out of integrity," which then becomes a rewarded way of life. But the longer they live out of integrity with themselves and others, the more it hampers other areas of their lives.

Many LGBTQ children hope that someone will see through the pretending—that someone will say, "I can see something is wrong; let me help you." But this rarely happens. And the truth is that LGBTQ teens do *not* want others, especially their parents, to ask them about their sexual orientation, because this kind of pressure can keep them in the closet longer. Read more about this in Chapter 13 on teenagers.

Self-Perception as Hopelessly Flawed

In the early stages of coming out, many LGBTQs believe that they are hopelessly flawed. Not yet self-accepting or having formed their full identities as LGBTQ individuals, they feel that they are faulty. They also feel ashamed—an emotion different from guilt. Feelings of guilt lead to self-messages like: "My behavior—what I did—is wrong or bad." The self-message of shame is: "My identity—who and what I am—is inherently wrong."

My clients have told me they will not and cannot come out to certain people in their lives, as they do not want to ruin how they are perceived by them—even when coming out would not jeopardize their safety, job security, or housing. They say things like: "It would ruin how they see me," or "Then I will be seen only as the LGBTQ friend." This type of self-talk and these beliefs inherently suggest that these clients believe something is wrong with them.

As a therapist, you can say to your client, "So what if they see you as their LGBTQ friend? What does that mean to you?" or "Why don't you want to be seen as their LGBTQ friend?" or "Talk to these people and tell them that you feel that your sexual orientation and gender identity are just a part of you and not *all* of who you are." It is important for clients to understand that they cannot manipulate how others will see them. Exploring their underlying feelings about why they do not wish to be seen in this way may reveal their feelings of being flawed.

Feeling flawed extends beyond one's sexual orientation and gender identity. It permeates how LGBTQ individuals feel overall in terms of gender, self-esteem, personality, and relationships with others.

Confusion About Sexual Orientation

Childhood sexual abuse will disorient you, not sexually orient you. It does not create sexual orientation, only confusion. Those who have been sexually abused in childhood often experience a sexual disorientation as to what their true sexual orientation and sexual interests are. In other words, sexual abuse will not shape someone's sexual orientation. They will be in your office wondering if the sexual abuse caused their sexual orientation and might they be heterosexual if it were not for the abuse. I have even had clients come in wondering if they are LGBTQ because were sexually abused even if there is no memory or indication of this. This stems from the covert cultural sexual abuse where LGBTQ clients are forced into examining a heterosexual identity and not having the freedom to explore what is natural for them.

Self-Hate and Self-Blame

LGBTQ individuals internalize the hate we see and read about in the media and watch others inflict on LGBTQ people. This is called *internalized homophobia*, which was addressed in Chapter 2. Those who cannot pass as straight receive it directly. This self-hate is learned at an early age. I believe it contributes to self-destructive acting-out behaviors like drug and alcohol abuse, unsafe sex practices, and other self-harming behaviors.

Not only do LGBTQ individuals feel responsible for the homophobia and microaggressions coming their way, but they also find people who will fulfill this belief, as the following case illustrates.

The Case of Arif

Arif, a 30-year-old Chaldean single male who self-identified as a gay man, came to me for therapy after a year with a therapist he felt shamed him for letting down his family by being an out gay man. Arif's family blamed him for not being loyal to their culture, which strongly advocated marrying and having children to carry on the family name. Arif's therapist sided with his mother and father, stating she could empathize with how hard it would be to have a child go against the cultural grain. Additionally, Arif wore his hair long and had mannerisms that were traditionally feminine, which his therapist interpreted as being an "in-your-face" expression of his gayness and invited abuse and ridicule from others.

Within the Chaldean culture, homosexuality is completely unacceptable—particularly for males. Arif's therapist was also Chaldean, and Arif hoped she would understand his plight. To his dismay, he received from her the same judgments he experienced with his family. He felt his therapist, along with his family, must be correct and that he was doing something wrong by being out and open as a gay man and inviting negativity.

Arif filled me in on his history. He initially told his family he was gay during college, at the age of 21. His family threatened to cut him off financially if he "chose that lifestyle," so Arif stopped talking about it. After graduation he took a job out of state to avoid having to deal with his family's negativity and to make a life for himself that supported his gayness. During his time away, he enjoyed living a normative gay identity with gay and lesbian friends.

Several years after his move, Arif was let go from his job. Unable to find a new job and no longer able to support himself, Arif decided to move back home to Detroit. His parents told him he had a rent-free place at their home—and promised to pay for his therapy—as long as he did not talk about being gay and he considered changing. He agreed to this but knew in his heart that change was not possible.

Arif's therapist explained to him that his homosexual interests might be a rebellion against his family, as he had a strained relationship with his father, whom Arif felt never liked him much as a child. She interpreted his need to be out to his family as an act of aggression and hostility. "It is okay that you are homosexual, but you don't need to act on it, and you don't need to make it part of their lives as well," his therapist told him. "Your parents are older, religious, and set in their ways. Why do you seem to need to do this? They are letting you live with them rent-free until you get back on your feet. They are paying your bills and your therapy. What more do you want from them?"

At first Arif took his therapist's words to heart, wondering if he was asking too much of his parents, who were already doing more for him than most parents would. "I've already made them suffer enough," he told himself. "I'm ruining everyone else's life as well as my own."

Then Arif met some other Chaldean men at a local bar and discovered that most of them were living underground lives, marrying the women their parents wanted them to marry, having children, and having sex on the side with other men. Arif did not want to live this way. He decided that he was with the wrong therapist, terminated with her, and started therapy with me.

Arif: Clinical Interpretation and Treatment

When Arif entered therapy with me, it did not take me long to assess how depressed he was and how damaged he felt about being gay due to his family and his past therapist. I helped him see that his family, his culture, and his former therapist were blaming him for his homosexuality and for wanting to overtly be his authentic self and live in integrity. I commended him for his attempts.

The arguments his therapist and family had made sounded logical to Arif, since he believed that his gayness was simply a behavior. I said to Arif, "But what about talking about where and with whom you went out with at night? What about wanting to talk about dates you go on or give them an idea of the places you frequent in case something were to happen to them or to you and they needed to get in touch with you?"

Living a lie might work for his family, but would it work for Arif?

I validated the therapist's well-intended attempts to help Arif in a tough culture where patriarchy and masculinity are revered and homosexuality is seen as being less of a man—and even a cause for being put to death in some Middle Eastern cultures. At best, she was trying to protect both Arif and his family and cause the least amount of distress for both. However, to me she was requiring change of Arif rather than of his family, which was where the issue truly lay. This was feeding into Arif's already low self-esteem and feelings of self-blame about causing his parents hardship.

I told Arif that he was not committing a crime in trying to be close to his family and be his authentic self with them. I helped him remove the blame from himself and explained that what he wanted in terms of being out and open was nothing different than anyone else wanting to be and feel "known" to those they love. He knew this to be true. Living out of state helped him meet other men and women living as out gays and lesbians, and he knew that was how he wanted to live.

Arif's therapy centered on his low self-esteem and his depression. He was trying to suppress how negative he felt about himself for being gay. I commended him for knowing somewhere within his psyche that something was wrong and for seeking out a gay affirmative therapist because of it. I urged him to go to gay and lesbian support group meetings and deal with his internalized homophobia, which both the former therapist and his parents, along with his antigay culture, played into.

Arif's physical mannerisms made his family uncomfortable but were part of who he was. His prior therapist believed they were contrived and had Arif believing this as well. I encouraged Arif to write a letter to the therapist expressing his disappointment in the work they did together and explaining that it further worsened his depression and self-esteem. Arif did this and felt empowered by doing so, even though the therapist never responded.

Eventually Arif found a job in Detroit and was able to move out of his parents' house. He continued working to encourage his family to accept him. This was no small task, and certainly success was not guaranteed, but it did improve Arif's self-esteem, and he no longer felt that being a gay man was something to feel badly about or that he was doing something wrong that needed blame or punishment.

Belief That People Who Care for Them May Abandon Them, Harm Them, or Kill Themselves

Children who are sexually abused—especially by caregivers—learn that to get their need for love and nurturing met they have to comply with the ongoing abuse or risk being abandoned and rejected. Their physical and emotional survival needs are linked to complying with the perpetrator. In fact, it is common for an abuser to abandon the abused child once the victim outgrows his or her desirability to the offender.

Parallel to this is that LGBTQ individuals often fear being abandoned or harmed. They also worry that loved ones may harm themselves upon learning the news of their sexual orientation and gender identity. "Trauma at any age, but particularly trauma that is inflicted by caregivers, generally has a profound effect on the capacity to trust" (van der Kolk, 1996, p. 196). Given that LGBTQ children have been born into the "enemy camp," where families may hold negative beliefs about homosexuality, it makes sense that they worry they will be harmed or abandoned. They do not trust that their families will love them enough to work things out and accept and understand who they really are.

Also like the sexual abuse survivor who worries about the well-being of others in the family if they tell about the abuse, LGBTQ individuals worry about the well-being of their family members as well. You will hear things like, "I cannot tell them—it will kill them," or "It will give them a heart attack. They are already not well, so why put this type of stress on them?" Here we clearly see the cognitive distortions. No one dies from bad news. I often joke with my clients that I have never heard of a death certificate that reads, "Died from knowledge of homosexuality of a loved one." This helps them see the cognitive distortion more clearly.

It is important here that you check out whether this is a cognitive distortion or whether it is true. Sometimes LGBTQ individuals *are* abandoned by their families, friends, and colleagues if and when they come out. Their families' dreams for them have been shattered. Friends may not want to associate with someone who is LGBTQ. Their work environments may turn hostile. Even though things are so much better overall for LGBTQ folks among younger people, particularly millennials, there are still many areas of concern. For example, they may lose their jobs or housing. It is still legal everywhere in the United States to be fired or kicked out of one's rental property just for being gay.

Moreover, the threat of such losses is used to keep LGBTQ people silenced and closeted. Your work as a clinician is to help the client review which people they wish to tell and what the possible outcomes will be. We will address that in Chapter 7, on coming out. Issues to examine around this cognition are those of trust, power, and safety. Once your clients go through some conflict—even major conflict—and negotiate it successfully, they will be empowered to do it again and remove this cognitive distortion.

Cognitive and Behavioral Symptoms of PTSD

The psychological aftermath of sexual abuse in adulthood again parallels that of covert cultural sexual abuse in that both lead to a similar set of dysfunctional behavioral symptomology, with results that include:

- Inappropriately sexualized affection
- Preoccupation with sex
- Deadening of all feelings to avoid sexual arousal
- Isolation from others
- Short-lived relationships
- Settling for very little
- Self-abuse, self-injury, and suicide

Inappropriately Sexualized Affection

Men—gay, bisexual, and straight—sexualize touch more than women. There are many reasons for this. In large part, adults stop hugging and touching boys around age 8—much younger than they do for girls. Males turn to sex for the touch that used to symbolize validation and support. Our culture permits women to touch men, children, and each other with affection, caressing one another's hair and clothes and even holding hands, without anyone thinking it's odd or inappropriate.

Many gay men use sex to fill a void in their lives and to feel wanted; they then confuse this for love. Sex offers instant pleasure and pseudo-intimacy. It is easy for gay and bisexual men to get caught in frequent sexual hookups, because they are looking for connection through the lens of sex. This often leaves their relational intimacy shallow and superficial—but shallow intimacy is better than the total loneliness and isolation that follow in the wake of covert cultural sexual abuse.

The sexualized touch also helps remind gay men they *do* exist—countering the invisibility they experienced growing up. Sex is a way to remind themselves that they're still "there," without having to exert much emotional or mental work.

All of this leaves gay men vulnerable to developing out-of-control sexual behaviors and other sexual-related disorders, which I discuss in Chapter 9.

Preoccupation With Sex

Like sexual abuse survivors, gay and bisexual men often have sexual difficulties that include out-of-control sexual hookups or trying to meet nonsexual needs through sex. Gay and bisexual men tend to be more focused on sex than lesbians. This is not a gay thing but rather a guy thing. Growing up, males receive less affection through touch and emotion, particularly from other males, and gay and bisexual men learn to exist and tolerate affection with other men through sex. Sex is often their initiation into gay and bisexual manhood, which makes them vulnerable to sexual compulsivity (Kort, 2002).

Through the lens of covert cultural sexual abuse, an LGBTQ child is like a sexual abuse survivor: In response to his vandalized sexual development, he develops hypersexuality. That's often because when adults recognize that a child is gay, they project adult sexuality onto him before he's developmentally ready to be assigned that adult sexual role.

In Chapter 9, I describe how this manifests among gay men and can become sexual compulsivity.

Deadening of All Feelings to Avoid Sexual Arousal

LGBTQ individuals may respond to covert cultural sexual abuse by deadening all sexual feelings. This is different from people who simply have low desire. People who have low desire are not usually *avoiding* sex. They simply are not often inclined to engage in sexual activity. Closeted LGBTQ individuals, on the other hand, try to *repress* their desire and are rewarded for doing so. They learn to have an underlying obsessive hatred and fear of sex, which they avoid by squelching their libido.

Isolation From Others

Like the sexual abuse survivor who feels alone, LGBTQ children also feel alone. The secrecy and invisibility inherent in growing up LGBTQ isolate these children from one another. They do not see each other and are not mirrored in a way that affirms their existence.

LGBTQ children do not experience a sense of belonging. Some schools have groups called gay-straight alliances, which bring LGBTQ and straight students together as allies and give LGBTQ students a sense of belonging. However, many schools do not offer this, and even in those that do, it takes a brave young soul to attend.

This is why it is essential that therapists provide homosocial resources to their LGBTQ clients and, when possible, place them in LGBTQ group therapy. Many gay community centers offer social groups that counter isolation.

It makes sense that to ease their pangs of isolation, many LGBTQ people use alcohol or drugs. To achieve an illusion of belonging, they may hang out at bars, clubs, and circuit parties, or console themselves with porn and gay chat rooms.

Social media can provide a sense of community for LGBTQ adolescents. This has both positive and negative outcomes, which we will explore in Chapter 13 on working with teens.

Short-Lived Relationships

As noted earlier, it is a myth that LGBTQ relationships are inherently short-lived and bound to fail. However, covert cultural sexual abuse often profoundly affects an LGBTQ individual's ability to attach to partners. Like sexual abuse survivors, LGBTQ individuals tend to enter short-lived relationships because their love map and capacity for intimacy have been vandalized—overlaid with someone else's sexual agenda. Internalized homophobia also can limit LGBTQ relationships. Finally, heterosexism demands that LGBTQ people role-play heterosexuality. This is explored further in Chapter 10.

Settling for Very Little

Covert cultural sexual abuse sends the message that LGBTQ people—especially those who choose to be out and open—don't deserve much happiness in life. It follows that people treated as basically worthless will, sooner or later, give up and begin compromising. They may stop attempting relationships completely, or enter into relationships with partners who treat them as unworthy inferiors—whose verbal, psychological abuse only validates their lack of self-esteem.

Self-Abuse, Self-Injury, and Suicide

The rate of adolescent suicide in gay and lesbian teens is 30% (Massachusetts Youth Risk Behavior Survey Results, 1999). Many say the number is inflated; some say it's higher. But I believe this is a fair number when you consider those who attempt suicide and fortunately don't succeed. Also, that number probably includes straight and questioning teens who, because of homophobia, worry that they might have a same-sex orientation. Prepubescent boys often experiment sexually with one another, but that curiosity does not make them gay. More about this in Chapter 13.

Victims of sexual abuse often cut themselves at some point. This behavior is an attempt to bring their inner pain to the surface. I believe that gay male barebacking (unprotected anal sex) and risking HIV exposure can be analogous to cutting behavior.

"Bug chasers" intentionally try to contract HIV, so they can empathize with others who are "poz" and can achieve a sense of belonging. Some gay men purposely infect other men with HIV without their victims' knowledge. The rage inherent in this violent act derives from the self-hate they experience, which in my opinion stems from covert cultural sexual abuse.

The Case of Art

A 24-year-old man named Art came to me after engaging in high-risk sexual acts in an attempt to become infected with HIV. He told me he had been having unprotected anal sex with guys at circuit parties, baths, and public restrooms. Earlier he had contracted hepatitis B, had it treated, and ignored the potential risk of receiving it again. He'd also contracted genital herpes and gonorrhea.

Art told me that he was intentionally continuing to have unsafe sex with others. "I don't care anymore. If I get the virus, there's nothing more I can lose."

"I know I will catch HIV at some point," Art said. "At least then, I won't have the anxiety of worrying about getting it." He added, "I was not out in the 1970s, when sex for gay men was free and easy. I'm not going to deaden my pleasure with latex."

Art was depressed about being rejected by his parents, who said they could not tolerate having a gay son. They cut him off financially, which caused him to drop out of college and live on his own. He tried to contact them, but they would hang up. His siblings also wanted nothing to do with him. He hated himself and his life more and more.

Art told me that he knew he was gay from an early age. He dressed in girls' clothes and enjoyed playing house and school with the girls in his neighborhood and his sisters. He was teased, humiliated, and bullied by other boys his age. His father told him he was a sissy, and his mother tried to get him to play with males and bought him male-oriented toys. Throughout his childhood, Art believed that he was bad, wrong, and that he'd let his parents down.

Art explained that he felt that if he got AIDS, his parents would see how much he was suffering. He believed it would make him less depressed. When I asked him why he thought this, he replied that it would help him cope with the assaults he received from his family and others who had teased him in childhood for being a girly boy. "If I got AIDS, it would say to the world exactly what I have felt all my life—that I am depressed, and I am dying inside, and nothing can stop it."

He went on to tell me, "AIDS would be perfect for me. It would give me an identity. It would concretize my pain so that others can understand how much I suffer. It is a virus that can infect my body and destroy me just the way the abuse has destroyed me on the inside. Finally everyone will understand what happened to me."

Art: Clinical Interpretation and Treatment

I've listened to other men involved in these risky sexual behaviors, and I often view them as victims of self-abuse. It's like the survivor of childhood abuse asking (if not consciously), "See how damaged I am? You don't believe me? I'll show you," and revealing his scars for all to see.

I see these men as no different from the sexual abuse survivors who cut themselves. They are trying to destroy the inner feelings of pain from the abuse and avoid the truth—the truth being that *they* are not the ones who are damaged; those who have *done* the abuse are. They are willing to protect their perpetrators to the end even if it means death.

Through engaging in high-risk behaviors, Art was reenacting his original trauma of being bullied, teased, and humiliated. "More commonly, traumatized people find themselves reenacting some aspect of the trauma scene in disguised form, without realizing what they are doing" (Herman, 1992, p. 40). The therapeutic task was to help Art see that he was victimized as a child and connect to that. His anger needed to be directed toward those who harmed him, not toward himself. He learned shame at a very young age, and now as an adult it was time to put the shame back where it belonged—onto the others who placed it on him. The shame was what was *done* to him—not him.

If I were to see Art today, I would educate him on PrEP, Pre-Exposure Prophylaxis. There is now an anti-HIV medication that keeps most HIV negative people from becoming infected when they have sex with someone who is HIV positive. It is sold under the name Truvada® (pronounced tru vá duh) and is approved by the FDA. PrEP is discussed further in Chapter 9.

Dysfunctional Coping Mechanisms

Trauma symptoms are often kept at bay by LGBTQ individuals in four general ways—by displacement, repression, overcompensation, and dissociation—all of which are attempts to shield oneself from the trauma.

Displacement

One syndrome I often see in clients—and even suffered from myself—is displacement. The client diverts or channels his innate impulses into some other fixation that's more acceptable, easier to "explain away." Think of the football fanatic who releases his aggression vicariously on the gridiron, or the abused child who buries his head in books.

As a child, I had effeminate mannerisms and played only with girls. I was very much the gay little boy, and everyone knew it—even me. My peers bullied me, spat at me, and beat me up for being gay. Even some teachers laughed at me. Then, in middle school, I became obsessed with a 1970s singing trio, Tony Orlando and Dawn, who served as objects of displacement for my homosexuality.

I discovered that other kids would tease me for liking this singing group—which made me want to like them even more. I became obsessed with them and bought every TO&D iron-on decal I could find. My peers—even some teachers—made fun of my wearing a different one to school every day. But I wore them proudly. I didn't like being made fun of but pushed it more and more, not really understanding why. Now, years later, I see that at the tender age of 11, my obsession allowed my peers to ridicule my star worship rather than harass me for being gay. It feels vastly more comfortable to be mocked for what one *likes* than for what one *is*.

Repression

Some who experience trauma avoid and block the feelings of emotional arousal they would have if they let the information about the trauma in. For example, if a woman is sexually abused, she might become asexual to avoid having to reexperience the trauma. The same phenomenon occurs with survivors of covert cultural sexual abuse, as the case of Diane illustrates.

The Case of Diane

Diane was a 33-year-old woman recovering from addiction to alcohol. She had tried sobriety on several occasions and was unsuccessful. She was referred to me for having "possible" repressed sexual feelings. The chemical dependency therapist who had been working with her thought Diane might be lesbian based on her mannerisms and the way she wore her hair and clothes. I made a note of the therapist's remarks but didn't make any assumptions about Diane—I appreciate input from other therapists but never accept their conclusions before talking to a client myself.

As Diane became sober, she began to wonder if she might be "homosexual." She had been instructed not to talk about this during her drug and alcohol treatment, and Diane obeyed. Now, however, she found herself interested in women and entertaining lesbian fantasies while masturbating, albeit infrequently.

Diane had a stereotypically masculine presence: She was tall, spoke aggressively, played sports, dressed in pants and T-shirts, and kept her emotions bottled up. As a child she had been drawn to sports and male-oriented toys. She knew she was different, but did everything she could to not let it show, pretending to be interested in girlish things.

Like many gay children, her self-awareness and eventual coming-out were delayed by a religious upbringing. Her Lutheran family was rigid in terms of rules and gender roles. Determined to please them, Diane became rule-oriented and believed—as they had taught her—that the Church's teachings were law. She also complied with her self-absorbed and narcissistic mother who demanded obedience. Some of Diane's siblings rebelled, but not Diane, who badly wanted her mother's love and acceptance.

Diane enjoyed the company of other women and felt different around them, but she told herself that her feelings were nothing more than a desire for friendship. She did not have an inkling that she was lesbian until she became sober.

Diane married at 24 and lived heterosexually for years—as many gay clients do. She told me that she never felt connected to her husband or her friends. She never enjoyed intercourse but engaged in it to please her husband. Obedient to heterosexist norms, she subordinated herself to his wishes as she'd done in her family, particularly with her mother.

Though her husband was kind to her, it was clear she responded to him by avoiding her own needs and always deferring to him. The only time Diane had a sense of herself was when she played sports. Then, she'd allow herself to become aroused emotionally, and her passion could surface. Through sports, Diane met a few lesbians and thought she might be a lesbian, too. However, this was not an option for her, as she was married; she could not allow herself to go against her church and her family.

Diane: Clinical Interpretation and Treatment

Given Diane's symptoms of repressed sexual feelings, I felt it was important to ask about any childhood sexual abuse. Her inability to connect to others and dissociation from her sexuality fit the pattern. But nothing in her history indicated any sexual abuse, either covert or overt—so I ruled that out.

Next, we explored Diane's possible repressed lesbianism. Growing up, she was not aware of any sexual feelings toward anyone, male or female. Diane prided herself on living out her childhood mission of being a good little Lutheran girl. This supported her avoidant, dissociated stance and kept her from exploring her inner self.

She and her husband eventually divorced, but neither bothered to examine why the marriage failed. Once we identified Diane's codependency, she began to identify her needs and make it a priority to act on them first.

During therapy, she realized that she had suppressed and avoided her own needs to the point of not knowing who she really was. It was time to stop being passive: Diane now knew that if she did not deal with her avoidance issues, she would lose her identity all over again. Diane was a lesbian and began the coming-out process.

As Diane began questioning the religious tenets of her church and examining her relationships with her family and former husband, she became more aware of her individual identity. She became increasingly comfortable with her feelings of attraction toward women and eventually allowed herself to act on those feelings.

Overcompensation

People overcompensate by becoming the best little boy or girl in the world and excelling in everything—academics, sports, household responsibilities, and so on. Often these individuals act out of shame; they feel defective and flawed.

In some cases, gay male children become hypermasculine and overly focus on male-oriented behaviors and sports. They may even become promiscuous with girls to reinforce that they are heterosexual. Lesbians may become hyperfeminine in ways that do not match their inner sense of femininity but show the external world they identify with mainstream feminine women.

The Case of Philippe

Philippe, a 40-year-old executive, came to therapy because he could no longer keep up with the pace of his life. Heterosexually married with three children, Philippe was struggling to maintain his "perfect" appearance.

He recalled that in middle school he could never wholly relax, except when resting in his bedroom. Hiding an increasingly significant part of his identity—that he was gay—took so much mental and emotional energy that Philippe became secretly ashamed of himself. He applied much of the homophobic talk he overheard to himself.

As a teenager, Philippe overcompensated by developing a false persona to pass as straight. He pleased his parents by becoming overresponsible and excelling at school and sports, all to avoid being disparaged as the flawed man he felt he was. Philippe realized that if he received good grades and did exactly what his parents, teachers, and other authority figures wanted—even anticipating their needs before they asked him to do something—he would be rewarded and praised. He felt that if they really knew his thoughts, feelings, and desires, he would be rejected.

As an adult Philippe became a workaholic, but his workload was beginning to overwhelm him. He presented as emotionally shut down; he intellectualized his inner and outer worlds. He was suffering from depression over his anxiety that he was not performing well enough as a husband, father, or employee.

Philippe: Clinical Interpretation and Treatment

Philippe was working hard to cover up that what he felt was damaged and corrupt— his homosexual self. Winning awards for employee of the year, father of the year, and best husband in the neighborhood is all fine and good, but it will not erase the feeling of being damaged goods. Philippe was working overtime, and I helped him see that he was no longer going to be able to maintain a perfect exterior without damaging himself physically and certainly psychologically.

Philippe went on antidepressants and gradually began slowing down his work performance. He attended a gay and bisexual married men's group in the area and spoke about his shame and guilt for being a gay man in a heterosexual marriage with children. He was able to see that he was pushed into making decisions that were not in his best interest or others' best interest because he wanted to please and be accepted by others. This trumped everything in his inner world.

Dissociation

Trauma specialists speak of the integral aspect of dissociation when trauma is happening—and long after it has occurred. Basically, an individual isolates the memory of the painful event and stores it in another compartment of the mind, along with any associated strong feelings and emotions. We know that children who are abused at home dissociate to get through each day and be functional at school, sports, religious institutions, and anywhere they need to perform. The dissociative split allows the rest of the personality to achieve and thrive as if nothing has happened. Dissociation can help suppress anxiety-provoking knowledge about the self and make life more manageable. As trauma survivors begin the process of reintegration, those repressed memories can leak out and interfere with everyday functioning. The individual is left disconnected not just from himself, but also from others.

The way LGBTQ children dissociate is by going into a heterosexual trance. They literally grow up believing that they are heterosexual and deny homosexual feelings and impulses by renaming them or giving them different meanings.

The Case of Elana

Elana, 35, came to see me after frustration with her past therapist, whom she felt was imposing negative judgments and not allowing Elana the freedom to decide for herself whether or not she was lesbian. Elana was having difficulty identifying for herself whether or not she was, in fact, lesbian; she had recently fallen in love with a woman and developed sexual feelings for the first time.

Prior to meeting this woman, Elana had been with, and was attracted to, only men. Her sexual experiences with them were less than satisfactory, and she blamed them each time for not satisfying her enough. She was currently living with a fiancé of 3 years and was not sexually satisfied, again holding him accountable for meeting only his needs sexually and not hers.

When Elana enrolled in a graduate-level class at a local university, she immediately found herself drawn to a female teaching assistant, Gayle, who was around her age. Week after week she would look forward to the class, not for the content but to be around Gayle. She began to recognize that she more than simply liked Gayle; she had sexual and romantic feelings toward her.

Elana met with Gayle after class to get "extra help" on her homework, though Elana had other intentions. She felt compelled to move toward Gayle and see if Gayle felt the same way. Elana had never acted this way before.

After the class ended, the two women became friends. Eventually Gayle came out to Elana as a lesbian, and Elana found herself hoping something could happen between them. "I had never felt that way before—ever!" she told me. "Not even with my fiancé."

Over the next year Elana and Gayle decided to take a vacation as best friends. Before going, Elana told Gayle about her feelings, and during the vacation their friendship turned romantic and sexual. Upon returning from the trip, Elana felt tremendous guilt and shame, and she entered therapy. She told the therapist that she did not self-identify as lesbian at all. She also did not see herself as a woman who would have ever cheated on her fiancé. Yet she was engaging in lesbian sex and romance—and was cheating.

Elana's previous therapist asked her if she had ever had any indication before that she might be lesbian. She asked about Elana's history, which was stereotypically female and gender conforming in an ego-syntonic way. Elana had dated boys during adolescence and fallen in love and gotten her heart broken by several men before becoming engaged to the man she called "the love of my life." She was not attracted to other women; even now, the only woman she had sexual feelings toward was Gayle.

Elana did have a history of being sexually abused by a best friend's brother at the age of 14. One night she awoke to find him kissing her breasts, with his finger in her vagina. She froze and pretended to be asleep, not knowing what the boy would do. She lay there until he breathed heavy and she felt warm fluid hit her face. Startled, she jerked back, scaring him out of the room. Thinking he had urinated on her, she wiped it off and never told a soul.

Elana's therapist was convinced that because she had no history of typical lesbian-type behaviors—like being a tomboy or feeling attracted to other girls—that Elana was not lesbian. The therapist told Elana that she was acting out her sexual abuse and once the abuse work was resolved she would no longer desire to be with Gayle. The therapist also told her to stop her relationship with Gayle, as it was cheating on her fiancé.

Over the next year Elana couldn't stop seeing Gayle, even though she knew she was going against therapeutic recommendations. The therapist continued to condemn the behavior and helped her to work through the trauma of having been raped by her best friend's brother. Elana went back and forth wondering about her identity. Was she straight and in love with a woman or was she a lesbian engaged to a man? She didn't know.

Elana: Clinical Interpretation and Treatment

Elana was completely dissociated from her sexual identity. She adapted and adopted heterosexuality as a means of survival. The therapist, in my opinion, made a poor judgment connecting her lesbianism to her sexual abuse. The fact that Elana did not have an inkling about her sexual identity is the norm for those growing up gay and lesbian—particularly for women, as I discuss in Chapter 7. Connecting the abuse to her homosexual behaviors was something to consider but not to make as a final decision. It is the client who should have the final say on his or her sexual orientation—not the therapist.

The sexual abuse Elana experienced only served to confuse her; it wasn't an acting-out behavior. What the therapist should have done is help Elana work through her sexual-abuse issues while simultaneously helping her with her identity crisis. Elana also needed to decide what to do in terms of her fiancé and living out of integrity. This was a major concern for her, as she did not want to want to lose him or hurt him.

It is understandable how, from a developmental perspective, this shame and trauma causes a natural splitting. Lesbians and gays hide anything that might expose them. Many will tell you in therapy that they changed their speech, their walk, the way they dressed and moved their hands, and their interests. To avoid being discovered, they bury a frozen inner self—a splitting that causes problems with identity and relationships.

Because of this splitting, many of your clients will appear characterological—that is, they will present with borderline or narcissistic personality disorders. Your job is to understand if the client's problem is characterological or a result of the splitting.

To help one client of mine connect with himself and stop the dissociation that contributed to his self-abuse, I had him write a letter to his perpetrator, who had infected him with HIV.

The Case of Terry

Terry was hiring male escorts and paying for sex when he traveled for his job, which he did on a regular basis. He no longer felt any sense of belonging within the gay community. As a clean-cut man in his 20s, he had exercised religiously, shaped his full head of hair in a style common among gay men, worn the right clothes, and gone to all the right clubs. He was constantly sought after by other gay men—and even some straight ones. But as he entered his later 30s and 40s, his job grew busier, and he no longer worked out like he used to. He gained a good 40 pounds, lost most of his hair, sported a goatee to make up for it—and no longer attracted men as he once had.

Throughout much of his adult life, Terry had attended circuit parties. Now, most of his friends were dead from AIDS or other health problems stemming from wear on their bodies, or were addicted to party drugs to the point that the only way he could socialize with them was to use as well. Otherwise, they had nothing in common. Terry had never learned to create much of an identity beyond the superficial one that he adopted at these parties.

No longer feeling attractive, Terry didn't feel entitled to claim a space in the gay community. So he began paying hustlers for sex. As he told me, this was easier than risking rejection and criticism in the gay bars or online. He was a bottom and found that paying a rent boy circumvented the relational and social work of cruising.

Terry ensured that the rent boys wore condoms, and for the most part they were affirming and kind, behaving nicely toward him. But after they left, he felt lonely and depressed. He grew increasingly uncomfortable with this solution and recognized that he might even have a sexual addiction.

Then, one night, Terry was receiving anal sex from an escort and felt him pull out his erection. When the man reinserted, Terry experienced a different sensation, but he never suspected that the man had removed his condom, as they had talked beforehand about the importance of safe sex. He realized what had happened when he felt the dampness running down his thighs. He was frozen in shock. Neither of them said a word as the escort put his clothes back on and left.

Terry: Clinical Interpretation and Treatment

For therapeutic reasons, I asked Terry to write the rent boy an anger letter, even though he couldn't mail it because he couldn't find the man's address. The point was to help Terry understand that he was acting out from covert cultural sexual abuse, access his anger instead of his depression, and get beyond the distorted belief that he somehow "deserved it."

I wanted him to read the letter aloud, but he asked me to read it instead. He said he did not want to weep and wanted to distance himself from his feelings because this was so hard for him. So I read it aloud. I'm reprinting it here with Terry's permission.

You won't remember me. We had a brief encounter in my hotel room last year. Our meeting was probably nothing out of the ordinary for you—you must have many such encounters in your line of work. But it changed my life.

You infected me with HIV, and I have to believe you meant to. Our encounter had been safe right up to the point when you deliberately removed our protection. After 6 weeks, I had the symptoms of acute HIV infection and was diagnosed as positive.

Since then, I've been holding myself to blame: I was a consenting partner, aware of the risks with someone I'd met on the Internet, and had taken such risks for some time. Maybe my luck was bound to run out.

On reflection, though, that's too easy. The fact is, on my other encounters, the play was always safe. So why did you remove our protection? Was it just recklessness on your part, a wish to play dangerously? I think you knew you were positive and had every intention of passing on the virus. But either way, what you did was wrong, and had the same consequences I now have to live with.

I can't change what happened, but believe me, I agonize over how it did. For a brief physical pleasure that would otherwise be soon forgotten, I must suffer the memory of how easily and cheaply you cut my life expectancy. For the time I have left (hopefully years, not months) I will suffer a reduced quality of life to protect my health. I may never find a life partner. Perhaps worst of all, what will this do to my family and friends?

Were these thoughts going through your head when you went out of your way to infect me? Did someone pass the virus to you in a similar way? And therefore, drive you to seek revenge on others? I can only imagine this is the retribution you sought.

How easy it must be to become a victim, blaming everyone but yourself and making a career (literally) out of passing on the infection. But you have to stop. You have to get the anger out of you and stop the chain of suffering. I am trying to find room in my heart for forgiveness, trying hard to control my anger and act responsibly towards others and not become a risk to them in the way you were to me.

I guess I'll never know your reasons or what became of you. It's ironic that you won't remember me, and I will never be able to forget you.

CHAPTER 6

Developmental Insults

If you can't get rid of the skeleton in your closet,
you'd best teach it to dance.
—George Bernard Shaw

Sometimes your LGBTQ clients will remain stuck—unable to move forward in their personal lives and relationships—even after you have implemented all of your knowledge about growing up LGBTQ (in terms of the trauma and covert cultural sexual abuse), have made a correct diagnosis, and have assessed them perfectly in terms of the *DSM-V* and *ICD 10*. I have found that in these cases, the issue they are struggling with is not about being LGBTQ at all but rather relates to a developmental insult and wound that is blocking them.

These developmental wounds often appear to be related to the clients' sexual or gender orientation, but in truth the issue has little or nothing to do with the client's orientation. The client's orientation may be what is forcing the developmental wound out, however. In other words, the block in their life around being LGBTQ is a symptom and not the problem. Additionally, developmental insults sometimes leave clients with apparent disorders of character and personality. Other times, a client may seem mood disturbed. But neither may actually be the case.

I highly recommend Jean M. Baker's (2002) book *How Homophobia Hurts Children*. This book offers an excellent overview on LGBTQ identity development. LGBTQ children go through the same stages of development as heterosexual children, but their sexual or gender orientations present unique hurdles centering around their perceptions of being different from both their peers and their parents.

In this chapter I discuss some of the most common developmental injuries I've seen in my office with adult LGBTQ individuals, and I talk about how they might manifest in your office. I have found that Erik Erikson's developmental stages of attachment, exploration, identity, competence, concern, intimacy, and responsibility can be used as a framework to help your clients get unstuck.

For example, being stuck in the identity-confusion stage of coming out may reflect a developmental error in the client's childhood identity formation. (See Chapter 7 for a detailed description of the stages of coming out.) Being stuck in the identity-tolerance stage of coming out may reflect a developmental injury during the childhood exploration stage. As you identify these developmental insults and help clients heal from them, you will find that the therapy begins moving forward again.

Attachment

Attachment style and the ability to bond with others are determined early in childhood (Ainsworth, Blehar, Waters, & Wall, 1978; Bartholomew & Horowitz, 1991; Siegel, 1999). Humans are all born wired for attachment to our caregivers. Three developmental processes are created that are then associated with a child's development of emotional competence, a sense of well-being, and skills for successful relationship development. These processes include the need to be physically close to a primary attachment figure; when upset having an emotionally secure, stable attachment figure to turn to for soothing; and after repeated experiences with the attachment figure, an internalization of the relationship as secure so that the child can hold it in mind for a sense of comfort when physically distant from the caregiver (Solomon & Siegel, 2003).

The effectiveness of how children go out into the world is based on how they learned to attach and build a secure base with their caretakers. This "template" becomes the basis for all future close relationships throughout childhood, adolescence, and adult life (Bowlby, 1988).

According to psychological attachment theory, mothers need to be available to their babies at least 60% of the time, to touch them and attend to them in loving ways. Their children then grow up into healthy adults who can attach to others. Otherwise, problems occur, creating unhealthy attachment disorders—vandalized forms of the ability to bond to others through love and friendship. In its most severe form, the sufferer cannot form attachments and becomes isolated and a loner. Knowing this is crucial to understanding what may be disrupting your client's attachment to friends, partners, and even you as the therapist.

Attachment and Internalized Homophobia

It would make sense that if individuals form an insecure attachment in the first year of life, they might have later problems with coming out. Internalized homophobia has also been found to be related to one's attachment style. Mohr and Fassinger (1998) indicated that attachment insecurity increases fear associated with the tasks of identity development, thereby compromising exploration that may be critical in developing a positive LGBTQ identity. Participants in their studies who had insecure attachment styles, especially the avoidant type, were more likely than others to fear judgment based on their orientation, less likely to disclose their sexual or gender orientation to work colleagues and heterosexual friends, less likely to identify with or interact with others in the LGBTQ community, and more likely to report high internalized antigay values.

Clients demonstrating developmental blocks around attachment issues may have come out to themselves but have great trouble trusting you as their therapist. They may not share their feelings with you for a long period of time, much as they want to. In other cases, these clients may ultimately come to trust you but not trust anyone else, regardless of your efforts to reassure them that it's safe. They may seem paranoid—which is not surprising given that growing up LGBTQ requires a high level of paranoia.

The Case of David

David was a 28-year-old gay male who came out in college to himself but not to his family or any of his friends—all of whom were straight. He also never established a social life with other LGBTQ people. He entered therapy with a straight clinician, Rachel, over depression, which he attributed to feeling lonely and isolated.

Over the first few months, David's depression improved as he met with Rachel on a weekly basis. Eventually Rachel started to talk with him about why he was not out to his parents or his straight friends.

"They would never understand, and I have such good relationships—I don't want to jeopardize them. Besides, they don't need to know what I do in bed," David responded. He denied any problems growing up. He believed he had normal, hardworking parents. He was the oldest of three, with two younger sisters. He denied any abuse or neglect and felt if there were any problems it was when he was a teenager and he used marijuana. "My parents caught me and we fought a lot about it, but I eventually stopped, and we stopped fighting too."

Rachel began working on David's internalized homophobia and fear of rejection and abandonment, teaching him these concepts in terms of gay affirmative therapy. It all made sense to David, and yet he was resistant to doing anything about it. He would agree with Rachel and come back the following week without having made any progress in the coming-out process. After 2 years in therapy, David was in the same place socially as he had been when he entered therapy.

Rachel sought me out for supervision, and I encouraged her to address David's lack of follow-through more directly, challenging his assertion that he wanted to end his isolation. If he really wanted to become less isolated, why didn't his behavior indicate this? I was sure she would invite negative transference from him, and sure enough, she did. I believed that within the negative transference would lie other issues that he was not able to consciously speak about.

In her next session with David, Rachel commented on how he agreed with her in every session, developed plans about going into the LGBTQ community at his own pace, and then inevitably failed to follow through on these plans. David offered some polite responses, but Rachel stayed with her gentle confrontation of him. Finally, David accused her of having an agenda for him. "I am not going to be a flag-carrying gay guy. I don't need to come out to anyone—I just need to meet some gay friends," he told Rachel. This only reinforced Rachel's assessment that GAT was what David needed in terms of addressing his internalized homophobia and coming-out issues.

In the next supervision with me, I told Rachel I thought differently. I had seen clients like David before and felt that his resistance to making behavioral change was taking too long given that he had been out to himself since college. I coached Rachel to stay with the negative transference and challenge his lack of behavioral change in a supportive but stern manner.

In the next session, Rachel did just this, and David started to get angry. "So are you going to fire me as a client if I don't do what you ask?"

"Why would you ask me that?" Rachel replied.

"Because you seem invested in making me more out than I want to be, and you are rushing me and being critical," he told her.

Rachel knew this was not the case and explored this with David.

"I'm not used to someone being on me so much like this. You haven't been this way before. I know you mean well, but get off my back!" David shouted. Then he started to cry. "I'm sorry. I didn't mean that. Please don't let me go as a client. I will try harder!"

Here was the material that needed to be addressed. Something was lurking that Rachel could not see before. She sat with David and asked him what it was like when his parents pushed him in directions that were in his best interest. And the rest of the story came out.

"They didn't really push me in any direction. They traveled a lot. My father's work demanded a lot of travel, so we were with a nanny most of the time," he reported.

"But why did your mother go with him so often?" Rachel asked.

"She liked to travel," David said.

"So they did not track you much or very well? Is that fair to say?" Rachel asked.

"They did the best they could," David replied.

"But David, they needed to be around more to encourage you and nudge you to be everything you could be. Children need a parent tracking them closely, looking over their shoulder, making sure they are on the right path. Your parents didn't do a good enough job in that. So when I try to be the good parent to you in coaching you toward the very things you asked me to, it makes sense that you try to push me away or think I will push you away. That must have been your defense as a child."

David agreed, and this became his working space in therapy. The issue was less about being gay and more about having an insecure attachment issue from having been left so often by his parents.

Exploration

It takes inordinate courage for lesbian, gay, bisexual, transgender, and queer individuals to explore the LGBTQ community. Even going to a social gathering looms as a huge challenge. If this persistent difficulty keeps clients from exploring avenues for socialization and establishing a peer group, explore what their caretakers were like and what the rules and norms while they were growing up were. Did their parents foster exploration and a well-rounded curiosity? Did they give them a sense of confidence that they could explore their own world and be okay? Or did they instill rigidity, warnings, doubts, and caution?

In this second developmental stage, a child needs to learn how he differs and is separate from others. It is also a time for developing an innate curiosity about the world. If this exploration is thwarted or made threatening, the child may grow up to have difficulty separating from the family and developing a healthy curiosity about his own culture.

If this stage of development goes well for LGBTQ children, the coming-out process will be easier for them as adults. But if it doesn't, their sexual and gender exploring and coming-out may be fraught with much more turbulence and angst.

For example, a client may be reluctant to explore the LGBTQ community. You may have great ideas and suggestions about going to local LGBTQ community centers or different groups, but the client simply won't go. The client may have trouble meeting others and adjusting to going from a straight lifestyle to a nonstraight one, and may blame the LGBTQ community for this. In fact, however, the issue is more about a vandalized exploration stage than about the community.

One needs a healthy sense of being able to explore the world, particularly a new culture like that of the LGBTQ community, which is not visible and very foreign to most people. Finding it and navigating through it can be scary. Clinicians need to be familiar with how to guide clients toward the best types of groups and organizations.

It is extremely important for the straight clinician to constantly push LGBTQ clients out into LGBTQ social groups. Allowing their reactivity around this to surface will help you know what direction to head in terms of their therapeutic work.

Obtaining a good family and social history is essential here. Questions to ask when clients seem stuck in this stage include: "What messages did you get as a child about being away from your parents?" and "Were your parents overprotective?"

Identity

To avoid pathologizing LGBTQ individuals for the ways in which they create their adult identities, you need to be aware of what's normalized within their communities. For example, in one of my gay affirmative trainings, a straight woman said she was bothered by the way gay dating personal ads spell out what men want sexually in terms of body types, top or bottom practices, and even fantasies. It made sense that a heterosexual woman might be offended by a man's personal ad leading off with what he enjoyed and wanted sexually, as that's not culturally acceptable in the straight world. But I explained to her that it was normative among gay and bisexual men to do that. In general, a gay or bisexual man creates his identity through his body and his sexual practices. Understanding why this is so from a developmental point of view is crucial.

The longer clients remain closeted and suppress their core identity, the more likely they are to display behaviors that mimic psychiatric disorders, actually create full-blown psychiatric disorders, or mask genuine disorders through acting out. This is addressed further in Chapter 12.

Often you can identify what stage of psychological development LGBTQ clients are struggling through based on their progress in coming out. Failure to develop a positive LGBTQ identity in childhood is perhaps one of the biggest deficits that LGBTQ people can suffer. By this I don't mean sexual or gender identification, but rather the normative identity development that all children and teenagers should successfully undergo. For LGBTQ children, their inner core becomes forbidden, their true identity walled off.

To develop a secure sense of self, children create their identities through playing with toys, usually between the ages of 3 and 4 years old (according to Erikson's model), and later through playing with others in school and on the playground. But, as I mentioned earlier, many LGBTQ children have their toys of preference taken away from them and are shunned on the playground. Suffering this kind of developmental insult can produce later problems in identity formation. It can manifest by way of cognitive distortions in terms of clients believing something is inherently wrong with them.

Every child should have a sense of belonging. But from childhood on up, LGBTQ individuals have been taught—if only by subtle slights—that their essential identity is disappointing, inferior, and something to be despised.

A new time of identity formation occurs in adolescence (Erikson, 1997)—but not for the LGBTQ teenager. For them, this second stage of identity formation occurs in adulthood, though more and more teenagers today are coming out earlier.

LGBTQ identities are very different from one another. That said, certain commonalities do exist.

These days LGBTQ children, teens, and adults are walking into our offices claiming their identities in many different ways. We will talk in Chapter 13 about how therapists can address the fluctuating identities of their clients when they are children and teens. LGBTQ adults, especially those of the older generation, didn't have permission to explore different and various identities. So many older LGBTQ individuals could have been spared shaming about their gender had they had permission to do what today's young LGBTQ kids and teens are able to do in terms of experimenting with different gender identities.

Gay Men

A common stereotype of the gay man is the slim, effeminate, soft-spoken individual. But many gay men take the opposite tack, striving to achieve a type of hypermasculinity. Here you will see the developmental wound in full bloom. These men have overidentified with the macho, patriarchal, bully-type male in terms of their overly muscular physical builds and their cognitive beliefs on what it is to be a man.

Gay men, and some straight and bisexual men, are punished from childhood for their natural desire to be softer and gentler and have romantic feelings for another male. The resulting developmental wound is to be out of integrity with one's self in terms of masculinity.

After years of being called "pansies," "sissies," and "mother-dominated mama's boys," and after years of being referred to as "more like women," "underdeveloped in their masculinity," "less than a man," "weak," "innately vulnerable," and "cowardly," it is no wonder that some gay men go to such extremes to project a masculine identity. Unfortunately, however, avoiding such slights by becoming hypermasculine constitutes a trauma in and of itself.

Straight-Acting Guise

"Circuit boys" are gay men, usually age 21 to 50, who attend circuit parties across the world. These events cram together shirtless gay men who dance to loud, rhythmic music and often do drugs and have sex right on the dance floor. These parties have different themes and usually run all night, into the late morning and even afternoon. It's a bit like a gay-boy sleepover that was missed out on during childhood.

The typical circuit boy is muscular, sometimes overdeveloped. He may abuse steroids. Some psychologists refer to this hypermasculine look as *muscle dysmorphia*: The man doesn't see himself as being as muscular as he "should be," even though he's developed far beyond buff. In these men's eyes, the more masculine looking they are, the better; it is an unconscious attempt to cover any femininity.

To achieve a sense belonging, these men want to be "a man among men," which they failed to be while growing up. When I am around circuit boys, I often feel surrounded by the very bullies and homophobes who ridiculed and humiliated me when I was younger. I have to remind myself that these are my gay brothers, and that they only *look* like those other, patriarchal men.

Like sex parties and sex clubs, circuit parties offer many gay men a niche, a place where they can finally fit in—which makes such parties so compelling to so many. Observed from the outside, circuit boys seem to exude freedom, connectedness, and authenticity. But circuit parties are fueled by drugs, alcohol, and barebacking. Many circuit boys fly from city to city to attend the parties, worshiping the DJs and enjoying pseudointimacy with one another. To achieve a sense of belonging, these gay men risk STIs and HIV infection, overdosing on drugs or alcohol, and recklessly wasting time and money on the next party they can find. They often spend all of their free time on superficial people they describe as their "close friends" even though they see them only a few times a year and only at these parties. They miss out on real relationships, careers, family—and, inevitably, on life.

When the party is over, men in their 40s and 50s will come to see you, regretting having expended so much on something that gave so little in return. I see this as a direct result of covert cultural sexual abuse.

Misogyny

Another way to identify a developmental insult at the identity stage is to track the language of woman hating by gay men. Aversion to women does not create orientation, though it can contribute to anger toward women and anything feminine. Some gay men do hate woman and are misogynists. Others appear to be antifemale but instead are showing their identity wound by shaking off anything female within them to reaffirm their own masculinity.

A gay comedian once quipped, "I like my women like I like my coffee. I don't like coffee." His audience laughed uncomfortably. Some women in the audience booed him. Did he mean he just wasn't interested in women sexually or romantically, or that he hated them?

Femininity is not generally acceptable among gay men. Countless times I have heard gay men say of their more effeminate counterparts, "If I wanted a woman, I would be straight," in a negative and hostile way. Many gay men accept and tolerate drag and feminine talk and behaviors among friends in the culture but declare this taboo in relationships. Just read the many personal ads seeking "straight-acting" guys, or "masculine, no fems."

Some gay men refer to each other as *she* or *her* or *Mary*. Although this can be said in jest—a way of "owning" femininity through humor—there are times I think it goes too far and becomes a way to channel hostility, sexism, and misogyny. It is a manifestation of an identity developmental wound that should be explored in therapy.

Questions to ask your gay male clients are:

- How were you treated by your parents in terms of masculinity?
- What were the gender roles and stereotypes in your family?
- What happened when you did or did not conform?
- How were you treated by your peers for the type of male you were?
- What was your relationship with your mother like?
- How did your father feel toward women?
- Where did you get the strongest messages about what it meant to be female and an atypical male?

Lesbians

Much of lesbian identity, especially in the 40-year-old and up generation, is tied to relationships and to politics. Having been suppressed by patriarchy, sexism, and heterosexism, lesbians take a different route when coming to terms with their identity.

The Lesbian Anti-Ideal

By trying to look as masculine as possible, gay men try to become like the straight men who demeaned them as teenagers and excluded them from the male fraternity and spurned their advances. But lesbians do the opposite. Historically, many lesbians (of the 40-and-older set) passed through a stage—perhaps during the coming-out process—during which they stopped shaving their legs and underarms and stopped using makeup, dyeing their hair, and wearing nail polish. This was done in an effort to distance themselves from the patriarchal sexist norms that so many straight women endured. After coming out, lesbians often cut their hair short, wear more comfortable shoes, and adopt a less traditionally feminine appearance to counteract the myth of acceptable beauty and what it means to be a woman (Krakauer & Rose, 2002). This defiant phase can settle into a way of life in which a lesbian decides that wearing as much makeup as she used to and dyeing her hair isn't what she wants or needs for herself as she develops her identity. This is necessarily not due to a developmental wound; rather, it can be a way of developing a healthy identity.

Lesbians also use their "physical appearance to be recognized by and to recognize similar others" (Rothblum, 1994). In other words, adopting such an appearance allows lesbians to identify one another and become distinct from women in the dominant culture. Appearance norms are one way to establish a group identity.

Among lesbians, identity issues relating to physical appearance are different from those of gay men and have changed over time. As Barron (1998) stated, being a lesbian "is a body issue":

> Becoming lesbian is partly about reclaiming the neutral from being defined as masculine. For instance, hairy armpits are not masculine; they are human and as sensual as a woman's bush. Shoes that allow one to walk naturally are not masculine; they are human. (p. 9)

Barron went on to say that her lesbian identity is about caring less about male approval or disapproval. This concept of the damage male patriarchy has done to women comes out in the competence stage as well.

Younger lesbians these days do not exhibit the same stage of coming out that focuses on fighting off patriarchy. Society has become (relatively) more tolerant of gender nonconformity, and in general younger LGBTQ people may have experienced less hostility at being "different."

Politics

For lesbians, how they identify themselves takes on far greater meaning than for gay men. For many of them, being referred to as "lesbian" rather than "gay" is extremely meaningful. I used to advertise my workshops for lesbian and gay male couples with a flyer that read gay and lesbian couples workshop. When I spoke to other therapists and lesbians, they told me that many lesbians would not come because the flyer did not read *lesbian and gay* couples workshop. In fact, lesbian couples regularly tell me that if I don't have female assistants—preferably lesbians—that they will not attend.

I must admit that at first I thought it was ridiculously nitpicky for anyone to use wording and gender as reasons for not attending a workshop. But I've come to understand that behind this apparent pettiness is profound logic. To date, the best overview of some reasons behind this issue is in Adrienne Rich's article "Compulsory Heterosexuality and Lesbian Existence" (1980). This still-popular, commonly referenced article describes how patriarchy and sexism—characteristics of male power over women—render lesbians invisible, forcing them to face an additional level of trauma. In other words, what might be misconstrued as lesbians' anger over slights and preconceptions is really about *existence.* In fact, Rich uses terms such as *lesbian existence* and *lesbian continuum* instead of *lesbianism*, a word she feels is limiting in terms of what it means to be a lesbian.

Clinicians can understand lesbian clients more fully—as I have managed to do in my workshops—by thinking along these lines rather than assessing them wrongly as hostile feminists. Validating their anger, mirroring their experience without judgment, and holding a safe space for them to talk about these issues are what they need.

The Relational Identities of "Butch" and "Femme"

This concept—or dichotomy—was more prevalent in the 1950s, when one female partner often dressed in a more "feminine" manner and the other was more masculine. This allowed lesbians to identify one another as well as express themselves as separate from the dominant culture (Myers, Taub, Morris, & Rothblum, 1998).

Some lesbian couples still do role-play, with the "butch" engaging in "packing," or wearing a dildo to represent the "male" role in their relationship. They refer to themselves as stud/fem and are often African-American. She is stereotypically more masculine in dress and behavior, sporting short hair and men's clothing, whereas the "femme" pays attention to her makeup and dress. Many therapists think that a butch lesbian is "trying to be a man," but this is not the case. The butch is usually trying to take on the character traits of being empowered and in control. Again, therapists must recognize whatever homophobia and prejudices this may evoke in them.

Adopting butch and femme roles is not necessarily an indication of a developmental injury. However, in some cases, it may be. For example, some lesbians assume a hyper-butch persona, acting as if nothing can bother them and projecting an attitude of not caring about a thing. They are often confrontational—with straight people, men, and other lesbians alike—and come off as having a chip on their shoulder. Underneath, however, these women are extremely sensitive and care deeply about being accepted. This may be the lesbian version of the circuit party/boy: the adoption of the masculine identity they were never allowed to have as children, now manifested as hypermasculinity. You can see how both of these personas ultimately cause further abandonment and emotional pain for these gay men and lesbians.

Misandry

Rosanne Barr had a standard joke in her stand-up comedy act where she says, "I don't know why people think lesbians hate men. They don't have to have sex with them!" Everyone laughs because they know the stereotype of lesbians hating men and they know how some straight women despise men for not meeting their sexual needs.

In fact, some lesbians do hate men and build their identities around anything that is not male. They might decide to spell *women* as "womyn" and distance themselves from anything that has to do with men at all. As a clinician, you have to assess whether this is healthy or unhealthy: Is it a case of true male hating or simply an attempt to honor their identity as separate from the patriarchal model?

A *misandrist* is the respectable feminist equivalent for the misogynist, according to the *Oxford English Dictionary*. *Misogyny* was a known word in Latin and Greek and according to the *Oxford English Dictionary* was first used in English in 1656. *Misandry* was first used in 1898, three hundred years later. Some books—*Misogyny, Misandry, and Misanthropy*, for one—use the word in their titles, as do some articles. But little is out there to explain the concept fully.

Both misogyny and misandry are gender-neutral: Misogynists and misandrists can be either men or women. In general, however, usually women hate men and men hate women. Perhaps because of the horrors of sexism, our culture had to go very far in one direction and only look at what men have done to women. Some accuse feminist activists of being misandrists, and some are—but most aren't.

The developmental wound here for lesbians is that of having to be hyperfeminine and behave and dress in ways that were not in line with how they saw themselves as the types of females they knew they were.

Clinicians catching this language and mindset in their lesbian clients can ask them how they have been treated by males—especially by their fathers and older brothers. You can ask your lesbian clients:

- What was your response to how your father wanted you to be?
- What were you rewarded for and punished for in terms of the type of female you were?
- What were your family of origin's rules about gender—overt and covert?
- What kind of a woman was your mother in relationship to men?

- How were you taught to be female?
- Did your mother go along with what the traditional female should be like, or did she give you some leeway to be the kind of girl you were?

Treatment

Clinicians need to teach their clients about betrayal bonds and explore the ways they may have been betrayed in terms of gender formation growing up. It helps to explore how their internalization of the perpetrators' characteristics might have manifested. These clients often feel unique and enjoy the "special" way they are in terms of how they live, dress, and keep their patriarchal stance. Clinicians need to help disrupt their beliefs around their uniqueness and the meaning they have attached to them by teaching them they may be continuing the same bad behavior that they were victimized by in childhood. In other words, show them that what they are doing is perpetrating the original abuse by doing to themselves what was done to them.

Competence

In the fourth stage, the child develops a sense of personal power and a drive to achieve. If negatively influenced, the child may feel incompetent now and later in life, or overly competitive with others. Many gay boys who aren't athletic and don't do well at sports are made to feel incompetent and belittled by coaches who deride them for not being a "team player." Gay athletes feel that by "passing"—by fitting the patriarchal ideal of what it is to be male—they're essentially phonies and that if others knew the truth, they'd be devalued and outcast.

Gay men and lesbians are highly competitive with each other as a result of wounds in this stage, which disrupt their ability to form cohesive groups. Their extensive past wounding leaves them feeling incompetent. Every child needs to feel that what he does and thinks about is competent. If he doesn't get this from caretakers or authority figures, he'll grow up to feel incompetent, competitive, or both. We are taught that how we think, act, and feel is wrong. How can we support and empower each other if we can't do it for ourselves?

Clinicians should look for overachieving traits in LGBTQ clients. It is common for LGBTQ teenagers to adopt this strategy to hide their nonstraight or noncisgender identities. Their adaptive thought and behavior is: "If I overachieve, people will like me and not see me as the damaged goods I am."

As an openly gay therapist writing books, doing trainings, and giving public lectures and workshops, I have had my share of negative transference from LGBTQ individuals. I've also noticed differences in how I am treated by lesbians and how I am treated by gay men.

At almost every public lecture I do, I am confronted by either a lesbian, bisexual, or gay person who, although well-intentioned, wants to add his or her expertise and story. It starts as a question, but soon it turns into a presentation, and suddenly I have a copresenter. Rarely, if ever, have I had a heterosexual individual do this.

At first, I was taken aback by this and did not know what to do. I would politely find an opportunity to ask them to sit down and wait for the question-and-answer part of the presentation, but this only served to make the speaker angry and give me a negative evaluation.

Later I discovered that what was happening related to the fact that as a group we have been silenced and held incompetent. In standing up in front of a group of people and sharing my expertise, I am breaking all the rules. Unconsciously, participants are feeling permission to do the same. However, it is inappropriate for them to interrupt my presentation, and it would be inappropriate for me to interpret their interruption. Usually what they have to say is solid and good—it's just bad timing.

I have had LGBTQ individuals tell me after a talk that they could do a better job than I did. One woman actually had me removed from a speaking engagement and used herself as the replacement. Others have told me what I need to include to be better at what I do.

Now I begin my talks by saying, "There will be one or more of you in the audience who will experience a reaction to what I am saying either positively or negatively, and you are going to want to add to my presentation. You will think you are raising your hand to ask me a question, but once you start talking you will find yourself becoming my copresenter, and I will be in a position of having to interrupt you and ask you to sit back down and wait. To avoid that, please know I provide time at the end of my presentation for you to add anything you wish, as I learn from you, too. Until then, please keep any questions you have to simply clarification of my thoughts and not adding any of your own opinions yet."

By saying this, I am letting them know that they will have a voice, that their opinion counts, and that they are competent. I never say that my opening remarks are directed at LGBTQ individuals, because that would be offensive to them, but the truth is that it is usually a gay man or lesbian who wants to contribute. I also do want to hear what they say, as it might help me say it better or differently next time, and I may even learn something I did not know.

As a straight clinician, you must be prepared for this kind of negative transference as well. Remember that it is coming from the pain of being silenced and rejected, and that what the client needs is your validation and willingness to listen. You will represent all the straight people in their lives who invalidated them and deemed them incompetent. This is different from what I represent to them as a gay male, cisgender, white therapist.

Concern

Most children develop healthy empathy for others—as long as those others are heterosexual. In fact, children are strongly encouraged *not* to feel concern or show positive regard for gays and lesbians, including their peers. Males, in particular, are rewarded for showing contempt and disgust for anything or anyone that seems gay. Gay and lesbian children, too, are encouraged to empathize with heterosexuals only and to "edit" their own identity development by developing a distorted self to present to the world.

Any adolescent's peer group becomes a vitally important influence. As adolescents develop a stronger sense of self, they separate from—if not actively rebel against—their parents' values. But in most schools, LGBTQ peer groups do not exist. Passing as straight bypasses the normative process of developing one's true identity.

The degree of psychological damage depends on how the adolescent adapts. With their sense of belonging critically impaired, they may withdraw and isolate themselves. Not until the coming-out process begins can their identity development take place, as they find their niche in the LGBTQ community.

During this stage, which Erikson termed the "identity crisis," teens refine their authentic self. To figure out who they really are, they hang out with like-minded peers who offer a sense of belonging. They try to choose a coherent self-image from many different templates: jock, leather-jacketed rebel, SAT scholar, computer geek, "most popular" or "most likely to succeed," or just an all-around good sport. Socially isolated teenagers are often believed to be gay—even if they aren't—and because everyone wants to avoid them, they remain isolated.

Later, as a delayed step in achieving a sense of belonging, gay men will desire to start a diet or increase a workout regimen—hoping to become the very types that other gays find attractive. Their sense of identity is often created by achieving perfect gym bodies: sculpted chests, buns of steel, and well-defined biceps. LGBTQ individuals may also work to ease the negative impact through sex, overachievement, and politics—and by joining a subgroup with extremely (often obsessively) narrow interests. All of this is an attempt to go against the grain of the way they were influenced at an early age—or, as psychologists say, imprinted.

To build a sense of one's own worth, one needs a feeling of belonging. This is the essential starting point from which one can add, remove, and modify where one came from originally and where one is headed—emotionally, mentally, and psychologically. In psychosocial development, this is a crucial stage for every child to complete successfully. The foundation of a sense of belonging begins with the family you're born into and continues with your socialization in school, on the playground, and in your house of worship. It is in these places that you learn relational skills and how to get along with others.

Often developmental wounds occurring in the concern stage will manifest in clients talking about someone different within the gay community in a negative way. They will talk disparagingly and contemptuously about certain people. You might mistakenly identify it as internalized homophobia, as it will look similar. But you will notice that the client lacks concern not only for other LGBTQ individuals but also toward others who are different. The way the client presents it will seem at times juvenile.

For example, I had a 24-year-old lesbian client who was primarily a loner but wanted to be in a relationship and have other lesbian friends. She described herself as a "gothic"-type woman, wearing dark makeup and with dyed jet-black hair falling over one eye. She said that people needed to love her the way she was and if they didn't, they could "kiss her behind."

I placed her in a singles relationship group mixed with straight, lesbian, and gay individuals. It was a 6-week group, and I learned a lot about her during those weeks. She was judgmental of the conservative lesbians coming from work in their business clothes, the gay men wearing their "typical" muscle shirts, and the "totally predictable" straight individuals. Her concern for others was almost completely absent, yet she desperately wanted it for herself.

Even in the goth community she felt isolated and was judgmental about the members who attended the bars and goth functions. I gently confronted her on her extremely judgmental attitudes and beliefs, and we talked about how she worried that others would treat her the same. She had always felt different growing up and was an outcast. Even at home her parents questioned why she chose the goth lifestyle and criticized her.

Her wound was not about being lesbian as much as it was about her sense of belonging and not feeling as though she fit in. As a result she developed a judgmental attitude toward others to keep them at bay. Once she realized this, her work in therapy became about being more empathic and accepting of others. It was shocking to her to learn this about herself, because she had always seen herself as open and nonjudgmental.

Intimacy and Sexuality

For LGBTQ individuals, perhaps the biggest developmental hurdle is not being able to experiment, sexually and romantically, with their own gender and being forced to role-play at heterosexuality.

According to Erikson, adolescence, between ages 12 and 18, is the most crucial stage, when all the earlier stages of growth become integrated. Do young people display a strong sense of independence, a sense of basic trust, and strong feelings of confident competence? Do they feel in control of their lives? If individuals can manage this stage successfully, they will be ready to head out into the world in a healthy way, ready to plan for their future. But if not, the teens will feel frustrated and incompetent, have difficulty making decisions, and remain confused about their sexual orientation, future career, and general role in life.

LGBTQ adolescents face even more challenges than the common ones Erikson talks about. They feel confused about their sexual identity largely because they're not allowed to explore it in a positive, instructive way.

At this stage of development, love relationships become central. Erikson believed that no matter how professionally successful one may become, one is not *developmentally* complete without intimacy. If all goes well, the young adult will bond with others and enjoy a secure sense of identity. If not, he'll avoid commitment and feel unable to depend on anyone. Many gay men find themselves isolated in just this way, because homophobia and heterosexism have kept them from developing intimacy.

Falling in love places anyone—LGBTQ or straight—in an endorphin-altered state. For LGBTQ individuals still in the earlier stages of coming out, developing crushes can accelerate the process (Coleman, 1981/1982). Romantic love supercharges the desire of wanting to tell the world that "gay is good" and to tell others that now they have a partner. Achieving the traditional cultural promise of a committed, loving relationship offers LGBTQ individuals "proof" that those who told them that same-sex relationships can't succeed were wrong.

Sexual Abuse

During childhood, overt sexual abuse can vandalize healthy development. As I noted earlier, there is no evidence that sexual abuse can shape, much less create, anyone's sexual orientation—it can only confuse young people about what their orientation really is and what actually happened to them.

Sexual abuse can contaminate anyone's ability to love and have healthy sexual boundaries. Sometimes clinicians overlook sexual abuse when their clients come in with intimacy and sexual problems, simply because they don't want to be politically incorrect by assuming that because the clients are LGBTQ, they have been sexually abused. However, it is okay to ask. With good therapy and healing, abuse victims can come to know their true sexual and romantic orientation—be it LGBTQ or straight.

The Case of Darren

Darren, 42, came to me regarding problems in his relationship with Spencer, his partner of 5 years. The two had moved in together just 3 months before, and Darren no longer knew if he wanted to stay with Spencer. Darren enjoyed the sexual openness that the two had shared before moving in together. He had promised that once they moved in together, they would be monogamous—but now he was having second thoughts. He wanted to be monogamous, but he also felt compelled to play around.

"Most gay male couples do this," Darren told me, "and I want to be able to be one of them. I always thought I wanted monogamy, but now that I'm living with someone, I can see I don't."

Darren had wanted a relationship for some time. He had come out at the late age of 30, dated many different men, and had short-term relationships with some of them, but he never found anyone he felt secure and in love with—until he met Spencer. Darren explained that Spencer was right for him in almost every way. He was a successful landscaper with a flourishing business, and he was very masculine. Though he enjoyed men, he wanted children. Darren couldn't believe he was willing to sacrifice this relationship, for which he had waited for so long, just to be nonmonogamous.

I obtained Darren's history. He said that as an only child, he was left alone most of the time while his mother worked. His first sexual experience was at age 13 with a 35-year-old man named Hans. Hans had taken a special interest in Darren and took him out for ice cream, to the movies, and to sporting events. Darren slept over at Hans's house when his mother worked late.

As Darren told me this, I asked, "So you were sexually abused?"

This made Darren irate; he insisted it was *not* sexual abuse. He explained to me how his mother had worked two jobs after his father's death, and she'd become friends with Hans from work. When Darren was 13, Hans introduced him to oral sex by fellating him. By then, Darren knew he was gay and wondered how Hans could tell. "He must have known I was gay, or he would not have given me my first sexual experience," Darren told me.

Over time, Hans "taught" Darren how to fellate him in return, how to masturbate, and eventually about anal sex—with Darren being the receiver.

When Hans took a job in another state, Darren's mother paid for Darren to spend weekends and a couple of weeks in the summer with him. They spent their time together doing things that Darren enjoyed, including being sexual. "Hans was the father I never had," Darren told me. "Hans was my first love."

Darren: Clinical Interpretation and Treatment

In my mind, there was no doubt that what Darren experienced with Hans was sexual abuse. In working with him, I took many opportunities to point this out, explaining that a 13-year-old is not developmentally ready to handle adult sexuality, especially not with a 35-year-old. But Hans's abuse had felt like love to Darren, and he wasn't going to let me or anyone else get in the way of what he believed.

Spencer had also told Darren that Hans was a perpetrator, but Darren got angry with him, too, and soon Spencer stopped talking about it.

I explained to Darren that there had to be some reason why he felt compelled to sabotage the relationship of his dreams by acting out sexually. He agreed that something was driving him, but denied that it had anything to do with Hans.

Darren was willing, however, to hear my thoughts on sexual abuse, despite refusing to connect them to Hans. He was also willing to consider that covert cultural sexual abuse was contributing to his urge to be promiscuous. He was willing to read the book *Victims No Longer*, which I hoped would help him realize that Hans's behavior was abuse, but it didn't. The more I pushed him to understand what Hans had done, the more he rebelled and started skipping appointments.

I decided the only way to help Darren understand what he had suffered was to put him in group therapy with other gay men—to reduce the negative transference he was placing onto me. In other words, he was projecting his problem onto me, taking the accountability off Hans. My simply identifying it as abuse caused Darren (albeit unconsciously) to blame me for calling the problem what it was.

Darren agreed to enter group therapy. Over the course of 6 months, he began to accept that what Hans had done was actually a "form" of sexual abuse and was interfering with his desire to remain monogamous.

However, Darren made it very clear to me and the group that even though he saw that what Hans had done was a form of sexual abuse, he still believed that Hans had loved him and that if not for Hans, he would have had no love growing up. Darren said he would not let the group or me take that away from him.

In my years of practice, I have met many gay men like Darren—gay men who were sexually abused by a much older male. But because it was done in an affectionate way, they viewed it as their "first sexual experience" and not abuse.

This is akin to the straight male whose first sexual experience is with a much older woman. The difference is that it's been easier for me to help straight men understand what happened to them than to help gay men see the abuse for what it was. The difference, I believe, lies in the isolation, loneliness, and feeling of being disenfranchised that gay children grow up with. When a perpetrator approaches them in a friendly way, they perceive it as love and not abuse, because covert cultural sexual abuse has made them feel so unlovable.

It is important to explore the developmental insults that might be related to clients' lesbianism and gayness but are not the main source of it. Darren is a great example of this: His sexual abuse affected his homosexuality, but his homosexuality was not the real issue.

Responsibility

When treating overly responsible, "workaholic" LGBTQ clients, it is appropriate to consider that they are responding to covert cultural sexual abuse by trying to be "the best employee/partner/family member possible." However, it is also crucial that you tease out any possible developmental wounds related to the client's family dynamics to assess whether this overachieving behavior stems from growing up LGBTQ or from something else.

The Case of Joey

Joey was a 32-year-old gay male who lived with his mother and father. His two sisters, both much older (ages 42 and 45), were married and living out of the house with children. Joey had been out since he was 16 and felt that he needed to stay home and care for his elderly parents (ages 80 and 81). He believed in family and giving back what he felt he received—a good childhood.

Joey came to therapy due to feeling depressed, which he thought might be about not having long-term relationships. He'd had one that lasted a little over a year, but when it came time to talking about moving in, Joey refused to move out of his parents' home. His boyfriend, however, did not want to live with Joey's parents. Unable to come to a compromise, they broke up. "If I cannot get a guy who understands my situation, then they are not for me," Joey told me.

"Understand what situation, Joey?" I asked him to explain.

"I had understanding parents who did not give me a hard time about being gay when I told them at age 16. I was bullied and harassed, and they were there for me. In turn, I did everything I could for them. My sisters were useless and would not drive them to their doctor's appointments or come by to see if there was something they needed. They started their own lives and families and never looked back," he said angrily.

In fact, this was not the case, as I learned when I asked further about the situation. The sisters came around and called quite often, but Joey would intercede and do what his parents needed, telling his sisters not to bother. Joey did not rebel during his adolescence as his two sisters had. "They gave my parents hell, and I vowed never to do that," he said.

"Why?" I asked. "That is the job description of an adolescent—to develop an identity through a bit of rebellion."

Joey then told me that his father and mother had always seen him as the good child. They'd told him they never had to worry about him and he always did the right thing.

Joey was a "surprise" to his family, as he was unplanned. He knew this growing up and made the decision to be there for his parents as much as he felt they were there for him. His parents never encouraged Joey to stop what he was doing, to get an adult life, or to move out. When I explored this with Joey, I received a verbal shower of anger and rage. He believed I was trying to fault his parents when I was only trying to understand why they were not encouraging him to move on.

Joey: Clinical Interpretation and Treatment

Perhaps if Joey had not been not gay, the same dynamics would have held for him in terms of his overresponsibility for his parents. However, it seemed to me that the issue related both to his being gay and to developmental issues. His parents' unconditional acceptance of his gayness made him feel obligated to them, and the fact that he was a "surprise" who arrived late in their lives perhaps made him feel like he owed them something extra to make up for their inconvenience.

I explored this gently and paced myself slowly, bringing these things up and tying them back each time to his lack of adult relationships and friendships. I told him that as long as he was preoccupied with taking care of his parents and not asking his sisters to share the responsibilities, he would remain alone and isolated. I worried aloud with him that after they passed away, he would be alone. I also suggested that his focus on his parents was preventing him from offering his caretaking "expertise" in other situations that would benefit from it. This motivated him to divert some of his caretaking away from his parents and toward others in the gay community. He got involved in some grassroots gay organizations and eventually began forming relationships with people in the gay community.

Lesbians and gays often become overly responsible as children to cover their inherent feelings of being damaged. Family members often support and reward this behavior without helping them see that they don't have to be as overresponsible as they are. When this is the case, it is important to look at how the family dynamics are being played out.

It is important as a clinician to look under every rock and rule in or rule out every possible cause of a client's problems. Developmental wounds play a part in all of our clients' lives. No parent can successfully get a child through each developmental phase without some wounding occurring, whether severe or light. Examining this with your clients can help them understand where they might be stuck and how to move forward.

CHAPTER 7

Coming Out

We do not choose to be gay . . . we are chosen.
—Suzanne Westenhoefer, lesbian comic

Most clinicians don't realize that the coming-out process has predictable, observable stages. Once you become familiar with the stages, you can help clients know which one they are in—and what they can anticipate.

The stages do not necessarily occur in order. Clients may jump back and forth, skip one or two, or linger in some as well. Along the way, those going through the coming-out stages struggle with internalized and outward homophobia. Some linger at one stage longer than others. It may be years before they move on.

As the therapist, you have to walk a fine line. It's essential to proceed at your clients' pace, not yours. Rushing them can prompt them to regress in stages or stay stuck in the one they are in. It can also traumatize them, as I talked about in Chapter 4 on covert cultural sexual abuse. However, not coaxing them along and failing to advise them on when and how to move to the next stage can stall their process.

Keeping the covert cultural sexual abuse trauma model in mind is crucial when working with clients in the coming-out process. Remember that coming out demands that clients relive the trauma that put them into the closet to begin with, which can result in trauma symptoms (as discussed in Chapter 5). This is often not understood by clinicians, who may treat the process as a "coming-out issue" and nothing more. Within the closet are more issues, such as family-dysfunction issues, bullying, and gender shaming, to name a few. Re-experiencing these traumas of suppressing one's identity can lead to many problems, which clinicians need to anticipate.

The Case of Maggie: Coming Out and Negative Transference

Maggie, 28, had recognized her lesbian feelings for many years. She knew that to live an authentic and affirmative life, she would have to act on these feelings and no longer hide and suppress them. To discuss this, Maggie chose a straight therapist, Barb, who was gay friendly and gay affirmative. She encouraged Maggie to approach gay and lesbian settings where she could build solid relationships with others like herself.

Barb, unaware of what was available, referred Maggie to a lesbian bar that she had heard of from her other lesbian clients. The following week, Maggie returned to therapy and reported being—in her words—"turned off" and "disgusted" by the women she'd met, who behaved in a "masculine manner." She was also appalled at being approached by several straight men wanting to "score" with a lesbian twosome. Barb aligned with Maggie's experience by saying, "I don't know why so many lesbians are masculine." Inadvertently, she also echoed Maggie's annoyance at straight men trying to pick up lesbians.

Next, she referred Maggie to a local gay and lesbian community center, where Maggie also saw masculine lesbians, some of whom came on to her—even those already in relationships. Maggie commented that lesbians must be unable to commit and that they all seemed like they wanted to be men. "If I wanted a man, I would not be coming out!" she said.

Disappointed in the lesbian community, Maggie was now disinterested in investigating any further. She was angry with Barb for not better preparing her for what she would expect to find at the lesbian clubs, accusing Barb of being unaware and incompetent. Maggie even threatened to find a gay or lesbian therapist who would be better able to help her. Although Barb supplied her with names of some lesbian therapists in the area, Maggie never followed through and stayed in therapy with Barb. Barb sought supervision and became informed on resources that she passed on to Maggie, but Maggie remained angry with her during treatment.

Maggie: Clinical Interpretation and Treatment

Here, problems arose because the therapist didn't know how to navigate an LGBTQ socialization process for someone just coming out of the closet. Barb assumed that a lesbian bar could serve as Maggie's first introduction to the "lesbian scene"; however, she should have cautioned Maggie that some straight men and swinging couples tend to frequent these bars—even though the management tries to keep that to a minimum.

Next, Barb should have addressed Maggie's internalized homophobia about masculine lesbians, which was manifested in Maggie's being "disgusted" by them. By validating Maggie's sense of disgust (by saying she did not know why they acted like that either), Barb fueled Maggie's internalized homophobia and increased her reluctance to attempt more homosocialization. Barb needed to tell Maggie that her reaction to seeing masculine women was her own internalized homophobia, that it was normal to feel this way in the early stages of coming out, and that it would diminish over time as she became more comfortable with her own lesbianism.

Maggie also needed to be aware that she could enter the lesbian community through many different doors. To help ease Maggie's transition—particularly at this early stage of coming out—it was Barb's job to know about the alternatives, and to treat Maggie's internalized homophobia, not inflame it.

Finally, Barb needed to address Maggie's unconscious negative transference toward her for not preparing her for what to expect in the lesbian community. The real source of Maggie's anger was probably related to her parents and society, who had let her down and did not prepare her for a lesbian identity. Unlike heterosexual children, LGBTQ children do not receive a road map on how to socialize and date.

When Barb sought me out for supervision, I asked her to address Maggie's negative transference toward her about Barb's being heterosexual. I knew this had to exist, as Maggie kept belittling her skills and threatening to see a lesbian therapist. It seemed as though Maggie needed to deem Barb incompetent and keep her that way to stay closeted and not move forward in her coming-out process.

Barb asked Maggie whom she thought Barb was standing in for, given that Maggie had so many negative feelings toward Barb for not helping her more. At first Maggie was defensive, but she then began to cry as she got in touch with her feelings of being left on her own without help from her family and friends. She badly wanted to talk to them about her feelings. She had even told her sister she thought she was lesbian and asked her if she would go with her to the bars, but her sister declined. Her mother was insensitive to her struggle of coming out, saying, "Well, this is what you wanted, so this is what you get."

With this breakthrough, Maggie was able to get in touch with the lonely feelings she'd grown up with and denied all of her life. Now, as Barb addressed the covert cultural sexual abuse Maggie had been subjected to, Maggie recognized how abandoned and rejected she had felt all of her life. She began feeling more positively toward Barb, and the therapy began to help her continue in the coming-out process. Maggie started attending lesbian functions once again and worked on her internalized homophobia, finding lesbians with whom she felt she could relate.

If Barb had seen Maggie's crisis only as a coming-out issue and interpreted Maggie's unhappiness with the therapy as a sign that Maggie was unhappy with Barb's sexual orientation, she would have missed the hidden issue of covert cultural sexual abuse. Negative transference is always an important therapy tool that can be used to uncover hidden information—but only if clients are willing to stay and work through it, and if therapists can tolerate their clients' being angry with them for a while. Fortunately, Maggie and Barb were able to use the negative transference to help Maggie.

The Six Stages of Coming Out

Various theorists have developed and defined the stages of coming out and discussed how clinicians can use them as a framework and tool for clients. By discerning which stage a client is going through, you can best prepare him or her for the next one.

Vivienne C. Cass's Homosexuality Identity Formation model (1979) best reflects the stages I've observed in my clients. According to her, the stages of identity formation are:

Stage 1: Identity confusion
Stage 2: Identity comparison
Stage 3: Identity tolerance
Stage 4: Identity acceptance
Stage 5: Identity pride
Stage 6: Identity synthesis

These stages are not necessarily linear or consecutive. Many individuals go from Stage 1 to Stage 3 and back to Stage 1, depending on many factors, such as their personalities and the circumstances in their lives.

During the first three stages, clients are most at risk for stopping the coming-out process and regressing back into the closet. Here they may even seek out reparative therapy. These are the most vulnerable stages in that clients' emotions are raw and their sensitivity to judgments of others is high. Safety, both emotional and physical, is crucial during these early stages. The work during these stages is often internal in that clients are mentally and emotionally deciding within themselves what their identity is, comparing themselves to others, and deciding whether or not they can tolerate it. Your job as a clinician is to help them remember the reasons why they wanted to come out to begin with. It is also important to allow them to start and stop at their own pace. Pushing them too hard can retraumatize them. Just as with other trauma survivors, the goal is to let *them* feel in charge of their own psychological material.

The final three stages are more affirmative, as clients become increasingly certain that they are on the right track and can accept and claim their authentic LGBTQ identities. The work is more outwardly focused; clients venture out into the non-straight world and begin learning relational and socialization skills that help them become more social and intimate with other LGBTQ people. Therapists need to assess what is creating any difficulties or snags for their clients during this time and watch for any developmental injuries such as issues pertaining to a dysfunctional family of origin or repressed memories of abuse. Depression and anxiety may also surface and interfere with the coming-out process.

Stage 1: Identity Confusion

Those who begin to acknowledge their attraction to other members of the same sex may not see themselves as even remotely gay. This isn't pretending; they still honestly identify themselves as heterosexual. At this stage, their homosexual feelings are completely unacceptable to them. They are looking for anyone who might tell them they are not gay.

Men may have sex with other men but define it as something other than gay or bisexual behavior. Terms like "on the down low" and "kinky" can help a man stay closeted to himself. Women might be sexual with other women and consider it merely experimental, or they may think of having sex with another woman as something for their male partner and his desires—not theirs. For many people, that may be true. For others it is the beginning of a natural gay or lesbian identity surfacing.

Once individuals recognize that a homosexual nature does exist within them, they often become very sensitive, highly anxious, and self-conscious. This is the beginning of potentially reexperiencing their trauma symptoms. Pushing them too far in this stage can cause too much psychological discomfort and potentially keep them from moving on to the next stage.

Many clients at this stage do not use the words *gay, bisexual,* or *lesbian,* as it would reflect affirmation and positivity. If anything, they'll usually self-identify as "homosexual" or "heterosexual with homosexual fantasies." Therapists need to stick with their clients' terminology to avoid rushing them or blocking them from continuing with their process, again keeping in mind the covert cultural sexual abuse and trauma.

At this stage, clients are ready to seek information, often by logging onto the Internet to explore various websites about sexual orientation. They are also vulnerable to getting married heterosexually, genuinely hoping for the best. Your job here is to support clients in being honest and open with their potential opposite-gender mates about their homosexual urges, thoughts, or feelings so that their potential partners can have informed consent.

When clients enter your office in this stage of coming out, it is an opportunity to intervene and help them identify and understand the true nature of their sexuality.

The Case of Drake

Drake, a 24-year-old college student, came to me after completing a recovery program for alcohol addiction. He told me he thought he "might be homosexual" and hoped that his sobriety would make his homosexual feelings go away—but they only grew stronger.

Drake filled me in on a history of what he called "being a little kinky." He told me that he'd experienced homosexual urges since he was 12, when he started masturbating, but thought they would go away. He was not, he believed, innately gay. When he told his chemical dependency counselors about his homosexual feelings, they told him it was related to his distant relationship with his father and brothers. Drake was the only nonathletic child of four boys, and his father took a strong interest in his brothers and not in Drake. Counselors promised him that once he became sober, worked on his "father hunger," and found a girlfriend, his homosexual urges would disappear.

However, Drake was not hopeful about this. The vast majority of his masturbatory fantasies were about males, and when he viewed heterosexual pornography, he focused primarily on the male bodies and on what the males were doing to the females.

He told me he could not imagine a gay life. He always dreamed of having a "normal" life with a wife and children. Being gay was not an option for him. He had a high level of social anxiety and knew that if he lived a life as a homosexual, he would not be able to tolerate the negative judgments.

Drake: Clinical Interpretation and Treatment

Many well-intended therapists explain homosexual feelings as stemming from anything other than an innate homosexual orientation—especially when clients doesn't see it as part of their identity and are in conflict with the feelings. The belief is that clients will eventually recover their innate heterosexuality through work on whatever "caused" the homosexual feelings. This does tremendous psychic damage to those who are truly LGBTQ. It discounts the possibility that the client is beginning a process of self-recognition of being LGBTQ and is in the identity-confusion stage.

My work with Drake was to help him decide this for himself. I educated him about the many possibilities that exist when people have homosexual feelings and interests: There are heterosexual men who have homosexual feelings, fantasies, and behaviors but are not gay or bisexual. Their sexual tendencies with men are a result of early childhood sexual abuse, father hunger, availability, and opportunity, just to name a few. I used the word *homosexual* when working with him, as this was the word that *he* used. When I slipped and use the word *gay*, he would cringe and worry that I thought he actually *was* gay. What I thought mattered greatly to him. I explored this as negative transference (as he knew I was gay) and asked if he thought I had an agenda to make him gay. (If you are a straight clinician, you may ask your clients if they think you have an agenda to make them straight.) He replied that he did think that. I reassured him that this was not the case and we explored the weight he gave to me about determining his sexuality. I told him it was normal for him to feel this way and that my only agenda was to help him resolve any shame around his identity and coach him to look within for the answers.

We started the work about Drake's distant relationship with his father, as this was in the forefront of his concerns. He talked about it in detail, and during the course of the work he told his father about his grief and anger over their strained relationship. He had always wanted his father to mentor him and support him in becoming a man, but his father worked long hours and seemed disinterested in him. Over the first year in therapy he became closer with his father, and he did not act on his homosexual feelings other than to masturbate while looking at porn. He tried to prevent any homoerotic thoughts and fantasies but always found himself "relapsing," as he called it.

In the second year of his therapy, Drake admitted that his homosexual feelings persisted and in fact were stronger. This is common to all people in this stage of coming out if they are truly gay or lesbian—their innate homosexuality surfaces. He could admit now that he was "homosexual" but would not use the word *gay*.

I told him that if he wanted to know if his homosexuality was about more than just sex, he needed to homosocialize. I warned him that doing this, however, could expedite his coming out if that was what was happening here. I told him that if he did not want this to happen, he needed to think about it. Again, I was helping him make his own, conscious decisions by openly stating the consequences of them. I gave him a list of local LGBTQ 12-step groups for his alcoholism and a calendar of community LGBTQ events. This made him very nervous, but he believed that he needed to follow through and took the literature.

After this session, Drake missed his next scheduled weekly appointment with me. Usually this means a client is acting out his resistance or transference, so I called him to ask why he missed. He denied that it had to do with our discussion of his socializing among gays and said he'd forgotten—even though he'd had the same weekly appointment for the last year.

I realized that he might have felt pushed toward the next step too fast. Even though he had told me he wanted to be pushed, his behavior said otherwise. I pointed out this discrepancy to him and he agreed that the idea of going into the LGBTQ community was too scary for him; however, he knew he needed to do it. He asked me to coach him more and lean on him to go. I interpreted this as his father transference directed toward me and translated the word *coach* to *father*, as his father did not mentor him into becoming the man he wanted to be. I told him that this positive transference of the good father directed at me was a good sign, as it was an opportunity to work through in a reparative way his negative issues with his father. I told him that I could be the "good father" therapeutically for him, and we talked about it. I did as he asked, and we agreed if it was too fast for him he would speak up about it, which at times he did.

I also kept in mind that Drake's socializing with the LGBTQ community would potentially activate his trauma symptoms from the covert cultural sexual abuse, which were kept at bay by being closeted. I talked with him about this, explaining what covert cultural sexual abuse was, and told him that he might experience traumatic and dysregulated feelings and that they were normal given his history and the stress he displayed about coming out.

Ruling Out MSM and WSW

Men who have sex with men (MSM) and women who have sex with women (WSW) are not necessarily gay or bisexual. When they show up for therapy, a therapist may, in an effort to avoid being homophobic, immediately label them as homosexual and place them in Stage 1 of the coming-out process. But this may not be true. Behavior is not always attached to one's sexual or romantic identity. There is a difference between sexual orientation, behavior, and fantasy. A client's fantasy or behavior might be a manifestation of childhood sexual abuse or an escalation of sexual addiction, where "taboo" behavior adds a thrill. Some bisexual or biattractional tendencies have nothing to do with a person's core sexual identity. Furthermore, sexuality is not a dichotomy of gay versus straight but rather exists on a continuum, including everything in between. More about this in Chapter 16 on sexual fluidity.

One's sexual *preference* takes into account the desired sexual actions and fantasies with a partner, whereas sexual *orientation* encompasses a sexual *identity* with all the thoughts, feelings, fantasies, and emotions that cause us to become sexually excited. Thus, there is a distinct difference between a gay man and a "male who seeks sex with another male." A gay man's sexual orientation is characterized by lasting aesthetic attraction to, romantic love of, and sexual attraction to exclusively others of the same gender. A gay man's sexual thoughts, fantasies, and behavior are aligned. It is an identity based on affectional, emotional, spiritual, psychological, and sexual feelings exclusively or mostly toward men. Although some gay men can enjoy women as part of their sexual fantasies and behaviors (for instance, being sexual with a woman while with another man and his wife), the gay man is mostly if not totally attracted to men and left cold by the woman if a man is not involved. I often explain it to my clients this way: If a gay man were walking on the beach, he would be sexually drawn only to men; he wouldn't notice women in such a way.

MSMs, on the other hand, might fantasize about sexual contact with men, but on the beach, they're staring at women. They sexually and romantically desire women, not men. These are heterosexual men who engage in sexual behavior with other men for a number of reasons. They are attracted to gay sex, not to men as a whole. They are not gay, nor are they bisexual. Their same-gender sex acts are about physical release and sexual behaviors, not about attraction to or desire for another man. MSMs are turned off and left cold by naked images of men. Instead, they are sexually aroused by and attracted to women. These men typically want to bond with and need affection from other men. Their behavior may also reflect a desire to experiment, or an expression of problems and conflicts with their sexual feelings and desires—which have nothing to do with being gay. More often than not, these are the men whom I counsel or whose wives come to me in such frantic states.

Informing clients about the stages of coming out will help them understand that their ego-dystonic state is likely to be short-lived. However, if this stage persists beyond 2 years, it is likely that the issues involved are not about homosexuality but rather about a developmental insult that occurred in the childhood identity-formation stage. You may need to delve into issues such as how the client's identity development was handled during childhood.

Stage 2: Identity Comparison

During this stage, clients begin to accept the possibility that they *might* be homosexual. They still typically don't describe themselves as "gay," because they associate the word with a particular way of life. The word *homosexual* lets them start exploring from a "safe" distance.

Some clients may accept their *behavior* as gay or bisexual while still rejecting homosexuality as their core identity. Or they might accept a homosexual identity but, paradoxically, inhibit their gay behavior by, for example, deciding to heterosexually marry and have anonymous "no-strings" sexual hookups with men. Of course, this kind of compartmentalization—a fracturing of behavior and identity—leads to problems later on. Suppressing the coming-out process, we know, will lead most LGBTQ people to a life of depression. For some, however, continuing to come out can also lead to a period of depression. More about this later in this chapter.

Some lesbian and gay clients may attempt to embrace a heterosexual identity out of internalized shame and guilt. These clients are particularly vulnerable to the promises of reparative therapy. Because of their self-hate and hope for a "cure," they are eager to be rid of these unwelcome thoughts and feelings.

Some will also seek out sex-addiction treatment. I have had clients say they would rather be labeled a sex addict than be a homosexual. Sadly, these clients will seek out a therapist and tell the therapist they struggle with same-sex attraction and that they are not homosexual but find it to be a compulsion or an addiction. Trained sex-addiction therapists will follow the lead of the client and provide sex-addiction treatment interventions. The problem with this is that it contaminates the coming-out process for the client by pathologizing their process rather than honoring it.

Intersectional Identities

I talk about intersectional identities in Chapter 2. In Stage 2, these become most important in terms of whether the person will continue with the coming-out process or not. Some clients, after exploring and experimenting, may decide to pursue a heterosexual life but do so *not* out of shame or guilt—they simply don't connect to a gay identity. Just as adults raised in one organized religion may decide to convert to another, people are entitled to choose the identity that fits them best. They don't change orientations; they change how they live out their identity. In other words, they are still inherently gay or lesbian, but they self-identify as heterosexual and decide to live this way.

When treating clients in this stage, it is important that psychotherapists (particularly LGBTQ therapists) not force the issue of whether their client is gay, straight, or bisexual, as doing so can cause damage. Again, I cannot stress enough that it must be the *client* who leads the way during these early stages, with you helping in the background.

The Case of Rita and Intersectional Identities

Rita, a 30-year-old Catholic woman, had known since childhood that she was homosexual. In recent months, she had made efforts to come out as a lesbian: She bought books on lesbianism and surfed the Internet for information on lesbian life, and she was attending a lesbian social group at her local LGBTQ community center. However, she was having no success in accepting and embracing her lesbian longings. The problem was the strong conviction of her religion. Rita simply could not reconcile her Catholicism and homosexuality. These were her intersectional identities.

Rita had read about Dignity, a supportive Catholic organization for LGBTQ individuals, but she decided not to look into it after she discovered that it was not sanctioned by the Church. After many months of struggling over the decision of whether or not to come out as a lesbian, Rita decided to live a heterosexual life. This prompted her to see Jan, a Christian psychotherapist, who in turn asked me to supervise the case.

Jan was struggling with how to approach Rita: Should she encourage her client to attend a Dignity service, or should she support Rita's decision to seek out groups that help people who are LGBTQ to live heterosexually? The problem with these groups is that they don't see *any* homosexuality as positive.

Rita: Clinical Interpretation and Treatment

I supported Jan's telling Rita that any decision should come from within herself and not be based on internalized shame and homophobia, which—as Rita needed to understand—can only block the process of either coming out or deciding to live a heterosexual lifestyle. I advised Jan to help Rita understand that for most individuals who have a homosexual orientation, coming out is the appropriate and best option. But for others, it's not—especially if the client is struggling with other issues such as religious beliefs and a religious identity. I informed Jan about the inherent sexism, homophobia, and heterosexism of reparative therapy, and had her address this with Rita to assess for herself how much of her desire to distance herself from homosexuality was about self-hate. These factors should not influence a person's decision to not define as gay.

Rita ultimately chose to keep her homosexuality at a distance and left therapy. She recognized that reparative therapy was not effective for her and instead chose to attend a Catholic group that promoted chastity for homosexuals. This supported her intersectional identities in that her religious identity trumped her lesbian identity. As a therapist, in doing no harm, we need to honor where the client is at.

Jan felt that she had failed this client. She believed that successful therapy for Rita would have entailed helping her to come out as a lesbian. I, however, disagree. Although coming out is the best answer for most LGBTQ clients, it was not for Rita. She made an informed decision to not self-identify or live as a lesbian because of her strong religious beliefs, and Jan needed to accept this decision. Jan had succeeded in providing a space for Rita to decide for herself how she wanted to self-identify, which is all we can ask for as therapists with any client.

I have helped many clients reduce or eliminate the shame they felt about their homosexuality, but then supported them in living heterosexually because that is what *they* wanted. I am aware of the fact that living a closeted life often leads to depression—something no therapist would want to foster in a client—but ultimately my main goal is to help clients live how *they* want to live, not how I personally think they *should* live. Although this is politically taboo in the homophobic climate in which we live, clients have a right to make their own decisions about how they wish to live their lives. Some simply cannot adjust to a homosexual identity or lifestyle.

I support these clients to be out and open in terms of their homosexual feelings. I encourage them to be up-front and honest with a partner when they enter in a relationship with the opposite sex so their partners have informed consent. However, many clients do not do that, and it is not for me or any other therapist to impose our values onto the client. It is their life and their choice. Nor do I try to fool these clients into thinking they can change their orientation. They do not change their sexual and romantic orientation. Instead, they create a heterosexual life for themselves.

LGBTQ clients who decide to live a heterosexual life need to be warned of the possible depression this can create, and I refer my clients to studies that show this. I also warn them that their defenses against homosexuality may eventually wane, explaining that this can cause problems for both them and their loved ones if they are married and have children. But again, the clients are the ones who have the responsibility of deciding for themselves how they want to live their lives.

That said, you should recognize when it is best to coax or coach a client questioning with how to self-identify. Giving clients too much room to explore *not* being gay might result in their staying closeted and aligning with what they think you (and others) want for them. Avoiding this can be tricky; you need to have a solid working relationship with your client. Generally the best approach is to avoid framing the issue as an either/or, coming-out/not-coming-out decision. Instead, explore what will work best for the client now and in the long term.

During this stage of the coming-out process, clients who are on their way to a healthy LGBTQ identity begin to feel positive about being *different*. They like that there is something inside them that is waiting to come out and be expressed, and they feel special inside themselves. The shame about their sexual secret turns into something ego-syntonic and integrated as part of their sense of self.

Your job as a therapist is to support this shame reduction by helping clients honor their specialness and uniqueness. Clients may worry that you, especially if you are a straight therapist, will not understand their feelings of being special—or they might not tell you about them at all for fear that you will think they are strange.

You can predict for your clients that during this stage a feeling of specialness and uniqueness arises and that is normal and healthy in the coming-out process and part of moving to the next stage.

Stage 3: Identity Tolerance

At this stage, individuals accept the likelihood that they're homosexual in a positive way and begin to move toward describing themselves and their identity as gay, bi, or lesbian. This entails "trying on" a homosexual identity to see if it fits. Clients may still hesitate to venture into LGBTQ culture, but they do begin to see a need to end their social isolation and loneliness.

Clients' experiences moving toward homosocialization within the LGBTQ community have a significant impact on the rest of their coming-out process. If the experiences are positive, the individual will continue moving forward in the coming-out process and begin an affirmative identity. If they are negative, the individual might stall or revert to Stages 1 or 2.

When clients have negative initial homosocialization experiences, it is your job as a therapist to be supportive and validate that they had a negative experience but assure them that this is just one negative of the many positives they will have. Remind them there are positive and negative things they will experience and normalize that attaching to the negatives is their internalized homophobia. For example, one of my former clients—an attractive 57-year-old man—came to a session very upset. He had just begun going to gay bars and said that he felt invisible, as though men were looking right through him. He had never had this experience with women and always found at least one woman—even if unattractive—to talk with. But at the gay bars, he had no luck at all. I explained to him that in the gay male culture, being over 50 can be difficult, particularly at gay bars where youth is revered.

He was also upset because he saw men having sex in the bathrooms and back rooms, and he concluded that the heterosexists and homophobes were correct in thinking that the entire LGBTQ community is strictly sexual. I challenged this homophobic thinking by saying that if the entire LGBTQ community were like this, lesbians would be acting the same way. In my judgment, what he witnessed was a *male* experience and couldn't be generalized to the entire gay population. I told him it is a "guy thing, not a gay thing." I also told him that it was unfortunate that he had these experiences, but that they were more about the bars than gay males themselves. This helped the client understand that he simply had to find other venues—and there are many—where he could mingle with men who would want to connect with him on a more meaningful level.

Other clients are afraid to achieve this stage, or fear that they'll get stuck in it. "I don't want to become a gay man waving a rainbow flag around," they say. I reassure them that this needn't happen and also explore their potential homophobia. I teach them that they will be able to become the kind of LGBTQ individual they wish to become and will find or create their own niche.

By the end of this stage, clients have learned that there are both healthy and dysfunctional LGBTQ people, just as there are healthy and dysfunctional straight people. There are also hundreds of subsets within the LGBTQ community. If clients feel overwhelmed, help them explore what niche they might feel most comfortable in. Make sure you inform them that there are many niches to choose from—they just need to search.

Culture Shock

Therapists must also understand the culture shock clients experience when they first step into the LGBTQ community and help their clients anticipate this. Like all communities—whether they are religious, ethnic, professional, and so on—the gay community has its own social customs. Clients who have not been exposed to such customs may not know how to interact with or respond to other LGBTQ individuals.

For example, I remember the first time I entered a gay bar. I was 19 years old, alone and frightened. I ordered a drink and stood near some other men who were standing at a wall. Unbeknownst to me, I was at the "meat rack" (a place where men who want to be chosen for quick sexual hookups congregate). I soon noticed a man staring at me intensely. Every time I looked away, he'd always be there when I turned back. I tried walking to another part of the bar, but he still glared at me.

I recall thinking that my mother was right—going alone to gay bars would get me killed, and this was the man who was going to do it. Though I can laugh about it now, at the time I was frightened, self-conscious, and overwhelmed. Fortunately a nice man started talking to me, explaining that that guy was "cruising" me (giving a sexual pred-atory stare to initiate immediate anonymous and casual sexual contact). I was lucky to have been befriended by this man—many first-timers have no idea what is going on.

Another problem occurs when gays and lesbians interpret this culture shock as a sign that they are not gay or lesbian or, even if they are, they are not meant to live their lives as such. This is again where they are vulnerable to going back into the closet and into Stage 1. They get scared by looking around and not seeing images that mirror them or what they would like to be. They do not feel psychologically safe; returning to the closet is about returning to safety.

The clinician's job is to help clients stay emotionally safe and assure them that there are plenty of environments where they will see themselves reflected in the way they wish. It is crucial as a clinician that you know of other LGBTQ groups and activities to talk about and refer them to.

Stage 4: Identity Acceptance—The Beginning of a Gay Adolescence

This is when people move from simple tolerance to accepting themselves as LGBTQ. They discover a new sense of identification and belonging in the LGBTQ community as a whole. They feel increasing anger at homophobic segments of society, which is healthy for this stage of identity development. All the doubts and self-hatred they once directed inward are now turned outward at more deserving targets.

At this time, individuals begin to process conflict between their own self-perceptions of their homosexuality and those of society. They begin to become more vocal and take small risks. They also may distance themselves from people and situations that would disrupt their new way of thinking. This healthy reaction is very similar to that of adolescents, who have just gone through puberty and start identifying with their burgeoning sexuality. Just as teenagers experience an acute need for privacy in which to forge their new identity—closing their bedroom doors, adopting music and fashions they know their parents won't like, and bonding with peers who recognize their newfound sexual selves—the "newly gay" distance themselves from family and old friends to explore their privacy. Few parents delight in a teenager passing through this stage, but school counselors and therapists know it's nothing to worry about—it's a necessary, appropriate step toward a sense of belonging and a personal identity. Friends of a "newly gay" person may feel the same. Like adolescents accepting their new sexual identity, newly gay men and lesbians of any age may choose new friends and hangouts, if only to shield themselves from gay-negative views—theirs or anyone else's.

The Case of Jeff

Crying in his therapist's office, 48-year-old Jeff talked about the years he'd lost by staying in the closet. He'd recently begun meeting many young gay men in their 20s and 30s and imagined what his life would have—could have—been like had he been out and open in his younger years. He did not regret having married; he deeply loved his wife and the son they had together. But he said he also was depressed at having missed out on having a gay youth.

Jeff expressed anger at society for pushing him into a straight life and anger toward his conservative family, whose beliefs he described as "Republican and narrow." His blue-collar father and his stay-at-home mother lived in a working-class neighborhood that he described as "macho guyville."

Jeff had recently begun separating himself from heterosexuals, whom he accused of being antigay, and dropped most of his straight friends. He grew increasingly distrustful of straights, frequently calling them "breeders" who were insensitive to the needs of gays and lesbians.

Jeff's therapist responded to these comments by pleasantly replying, "Not all straight people are like that." He also tried to help Jeff see that he at least had begun coming out before it was too late in life, and that his discomfort was not the fault of straight people but rather of his having been raised in an environment of patriarchy and heterosexism. But Jeff did not want to hear this. Because his therapist was straight, Jeff had even more ammunition for his anger, and he used his therapist as the target of his negative transference at heterosexist straights in general.

I advised the therapist to mirror Jeff's anger rather than challenge his logic. That is, instead of trying to curb Jeff's anger by being reasonable and rational, it was more practical to understand the source of the anger and to locate Jeff's progress in the coming-out process.

It was also important to help Jeff through his grief over losing heterosexual privileges, as well as over not having been able to explore his gay orientation during his youth. Now that Jeff was identifying with part of a marginalized subculture, he was angry at how unfair this was. The therapist needed to validate Jeff's grief and loss and help him work through his feelings, not argue about them.

Grief and Loss of Heterosexual Privilege

The case of Jeff illustrates one of the common aspects of Stage 4: As clients take more risks, entering gay affirmative establishments where people of all ages are out and open, they typically begin experiencing grief and anger over their "lost" years of living heterosexually.

Using Elizabeth Kubler-Ross's stages of grief in dealing with death and dying (2003) can help you assist your clients as they go through the sorrow of losing heterosexual privileges:

1. *Denial.* During this stage, clients are in denial about the loss they are going to experience by switching from living as a straight person to now identifying authentically as gay or lesbian. They also deny other people they tell the right to have their reaction to their sexual and romantic identity, and deny any other reality but their own.
2. *Anger.* The anger begins to grow toward heterosexism, which has forced them to play it straight. Heterosexuals become the target of their anger, as if all heterosexuals are heterosexists.
3. *Bargaining.* This happens more in the early stages, where clients try to keep their homosexuality at bay and bargain with their higher power that they will be good and hope the feelings go away. In this stage they might consider only being out in certain places to ensure everyone else's comfort and forgo their own. This bargaining is an attempt to help keep the peace.
4. *Depression.* So many circumstances add to this stage—from coming out later in life to heterosexually marrying to getting infected with HIV. Whatever the depression is focused on, it is real and usually predominately about the loss of heterosexual privileges.
5. *Acceptance.* In this stage, clients fully accept that they are—and want to be—truly gay or lesbian. This prompts Stage 5, in which they force the world to just get used to it!

While waiting for others to adjust to their news, clients must brace themselves for the distancing or loss of friends and family relationships or even their livelihood. These losses may also trigger feelings about other past losses the client may have experienced.

Stage 5: Identity Pride—Gay Adolescence in Full Force

In this stage, gays and lesbians immerse themselves in their subculture. They have much less interaction with heterosexuals and often begin to confront straight people. They do not distinguish between straight people who are heterosexist or homophobic and those who are not. All their previous repression is now explosively directed outward, and they want to come out to the world. They devour gay books, magazines, and weeklies, absorbing all the culture's earmarks and trademarks. Disdain for the straight world surfaces; they tend to think it's "them against us." The person in Stage 5 also begins correcting heterosexuals who assume they're straight (Kort, 2003).

This stage energizes the best activists. The combination of anger and pride impels them to become heavily, passionately involved in gay rights organizations and gay pride marches. Those in the forefront of these marches are often predominately those in this stage of coming out.

Stage 5 individuals are teenagers trapped in adult bodies—and minds. Again, like adolescents, who do all kinds of things to underscore their "emerging" as individuals—dyeing their hair, shaving their heads, piercing themselves, wearing T-shirts with slogans that discomfort their elders—gays and lesbians assume a similar "in-your-face" attitude. They delight in shocking behavior that's over-the-top. They relentlessly tell everyone they're gay. They wear T-shirts that say I can't even think straight. They're rebellious and promiscuous. They French-kiss in public. They love to draw attention to themselves, but their critics—and they themselves—don't real-ize that this is only a phase of development that they missed at their age-appropriate time. The difference is that their "gay age" doesn't match their chronological age. Whereas such behavior is appropriate for teens, it doesn't seem appropriate for adults.

Therapists who aren't aware of Stage 5 behavior may misdiagnose clients as suf-fering from oppositional disorders, personality disorders, or sexual addictions. These therapists may also unwittingly shame their clients by displaying their own discom-fort over their clients' Stage 5 behavior.

Homophobes like to condemn lesbians and gays for their "bad" behavior on the grounds that being "promiscuous," obnoxiously vocal, and indulging in too much partying and chemical abuse exemplifies what gay life is all about. However, that acting-out behavior is a stage of coming out—usually lasting only 2 to 3 years—and has little to nothing to do with gay identity. Typically, clients are relieved to learn that they're only going through a stage, as they feel uncomfortable about being com-pelled to act this way.

The Case of Roger

Recently divorced from a heterosexual marriage, Roger was a 50-year-old execu-tive at one of the Big Three auto companies and a father of two teenage sons. He sought therapy after 2 years of promiscuous behavior. Worrying that gay life was "all about sex," he told his therapist that he'd met many men with whom he'd hoped to share romance, but after having sex, both safe and unsafe, they would drop him. He repeatedly promised himself to stop having sex with men, but found himself doing it all over again.

Though he took pride in being authentic, true to himself, and able to act on his being gay, he also felt chagrined at what he saw in the gay male community as well as at his own lack of sexual boundaries. He'd never before exhibited any sexual acting out or impulse-control problems. He admitted that his behavior was putting him at risk of contracting STDs.

Ashamed by his behavior and not feeling understood by his therapist, Roger made an appointment to see me. He told me his past therapist had chastised him for conforming to the promiscuous behavior that the media portrayed as being typical for gay men. Astounded by the therapist's remark, Roger stopped seeing him.

In assessing Roger's behavior for a diagnosis and treatment, I asked questions that explored possible sexual compulsivity, bipolar disorder, borderline personality disorder, and reenacting of childhood sexual abuse. The behavior of individuals in Stage 5 imitates these syndromes, so it's vital that you make these distinctions in order to plan appropriate treatment. Roger's behavior fit many criteria for these disorders, but it seemed to me that his promiscuity derived from delayed "gay adolescence." I talked with him about Stage 5 to help him make sense out of why he was experiencing a loss of control. I explained that it is not uncommon for gay men—particularly heterosexually married men—who have long repressed their needs to become sexually compulsive for a *temporary* period. As discussed earlier, they can act like teenage boys whose hormones suddenly kick in.

During Stage 5, reason goes out the window. I suggested that Roger remove the gay pride bumper sticker he'd put on his car because his 16-year-old son drove it, too. It made sense that he wanted to proclaim his identity, as any "adolescent" would, but his son might have to explain to his pals what the sticker meant. I reminded Roger that his son was straight, and that he needed to be sensitive to his son's feelings. Roger agreed that he had placed his own "adolescent" needs over his son's genuine ones.

Roger wept while we talked about this. He felt ashamed about the way he had treated his son. He knew better than to act like this, but his antiestablishment feelings were very strong. However, learning that his behavior could be understood as a stage in his coming-out process relieved him of the toxic shame he felt and allowed him to do right by his son. Roger removed the bumper sticker.

As Roger's coming-out process unfolded, his urgency and compulsive acting out diminished to a normal frequency, as it naturally would for anyone moving toward identity development after a delayed adolescence. He became more in control of his sexual life, and he began to date more and have boyfriends for months at a time.

Many men and women in this stage beat themselves up and experience high levels of shame over long-suppressed behaviors that they now feel compelled to act on. The therapist's job is to help them understand what is happening to them and how best to navigate it.

Individuals in Stage 5 often proclaim that they're gay and proud even if they don't yet fully understand their own behavior and feel a little foolish. You may also detect tremendous grief inside them: They wish they'd made this change years earlier in life. Although their behavior can be mistaken for a midlife crisis, I redefine it for them as a life-awakening opportunity and educate them on the stages of coming out, reassuring them that they're just in the "adolescent" stage of "identity pride"—a necessary step for their eventual self-actualization as gay or lesbian. Upon learning the name for their experience, they almost always breathe a sigh of relief.

Stage 5 can last up to 2 to 3 years. It can be painstaking and fraught with emotional turmoil—humiliation, frustration, and heartbreak. People in this stage frequently meet potential flames who swiftly flicker out. (Formerly married clients who come out later in life tend to have forgotten the trial and error involved in dating and naively expect that "love at first sight" will evolve into a long-term relationship.)

Therapists need to remind clients who are experimenting with sexuality and promiscuity of the importance of safe sex. Clients in Stage 5 need to monitor their sexual behaviors. They also need to remain alert for signs of dependence and abuse if they're using drugs and alcohol.

If your client remains in this stage longer than 2 to 3 years, it's no longer merely a stage. Using your clinical skills, explore the possibility of a mood or personality disorder (see Chapter 12), sexual compulsivity, or chemical abuse or dependency. You should also begin exploring if they are stuck in some unresolved trauma or stage of development from childhood (see Chapter 6).

Stage 6: Identity Synthesis

At this stage of integration, the "them-and-us" concept breaks down. LGBTQ people begin to understand that not all heterosexuals or cisgender individuals are hostile. Like older adolescents, they can now relax their militant stance and reintegrate themselves into society. They understand that there are "good straights" as well as "bad straights," that heterosexism and homophobia needn't dominate their lives, and that they can relate to LGBTQ people without any loss of self-confidence.

As I mentioned earlier, these stages do not always occur in the order presented; they are simply meant to be used as a guide for therapists, just as Kubler-Ross's stages of loss are. For instance, although most lesbians and gays do go through Stage 5 and have a gay adolescence, some don't. Anticipating it for clients is the best approach, so that if and when they experience some of the symptoms and dynamics particular to the stage, they will know what is happening to them.

Even with the recent increased acceptance of LGBTQ people, these stages persist. Children and teenagers are still not allowed to explore and know their homosexuality or gender nonconformity, so a coming-out experience will always need to occur for the identity to be integrated.

What *has* changed with time is that LGBTQ people are coming out earlier. They are feeling safer and witnessing a shift in acceptance for the better. An observation I have made, and others have concurred with, is that many of today's young LGBTQ individuals, who are coming out more in late adolescence and young adulthood, tend go through the stages faster and sometimes all at the same time, being angry and proud and tentative and outspoken all at once and vacillating rapidly between feeling ashamed and apparently secure. Knowing this as a clinician can help you normalize it for yourself and for your clientele.

Phases of Coming Out

In addition to the previously described stages, there are also *phases* to coming out. The phases are:

- Coming out to oneself
- Coming out to close friends
- Coming out to family

Typically, LGBTQ individuals come out first to themselves, then to close friends, and finally to family. Your job is to normalize and anticipate each phase so that clients understand what they are going through. A good book to help your clients deal effectively with the coming-out stages and phases is Michelangelo Signorile's (1996) *Outing Yourself: How to Come Out as Lesbian or Gay to Your Family, Friends, and Coworkers.*

Usually years of self-exploration precede coming out to oneself. From a psychological perspective, safety and security are extremely important. Individuals then come out to friends (especially gay and lesbian friends), as they are the next safest. Being rejected by friends is more tolerable than losing relatives. Friends may serve not only as a sounding board but also as a practice ground.

As you guide clients in their coming-out process, tell them what has worked for other clients during the same phase. For example, gay males have a better and easier time telling their mothers first and then their fathers, whereas lesbians have it easier when telling their fathers first and then their mothers. Generally the parent of the same gender as the client has a more difficult time being accepting. Also tell clients that it is important to come out to themselves and feel solid first, and then to close friends before their family, as they will probably not receive the support they would like from their family and will need their friends at that time. Also encourage clients to make some new friends—preferably gay and lesbian—so that they have support-ive individuals to turn to if they are met with distancing and rejection from their family and straight friends.

Coming out to family—especially parents—is the hardest, bravest thing your cli-ents will ever do. Few gays and lesbians want to hurt their parents, and they know that this information very well might cause hurt and other feelings they're not eager to engender. These issues are discussed in more depth in Chapter 8.

Gender Differences

Lesbians generally come out later than gay men (Hanley-Hackenbruck, 1989). One reason is that girls can touch, hug, and kiss each other, and even dance together, without raising an eyebrow or being labeled "queer." Women also tend to act on their acknowledgment several years later in life. They tend to realize their orientation in a special same-sex friendship, whereas men tend to seek sexual experiences for their own sake, not necessarily in any long-term relationship context.

Once a man falls in love with another man, he's forced into awareness that his feelings are more than sexual. Men are not supposed to have any feelings at all, let alone romantic feelings toward another man. Men learn they'd better keep their emotions at bay. Thus, when feelings arise toward another male and can no longer be pushed aside, a man must recognize that he might be at least bisexual or sexually fluid.

For women, it's just the opposite. It is when she has sexual feelings for another woman that her awareness of being lesbian surfaces. Our society permits women to love each other, use terms of endearment, and even touch each other affectionately. However, having *sexual* feelings toward another woman will prompt the woman to consider her lesbianism.

The Case of Caroline

Caroline was a 36-year-old mother of three children. She was married to her high school sweetheart. Overall she was happy with her husband—it was a safe and secure marriage and she loved him very much. But they'd always had sexual difficulties.

He wanted to please her, but no matter how he tried, she didn't respond, and she blamed herself. At first, Caroline told herself that she had a low libido. Later, she blamed her husband for wanting sex too often. Over the years, it became more of a chore for her; she dreaded sex and complied only to please him. She did not think this situation was problematic, however, as she talked to other married women who were in similar situations.

Then Caroline met Tina, a 30-year-old lesbian who was involved in one of the sporting events Caroline attended. They became friends and it was obvious that Tina was interested in Caroline. Caroline felt flattered and told Tina she was straight. Tina said she was more interested in straight women than gay women and saw this as challenge. Tina, a masseuse, offered Caroline a free massage, which she accepted.

Tina began giving Caroline, who was naked, an erotic massage. At first, Caroline fought the arousal she began to feel, but ultimately she decided to enjoy it. She realized that she'd felt sexual feelings upon first meeting Tina—sexual feelings that were becoming increasingly difficult to hide. The two began having sexual contact. Caroline felt herself come alive sexually, experiencing feelings she never had with her husband. For the first time in her life, she had no trouble becoming and staying aroused.

The relationship between Caroline and Tina became a yearlong affair during which Caroline realized that the sexual trouble in her marriage was not from her poor libido or her husband's overactive libido. The issue was that she was lesbian. Never in her life had Caroline thought of herself in this way. She'd coached her children's sporting events and was involved in adult women's sports, but she never thought of the women she met as anything more than friends. Now she was angry that she had suppressed her own sexual identity for so many years, depriving herself of enjoying a full sexual experience with another person.

Caroline's therapist, however, did not think Caroline was a lesbian. She told Caroline that women have a more fluid sexuality than men do and that one can fall in love and even have sex with another woman but not be lesbian. The therapist also said that if Caroline were truly a lesbian, she would have had some inkling of this earlier in her life. The therapist was relying on what she'd heard from her gay male clients, who said they recalled always being aware of their sexual orientation.

Because she'd never been attracted to women before, Caroline was relieved to think that she wasn't lesbian; it meant she could return to her happy life with her husband and children. The therapist worked with her to frame the behavior as a phase that would eventually pass. However, Caroline soon found herself sexually attracted to other women in addition to Tina. "I had been repressed my entire life," she said, "not realizing that my true sexual and romantic attraction was to other women." The "phase" was lasting longer than Caroline felt comfortable with.

Caroline: Clinical Interpretation and Treatment

Caroline's therapist was misinformed and uneducated about lesbians; she also didn't realize that women repress their homosexuality differently than men do. The therapist was aligning with Caroline's hope that she was not lesbian by promising her that it was not true given Caroline's past.

The therapist needed to be educated about not only male homosexuality but lesbianism as well. Although there are lesbians who report they knew something was different about them, it is more common not to know. Remember, we don't teach children anything other than heterosexuality, so there is no permission for them to know they are anything different. Women report that they had loving and strong feelings for their girlfriends, teachers, and coaches, but never considered it was anything more than a strong relational bond and attachment.

Caroline's therapist, whom I was supervising, admitted to me that she had had a sexual experience with another woman during her 20s, and it was nothing more than a sexual expression of their love for one another. It happened a few times and was a passing phase for both of them. I helped the therapist understand that this was not the case for Caroline. As a therapist, she needed to pay attention to the other things Caroline was saying in terms of her attraction to other women and diminishing desire for her husband.

Caroline was coming out, as most women do, with a lack of awareness that she was a lesbian. And Caroline's therapist needed to put her countertransference in check and acknowledge that her client was having her own journey.

Disclosure of One's Sexual Identity or Gender Nonconformity

I do not believe that all LGBTQ people must be completely out and open in every aspect of their lives. I have seen, however, that even when clients decide not to come out at work or within their families for legitimate reasons—because they know that they might be fired or lose their housing, for example—they still send negative messages to themselves. That is, they say to themselves, *There's something wrong with me or my relationships that I must keep secret.* This needs to be addressed therapeutically, but it often isn't. Clients use the old excuse that "there is nothing I can do about it."

For example, it may be unwise for a lesbian employee to come out at work and risk being fired. But she still has to face the emotional and psychological consequences of staying closeted. For example, at office functions, she'll have to edit out any references that might imply that she is lesbian. She won't be able to introduce her partner as anything more than a friend. She'll have to limit the number of times she takes phone calls from her partner.

Although it is true in these types of situations that coming out is not an option, clients need to safeguard against the negative messages they send themselves by being and staying in the situation. As a clinician, you can tell your clients that not coming out—while important in their specific situation—is not good for their self-esteem. To help them through the process, have them do some written work or self-talk reminding themselves why they are hiding and pretending, and encourage them to do the least amount of lying possible.

At the very least, clients should come out to themselves—which doesn't necessarily have to involve informing anyone else. Many people don't understand the need for gays to come out, saying, "It's nobody's business if I'm straight." But heterosexist society assumes that *everyone* is straight—unless they declare themselves otherwise. Gay men get asked about their wives or girlfriends; lesbians about their boyfriends or husbands. To answer such questions, lesbians and gays must lie, change the subject, or explain exactly why the question doesn't apply. Gays and lesbians often convince straight clinicians that they can't or shouldn't come out when they're actually suffering from conflict avoidance or trauma from their accumulated shame and concealment. Clinicians need to challenge their denial because visibility increases self-esteem.

Staying closeted results in personality disorders, which I address in subsequent chapters. Staying in an incongruent state, being out of integrity with oneself and others, and living a life of chronic deceit and concealment distorts one's personality.

Coming Out: A Lifelong Process

Coming out is not a discrete event or milestone but rather a lifelong process. Various life situations change over the years, necessitating new instances of coming out (for example, when someone begins a new job or makes a new friend). Changing doctors and disclosing one's sexual orientation to the new doctor can be difficult, yet it is necessary for the best possible treatment. Single clients may not have felt the need to come out to extended family and have told only when asked. However, when partnered, they often feel a desire to tell, with pride, that they finally found someone.

Whatever the life circumstances are, they change throughout one's life, and each situation is unique and calls for another coming-out.

Coming Out Is Not a Cure-All

National Coming Out Day, which occurs each year on October 11, encourages individuals to liberate themselves, promising happiness and increased self-esteem. But this positive message fails to acknowledge that locked within that closet are other issues waiting to come out: family dysfunctions, childhood trauma, grief, and loss, all of which have been hidden along with one's orientation. Your clients may tell you, "Okay, I have come out of the closet, told everyone there is to tell, and I feel worse than I did before!" Typically, they assumed that everything would fall into place once they came out. But as addicts in recovery learn, things don't always get better; sometimes they get worse. There's plenty of baggage in the closet that has to be addressed once the door is opened.

Repressed memories can leak out through the coming-out process, for example. I often refer to these issues as "dust bunnies" that need to be addressed along with sexual orientation. Depression can also arise from trying to release a lifetime of repression and erroneous messages and beliefs in a day, a weekend, or even a month of gay pride. As therapists, we need to anticipate these possibilities and treat them as they arise.

Treatment Considerations

As a clinician, you may have LGBTQ clients who display positive and negative transference around coming-out issues. Following are some brief guidelines for dealing with this.

- *Watch for clients' desire that you can cure them.* Some clients hope that while they're still in the early stages of coming out, you might have some secret behavior-modification technique to help them revert to being straight.
- *Realize that you are standing in for the good, accepting parent.* Many clients invest a great deal in their therapist's acceptance and approval—which they do not expect to get from their parents.
- *Anticipate that when the client is in Stages 1 through 3, you might become the target of their homophobia if you are an LGBTQ therapist.* Because of the shame

and repression of the clients' sexual identity, their homophobia and internalized homophobia are at their worst in these stages. It is important as a clinician to name the homophobia and help the clients understand the negative transference that is happening in your office.

- • *Anticipate that when the client reaches Stage 5, you might become the target of heterophobia if you are a straight therapist.* Because this stage is about seeing the world as "us against them," you as a straight therapist are likely to become the target of your client's negative transference. I recommend informing your clients that this is likely to happen.

- *Educate your clients that a full public declaration of their sexual orientation or gender nonconformity isn't necessarily the best decision for everybody under all circumstances.* Help them determine the social costs and psychological benefits for their particular situation.

- *Coach clients to be sure they feel comfortable about being LGBTQ before telling others.* They need to resolve their guilt or depression before coming out to family or other straight people. If they don't, others will assume that they're unhappy because being LGBTQ is not what they really want.

- *Inform your clients that they may surprise, anger, or upset the people they tell—at first.* Teach them not to react angrily or defensively, and to let others honestly express their initial feelings, even if negative. Initial reactions are seldom long-term or permanent. Any initial distancing usually changes over time—but clients should realize that in some cases, reactions like this can become permanent.

- • *Make sure that clients are well enough informed to answer questions with confidence.* Refer them to dependable books and websites they can quote as resources, if need be.

- *Help them never lose sight of their own self-worth even if people reject them.* Remind them that by coming out, they shared an important part of themselves. Ask them if they really desire a relationship with someone who rejects them for coming out. You can ask, "Were they *really* your friends?"

- *Remind clients that coming out is one of the most difficult things they'll ever do.* It won't always go well, nor does it need to—but most of the time, it is a very liberating experience.

Countertransference Considerations

Check your own countertransference by differentiating what *you* want for the client from what the *client* needs and wants. This is true for all your clients, of course, but it is especially important when working with LGBTQ clients during their coming-out process. Taking an overaffirmative stand, trying to be too gay friendly, can ultimately push clients out too fast for *their* comfort.

You also must remember that LGBTQ people can hold homophobic beliefs themselves. It is important not to align with their internalized homophobia as a result of your own unresolved feelings. For example, if you are uncomfortable with blatant vocalizations of gay pride, your countertransference may activate, or even fuel, a client's negative transference about people who attend gay pride events.

Following are a few guidelines about avoiding countertransference.

Remember that the decision to come out is your client's, not yours. Never pressure your clients into coming out before they feel ready.

Be clear about your own homophobia and heterosexism. Many therapists will be initially supportive and open to their clients' being gay—until the clients start addressing issues such as promiscuity, sex, and "in-your-face" activism, wanting a premature living-together relationship or gay marriage, and challenging religious teachings (which may include yours).

Get comfortable with your own sexual feelings and impulses. For example, it is not uncommon to have your unresolved feelings about your own unacknowledged and unresolved homosexual impulses and homoerotic feelings get in the way of treating gays and lesbians, particularly if you are working with someone of the same gender.

Remember that clients in Stage 5 may become angry with you. If you are a straight person, you represent heterosexists, so be prepared to deal with your clients' feelings about them. Tell your clients that anything they have to say about heterosexuals is perfectly fine in your office, so they feel safe in examining their grief and anger during this stage. Of course, this is not an invitation for them to abuse you as a therapist, but it is a time to hold a space for their anger and allow them to use you as an antenna for all the heterosexists who have betrayed them. You can teach them to vent appropriately and respectfully. Give them permission to vent with you as a stand-in for all heterosexists.

Sexual identity is on a spectrum, and your client might not be coming out gay or lesbian. It is important to keep in mind that while your clients may be going through a coming-out process, they might not be coming out lesbian or gay. They may come out as bisexual, transgender, or even straight with sexually fluid interests. You, as the therapist, will need to be alert to what they are telling you as they go through this process.

CHAPTER 8

Helping Families of Lesbians and Gays

We are the only minority born into enemy camp.
—A client to his therapist in Jack Drescher's
Psychoanalytic Therapy and the Gay Man (1998)

When I was 18, I told my family I was gay. My therapist, though helpful in other ways, had led me to believe my gayness was the result of a smothering mother and a distant father. So I dutifully blamed my mother for being overprotective and told my father it was his fault for leaving us to start a new family when I was 3.

I was angry. I wanted them to feel guilty. We all went into family therapy—with a new therapist who also believed that my being gay was the result of their shoddy parenting. "Joe," she asked, "why would you tell your family? And why did you tell them in this way?" What I really needed to hear was how brave and courageous I was for telling.

Finally, at age 21, I found the courage to come out of the closet completely, let my parents off the hook, and become responsible for myself by presenting my gayness in a healthy way. The second time around, my family was more accepting. We probably spent more time healing from what therapy did *to* us than from my coming out.

This chapter is about helping your LGBTQ clients and their families have an easier time coming out than I did. The first step for you as a therapist is educating yourself about the coming-out process as it pertains to family-of-origin issues.

Therapists working with LGBTQ clients and their families often apply their knowledge of minority families as a guideline. But that approach is flawed in a number of ways. First, most minority families are a *united* minority. Members learn how to think and behave as they see themselves mirrored in other family members. Most children of minority families are offered a prejudice-free zone at home, and their parents suggest ways of dealing with discrimination outside the home. Those who are LGBTQ, however, are minorities within their own families. Learning to role-play and pretend—even to themselves—that they are like the rest of their heterosexual and cisgender family contributes to problems for them and their families alike.

Some clinicians use the concept of adoption as a template for what it must be like to be LGBTQ within one's biological family. But that model also falls short, because adoptions imply that the children are coming from outside. Provisions and allowances are made to include those children and integrate them as full-fledged family members. Their differences are respected, especially if they are of a different race or ethnicity.

Another approach sometimes used by clinicians is to borrow from the guidelines for an adult child dating or marrying someone outside of the family's race, religion, or ethnicity. Because the LGBTQ adult is now interested in being with members of another minority, that paradigm seems to make sense. This model applies if one views coming out as a sudden change in the family. However, although the family may view their loved one's coming-out as a sudden change, it isn't a sudden change for the LGBTQ family member. In keeping with the LGBTQ affirmative belief that homosexuality and gender dysphoria are innate, it's vitally important to remember that those who are LGBTQ have been minorities from the start—they were born into their minority status.

In your LGBTQ clients' coming-out work, much of their anxiety and depression will focus on their families. They worry about letting them down and being let down by them.

As mentioned earlier, by the time LGBTQ individuals do tell their family, they've usually come out to themselves and their friends. Because one's family is seen as the highest risk for rejection and abandonment, clients worry about what reactions their disclosure will engender. They see coming out to family as risky, something fraught with fear and danger. For example, over the years, LGBTQ clients have told me,

"I cannot tell them—they're already too old. They won't understand."

I often tell my clients that they might regret not telling their parents after they are deceased and that they really need to think about this.

"They are very religious; they'll never accept it."

In some situations, especially for those in a minority situation such as being in a family of color or a rigidly religious family, it can be true. This is a loss for everyone involved.

"If I tell them, it will make them physically ill or even kill them."

Bad news doesn't kill people. And even if it did, that would indicate far worse issues than just not being able to tolerate that their family member is LGBTQ.

"They will never let me be alone with my nieces and nephews."

It is up to LGBTQ people to educate their families that sexual orientation and gender nonconformity are not correlated at all with pedophilia.

"Why do I need to tell them? They don't tell me about their sex lives."

Here is where I identify the internalized homophobia of my client reducing the idea of being LGBTQ to something that is primarily sexual. Telling your family you are LGBTQ isn't telling them what you are doing sexually any more than telling them you are heterosexual would. The work here is shame reduction and challenging the client's internalized homophobia.

Parents have told me such things as:

"I would rather my child be a murderer than a homosexual."
"It's all my fault! What did I do wrong?"
"They can change, but they don't want to."
"Why did he tell us this? Is he trying to hurt us?"
"Why can't my child just be lesbian, gay, or bisexual rather than being transgender?"

In a way, this last comment is progress for the nonstraight community, in that parents would want their child to be LGB under any circumstances. However, what they really mean here is that, in addition to the worry about their child not being straight, they have to also worry about the negative side effects and risks of hormone treatments and surgeries should their trans child decide to transition in those ways.

"They're my only son [or daughter]. I was counting on them to give me grandchildren."

Today coming out doesn't mean that parents won't get grandchildren. A 20-year-old client of mine was in a family therapy session with his mother who was crying at the thought of not having grandkids, to which he said to her, genuinely puzzled, "What makes you think I won't have kids?" Times have changed, and it isn't true that just because someone isn't straight, they won't produce children.

LGBTQ individuals usually *want* to tell their families to be closer to them. Their very urge to come out demonstrates their commitment to maintaining healthy communication, interactions, and closeness. But once they do, they'll have a whole new set of challenges for you to help them with.

Helping families build bridges across such a turbulent, difficult topic is no easy task. To effectively facilitate this process, you must know a client's family dynamics and issues as well as the client's own personal judgments and agendas.

Recognizing your own homophobia and heterosexism is essential. Growing up, we were all imprinted with some form of homophobia, and for any therapist to deny that would itself be a form of covert homophobia and a microaggression. It's too easy to get caught in your clients' heterosexist and heteronormative webs and collude with their reasons not to come out to their families.

The Case of Jennifer

Jennifer, a 30-year-old lesbian, came to Alice for issues around her coming out. Initially uncertain that she really was a lesbian, Jennifer began confirming her identity through her therapy with Alice and had a long coming-out process that lasted over 2 years. She developed a group of lesbian friends, began dating, and finally fell in love with another woman.

Now that her orientation was increasingly clear, she wanted to tell her parents that she was a lesbian. But she was concerned about how they would take it. She worried that, at ages 75 and 77, they were too old to be able to handle the information. "What would telling them now do for them or for me?" she asked Alice. "What if it kills them? It feels selfish, because it will do more for me than it will for them. I want them to live out the rest of their years in peace, not grief for having a dyke for a daughter! But I also want them to know who I am."

Alice concurred that Jennifer's hesitance was warranted. She added that bad news probably would not *kill* Jennifer's parents, but that it was something to consider. "What if that did happen?" Alice asked. "And what good would it do them? Is this for you or for them?" She also explained that Jennifer didn't need to advertise or promote her sexuality: "Most adults don't share their sex lives and behaviors with their parents, so why should you?"

Jennifer agreed with this. But she also felt torn; she was very much in love with the woman she'd begun dating, and she wanted to be able to share this happiness with her parents. Alice, however, cautioned her against it: "You are in romantic love and should enjoy this honeymoon period. But your parents won't be in the same place, so why do that to them?"

"But they might feel better knowing I have someone," Jennifer replied.

"But what if they don't? Then you've not only made them unhappy, but you may have harmed your relationship as well."

Jennifer accepted Alice's point of view and kept her new relationship a secret from her parents for several months. But as her love with her new girlfriend grew and she felt more assured in her lesbian identity, she spontaneously told her parents, expressing her excitement and hoping they'd be happy for her.

Mortified and angered, her parents at first did not believe her. Jennifer, crying, insisted that she was lesbian and tried to open up a dialogue with them. But they stopped the conversation and asked her to leave their house. Over the next few months, she had very little contact with her parents.

Alice questioned why Jennifer had told her family so impulsively. She thought that together, they had agreed she would remain quiet about it and keep her private life private so "no one would be harmed." Alice then explored Jennifer's "unconscious rage" toward her parents, manifested in what Alice called "acting out her hostility" by telling her parents so impulsively.

Assessment of Jennifer's Therapy

Alice was colluding with Jennifer's internalized homophobia, as well as expressing some of her own. What Alice should have done for Jennifer was prepare her: give her the pros and cons of coming out, tell her what she could reasonably expect following her declaration, and inform her about how other declarations typically had unfolded. But Alice lacked the information to help Jennifer effectively navigate her coming-out process. In addition, her agreement with Jennifer's concerns about her aging parents' ability to handle the news, and her advice to keep her "private" life private, were symptoms of her own countertransference and homophobia. No therapist would advise heterosexual clients to tell their parents that their new romantic interest was "just a friend."

The harm in not telling was twofold. Jennifer wasn't able to have her relationship respected, and by being evasive, she compromised her own self-respect by being out of integrity with herself as well as her parents.

Jennifer's telling her parents impulsively was not out of unconscious rage toward them. Rather, she was in Stage 5 of the coming-out process—identity pride. Experiencing the rush of exhilaration and excitement that anyone feels when starting a new romance, she wanted to tell the world about her identity and new love. Treating such behavior as "unconscious rage" is not just ineffective—it's actually damaging.

Realizing that her work with Alice was not helping her coming-out process, Jennifer terminated therapy. She and her parents experienced a temporary period of distancing—as is usual when families learn that someone they love is gay. But Jennifer's relationship with her parents had been close throughout her life, and after a couple of months, her parents did come around. They did not, however, want to talk about Jennifer's "news" and referred to her girlfriend as "your friend."

At this point, Jennifer needed support to deal with her parents' conditions. She needed to understand that while her parents' discomfort needed to be respected, her discomfort needed to be respected by them, too. She shouldn't have to be silent about who she was. At the same time, the parents didn't have to pretend that they accepted the situation when they did not. Both positions made sense; both deserved validation. She and her parents needed to explore a happy medium. Their way through this was dialogue and constant communication with both sides hearing and validating the other's points of view.

For example, would Jennifer's parents be willing to listen to information about Jennifer's life as a lesbian with some limits, and could Jennifer be okay with that? Could her parents be willing to stretch themselves and hear more than was totally comfortable for them—within limits of respectability, of course? Both Jennifer and her parents would need to stretch for the other in terms of their comfort zone; neither's reactivity should be allowed to trump the other. Both had points of view that needed addressing.

For a while Jennifer's parents would not ask her about her life, and Jennifer came to her sessions angry. I encouraged her to talk to her parents about her life anyway and let them have their reactions—which they did. I supported her in responding that although she could accept that they would not ask about her life, she would tell. Even if there was silence on the other end, it was better than her being silent.

After a while her family did ask about her life and her girlfriend. Elated, Jennifer talked about things going on. I encouraged her to tell her parents how good it made her feel to be asked.

However, at the first family gathering since Jennifer began her relationship, her parents said they would rather she not bring her "friend." Jennifer chose not to go and was angry. I coached her to express her feelings in therapy but to honor her parents' request and for them to honor her decision not to go if her girlfriend couldn't be with her. Before the next family gathering, Jennifer's parents did not ask about her girlfriend. Jennifer was determined just to bring her. I talked her out of that and convinced her to tell her parents that she really wanted to attend but only if she could bring her girlfriend. Her parents hesitantly agreed.

All of this took time and back-and-forth and communication. It is your job as a clinician to help your LGBTQ clients understand their family's perspective, just as the family needs to understand the perspective of the client.

Before Coming Out: Typical Family Patterns

When LGBTQ individuals do *not* come out of the closet, they follow three typical patterns to avoid their families' rejection or abandonment (Brown, 1989):

- *Maintaining a rigid emotional—and often geographical—distance from the family.* LGBTQ individuals may run away from home for a life on the streets—particularly in their teen years, when boys and trans females are old enough to get involved in hustling. They may move to another state or across the country—to gay meccas like Atlanta, New York, or San Francisco—keeping their private life secret from the family and visiting only rarely. They may also call and visit less to avoid being asked questions about their personal lives so that they won't have to lie.
- *Adopting the "I know you know" pattern.* Today, we'd call it "Don't ask, don't tell." According to Brown, "The gay person relates to his family . . . with the unspoken agreement that no one will talk about [his] personal life" (1989, p. 68). Everyone knows that his "friend" is more than that, but no one dares say so.
- *Selective sharing, as in, "Don't tell your father."* The gay son or daughter is officially out to one parent or sibling, who responds with support but with a warning not to tell certain family members.

Privacy Versus Secrecy

Obviously, these are unhealthy patterns. You can help your clients be more open with their families by explaining the difference between privacy and secrecy. Clients may tell you things like, "My parents don't tell me about their sexual behaviors, so why should I tell them about mine?" My response is usually that, of course, some topics, like finances and sexual practices, are nobody's business and should be kept private, but being LGBTQ isn't one of them. Being LGBTQ is not just about sexual preferences but also about whom you love and how you live your life (as already addressed several places in this book). Here you are helping the clients with their internalized homophobia.

Secrets keep people feeling ashamed and inauthentic. To be fully out and confident, an LGBTQ individual should tell his or her parents. The only exception is when the clients feel that telling the family will put them at risk for physical or mental harm or of losing the family for good.

Disclosure: Getting Your Client Ready

Most therapists and their LGBTQ clients struggle with when and how to tell their families. There's really no best time for this type of news. Before LGBTQ children can reveal something so deep about themselves, their families must first establish an atmosphere of affection, openness, and safety. Most of the literature advises not telling family members during the holidays or special occasions, as it can create a worse reaction and generate more problems for all concerned.

The most important factor is that clients should be fully out to themselves and to some friends for support, in case the reaction is very negative. They need to feel confident and positive in their sexual and gender identity; parents and relatives should not see them showing any ambivalence or negativity about being LGBTQ. This is an important point: Some LGBTQ individuals appear ambivalent because they weep, but those tears are often shed over the fear of impending rejection and abandonment, not because of any ambivalence about being LGBTQ.

Also, LGBTQ individuals need to understand that their families have a right to their reactions, negative or positive, and need the time and space to experience it. As the LGBTQ person comes out, the families immediately go into the closet. The family, in other words, is at Stage 1 of their own coming-out process of having an LGBTQ child, whereas their LGBTQ offspring might be at Stage 5 or 6.

A religious family, for example, might become more devout. If there's alcoholism, the drinking might increase even more. Family relations that were strained before become even more distant—and family members often blame all these changes on their LGBTQ son or daughter, who, to make things worse, tends to believe the family's dysfunctional reaction is somehow his or her fault.

Helping clients brace for their families' reactions is extremely important. A family's reaction to unexpected news in the past will indicate how it might react to this new development (Ritter & Terndrup, 2002), so you can ask clients how their families have handled previous crises and stressful situations. Under-standing that their families' reactions are not really about them can also help your clients not take things personally. Exploring these issues will arm clients with helpful coping strategies that allow their families to go through their own reactions.

After a Child Comes Out: Typical Negative Reactions

Kubler-Ross's stages of grief—denial, bargaining, anger, depression, and finally acceptance (see Chapter 7)—apply not only to the person coming out but also to the family members, who must deal with the sudden realization that many of their hopes and dreams for the LGBTQ family member are lost. Following are some of the typical negative reactions family members may have.

- *Seeing it as a "stage" or "phase" that won't last.* Often parents say things like, "So you *think* you might be LGBTQ?" or "Don't make too many decisions, as this might be a passing phase for you, dear." Parents of LGBTQ teenagers often ask, "How could she know at such a young age? She hasn't even been with a boy!" Of course, straight teenagers do go through phases when they experiment with others of the same sex; these teens know what they are doing, as I address in Chapter 13 on LGBTQ teens. Parents, then, of course are hopeful that their child's announcement is just this—just a stage. However, usually the LGBTQ teenager or young adult is clear that "this is not a phase or a stage—it is who I am and always have been and will always be." This is hard for parents to believe or understand, which is why they cling to the notion of it being a "stage."
- *Magnifying existing family dysfunction.* If the family is already struggling with a parent who is alcoholic or physically abusive—or if there have been marital problems, affairs, a divorce, or any other issue that exists within the dysfunc-tional family—family members may blame their child's sexual orientation or gender nonconformity on that. These dysfunctional family issues become exag-gerated and are used as an excuse for the child's LGBTQ nature. Blaming family dysfunction *is* the dysfunction in and of itself. Rather than deal with their dys-function, family members look at the symptoms as a way to avoid dealing with the real issues.
- *Refusal to acknowledge a romantic partner's existence.* Families who do not want to acknowledge their child's sexual identity or gender nonconformity often won't

talk about the significant other. They won't ask about him or her, nor will they recognize the person as anything more than a "friend"—if they acknowledge the partner at all.

- *Blaming the partner for "seducing" the child into homosexuality, bisexuality, or being transgender.* This is very common in families who don't believe their child is truly LGBTQ. They blame the partner for "turning" their child LGBTQ. This stems from the belief that sexual orientation and gender non-conformity can be learned. The family is also unconsciously worried that something they did turned their child LGBTQ, so they use the partner as a scapegoat.
- *For ethnic families, seeing the child as being a traitor to their culture and ethnicity.* These families view their child as turning his or her back on their culture and not reproducing and staying within their ethnicity.
- *For religious families, becoming more religious.* I have heard clients tell me that their families were not particularly religious before the child's disclosure but began "quoting the Bible" upon learning about their LGBTQ children. Some parents start attending church or synagogue regularly.
- *Taking it personally ("How could you do this to me?").* Some parents take a child's disclosure as a direct assault, as if their child is using his or her LGBTQ nature to hurt them and humiliate them.
- *Trying to send the child for reparative therapy.* One of my clients reported that his father regularly showed him religious pamphlets and books on organizations that promote "healing homosexuality."
- *Ignoring the issue, sending the inadvertent or deliberate message that "You don't matter."* For example, a family of a gay child that will never bring up anything about their child's gayness. If the child brings it up, they won't respond. They will ask their child if he "has a girlfriend yet" or if his partner "has found the right girl yet," totally dismissing that their child is gay.
- *Hijacking the child's process of coming out by making it their own.* Some parents make their child's coming-out journey their own by telling everyone they have an LGBTQ child and putting the spotlight on themselves rather than letting their child have his or her own "moment of fame." These parents often have not had much of an identity of their own and unconsciously see their child's coming-out as an opportunity to have an identity as a parent of someone LGBTQ. My clients who have parents like this are disheartened and feel that their parents are not being supportive but rather selfish. This is hurtful and frustrating to the child.

During the time of the "outing," judgments fly, and the result can resemble a witch hunt in miniature. Though it is usually the parent of the same natal gender as the child who has the most difficulty accepting the child's sexual orientation or gender nonconformity, other family members may have a hard time as well. They struggle to find reasons or excuses for the child's LGBTQ nature, and they look around for someone to blame—often the LGBTQ child but also other family members. To make sense out of something they don't understand, families search through past issues that they have long acknowledged but until now have been unwilling to confront: parental divorce, a distant or workaholic father, a controlling mother, an alcoholic parent, and so on.

Similarly, when the truth is spoken, other uncomfortable and unexamined truths tend to "come out of the closet" as well—making the core issue seem even heavier than it already is. I've had clients talk about how, once they told their families they were LGBTQ, other family secrets—such as their parents' sexually open relationship, a family member's chronic mental or physical illness, or a child's being adopted out of the family—came spilling out. These types of family secrets tend to come out because the child's disclosure makes family members feel that they, too, have permission to reveal their secrets. The important point to remember is that although this secret telling can be painful or shocking, it sets up a safe space for more honesty in the family.

The "Change Back" Syndrome

Family members often try to get the LGBTQ individual to return to who they thought he or she was—or who they want the person to be. Family members will do anything to get the person to *change back* so that they don't have to face the truth about the person or about themselves.

From family-therapy theory, we know the concept of homeostasis, which is that the family—or any organized system, for that matter—tends to resist change and seeks to maintain its customary organization and functioning over time. You can teach your clients and their families about homeostasis and how it is not helpful to the family, as coming out requires the family members to change and adjust to the news. It is helpful to predict with your LGBTQ clients that they will potentially be seen as the problem and that family members will work hard to "fix" the problem by talking them out of being gay.

You can also ask your clients how their families dealt with change in the past. This will offer some insight into what they might be able to expect.

Magnified Family Dynamics

When an LGBTQ son or daughter comes out, most families' existing dynamics become exaggerated. The family is plunged into a temporary crisis and reverts to old, familiar behaviors—dysfunctional or not. Current dysfunctional patterns may also be magnified, which the LGBTQ family member may be blamed for.

Families that are not very open or have a "don't talk" rule have an especially difficult time dealing with the coming-out crisis, as the gay family member is breaking the rules by raising a controversial issue. The same goes for families that are inflexible and rigid and families that have trouble letting their children grow up and differentiate (Laird, 1998).

The Case of Brenda

Brenda, a nurse, had spent most of her life living with her parents, caring for them as they aged. The last of seven children, she remained single while the others moved out, married, and started families.

For a while, Brenda had thought she might be lesbian, but she never acted on it—nor did she believe she ever would. In her 30s, much to her parents' and siblings' delight, she had explored entering a convent. But halfway through, she realized it was not for her and returned home.

When Brenda was 40 her father died, leaving her to live with her mother, who began to lean on her, asking Brenda to accompany her on errands and attend family functions with her by her side. Brenda's mother did not know how to handle finances or manage the house, as her late husband had handled most of these things. Brenda stepped in and helped her mother do this. Her family was accustomed to seeing her as the one who should stay home to care for her mother.

Then, Brenda fell in love with a female doctor, Darcy, who worked at the hospital. Though Brenda still cared for her mother, she spent more and more time at Darcy's house and was home less and less. Her mother complained to her other children, who then started calling Brenda, upset and disappointed that she was not doing her "job."

At first, Brenda felt guilty. But ultimately, with Darcy's help, she realized that her brothers and sisters needed to step in and help their mother, too, now that Brenda was creating a life for herself. Her siblings did not see it this way at all and grew angry when it became apparent that Brenda was not going to comply with "the family's" wishes and resume her full-time role as their mother's caretaker. Brenda then told them she was lesbian and had fallen in love. Although she still wished to care for their mother, she no longer wanted to do it alone.

The family—including the mother—accused Brenda of being selfish and looking out only for herself. They also blamed Darcy for "influencing" her to become a lesbian and abandon her place in the family. In an angry, reactive stance, Brenda moved out of her mother's home and in with her new partner, leaving her family to hold gatherings without her.

Brenda: Clinical Interpretation and Treatment

Brenda came into my office, crying that her family had rejected her. She told me that they had mailed her pamphlets on how to "heal" her lesbianism. This was very hurtful to her, but being alienated from family gatherings bothered her the most. She was considering leaving Darcy and going back to her mother and her place in the family.

Quickly assessing her family situation, I explained that this had less to do with her being a lesbian and more to do with her relinquishing the role of "good daughter," which she'd created to hide her lesbianism and be accepted by the family. When I asked what her mother thought of the situation, Brenda said her mother had "blamed" her for moving out and not continuing to care for her. She also refused to consider Brenda's lesbianism as authentic; she felt it was an excuse that Brenda was using to leave her.

I explained to Brenda that her mother had a covert form of narcissism, and I helped Brenda see that her mother had carefully groomed Brenda to be her mother's caretaker ever since Brenda was a girl. Brenda told me that her mother hadn't wanted a seventh child and had "accidentally" become pregnant. She even had admitted to Brenda that she had tried to abort by subjecting herself to strenuous exercise. It appeared that Brenda's mother decided to single out Brenda and use the girl for her own needs.

Brenda understood that this was probably why it had taken her so long to come out and lead an independent life. Now, her lesbianism was a convenient distraction for her siblings and a reason to be angry at her for forcing them to have to step up and care for their mother.

Knowing a client's family system is always imperative, but it's particularly so when homosexuality is involved. Homosexuality has many issues attached to it, including religion, sex, and politics, to name a few. Some questions you might ask a client about his or her family to get a sense of how the family might react to the client being gay are:

- Does your family talk about sex? If they do, is it too much, inappropriate, or within normal limits, in your judgment? If they don't, what happens when the subject comes up?
- How religious—if at all—is your family?
- How does your family deal with change? Tell me about the three most recent changes in your family and how the family members dealt with them.
- What are your family's politics? Have you seen this affect your family and if so, how?
- How does your family deal with differences among other family members? Are they open-minded and accepting or closed and rejecting?

The Case of Alan

Alan, age 25, was an only child. He came from a Baptist Christian home where he felt judged and learned that homosexuality would send him to hell. Throughout his childhood, he kept most of his inner world a secret, but after leaving home for college, he came out to himself and his friends at school. He also met and fell in love with a man, with whom he was in a committed relationship. Now, as he prepared to return home to look for employment after finishing an out-of-state master's program, Alan realized that he wanted to tell his parents who he really was and face their judgment in an effort to be closer to them.

Armed with literature and support-group handouts, Alan was prepared for any reaction they might have. To his surprise, when he revealed the news, his parents said they had always known. Martha, his mother, said she'd found some gay pornography in his bedroom, and Cliff, his father, said he "just had a hunch."

Although Cliff and Martha embraced Alan and told him they still loved him, they were not accepting of his being gay and told him they would pray for him to change. Martha voiced her worry that he would go to hell. Cliff was more critical, saying to Alan, "Well, this is *your* choice!" This comment led to an argument, in the middle of which Cliff turned and walked away—as he always had done in Alan's life. Alan expected his mother, who had always been accepting and supportive, to ask more questions and follow up with the information that he had given them, but in the days and weeks thereafter, neither she nor Cliff asked him anything about being gay. It bothered Alan, and the longer they "ignored" the issue, the more he felt rejected and isolated.

When Alan explained his feelings to me, I told him what I tell all of my clients: "You have to be the one to keep the dialogue going." It would be great if his parents asked follow-up questions and even planned to go to PFLAG (Parents, Friends, and

Family of Lesbians and Gays), but most family members don't know what to do—
or what to say or ask. To play it safe, they adopt a "don't talk about it" rule. I told
Alan that his job was to create a dialogue and insert new topics on being gay into
conversations.

Hearing this, Alan became angry. He felt it wasn't fair that he was expected to
do all the work in coming out to his family. This brought up his memories of being
emotionally neglected while growing up. If he did not talk to his parents about his
schooling and grades, they would never ask. He even had to rely on school counselors and friends when considering college, as his parents didn't encourage his attending or even ask about it.

Alan: Clinical Interpretation and Treatment

Alan had two issues to resolve. One was the typical way many families deal with
learning their child is LGBTQ—which is to be silent and distant. The other was
that he wasn't comfortable with the way his family normally operated, which left him
angry about his childhood. His work in therapy was dealing with his feelings about
having been neglected as a little boy.

I coached Alan to talk to his parents about his socialization while coming out, urged
him to mention what types of organizations he had discovered (including PFLAG),
and even suggested that he give them a copy of the local gay newspaper. I referred
him to several articles and the books *What the Bible Really Says about Homo*sexuality
(Helminiak, 2000) and *Prayers for Bobby* (Aarons, 1996; about a mother who prayed
for her son to change and ended up contributing to his suicide). Alan followed my
advice, but he often found things left, untouched, where he'd put them, and if he did
bring up the subject, his parents would not ask him to elaborate. So I encouraged him
to talk to them about their lack of follow-up questions. He worried that doing this
would cause even more problems, as they were already upset each time he brought up
his being gay. I told him that although it upset his family to talk about it, it upset him
not to talk about it—and that the three of them should address this together.

Alan did go to his parents about this, and they all wept together. His parents
said they didn't know what to say or do and were trying to avoid hurting him with
possibly ignorant and hurtful questions. Through her tears, Martha said she worried about his catching HIV and asked if he was being careful. For the most part,
Alan's father was silent but tearful and attentive to the conversation—even though
he looked away.

I asked Alan to have his parents come in for some family therapy sessions and
they did. It was apparent that Martha was in the initial stages of grief over the loss

of having a heterosexual son. Both the parents were cycling back and forth between denial, bargaining, and depression. They were not angry, however.

Over our next three sessions, I told Alan's parents that their son was clear about his being gay and wasn't going to change. I explained to them that when the gay or lesbian family member comes out, the family often has a hard time with it—initially. Gently, I told them that now *they* needed to do some work on accepting their gay son—that problem was theirs.

To this, Martha reacted angrily: "Are you telling me it's our fault that he's gay?" She then stated that she thought she must have caused Alan's gayness by being too overbearing and smothering as a mother. I normalized her reaction and educated them by saying that parents cannot cause a child's gayness, although it's typical for them to think they did. I told them the issue was not about Alan's gayness as much as it was about their acceptance.

Cliff commented that he still had trouble with Alan's homosexuality and said he would never accept it. "I don't think he has been with enough women to know," he remarked. "Maybe he's had bad experiences with them. With women, it wasn't easy for me at first either. I did everything to make this boy straight by putting him in Cub Scouts, sports, and even leaving my copies of *Playboy* around for him to see. But nothing worked!"

I asked Cliff about his own childhood relationship with his father. It came out that as a boy, he'd been sexually abused by a priest and a neighbor boy, and for a while he had felt confused about his sexual orientation. Nothing had ever been done about the abuse, nor had he told anyone until now.

Martha and Alan were in tears. For Cliff, this was the real issue: The news of Alan's being gay had brought out his own unresolved material. As mentioned earlier, this is a very common dynamic: When a child comes out, other family issues surface as well. And usually family members blame (or in Alan's case, ignore) the gay child rather than examining what is causing their distress.

Several weeks after this session, Alan gave the following letter to his parents.

Dear Mom & Dad,

I wasn't doing a very good job of educating you guys, because even with all of the reading I have done I wasn't totally prepared for talking with you. The bottom line is that I am who I am, and this is who I have always been. And I don't care what anyone says, this is not a choice. I was born this way and I finally get to be who I am and I can honestly say that I am the happiest I have ever been in my entire life, finally!

I don't ever want to hear "you can go back" or "it is a choice." I believe that God/Jesus/whomever made me this way and he wouldn't make something that he thought was evil or bad. True, people can turn into evil or bad, but I was not born that way because I am gay. And by the way, the Bible also says that God will be the one to judge us, not our parents or our siblings or our friends or anyone else, so I would also appreciate you saving the judgment for him to pass.

I know it may sound as if I don't care if you guys accept me or not, which is not the case, but I had to go into this whole process being true to myself and being proud to be who I am. And I can tell you with 100% certainty that I am. I hope that we can continue to have the same or a better relationship now that I am honest with myself and everyone around me, but if that is not possible, I totally understand. That is not to say that I am expecting you to come around today, tomorrow, next month, or even in a year or two. Take as much time as you need. I do understand that this comes as a shock and it takes time to adjust no matter how you end up dealing with or accepting it.

Please know that I love you both and I am the same person I was yesterday, and for my entire life for that matter. I am just much happier than I have ever been and I am actually very proud of myself for finally being able to be true to myself.

When you are ready (and again, I will wait for you to tell me), I would like to talk about how my significant other or whatever you would like to call him fits into this picture. I know that may not be easy but accepting me will also include accepting him as the wonderful human being that he is.

Talk to you guys soon.
Alan

Alan waited a good year before his father came around. He talked with his mother regularly, and though she cried each time he brought up his sexuality and his relationship with his partner, she listened. Ultimately his father's way of making peace was to say that it would be God's judgment in the end and should not be his. Although Alan was not 100% pleased with his father's "tolerance," I helped him see that this was the best his father could do given his religious beliefs.

What Parents and Families Need to Know

As therapist, you need to know how to help the parents in addition to the LGBTQ client—even if the parents never come in to see you. Family therapy sessions are particularly helpful, but you can also help your clients educate their families on their own. Parents receive little to no support from others for having an LGBTQ child. In terms of comfort and empathy, they actually would receive more support if the child had died.

Work by Caitlyn Ryan and her team at the Family Acceptance Project (https://familyproject.sfsu.edu), which helps families with an LGBTQ member, is one of the best resources available. The group's website describes their work as follows.

> The Family Acceptance Project® is a research, intervention, education and policy initiative that works to prevent health and mental health risks for lesbian, gay, bisexual and transgender (LGBT) children and youth, including suicide, homelessness and HIV—in the context of their families, cultures and faith communities. We use a research-based, culturally grounded approach to help ethnically, socially and religiously diverse families to support their LGBT children. (para 1)

Caitlyn and colleagues found that family support for an LGBTQ child is predictive of increased self-esteem, social support, and general health status. Family acceptance also protects against depression, substance abuse, and suicidal ideation and behaviors (Ryan, Russell, Huebner, Diaz, & Sanchez, 2010).

Parents need to know that their child's orientation is not their fault in any way. They need to be reassured that they did nothing to cause it, shape it, or develop it. The more you can help them understand they are not to blame or the cause, the more they will be able to accept their child's identity.

Next, it is helpful to talk to parents about the closet they are in now that their child has come out. They now have to deal with telling or not telling their friends and family that their child is LGBTQ. Prepare them for what they might feel when they hear homophobic slurs—mad, sad, afraid, ashamed—and what, if anything, they intend to do about it.

Discourage parents from telling their child not to tell certain family members. Remind them that it is their issue, not their child's. If they need some time before their LGBTQ child tells, that is fair, but making blanket statements like "I don't ever want you to tell so-and-so" is not fair to their child. Help parents see their own issues that arise around why they would not want certain people to know.

Also, it is important to teach parents and families that their reactions are their own. Their reactions have less to do with their child's identity and more to do with how they react to news that is upsetting. Help them understand what about their child's disclosure bothers them the most.

The following questions are helpful when working with parents:

- Do you feel it is your fault and if so, why?
- What is the general way you deal with sexual issues?
- How were sexual issues addressed in your family growing up?
- How were differences viewed among family members' personalities and interests in your childhood growing up?
- Is this affecting your marriage? If so, how?
- What concerns do you have about your child being out in the world as LGBTQ?
- Does this conflict with your religious beliefs, and if so, how?

For further support you can refer parents to PFLAG (Parents, Friends, and Family of Lesbians and Gays). There are chapters all around the country. The group's website (www.pflag.org) lists information about local chapters. It is especially helpful to have some hard-copy pamphlets and brochures for them to read. Educate them on the benefits of going to a support group of people who have experienced what they are experiencing and can share stories that may help them.

The Case of Mary

Mary, a 42-year-old mother, told me her 20-year-old son, Jacob, had just told her that he was gay—and she was sure this wasn't so. Her husband, Howard, who was Jacob's stepfather, wasn't interested in attending therapy, so she came to the appointment with Jacob. (Jacob's father died when he was 3, and Howard functioned as Jacob's principal father figure.)

Mary began the session by stating that Jacob "doesn't know what he is" and that she wanted to provide some help. Apparently, Jacob had come out to her only two months before. Mary was devastated, claiming that Jacob, her youngest, was closer to her than her other two children. She even stated that she felt closer to Jacob than to her own husband!

Jacob assured her that nothing had changed, that he loved just her as much as before. He said that he was *not*, in fact, struggling with his sexual identity and knew that he was gay—for sure. Mary took this as an affront. "Why are you trying to hurt me like this?" she implored.

Over several more sessions, it became clear that Mary's relationship with Howard had been weak for years. She had given very little to the marriage and received little in return. Able to ignore her marriage, she had put all of her energy into her daughter and two sons.

Jacobs's brother and sister had moved to other parts of the country, which she took as personal rejections. "I never believed I couldn't see my kids every day." The children kept in constant contact with her and visited with her four times a year, but that was not enough for her, she reported. She still felt alone and abandoned. Now, Jacob had told her he was gay, and he was spending less and less time with her.

I assured Mary that the fact that her son and daughter felt comfortable living elsewhere—and stayed in regular touch—was a sign of her good parenting. Her children felt secure, able to make their own lives for themselves. But Mary insisted that this was *not* a positive sign. I also praised her for having raised a gay son who was willing to share his authentic self with her, but this didn't calm her either. So we moved on to the real, underlying issue, which was her distant relationship with Howard.

I asked that Howard come to our next appointment, which he did—tentatively. Immediately upon entering the therapy room, Howard stated that he was there only "to support his wife," and he refused to participate in our conversations. I honored that, giving him credit for being there at all.

During the session, I explained to the parents that Jacob was on his way to a healthy gay identity, if not already there. The issue was really about them coming to terms with having a gay son—and a marriage based on parallel lives, with not much overlap as a couple or as parents. Howard worked many long hours and was an avid fisher. Mary had repeatedly asked him to spend more time with her, but Howard had rebuffed her. I recommended that if therapy continued, it should be marital therapy for Howard and Mary, without Jacob—which sent a message to the whole family.

Howard wasn't pleased with this suggestion, as he felt his marriage was fine and had no interest in working on it. But after Jacob stopped joining his parents for therapy, the three of us spent a number of sessions on Howard's ambivalence about marital therapy with his wife. Ultimately, he agreed to try it, and they created a stronger, tighter marriage.

Becoming more confident about herself and her husband, Mary was no longer so emotionally needy with her children. Their interactions were more appropriate. She also developed healthier relationships with her friends and relatives. She and Howard were able to resolve other issues in their marriage—all thanks to Jacob's integrity and courage.

It can be hard for parents to deal with the behaviors typical of an LGBTQ child or teenager coming out of the closet. They worry their child will be bullied, humiliated, harmed, and endangered either physically or emotionally. It is normal for parents to have these concerns. As a therapist, normalizing their child's behaviors (without condoning the dangerous ones) is important.

Following is an email I received from a concerned parent. It is typical of what many parents struggle with as their child goes through the coming-out process.

Dear Joe,

I hope you don't mind that I am sending you this email, but I am kind of desperate. My son is 20 (just finished his sophomore year in college) and told us a couple of months ago he is gay. My husband and I are coming to terms with this—we really are. We love Jordon and would do anything for him and we only want the best for him.

The problem is this: I think he is way too sexually active and sometimes practices unsafe sex. He seems to spend hours and hours on various gay male websites talking to guys. Then he goes out and hooks up with them (I think). While he was at college, we were obviously not there so we don't really know, but for the week that he has been home he has done this twice. I don't have a problem with him meeting gay guys and hopefully someday developing a deep relationship but I feel like he is kind of whoring around right now and I am torn apart inside. I'm not sure he tells us the complete truth about what he does—not that we want details. We did find out that he had tried drugs with these men he had met and we came down on him pretty hard about that. He swears he will never do it again and that he only did it a couple of times. Can we trust him? I'm not sure.

We really need help with this because it does not seem "normal" to me that he spends so much time talking on the Internet with guys. He is basically a nice kid, just with such low self-esteem that I am scared to death for him. Please let me know what you think—I know it's hard to say anything without meeting a person but WE ARE DESPERATE!

Thank you,
Ashley

My response to them was as follows:

Dear Ashley,

Although I cannot speak specifically for your son because I don't know him, I can tell you that what he's going through is normal. He sounds like he is in Stage 5 of the coming-out process, which is like adolescence, only delayed. Most straight teens do what he is doing in middle and high school, and straight teens don't have to go online because they can date openly and have the resources and openness to do it.

Your son is probably more like age 15 in the romance/sexuality department. It is *very* scary to hear he is having unsafe sex and experimenting with drugs. On the other hand, he is no different than any teen having unprotected sex and experimenting with drugs. I am just trying to give you a normative concept so you can see what he is doing is normal—just different in terms of his age and how he meets guys. The number one way gay men hook up is online. Honestly, it is better than the bars, where he could fall in with the wrong peer group who do drugs on a regular basis.

This is a stage he is going through, and it could last 2 to 3 years, as with any adolescent. After people get this stage out of their system, they settle down with Mr. Right or Ms. Right, just as your son will probably do.

It sounds like you and your husband have done all you can do. I would recommend keeping the conversations open and honest as they sound like they have been. Also, have you heard of PFLAG (Parents, Friends, and Family of Lesbians and Gays)? They would be a great support for you and your son. I also recommend the books *Beyond Acceptance* and *Always My Child*.

Your fears are valid regarding the unsafe sex and the experimental drug use. You have told him your concerns, and the best part is that you raised a son so honest. Now you have to honor him with your trust and cross your fingers. If you push too hard you could alienate him.

I hope this helps you and your family.

Sincerely,
Joe Kort

Establishing Rules for Discussing LGBTQ Identity Among Family Members

It is important to establish ground rules for discussing LGBTQ identity among family members. The subject is charged for many reasons, as the examples in this chapter have shown. Emotions run deep, reactivity runs high, and individuals regress to primal coping mechanisms, relying solely on the reptilian brain, which operates only on survival. Family members will do or say whatever it takes to get relief.

Given all this, rules have to be established for the family to engage in healthy communication about the disclosure of being gay. Following are some you can teach your clients:

- Keep the dialogue about being LGBTQ going, even if it makes family members uncomfortable. It is easy for the LGBTQ family member to give up if the rest of the family does not want to talk about it or stops talking about it. This usually just means that people don't know what to say. You can prompt parents to keep talking to their child about the child's homosexuality with curiosity, asking things like, "What does LGBTQ mean to you?" or "When did you first discover you were LGBTQ?" or "If I said anything before I knew that was negative, I want you to know I am sorry." Whatever comes up for the family members, they need to be encouraged to keep talking.
- Take time-outs. Everyone needs to have permission to say when and if they are overwhelmed and unable to continue the conversation. Everyone needs to agree to take a time-out and agree when the conversation will continue. The time-out should never be more than 24 hours, or family members might have a tendency to avoid it for much longer and months could go by.
- Within the dialogue, feelings should be addressed and revealed only in nonreactive ways and through "I" statements, such as "I have feelings about . . ." or "I am worried about . . ." In other words, if one or more people are having an overreaction, the conversation should stop immediately and only be resumed when reactivity can be contained. Emotional safety is the number one priority for all within these discussions. If people no longer feel emotionally safe, they need to be able to express that and ask for the family member talking to state his or her thoughts in a different way or take a time-out.
- Validate one another's points even if they are different from each other. It is easy to say that what someone is saying "doesn't make any sense" or is "completely ridiculous." Teach the family to refrain from making such statements and instead say, "What you have said makes sense *from your point of view*." This is not agree-

ment, but it does not negate what the family member doing the validating is thinking. The family member will have a turn to share his or her side of things. The issue here is for all individuals to hear one another out and to be validated and accepted for what they think even if they disagree.

- Teach the family members how to stay emotionally connected and empathize with one another. For example, a gay son or daughter might say, "It must be scary to think about my going to gay bars in areas you don't think are safe." A parent might say, "I imagine you feel angry that my religious beliefs make it hard for me to accept your homosexuality."

These rules and guidelines are often very hard for families to follow on their own. Having a few family sessions can be enormously beneficial, with the therapist there to facilitate and point out overreactions, judgments, interruptions, and anything else that is standing in the way of effective communication.

I would like to end this chapter with a story from the Talmud.

A king had fallen out with his son. Very angry, the son left his father's castle and created his own kingdom, many miles away. Over time, the king missed his son and sent a messenger, asking him to return, but the son declined his father's invitation.

This time, the king sent the messenger back with a different message: "Son, come as far as you can, from your kingdom to mine. And I will meet you the rest of the way."

CHAPTER 9

LGBTQ Sexuality

This I can say for certain: If you go to war with your sexuality,
you will lose and end up in more trouble than before you started.
— Jack Morin, *The Erotic Mind*

For over a year, I had been treating a heterosexual single client named Joyce. During a session following a romantic trip Joyce had taken with a new boyfriend, she reported that the vacation had gone well and that they had a great time sexually and romantically.

"And I also learned about shrimping," Joyce said excitedly.

"Did you like it?" I asked.

"Not at first," she said, scrunching her nose. "But I got used to it—especially the smell—and I had fun with it."

"What about the taste?" I asked.

"It was delicious!" she exclaimed.

"Delicious? I've never heard someone use that adjective," I replied.

"I'll try anything once," she said happily, licking her lips. "It was hard to get used to using the net while doing it!"

At this point, I realized that we were talking about two different things. Joyce was a highly sexual woman. During our work together, she had a number of different male partners—even a woman for a while—and was experimental and open to just about anything sexually.

"Joyce, what do you mean by shrimping?"

"We went to Maine and went on the water in a boat with a net, catching shrimp to eat later in the evening. Why? What did you think I was talking about?"

"I thought you were talking about sucking and licking toes—that's also called shrimping!"

We both laughed.

This comical misunderstanding illustrates how important it is that we clinicians be clear on the right questions to ask, know the sexual jargon and terminologies, and, most importantly, be willing to ask when we are confused or don't know the resources to give our clients.

Some straight clinicians—and even LGBTQ clinicians—erroneously expect LGBTQ sex lives to resemble heterosexual ones. They assume, for example, that there is the same frequency of sexual contact and that an LGBTQ person's views on monogamy and penetration are identical to those of straight people. This hetero-centric viewpoint is often what causes LGBTQ clients to consult with me. They say, "My straight therapist just didn't get it."

A growing number of heterosexuals—especially millennials—are no longer adhering to heterocentric and heteronormative sex lives. They tend to be more sexually fluid and open in their relationships, often identifying as poly.

Other clinicians may operate under the false assumption that gay men are more preoccupied with sex than straight men are or that lesbians are less interested in sex than straight women. These kinds of misconceptions can derail therapy.

LGBTQ clients—and many straight ones as well—often report sensing that their therapists don't want to talk about sexual issues. As one of my clients once said to me, "I was too afraid [my past therapist] would not like me or understand me if I told him about my sex life."

This chapter will help you learn enough about LGBTQ sex that you will be able to ask informed questions and treat your clients more effectively. Clinicians who can reassure their LGBTQ clients that they are informed about the pertinent facts will find that their clients feel much safer in confiding in them.

It is important for me to note here that many of the claims I make in this chapter are generalizations. I in no way, of course, mean to stereotype men and women—straight or otherwise—nor do I mean to suggest that I know everything about LGBTQ sex lives. But to present the types of problems you will see in your office, I make some sweeping statements. As you read this chapter, remember that there are always many exceptions to the rule.

Knowing Your Own Biases and Comfort Zones

Before you can listen to clients and be nonjudgmental about their sexual issues, you must be willing to explore your own feelings and beliefs about your own sexual behavior. You need to be aware of your heterosexist biases about sex and sexuality. You may, for example, be *tolerant* of a client's sexual identity as it relates to himself or herself (and to families, friends, and partners) but find that the details of his or her sexual life make you uncomfortable.

I don't believe that therapists are judgmental only about the sex lives of LGBTQ clients. Indeed, most therapists are uncomfortable with the erotic lives of *any* of their clients—especially when the eroticism is directed at them by way of transference. It is normal to be uncomfortable listening to LGBTQ clients, especially those of your own gender, talk about their sex lives. But because LGBTQ individuals have been insulted and stunted developmentally with regard to their sexuality, failing to acknowledge this area limits your ability to conduct full and effective therapy.

Clients always know when their therapists feel uncomfortable with a topic. I've had many clients tell me that when they tried to talk with their previous therapists about a sexual conflict or act, they were met with resistance. The therapists wouldn't ask them to elaborate or even mirror back what they said and would instead move on to an unrelated topic to escape their own discomfort or lack of knowledge.

Countertransference will inevitably enter the treatment room when your clients talk about their various sexual encounters, fantasies, experiences, and behaviors. As you read this chapter, monitor your own feelings, whether positive or negative. Let your judgments surface to consciousness so that you can either work on them or decide that addressing the erotic lives of your clients is not for you. The more uncomfortable you feel, the more you can understand your own values and honestly assess which clients you can work with and which would be better served by a different therapist.

The Case of Nancy, a Therapist

Nancy asked me for supervision regarding a lesbian client she was seeing. Jess, age 25, was in Stage 5 of the coming-out process (see Chapter 7 for the stages of coming out). She had begun meeting women online and at bars and was increasingly excited about her lesbian identity.

Jess had moved into a highly sexually charged phase. During sessions with Nancy, Jess would relate her sexual experiences and all that she was learning in great detail.

When she asked if Nancy was comfortable hearing about it, Nancy replied, "Yes." But she really wasn't.

In supervision with me, Nancy admitted that she was more comfortable listening to her gay male clients' sexual exploits. She feared that Jess was acting out with her in the therapy—perhaps eroticizing her and "purposely" regaling her with details about her sex life to see if Nancy had lesbian tendencies. Even though she'd told Jess she was straight, Jess repeatedly asked if Nancy was certain she was heterosexual. Jess also related that she, herself, had believed she was heterosexual before realizing she was gay. Nancy became increasingly uncomfortable and believed that Jess enjoyed making her feel uncomfortable.

Jess continued to discuss her sexual feelings toward other women—including Nancy. To avoid Jess's "advances," Nancy talked about her husband more than she normally would and actually brought in a photo of him and their children to solidify her straight status.

Now Nancy was feeling guilty, worried that her countertransference would become obvious. She realized that she needed to better understand what was happening. She asked me, "Is it okay to tell Jess that I'm not comfortable hearing the details of her sex life? I don't want to shame her in any way, but I do want the boundaries clear in the therapy room."

Nancy: Clinical Interpretation and Treatment

I immediately told Nancy it was normal for her to feel uncomfortable, given that she was a woman herself—and the object of Jess's erotic desire—and straight. But it was important to acknowledge her discomfort rather than try to be "politically correct" and pretend to adopt an attitude she didn't have. This was a relief to Nancy because she wanted to remain LGBTQ affirmative and keep working with lesbians.

Nancy and I also explored the normalcy of clients' romantic feelings for therapists. I asked her how she had felt when men expressed these feelings toward her. She said it had made her uncomfortable but that she felt more at ease working through the erotic transference with men than she did with Jess—who actually had never said she had *romantic* feelings for Nancy, just sexual ones. Nancy also admitted that with Jess, the erotic transference felt more aggressive.

I explained that for Jess and others who are in the midst of the coming-out process, it is normal to have positive transferential feelings toward the therapist, including sexual and romantic ones. The aggressiveness Jess displayed (goading Nancy into thinking she might have suppressed lesbian tendencies) might be due to the fact that she was in Stage 5—the "in-your-face" phase when many gays and lesbians think that everyone is (or should be) gay or lesbian.

I then asked, "Are you willing to explore your own sexual issues that might be interfering with your work with Jess?" Sobbing, Nancy revealed that when she was 13, an adult male neighbor had molested her while his girlfriend watched in obvious enjoyment. In her own therapy, Nancy had done a considerable amount of work around this and thought she was finished dealing with what the male neighbor had done. Now, however, she realized that she had never addressed her feelings about the woman who was there.

Jess's disclosure of her sex life triggered Nancy's memories of her perpetrator's girlfriend's erotic enjoyment of her abuse. Because it wasn't appropriate for Nancy to share her own sexual-abuse issues with Jess, I recommended that she work this through in her own personal therapy and supervision and view it as an opportunity to finally resolve her own sexual-abuse issues.

As a result of this conversation, some of Nancy's discomfort in working with Jess was reduced, but although she now realized why Jess was behaving in the ways she was, it still remained an issue. I advised her to talk openly with Jess about the possibility of an erotic transference to see Jess's reaction. Nancy could ask questions such as:

- "Jess, it's normal for clients to have sexual and romantic feelings for their therapists. I was wondering how you want me to feel about your expressing yours toward me?"
- "How do you imagine I feel about your having a sexual interest in me?"
- "How do you imagine I feel in return toward you?"
- "How do you want me to feel when you tell me that perhaps I am suppressing a homosexual orientation?"
- "If I *were* suppressing lesbian feelings, what would that mean to you?"

These are some standard questions that allow deeper work on clients' transference and help the client self-examine rather than focus on the therapist.

Nancy worried that these questions might embarrass Jess. Even if it were true that Jess had romantic feelings toward Nancy, Jess might lie to avoid the strain it might cause in their therapy. Nevertheless, I helped Nancy find the words to bring this out into the open, working it through to keep it safe for Jess to talk honestly about all of her sexuality.

I also advised Nancy to discuss with me her own discomfort over listening to lesbian sexuality. It was not appropriate for her to address her discomfort in detail with Jess. I suspected that Jess might be already picking up on it, as clients often do. It was normal for Nancy to feel uncomfortable, like any straight woman who was not familiar with the details of lesbian sex would. But if Nancy expressed some of her discomfort sensitively and admitted she was working on it in supervision to allow herself to listen to and help Jess, Jess might understand. Next, they could decide together if Jess should see another therapist—perhaps a lesbian—if Jess felt it was interfering with her therapy.

Many therapists don't agree with—and are uncomfortable with—any type of self-disclosure with their clients, arguing that a therapist's personal issues should remain outside the therapy room. I generally agree, but because LGBTQ individuals are hypervigilant regarding others' judgments, feelings, and discomfort, I thought it would be in Jess's best interests to hear Nancy express own her discomfort. This humanistic approach honors LGBTQ clients' possible perceptions and minimizes their viewing the problem as being about them, something they have done their whole lives.

Ultimately Nancy did express her discomfort with Jess's sexual discussions and assured her that she was working on the issues that were surfacing outside the consulting room. Naturally, Jess asked Nancy what those issues were. Nancy and I had anticipated this question, and I had coached Nancy not to respond to it. Knowing the reasons behind Nancy's discomfort would not be therapeutic for Jess. All Jess needed to know was that it was a source of discomfort and that Nancy was working on addressing it.

Nancy then asked Jess how she felt about hearing this. Jess sighed with relief, stating that she knew that Nancy was uncomfortable and was glad she admitted it. Jess also said that she felt honored that Nancy was taking time outside of their therapy to address the issues coming up. She said that this made her feel even more important to Nancy. Jess continued in her work with Nancy, and through supervision Nancy was able to get past her countertransference.

It is unrealistic to think that as therapists we don't have judgments about things our clients tell us—we do. It is being *aware* of our judgments and leaving them out of the therapy room if or when they interfere with a client's progress that is the challenge. Other times, the challenge is to use our judgments for the benefit of our clients. We do this best when we understand our own judgments and ways of thinking and feeling.

The Case of Glenn: Issues with HIV

Glenn came to see me concerned about not finding Mr. Right. During the intake I asked him if he knew his HIV status (a standard question I ask all of my clients), and he said he was HIV positive. He had been living with HIV for the past 13 years. Although he had some symptoms in the beginning, he'd been taking medication for 10 years and was symptom free.

I asked Glenn if he felt uncomfortable disclosing his HIV status and questioned whether this might be part of the problem around his dating. He said he did not like to disclose, as each time he had to expect possible rejection. I empathized with how difficult that must be for him, but he said it was not a central issue for him. The way he worked around it was by not telling dating partners until they asked.

"Is that before you have sex with them?" I asked.

"Sometimes, but not always," he replied.

Now I was concerned. "What about the men who don't know you are HIV positive—don't you feel an obligation to tell them?"

"No," he responded. "I play safe. I never do anything that is of risk with any partner. Besides, if they feel strongly about it, they should ask. In my opinion, every gay man should assume that whoever they are sexual with is HIV positive and play safe. Then no one has to disclose unless asked."

Now my negative countertransference toward Glenn was in full gear. Not being aware of the extent to which I was negatively judging him, I said, "Glenn, don't you think it is your obligation since *you* are HIV positive to let each man know before you have any kind of sex with him—even kissing?"

"No, Joe, I don't," he responded defensively. "It's painful for me to be rejected over and over again. As long as I always use condoms and never exchange bodily fluid, there is no reason to tell, because the risk is low."

"But the risk is *not* nonexistent. Do you kiss the men and let them fellate you without ejaculating in their mouths?" I asked.

Angrily he retorted, "Joe, don't you know that even though HIV can be found in saliva and precum, it is very unlikely to be contagious in those ways?"

"Yes, I know that, Glenn," I said. "It just seems like an ethical issue for the person infected."

"Why? I always tell the truth if I am asked. I never lie. Why does the responsibility rest with me only and not the man choosing to have sex with me?"

Glenn had a point. I had been thinking about the issue only in terms of my own view, which was that those with HIV have a responsibility to tell the unsuspecting sexual partner.

"You don't agree with what I am doing, do you, Joe?" he asked.

"Honestly, Glenn, I don't. But I don't know really where I stand on this, as I've never had this conversation before. You've given me a lot to think about, and I will do so," I replied.

Glenn: Clinical Interpretation and Treatment

Clearly I was having countertransference toward Glenn, which brought out his negative transference toward me in the form of defensiveness and anger. I had long had fears about becoming HIV positive during my single years. After I partnered, I felt safe from having to experience any of these dilemmas.

My conversation with Glenn exposed my bias toward the HIV-negative partner and against the HIV-positive one. I believed that HIV-positive people bore the larger share of the responsibility to tell potential sexual partners about their status. As a single man, I always asked guys before having safe sex what their HIV status was. But not all gay men do.

I don't know what the ethical answer is. I imagine for each person it is different. However, I had to determine where I stood on this issue in order to work with Glenn and other clients who chose to take this stand. I had to be able to articulate where I stood and what I was willing and unwilling to say about this touchy subject when speaking with clients.

On the one hand, I saw Glenn's point. Why should he have to tell if he wasn't going to be sexually unsafe? On the other hand, what about the men who trusted those with HIV to disclose and did not think it was polite to ask? I could see as I thought this through and talked with others supervising me that the words I chose to use in my discussions of this subject leaned in favor of the HIV-negative partner.

After some careful consideration, I decided how to manage my countertransference. I now tell all clients who are negative, gay or straight, to ask the person with whom they are engaging in sexual behavior about their HIV status—or to realize that they are taking a risk in not asking. I disagreed with Glenn's position about when to tell others about one's HIV status, and I make this position clear to clients who are HIV-positive and do not disclose. I want them to know where I am coming from as a therapist. I also explore with both positive- and negative-status individuals the psychological issues that would prevent them from telling or asking.

Clients who do not disclose their HIV-positive status and engage in *unsafe* sex must be informed that therapists have a legal obligation to report them. All therapists need to know their state's laws on reporting (guidelines vary from state to state).

The best source of information on this topic is Anderson and Barret's (2001) *Ethics in HIV-Related Psychotherapy: Clinical Decision Making in Complex Cases.*

Note that there are medications that can be prescribed to prevent HIV infection, which I will discuss later in this chapter when we come to gay male sexuality. Many gay men take this medication, which is more effective than condom use, but still not 100 percent effect. Regardless, I think it is important to have a sexual health conversation with a potential hookup before engaging in sex.

Educating Yourself: A Vital First Step

Before you can effectively address your lesbian and gay clients' sexual lives, you must become familiar with same-sex sexual acts and the terms used to describe them. The glossary in the back of this book discusses terms like *fisting, S/M, strap-on sex, top, bottom, rimming,* and other terms that clinicians often do not know. Some of these sexual acts are specific to gay men and lesbians; most are done by both, though dealt with differently.

To communicate with gay and lesbian clients, you must be fluent in two idioms— the jargon that gays and lesbians use among themselves, and the standard clinical equivalents. Likewise, a working knowledge of gay culture is just as imperative as it would be when working with any other minority.

As you learn the sexual language used among gays and lesbians, you'll discover that they often deal with sexuality very differently from heterosexuals. For example, it's common for gay men to state in personal ads—and on a first date—what they like to do sexually and whether they are a "top" (the partner who anally penetrates) or a "bottom" (the partner who is penetrated). This is done to attract like-mined partners and to dissuade men who aren't a sexual match.

In an LGBTQ clinical training I once gave, one female therapist was shocked to learn this. "If men did that in heterosexual personals," she said, "most women would find it a turnoff, and they wouldn't get many responses." But the gay male community is different. In fact, if a gay man *doesn't* put his sexual preferences (whether he is a top, bottom, or versatile) in his profile, he's not likely to get many responses!

Why the labels? Straight relationships enjoy the traditional generalizations of sexual compatibility. But before two men meet, it's difficult for them to determine sexual compatibility. Of course, when it comes to each individual's sexual preference, there are no absolutes. Some men use these criteria merely as a guide, whereas others view them as deal breakers before dating or sex.

The truth is that heterosexuals could also benefit from being a bit more open and disclosing about their sexual interests early on in a relationship to avoid sexual incompatibility later on.

Knowing sexual terms and behaviors is key to open, comfortable dialogue in the therapy room. It also helps prevent countertransference, as the following case illustrates.

The Case of Mark, a Therapist

Mark, a heterosexual male therapist, had helped a client, Luke, with the coming-out process. Luke grew deeply attached to Mark and grateful for all the therapist had done to help him feel better about coming out to himself, his friends, and finally his family. Now, they agreed, it was time for Luke to start dating other gay men romantically. When Luke began having sexual hookups, Mark asked him how things were going and discovered that Luke was only receiving anal sex, not reciprocating.

Luke stated that he had tried penetrating his partners and had successfully entered men but never achieved orgasm. He told Mark he preferred receiving anal sex.

Assuming that all gay men "share" in giving and receiving intercourse, Mark warned Luke that this might prevent him from finding a partner. I've heard many straight therapists say that they thought gay male couples "took turns" penetrating each other. The truth is that most gay men (especially those over 40) are generally either an anal penetrator or receiver, and they tend to want to know their partner's preference before entering into a hookup or relationship. Gay men under 40 report they are more versatile, both topping and bottoming.

Luke tried to take his therapist's advice, but he never enjoyed giving anal sex as much as receiving it.

Mark: Clinical Interpretation and Treatment

When Mark sought my supervision, I taught him the terms *top* and *bottom* and explained that gay men usually self-identify as either one or the other. Some men go both ways—calling themselves "versatile"—but this is more common among younger gay men. Being the bottom is still seen today as inferior to being the top among gay men—to the point that gay porn stars never identify as a bottom, only as versatile. Inherent in this is the sexist belief that being the receiver is feminine. (As the joke goes, "At a gay male wedding, the father of the bottom pays!")

Mark then said to me, "I don't mean to offend you, but is that like one playing the woman and the other playing the man?"

"It's not about male/female role playing," I explained. "It's just about sexual preferences and erotic enjoyment." I also explained that some gay men never engage in anal intercourse, only oral sex and masturbation. For them, this is still considered sex.

Now Mark was really confused. I had him read some books on gay sexuality, including Silverstein and Picano's (2004) *The Joy of Gay Sex*, and I encouraged him to admit to Luke that he hadn't understood enough about gay male sex. My concern was that he might have shamed Luke for not "acting like a man" in bed.

When Mark broached the subject, Luke revealed that he had indeed felt ashamed. He'd subsequently done some Internet research on gay sexuality and was considering switching to a gay male therapist who could "understand [him]." But he felt connected to Mark and wanted to keep working with him.

Mark's decision to seek supervision around his client's sexual issues saved his work with Luke. When I work with therapists, I try to debunk the erroneous beliefs they hold about gay and lesbian sexuality. One of the most common is the belief that genital penetration is the ultimate—if not the only—way to have sex and that any other practice is inferior. Many lesbians, for example, can fulfill each other sexually without penetration, and some gay male couples only perform oral sex or engage in mutual masturbation. In many therapeutic circles, it's believed that not having intercourse indicates a delayed, not fully developed sexuality—a bias from a heterosexist, patriarchal, sexist model. Many of your clients will also come in with this belief and will feel ashamed for not engaging in intercourse. It's your job as a therapist to normalize their sexual preferences and become educated and trained on the wide variety of healthy sexual behaviors and erotic interests.

Heterosexual Versus Lesbian and Gay Sexual Behaviors

In my role as a gay affirmative therapist and educator, I've heard both male and female straight therapists ask questions like those below, which amount to microaggressions.

- "If a lesbian needs to use a dildo, then why doesn't she just get a man?"
- "Why don't some lesbians want their dildos and sex toys to look like penises? Doesn't that reflect their hate for men?"
- "If a gay man is a top and receives oral sex but doesn't give it, then why not just be with a woman?"
- "Isn't it offensive and insulting to a potential partner if a person leads with sexuality, the way gay men do in dating?"
- "If lesbians aren't actively sexual with each other, then are they really lesbians?"
- "Why are gay men so promiscuous sexually?"

The answers to these questions might seem obvious, but they aren't to many clinicians. Many therapists still believe that homosexuality is defined *only* by sexual behavior and assume that if an individual is not being sexual he or she may not be gay. (Of course, sometimes straight men who don't want sex are "accused" of being gay. I won't try to explain this ironic inconsistency.)

Predictably, gay males and lesbians do behave sexually much like their heterosexual counterparts. Gay, bisexual, and straight, men are testosterone driven, lead with sexual urges, and have more sexual partners than women. Men generally can be sexual without any flirting or even knowing their partners' names. They need no attachment, before or after. Of course, there are women like this too, but they are the minority. Lesbian, bisexual, and straight women tend to be more relational. When being sexual, they usually value intimacy, attachment, and connection.

Whereas straight men are generally constrained by women's avoidance of quick, anonymous sex without intimacy, gay men are not confined in this way. In other words, the gay male community enjoys easy access to multiple hookups because of the absence of women to put on the brakes. This explains the more frequent sexual activity among gay men. It isn't that they are more sexual because they are gay; it's that they are male in a world without women. For better or for worse, the issue is about the differences between males and females, not gays and straights.

When addressing sexual issues in clients' lives, it is important to remember that you may experience negative reactions from gay and lesbian clients due to their hypersensitivity about the homophobia and misunderstandings you might carry if you are a straight clinician. If you understand that lesbian and gay sex has been judged as abnormal both historically and in psychotherapy up until very recently (see Chapter 1), you can anticipate their reactions and help validate and normalize them.

Often lesbians and gays will come to me after doing very good work with their straight therapists with the belief that their therapist could not understand or help them with their sexual issues. Sometimes this is assessment is unfair and untrue; the clients may simply not be giving their straight therapists a chance to show they *do* know a great deal—perhaps even more than the client does!

You can address this by asking your clients if they are concerned about talking about sexual issues with you. Invite them to tell you directly if they are holding back and give them permission to tell as much or as little as they want to. And finally, know your limitations. If you are uncomfortable with any parts of their sexual behavior and fantasies, refer them to someone who understands, is knowledgeable, and can help them.

Use of Pornography and Gender Differences

Straight men and women relate to pornography differently from LGBTQ individuals. In 2016, the Utah State Senate declared porn to be a public health crisis (Allred, 2016). Even Dr. John Gottman jumped on the bandwagon, identifying porn usage as a threat to couples' intimacy following a *Time* magazine cover story, "Porn and the Threat to Virility" (Luscombe, 2016).

Other research shows that pornography does not threaten relationships but rather adds to sexual responsiveness. (Prause, 2015).

But if this were the case, then why isn't porn in a health crisis in the LGBTQ community? Most of these discussions on porn as a public health crisis and "addiction" are heterosexist, meaning they focus on straight individuals and couples looking at porn and ignore the fact that gay men and lesbians look at porn, and it generally isn't a problem. (The "porn problem" for straight couples often comes down to: The husband likes porn and the wife "doesn't want it in the house." The issue is a disconnect between the two individuals, not really the porn. There is a lack of sexual literacy that blocks clear communication and intimacy for these couples.)

Most gay male couples have no problem at all with porn. It is common for gay male couples to openly discuss their porn practices and even view it together. In the gay community, viewing porn—kinky and otherwise—is okay. There is no shaming around it. Many lesbians openly talk about viewing both lesbian porn and gay male porn. They often watch it together, and rarely does a lesbian come into my office complaining that her female partner is watching too much porn.

Gay couples have on rare occasions come to see me with some of the same conflicts over viewing porn as straight couples. However, for straight or gay couples, it's never fundamentally about the porn itself but always about some other issue. Perhaps one of the partners has fallen into the trap of comparing himself or herself to the porn and believes that there is some "normal" way to go about sex, or perhaps intimacy is lacking in the relationship and it's come out as a disagreement around porn. I have never known such problems to be solved by doing away with the porn. If one partner is dealing with out-of-control sexual behavior, then I might recommend taking a break from the porn, but again, porn is not the problem. It goes deeper than that. For instance, if men are watching porn to avoid the relationship, that is a problem, so we look at the source of the avoidance. Has sex changed for them? Are they in a marriage where they want something different? Has he developed new sexual turn-ons that he hasn't been able to tell his wife about yet?

In the straight community, all too often there is the assumption, especially by women, that once the couple is together, there should be no need to view porn, that the relationship will forever banish the need for outside sexual stimulus. Practically speaking, this is never true, though I understand why women think this way. There is no understanding of male sexuality in our culture, only misconceptions and negative judgments. We know from many studies that men—whether married, single, religiously or culturally forbidden to watch porn—consume porn voraciously. When their partners discover this, too often it leads to one or both coming into my office, telling me of extreme reactions. Some wives insist on "lockdown," shutting off all the devices. There are fights, shaming, even divorce, because the heteronormative myth is that once there is marriage or commitment, both partners should be everything to each other, superseding the need for porn.

But think about this. If that standard is applied equally, women should have no need to, say, lock themselves in the bathroom and read romance novels by candlelight, or read *Fifty Shades of Grey*, or go to a romantic movie. Their romantic desires should have been fulfilled forever by the partnership. But it is understood that no matter how much or little she is getting at home, she still is drawn to watching and reading about others in romantic love, and even fantasizing about being with the male character in the book or movie. If she is not getting enough romance from her partner, she often turns to him and says, "I need and want you to be more like the men in my books and movies." While men don't like hearing this, they try to understand her need and know they have to work toward this because it will fulfill her.

The other way around is not true. When a man turns to his female partner and tells her that he would like her to engage in some of the things he is watching in porn, the man is shunned, shamed, judged, and often looked at with contempt and disgust. And yet I would argue that what he is asking is similar to what she is asking, only in a different form. She wants him to take all of her, and so does he. She wants to be told she is beautiful and his one and only, and so does he. She wants to be desired and pursued, and so does he. The difference is that she articulates this through emotional and relational ways, and he does so in sexualized ways in the erotic part of their relationship. No one should be judged or shamed about how they articulate their needs. If there were a more public conversation about this subject, more sexual literacy in our society, we would understand that men and women have different needs, different sexual and romantic fantasies.

Thus, the real public health crisis is a lack of sexual education. A step in the right direction would be to have a conversation with gay men and lesbians who watch porn and are not in crisis over it. It would be better if all children in schools could receive a proper sex education that included balanced representation of porn and all the ways that exist to be sexual that are not primarily heterosexual. There is no sex education in schools for gay boys, and so they have to turn to porn to get it. Discovering gay pornography is almost a rite of passage for young gay men. For sexually fluid men, or sexually repressed men, watching porn can begin to connect them to who they really are sexually.

Sex is messy, politically incorrect, taboo on many levels. Porn is not what we do in real life. Just like in other movies, it is fantasy. Straight people need to learn what porn means to men. Men objectify more than women, who are more relational. And it is a scare tactic to say that watching porn leads to infidelity. In fact, it is often a way to not engage in infidelity, an outlet that allows men to vicariously enjoy an act that they cannot do, like watching football—they can't play it, but boy do they enjoy watching it. Some may say, "See what porn did to you?" but my belief is that they are discovering something already within themselves, and they can use this self-knowledge to begin to move toward a more authentic sexuality.

This notion that porn is a public health crisis pathologizes men's natural curiosity about porn and their natural interest in watching it. I believe calling porn a crisis is a distraction. Actually, as long as people understand what it is and isn't, porn can be a means to explore and discover one's own sexuality. It is easy to scapegoat porn for destroying our relationships and our nation. Instead, why not make a greater effort to understand each other's sexual needs? This would get us much closer to understanding the underlying difficulties we have in relating to our partners.

In their book, *A Billion Wicked Thoughts: What the Internet Tells Us About Sexual Relationships* (2011), Ogi Ogas and Sai Gaddam refer to male sexual fantasies as "porntopia" and female fantasies as "romantopia." These researchers analyzed a year's worth of terms entered into the search engine aggregator Dogpile between July 2009 and July 2010. They found that 55 million of the roughly 400 million terms were sexual in nature. From their research they conclude that men's sexual fantasies are more about "sheer lust and physical gratification, devoid of courtship, commitment, durable relationships or mating efforts." They conclude that females are more interested in romance, essentially love stories in which "the heroine overcomes obstacles to identify, win the heart of, and ultimately marry the one man who is right for her."

In order to understand pornography and how to help those struggling with shame and experiencing feelings of loss of control around it, I recommend David Ley's book *Ethical Porn for Dicks: A Man's Guide to Responsible Viewing Pleasure* (2016), and Marty Klein's *His Porn, Her Pain: Confronting America's Porn Panic with Honest Talk about Sex* (2016).

Lesbian Sexuality

In general, less research has been devoted to women's health and sexuality than to that of men, and the same holds true for lesbians as compared to gay men. A larger body of literature exists on the positives and negatives of gay men's sexuality. Before the 1990s, the material that *was* available on lesbians mostly consisted of misinformation and sweeping, mostly negative, generalizations. The best book to date is sex-positive and informative: Felice Newman's (2004) *The Whole Lesbian Sex Book: A Passionate Guide for All of Us.*

Because therapists, like the lay public, are primarily misinformed, uninformed, or naive about lesbian sexuality, many therapeutic mistakes are made with lesbian couples and individuals. Even your lesbian clients may be misinformed.

Many American heterosexual males eroticize lesbian sexuality. Countless times, I've heard straight men admit that their biggest fantasy is to get two (or more) lesbians in bed with them. The problem is that they confuse lesbian sex with an erotic performance by straight or bisexual women for the straight male's enjoyment. That's because pornography depicts "lesbians" as primarily heterosexual women performing sex acts on each other to arouse a male voyeur. Lesbian sex, however, has nothing to do with men. Self-identified lesbians say that if they are going to be sexual with each other, they don't want a man in the room.

Many people assume that, for lesbians, sexual activity is unimportant, or even absent, because women typically don't push for sex. Women generally are taught not to be as sexual as men; some people believe women may be biologically less sexual. These assumptions are sweeping generalizations and are based on opinions, not research. The truth is that for both gay and lesbian couples, the partners are more likely to equally share responsibility for initiating sex. In heterosexual relationships, males tend to apply more sexual pressure than women.

Lesbians engage in sex roles of being tops and bottoms like gay males do, but they do not usually lead with that language in personal ads as gay men do. Many therapists erroneously think that lesbians rarely—if ever—engage in intercourse and only snuggle and kiss. The truth is that many have intercourse in a variety of ways, which you can ask about when you do your evaluation.

In a study by JoAnn Loulan, lesbian sexual practices were found to involve hugging, licking, snuggling; kissing all over the body; touching, kissing, licking, and nursing on breasts; oral-genital sex; insertion of fingers or tongue in the vagina; and masturbation. Overall the study showed that 70% of lesbian sexuality tends to focus on oral-genital sex as a large component of the sexual relationship (1987).

Thus, it is important to ask lesbian clients about their sexual behavior rather than making assumptions about their preferences based on the scanty literature about lesbians.

The book *Therapy With LGBTQ Clients: Working With Sex and Gender Variance From a Queer Theory Model* (Nichols, 2014) reports that lesbians do not look at sex in terms of male standards and heteronormative norms. Some lesbians using sex toys such as vibrators and dildos do not want them to resemble a penis. They don't always count orgasms, look at frequency, or need penetration. This book notes that lesbians spend more time on sex, have a larger sexual repertoire by spending more time on sexual behaviors that are considered foreplay by most people, are frequently orgasmic, are less likely to have sex because their partner wants it, complain of fewer pain disorders, and have lower rates of sexual dysfunction. However, they do complain sometimes of "lack of desire," which is sometimes a concern of heterosexual women, too.

When Sexual Abuse Is an Issue

There is a tendency to assume that lesbians are gay because they were sexually abused. This is a myth. Sexual abuse cannot create a sexual orientation. However, issues of past sexual abuse do come up in lesbian relationships. In fact, lesbian sex therapist and author Marny Hall reports that "lesbians report high levels of childhood sexual abuse" (Stewart, 2002, p. 14). Peggy is a good example of this.

The Case of Peggy

Peggy came to my office following a negative experience with her previous therapist. She had sought therapy because she experienced sexual dysfunction each time her partner, Bonnie, gave her oral sex. Peggy was able to masturbate herself and tolerate Bonnie's digitally masturbating her. However, when it came time to receiving oral sex, she would lose her erotic feelings and shut down.

In addition, she did not want to give oral sex to Bonnie. She was not bothered by the fact that Bonnie was overweight or by the smell of her genitalia, which she stated was normal and not unpleasant.

When Peggy brought up this issue with her therapist, the therapist speculated aloud about whether Peggy was actually a heterosexual who was turned off to men because of past sexual abuse. The therapist was actually correct in guessing that Peggy was a sexual abuse survivor, but she had made this assumption without even asking

Peggy about her history or doing a thorough assessment. Peggy had, in fact, thought that her current sexual dysfunction might be related to her past abuse, and it was a direction she wanted to follow in therapy. But the therapist's speculation that Peggy might not be a lesbian so angered Peggy that she terminated the therapy.

Crying, Peggy told me that her stepfather sexually molested her throughout her childhood until the age of 13. He would sneak into her room at night, get under her covers, lick her vagina for what seemed like an endless amount of time, and then leave. He would also take her to areas of the house that no one would enter, such as the basement cellar, lift her dress and pull down her panties, and lick her there. When she was very young—around the age of 4—he put her on top of the refrigerator and abused her there with cunnilingus. After the abuse, he would talk to her as if nothing had happened, and she felt afraid to tell anyone.

When Peggy was 13 her stepfather began attempting to digitally manipulate her genitals and told her he was going to use his penis. She pulled away and stopped it immediately, ordering him to discontinue his assaults permanently and threatening to tell on him if he didn't. He never spoke to her again throughout the rest of her teens.

Peggy knew that this past abuse was an impediment to her enjoying a good sex life with her partner. Although Bonnie was kind and considerate and did not force Peggy to do anything that made her uncomfortable, Peggy felt guilt and shame over not being able to have a more active sex life with Bonnie. Hearing her lesbian friends talk about the joys of getting and receiving cunnilingus caused her to feel even more shame and guilt. Peggy knew she was a lesbian and that she loved Bonnie. However, she worried that ultimately Bonnie would leave her if she did not deal with the abuse.

Peggy: Clinical Interpretation and Treatment

First, I validated Peggy's anger and concern about her former therapist's premature judgments. If a heterosexual woman entered a therapy office struggling with sexual dysfunction with her male partner, a therapist usually would not suggest to the client that she might be lesbian. Instead, the therapist would probably try to get to the source of the sexual dysfunction, with the understanding that questions about the client's sexual orientation might be appropriate in future sessions if the exploration of the sexual dysfunction didn't seem to be yielding answers.

Next was the work of dealing with her partner, Bonnie. Was Bonnie truly okay with how things were? Was there a chance she would leave Peggy because of this? I asked Peggy to bring Bonnie to a joint session so that we could talk about this. Scared but hopeful, Peggy asked Bonnie and they both came in. Crying, they both stated how much they loved each other and how they enjoyed sexuality in other ways. Bonnie said that even if their sex life stayed the same, it was enough for her; she loved Peggy that much. They enjoyed kissing and holding each other, took baths together, and each held the other while she masturbated. Bonnie did say that she would like Peggy to be able to give and receive oral sex at some point but that her primary concern was for Peggy to deal with her stepfather's sexual abuse.

The rest of my work with Peggy focused on having her talk through that abuse. I was careful to make sure that my being male was not going to interfere with her therapy. She said that my being a *gay* male helped her feel safe.

Lesbian Bed Death: Myth or Reality?

The term *lesbian bed death* emerged in the 1980s to express the idea that lesbian couples have sex less frequently than heterosexual or gay male couples do. It is often attributed to the research of Pepper Schwartz who, however, has denied having coined the term. Her book *American Couples* reported studies that show in lesbian relationships both partners eventually stop asking for sex and allow their sex life to die out. Also, these studies indicate that lesbian couples have the least amount of sex compared to gay male and heterosexual couples (Blumstein & Schwartz, 1983).

Today, the subject of lesbian bed death is very controversial, and the standards by which the studies were done have begun to be challenged. One criticism suggests that these studies were done according to heterosexist and heteronormative standards. The "lack of sex" was based only on factors such as penetration and orgasm. Many lesbians do not restrict their idea of sex to intercourse or even orgasm. They report that a sensual bath, sensual massages, or romantic nights in front of the fire naked count for sex. Also, according to Herbert (1996), "decreased frequency of sexual interaction does not appear to affect sexual satisfaction among lesbian couples."

In all relationships—gay, lesbian, and straight—sexual desire tends to decrease after the romantic love and honeymoon period wears off. Often, you will see a diminished interest in terms of frequency of sex and satisfaction. Although this is normative for most couples, research shows that the drop in erotic feelings does, in fact, happen sooner for lesbian couples than it does for gay and heterosexual couples. One reason for this may be the "dissolution of individual boundaries, a submergence of self in the larger arena of the relationship" (Hall, 1987, p. 138). This goes back to the enmeshed relationships lesbians create, wherein their individual boundaries are blurred and the "spark of differences that ignites eroticism disappears" (p. 138).

Author Esther Perel (2006) spoke of this very concept in her book *Mating in Captivity*:

> Love enjoys knowing everything about you; desire needs mystery. Love likes to shrink the distance that exists between me and you, while desire is energized by it. If intimacy grows through repetition and familiarity, eroticism is numbed by repetition. It thrives on the mysterious, the novel, and the unexpected. Love is about having; desire is about wanting. An expression of longing, desire requires ongoing elusiveness. It is less concerned with where it has already been than passionate about where it can still go. But too often as couples settle into the comforts of love, they cease to fan the flame of desire. They forget that fire needs air. (p. 37)

Past sexual encounters, both positive and negative, can also contaminate sexual expression due to powerful associations, as seen in the case of Peggy. Traumatic sexual experiences, such as childhood sexual abuse or rape, can negatively affect sexual desire and behavior. Covert cultural sexual abuse can be another explanation for lesbian bed death, as lesbians (more than gay men) tend to develop sexual anorexia as a result of the negative messages they receive about same-sex attractions when they are growing up.

Various writers and therapists have debunked Schwartz's theory (Hamadock, 1996; Iasenza, 1999). In her article "The Big Lie: Debunking Lesbian Bed Death," Suzanne Iasenza challenged the questions asked and the way in which the studies were implemented. She cited Pepper Schwartz's later work, *Peer Marriage*, which stated that heterosexual couples develop "peer" partnerships in which genital sex is not a primary part of their relationship (Schwartz, 1994). She argued that this would probably apply to lesbians and some gay males as well.

The reason for a therapist to be aware of, and understand, lesbian bed death is that it is feared by many lesbian couples. Also, there are many female couples who are together for many years and who no longer are sexual with each other. Whether or not that is a problem should be up to the couple and not come from an outside observer.

One of the things Marny Hall does with her lesbian clients who suffer from lack of sexual desire and intimacy is give the homework assignment of sending them to the local sex emporium. "I ask them to browse, pick out some erotica that appeals to them. Over the years, I've found that couples often come home from these excursions with porn that features gay males. They claim that it is more of a turn-on than the lesbian books and videos" (Stewart, 2002, p. 14).

It has been generally noted that lesbians enjoy watching gay porn. In an article by Elizabeth Stewart in *In the Family* magazine, the author debunked the myth that lesbians enjoy porn with more of a story line and emotional content: "One appeal of gay male porn . . . [is] that it doesn't get bogged down in plots, so there is less fast-forwarding to get to the 'good parts'" (2002, p. 13). Stewart found that lesbians do not like the women-on-women sex scenes in heterosexual porn because to them the women seem fake. What lesbians enjoy about gay porn is that the arousal of both men is "authentic, raw sexual energy" (p. 14). Although this survey was not scientific, many lesbians attest that this is true for them.

Gay Male Sexuality

Whereas lesbians struggle with the issue of being less sexual, gay males are confronted with the issue of being overly sexual. Gay men tend to establish their identities around sex and sexuality. This tendency may be intensified by the sexualized culture that exists among gay men.

Therapists treating gay male clients must remember that they have had to endure a lack of role models and images of men touching and expressing affection. Gay porn fills this lack, if only through sexuality. The gay man who lacks the courage to go to a gay bar finds porn the easiest, safest way to explore his sexuality. The closeted man knows that no one will judge him in a bookstore, X-rated theater, or especially on the Internet.

But using porn as one's initiation into gay manhood can feed into the feeling that being gay is forbidden and underground. Sneaking into a "dirty" bookstore can make one feel shameful, but also add to the excitement.

Many gay male couples feel shame that they are not having frequent sex with each other. The message—delivered both by the mainstream media and the gay community—is that gay men are sexual and constantly on the prowl. However, this is not necessarily true. Nor is it the case that all gay men enjoy anal sex. Some will come into your office feeling shame about this or thinking that something must be wrong with them.

Gay Men and Anal Sex

Gay men may choose to express their sexuality in many different ways. The "right way" is the way that works best for them. Lots of gay men love anal sex. They identify as tops; they identify as bottoms; they identify as both. But you as a therapist should understand that it is totally and perfectly fine if gay men never have anal sex.

Maybe they don't like it or it's not their thing. They are not a top; not a bottom. They're a "side." I wrote an article in *The Huffington Post* called "Guys on the 'Side': Looking Beyond Gay Tops and Bottoms" (Kort, 2013). Many gay men feel shame if they don't do anal sex. That's the result of ignorance and prejudice. No one should tell an individual gay man what he ought to do.

This is also true for nonstandard sexual interests and behaviors that don't hurt anybody. Part of the luxury of being a gay man is permission to play with fetishes openly, which is not the case for heterosexual men. For every 20 men with a fetish, there is only one woman. Heterosexual men have a lot more trouble finding play partners than gay men do.

Gay Sex Versus Guy Sex

It's true that some people say gay men are overly sexual, but I want to be clear: That's a *guy* thing, not a *gay* thing. If it were a gay thing, lesbians would be doing it, too. One benefit of being a gay man is that we get to have a lot of different kinds of sex that our heterosexual male counterparts don't. There's a freedom in that.

On the negative side, a culture without women does sometimes have problems with boundaries, with finding the "pause button." I had a male client once who answered a Craigslist ad that read: "My back door's open and my back door's open." He went to the man's house and, without any words exchanged, entered the house, engaged in anal sex with this man, and left. Most women would never respond so casually to an invitation like that for quick, anonymous sex. Women tend to want to know their partners. "Wait a minute. Let's learn each other's names. Let's go to dinner. Let's see if we like each other."

Many gay men are not into anonymous hookups or random sex, either. Often, these gay men feel ashamed about wanting a little courtship. I understand that they feel out of place, because it does appear that gay men are having sex everywhere, all the time. While that's the case for some gay men, it doesn't mean they have to do it. There's room for them, too. They're going to have to dig a little deeper and hunt a little more intentionally, but gay guys are out there who want what they want.

Gay Dating and Sex Hookup Apps

Some gay men like to meet other men for quick hookups. Grindr and other "gay apps" facilitate quick, anonymous hookups, but these apps can also be used for dating and for finding friends. (Teens also use these apps for various reasons; see Chapter 13.)

For many a gay man, especially when he is first coming out, the realization that there's so much easy access to hookups can cause him to overdo it. And then he panics: "Every time I try to stop, I can't stop, or I stop and then I go back. Oh my god! I must be a sex addict." But most men would go a little crazy when first offered unlimited easy sex. Give a straight guy an opportunity to get on a heterosexual Grindr and see lots of women eager for hookups, and he would also experience a struggle. Struggling with easy sexual opportunity doesn't necessarily mean your client has a disorder. Often, going overboard comes from being new to the apps, and sometimes it's from being newly single or newly coming out. Often, the obsession subsides.

As a therapist, be aware of the heterosexism and hidden homophobia that may contaminate your ideas about sex. Gay apps can become unhealthy, but they open up opportunities for men to connect, and that's healthy. Once, I myself had internalized homophobia about "excessive gay sex." Over time, I've become more sex positive and sex affirmative. I don't think we should put a wet blanket over the entire gay male community and say that it's wrong to want to connect sexually.

I also point out to my gay male clients that they can use the apps as dating opportunities. A lot of my clients use them that way. Yes, they're mostly for random sexual hookups, but that doesn't mean they can't be used to meet Mr. Right.

Gay Men, Aging and Sexuality

As a therapist, I see many gay male clients who are struggling with middle age. As a middle-aged gay man, I understand the struggle. When I was a younger therapist, older gay men in their 40s, 50s, and 60s would tell me that they "disappeared" at gay events, that other gay men—particularly younger ones—didn't notice them. I didn't believe them. I told these men that life is what you make of it, and if they were invisible, we needed to discover what they were doing to make that happen.

As I approached my later 40s, and now in my early 50s, I see exactly what they were talking about. I have literally been standing in a bar behind younger guys who turned around and bumped right into me as if I weren't there. Heads don't turn toward me the way they did when I was younger. As one ages, one notices these things.

I once told a gay male client in his 20s who was struggling with not feeling attractive that he was, in fact, a very handsome and hot guy, and that we needed to work on his self-esteem. I immediately followed this by reassuring him that I was not coming on to him. He responded, "Why would I ever think you were coming on to me?" That is when I realized he didn't even see me as a sexual being.

American culture worships youth and beauty, and even more so in the gay community. Historically when gay men reach a certain age, they tend to withdraw from the dating and bar scene, from interaction with younger men, afraid that they will no longer be seen as attractive, or will be seen as predators.

Unfortunately, the striving for a younger body and stronger libido is leading to an alarming trend I am seeing among middle-aged gay men: the use of crystal meth. This is not the answer. There are far healthier ways to retain a sense of virility, attractiveness, and relevance.

The Case of Jim and Daddy Fetishes

There is something going on in the gay community. Men 40 and older are being approached by younger guys, usually in their 20s and early 30s, and being identified as "daddies." There are even some websites for "daddies" and their admirers, one being www.daddyhunt.com.

But some older gay men don't know how to respond when approached this way. What often happens is that an older man is on Grindr or some other gay app, and suddenly a young guy contacts him, "Hey daddy!" or "Hot daddy!"

I've had gay clients tell me it's offensive. My client Jim felt that way. He was already self-conscious about his age. He was a midlife gay guy, and here's this kid calling him "Daddy." And to top it off—and this is really common—he *was* a father of two teenage boys. So to have some young guy contacting him for sex and calling him "Daddy" really creeped him out.

"Look," I told him. "This isn't about being a real daddy. It has nothing to do with incest. They want you to be a 'hot daddy,' but it's mostly just make-believe. These guys are sexualizing you, objectifying you. They're wanting you to enter into their fantasy."

I explored with Jim the possible benefits of taking on the "daddy" role, but he was still worried. "This kid wants to be my boy. I just can't deal with that."

"No," I told him, "he wants to be your b-o-i. He wants you to be playful and role-play a daddy-son relationship. There's nothing inherently wrong with this. You don't have to do it, Jim, if you don't want to, but you can also have fun with it. It's an opportunity to play with a younger guy who wants to play with you."

Jim was worried that the young men who approached him would be trying to get money from him. He feared they wanted a sugar daddy; they'd try to make him pay to play. But that's not usually what these guys want. True, these connections are not usually about relationships; the young men are not looking to set up house with an older guy. On the other hand, often the younger men are looking for more than just a little fun. They want connection and mentoring. They want to be blessed by a father figure.

Jim was also worried that these guys had to be psychologically messed up. "Why would they want this? Something must be wrong with them."

I do have a sense of what's going on, because a number of these young men have been my clients. They either have not been fathered well, so they've sexualized that neglect and are looking for a father figure in the erotic realm. Or they've been so well fathered that they want more of it. I've seen that side, too.

But while their sexual interests may be the result of childhood experiences, maybe bad experiences, that doesn't mean there's anything wrong with playing with them now. Their past might in reality have been a jungle of pathology, but sexualizing it now makes a garden for play. Yes, if there's a destructive, compulsive side, they will need to address that in therapy. Otherwise, it's harmless. And I salute their ability to have their fun. I don't see anything wrong with it.

PrEP, Pep, Condoms, and Sexually Transmitted Infections

Sexual play and hookups, while fun, can come with a price. You and your clients must educate yourselves on how to avoid sexually transmitted infections (STIs). One in four sexually active people get herpes. People are still contracting AIDS. From herpes to AIDS, STIs need to be taken seriously. This book is not the place to learn about them, although I'll touch on a few topics. You can begin online with the Centers for Disease Control (CDC) website: www.cdc.gov/std/.

Condoms are the first line of defense, but much progress has been made recently with antiviral medicines. To quote the CDC,

> Pre-exposure prophylaxis, or PrEP, is a way for people who do not have HIV but who are at substantial risk of getting it to prevent HIV infection by taking a pill every day. When someone is exposed to HIV through sex or injection drug use, these medicines can work to keep the virus from establishing a permanent infection. When taken consistently, PrEP has been shown to reduce the risk of HIV infection in people who are at high risk by up to 92%. PrEP . . . can be combined with condoms and other prevention methods to provide even greater protection than when used alone. (CDC, 2017, para. 1)

It is important for you to know the facts and be able to tell your clients how to play safe. When I have a client who is ignoring risks and having unsafe sex, I immediately suspect an underlying psychological cause. Unnecessary risk taking is one sign of trauma reenactment leading to problematic sexual behavior, as discussed in the next section.

Sexual Compulsivity and Out-of-Control Sexual Behavior

When I originally wrote this chapter I believed in the concept of "sexual addiction." I no longer believe that this is a useful framework for therapy. Research studies have continuously failed to prove that it is a common condition or even that it exists at all. I have also found the treatment model used by sex addiction therapists to be abusive and harmful to gay and bisexual men—and, in fact, to men in general.

The longer I was in the field of sex addiction treatment, the more I found both the label and many of the interventions antiquated, limiting, and sometimes even harmful—especially when working with gay and bisexual men. Sex addiction treatment began to reveal itself to me as simplistic, moralistic, and judgmental rather than truly diagnostic. The more I learned about healthy sexuality, the more I saw a number of problems embedded in the interventions within the model—negative messages of shame, erotophobia, biphobia, and homophobia—which were inextricably entwined in the treatment.

Over the last 10 years, I have become an AASECT (American Association of Sex Educators, Counselors and Therapists) certified sex therapist and supervisor, and I have learned a great deal more about helping people with problematic sexual behaviors from an informed sexual-health model, which is lacking in the sexual addiction field.

I know of clients telling their therapists, "I would rather be a sex addict than a homosexual." Some sex-addiction therapists, especially those who have a religious influence in their work, explicitly state that homosexuality is not an "authentic" identity, particularly for those who do not want it. Calling such sexual interests a "same-sex attraction" and an "acting out" of the client's sexual addiction, these therapists then treat the client as a sex addict and send him to Sexaholics Anonymous, which is overtly antigay. This type of sex addiction treatment becomes, at times, the new reparative therapy, which is widely considered unethical and, in some states, illegal. It might be coming from a well-intended therapist; however, it is still treating same-sex attractions as pathology rather than exploring the various ways sexual orientation can manifest. It does not help gay or bisexual men come out of their shame into their true sexual identity.

There can be cultural reasons to maintain that being sick and a sex addict is better than being a gay or bisexual man. I have had clients who are clearly homosexual, but because of their culture—such as Arab or Indian—cannot come out and never will. (See Chapter 7.) I never tell these clients that they are sex addicts or can change from gay to straight, or that they should manage their feelings because they are sick. Instead, I help them to accept that they are homosexual but they don't have to embrace the "gay lifestyle" or a gay identity. It is their choice. This supports a position of sexual strength and health rather than pathology or sickness that keeps them ashamed.

Clients come into therapy with many issues around sex. We need to help them manage their issues through a lens of appreciating their sexuality as part of themselves. It is important to understand sexual health and not label everything as "sexual addiction" or "out-of-control sexual behavior." For example, understood in the context of the gay culture, when a gay man first comes out he often experiences a period of hypersexuality—a delayed gay adolescence, which is completely normal. It is inaccurate to label him a sex addict, as he would be labeled in the sexual-addiction model. Many straight men enjoy watching gay porn, and this speaks to the sexual fluidity of many straight men. Without a therapist understanding sexuality, it can be easy to pathologize such behavior.

If It Isn't Sex Addiction, Then What Is It?

Problematic sexual behavior (PSB) is a *sexual health problem* in which an individual's consensual sexual urges, thoughts, and behaviors lead to troublesome consequences. "Consensual" rules out pedophilia, rape, or other sexual violence. "Sexual health problem" rules out mental illnesses such as bipolar disorder, borderline personality disorder, and various antisocial personality disorders.

Looking at consequences is the only rational way to evaluate how problematic a sexual behavior is. Having strong sexual interests is not necessarily problematic. Neither is having a lot of sex. Neither is having unusual sexual interests and behaviors, as long as nobody gets hurt by them.

Instead of looking at problematic sexual behavior as sexual addiction, I view it through the lens of a person being troubled by *out-of-control sexual behaviors* (OCSB), which is the phrase I prefer. Sometimes, a person's sexual behavior is truly compulsive and difficult to control, despite the consequences. Sometimes, it is "trauma reenactment" that can be treated by psychotherapy. However, a person can have strong sexual interests without there being a problem. A person who really likes something may simply want to do it.

You as a therapist may not be comfortable with a client's sexual interests, and even clients might not be comfortable with their sexual interests and may be experiencing consequences that are causing problems in their lives and in their relationships. However, there may be nothing inherently unhealthy about their sexual interests.

Client and their partners may just be (sexually) incompatible as a couple. Or religious beliefs may put clients at odds with their sexual interests. Or clients may feel that their sexual interests will be a threat to their relationships.

Some people really like sex. They have a "high sex drive." When would we (or should they) decide they are engaging in PSB? Put plainly, wanting or having lots of sex is not a disorder, as long as the consequences are not destructive. High-sex-drive people do not necessarily suffer from a psychological problem.

The issue of consequences has many layers. Legal consequences cannot be ignored. In places where sodomy is illegal, couples engaging in anal sex must consider the trouble they might get into, even though anal sex in itself isn't unhealthy. Social consequences may also be a factor. Being gay is still socially unacceptable in many subcultures of the United States, and being out can have consequences, even though there is nothing wrong with being gay. Personal consequences include risk of disease, spending too much money, spending too much time, or otherwise harming yourself, without directly harming anyone else. It goes without saying that any behavior that harms others is unhealthy and must be stopped. How long should a person be allowed to put only himself or herself at jeopardy before an intervention is called for? This question has no easy answer.

One final point: No matter how unusual a sexual fantasy might be, it is not automatically "problematic." Problems are defined by consequences, and only behaviors have consequences. Yes, individuals, society, the law often define "problematic sex" by type or category, but this is not psychologically justified. Even so, to protect yourself, you should keep in mind that behavior that seems to you to be "obviously innocent" may get your clients into trouble with their neighbors or the law. After all, until recently (and in many places still today), being gay was a crime.

What Is OCSB?

Therapists Douglas Braun-Harvey and Michael Vigorito (2015) use the phrase *out-of-control sexual behavior* (OCSB) to capture the sexual behavioral issues of clients who want to do one thing while doing another and experience a feeling of being out of control as a result. OCSB is offered as an alternative concept to "sexual addiction."

OCSB puts the emphasis on what the individual wants. OCSB does not commit itself to a (rigid) addiction model. It focuses on the point of view of a client who comes to see a therapist with concerns that his sexual behavior feels "out of control." (Such clients often come in claiming they are sex addicts, or at least they fear they are.) The therapist works as a partner with the client to develop a reasonable plan to make things better. OCSB rejects the idea that treatment should be imposed on the client by an outside "authority," as is the case with some sexual addiction treatment programs.

OCSB represents a perspective in the therapeutic community to stop being sex negative, to focus on problems people are actually having and stay away from moral and religious rules and regulations. Being gay isn't bad; masturbating isn't bad; porn isn't bad; BDSM isn't bad. Calling these behaviors "bad" is essentially a moral judgment, and we therapists want to focus on the practical problems people are having, not moral theories.

It is very common for certain types of people to *think* they have OCSB even when an outside observer might not reach that conclusion. By our definition of OCSB, these people do have OCSB, because their sexual behaviors are troubling them. These individuals are often characterized by their *attitude* toward sexuality. They tend to share some of the following characteristics: They are religious, have negative attitudes about porn, are judgmental about (their own and other people's) sexual morality, are more depressed, have substance abuse problems, are more prone to sexual boredom, and have naturally high sex drives. I see in my clients with OCSB significant shame, especially sexual shame. They usually have a lack of accurate sex education and commonly fight their natural sexual desires, especially fetishes and kinks.

My gay clients who are in their "gay adolescence" (Stage 5 of coming out; see Chapter 7) are often suffering from OCSB because they are so eager to enjoy their natural gay sexuality after denying it for so long. A male adolescent's inability to control his sexual behavior might be expected because of his adolescent impulse-control issues and the newness of sex for him and his inexperience with it. If an older man is obsessed with sex, then his behavior might lead him to conclude that he has OCSB. However, newly out gay men will often focus excessively on sex, even if they are older. Gay adolescence usually transitions into more mature sexual behavior within a few years.

A client's sexual behavior is "out of control" only if he decides it is. You might suspect that he is exhibiting OCSB, but that is a conversation to have with him and to explore why. Again, getting into trouble around sex doesn't necessarily mean your client is at fault. The trouble might be circumstantial, not inherent. It could be grounded in religion, culture, or the tastes of the people around them. Any of these things can create conflict for them, but it doesn't mean there's something wrong with them.

On the other hand, if a client is constantly putting himself at risk with his sexual behavior, and regrets it but can't seem to stop, then he may indeed have a problem with OCSB.

The Case of Colin and OCSB

I recently had a client, Colin, who came to consult with me about his "sexual addiction." He was ashamed because he enjoyed what he called "compulsive masturbation" and looking at pornography of men with big penises. He had been working with a series of therapists who told him in no uncertain terms that his masturbation was compulsive. They said that he ought to want to express his sexuality in a loving, committed relationship. He wasn't in such a relationship (they said) because of his "addiction." His therapists had recommended 12-step groups for sex addicts, and he had dutifully attended these groups.

Colin: Clinical Interpretation and Treatment

When I asked Colin if being in a loving, committed relationship was what he wanted, he responded, "Shouldn't that be what I want?" I replied that he should want whatever *he* wanted. He had a full social life and very close friends. He had a prior partner of 10 years whom he loved, but it didn't work out, though they remained friends. He was neither yearning for another partner nor excluding the possibility. I asked him to consider whether masturbation and fantasy were actually what he wanted.

When I was a sex-addiction therapist, I would have pushed someone like Colin to wonder why he was "avoiding" relationships, and I would have attempted to convince him that his compulsive masturbation was interfering with his life. I would have directed him to 12-step programs to stop the masturbation, to work on dating and finding himself a partner.

I would have examined his childhood with him for sexual, physical, and emotional abuse. Anything we found would have been explored as possibly contributing to his "addiction." We would have come up with nonsexual ways he could self-soothe to make it easier for him to give up masturbation. If Colin had continued to masturbate, in my role as a sex-addiction therapist I would have been forced to conclude that he was "slipping" and "relapsing" and never "recovering" until he stopped.

However, my approach to help Colin was different from this. I examined with him—from his point of view and his values—whether or not *he* felt his sexual behavior was compulsive and interfering in his life. In fact, he told me that he enjoyed what he was doing. He was open to the possibility that someday someone special might come along, but a relationship was not high on his list of needs. He had assumed it should be, because that's what his sex-addiction therapists had told him.

Colin and I did talk about his past to see what parts might be driving how he expressed his sexuality—not assuming we'd find something pathological, but rather just for understanding. Using the perspective of OCSB, even if Colin's masturbation and porn use could have been linked to childhood neglect or abuse, I still would not have labeled his sexual behavior a problem unless he thought it was one himself.

I encouraged him to let go of any shame that he had about how he enjoyed himself. I didn't say he had to be in a relationship. I didn't try to move him in any particular direction. This was very different from my training as a sexual addiction therapist, in which I was taught to push the client toward "relational sexual health."

All of us have threads from our childhood that influence our sexual desires, fantasies, and behaviors. You have an opportunity to learn to play with your sexuality and claim it as your own rather than fighting it throughout your life.

Confusing Fetishes With Compulsive Sexual Behavior

"I keep going back to this same thing over and over again. I try to stop, but I can't stop. I can't control it," reports your client. This is what might be called a compulsion: an interest or behavior with failed attempts to stop, spending more and more amounts of time engaged with it, wanting it more and more. But this pattern also captures any hobby or profession that becomes more and more engrossing, from watching football to playing video games. Many of the young scientists and engineers I've interviewed have been utterly consumed by their profession, spending almost all their time on it, often neglecting other important things in their lives. But sex is less respectable in our society than science or engineering.

Expressing your natural sexuality is not necessarily unhealthy, and "trying to stop" something so fundamental to your nature is bound to fail. As the late psychologist Jack Morin famously summarized, "If you go to war with your sexuality, you will lose, and end up in more trouble than before you started" (1996). Fetishes can feel especially like compulsions; their pull is so strong. But most fetishes are harmless. The harm comes from fighting your own sexual nature. If you are at odds with your sexuality, fighting it will contribute to your grief around it.

Clients may be turned on by spanking, and may be spending too much time and money on their computer with spanking porn. The problem is not the fact that they are turned on by spanking, which they cannot change. The problem is the time and money that they need to manage more effectively. If they are struggling with a psychological compulsion—perhaps they are reenacting childhood trauma—then they may need therapy to give them control over the compulsion. But being turned on by spanking is inherent to their sexuality. When they have successfully completed therapy and can now manage their time and money, spanking will still turn them on. This remains true even if they never look at porn again.

A celibate priest is still a sexual person, merely one who has chosen to not act with respect to his sexuality.

Some "authorities" and leaders of the sexual addiction community have an extreme overreaction to fetishes. They say things like, "All violence is bad and must be stopped" in response to the mildest forms of BDSM play. I take the position that nonstandard sexual tastes are not necessarily bad. Men are especially likely to have fetishes (20 times more likely than women). How you're wired, what you're into . . . it may be nonstandard, but it's not necessarily bad.

Childhood Sexual Abuse: Trauma Reenactment Versus Trauma Play

There are several important points to make about the consequences of childhood sexual abuse.

First, childhood sexual abuse can be a significant trauma that a person carries as a heavy burden into adulthood. An abused person may have a compulsion to act out sexual scripts that reflect the abuse, even if he has "forgotten" that he was abused. This unconscious process is sometimes summarized as "turning trauma into orgasm." Until the source of the trauma is resolved, the sexual reenactments never end. In other words, unresolved childhood sexual abuse can lead to compulsive sexual behaviors. The adult abused as a child often requires psychotherapy to break the control that the compulsion has over his life.

Second, when a man abuses a boy who is straight, the boy sometimes grows up to feel a compulsion to have sex with men, even though he is not gay or bisexual. I discuss this situation at length in my book *Is My Husband Gay, Straight, or Bi?* (Kort & Morgan, 2014). When the trauma of the abuse is resolved in therapy, the straight man is no longer drawn to sex with men. He was not gay or bisexual. Being abused cannot change a straight boy's orientation, but when the straight man is drawn to want sex with men, he is often confused and thinks he may be gay or bi.

Third, a boy who is gay may be damaged by abuse. When the abused boy grows up, the gay man must deal both with the trauma-induced compulsion to act out sexually with men and also his own gay sexual nature. This confusion can significantly prolong his coming-out process.

Therapy is generally required to resolve the trauma of sexual abuse, whether the man is gay, bi, or straight. Many men who come to my office for treatment of OCSB learn that the origin of their compulsion is in childhood sexual abuse. Whether he is gay, bi, or straight, the man has been damaged by the trauma of the abuse, but his inherent orientation has not been changed by it.

Gay men are taught early on not to be intimate with each other, let alone be open to their families or classmates. Abuse that begins early in a gay boy's life leaves him extremely susceptible to intimacy issues.

Sexual abuse can shape fantasies, but that's not necessarily something that has to change. A client of mine suffered sexual abuse when he was a child. It had been perpetrated by his best friend's father. The man was significantly hairy, and now, as a direct result of the abuse, my client was into hairy guys. And that's okay. Yes, the father of his best friend should never have abused him, and there were negative consequences that my client had to deal with in therapy. But being into hairy guys was not one of the consequences that needed to—or could be—changed.

One final point: There's a body of published research that shows "abused" and "traumatized" don't always go together. Not everyone who has been sexually abused is traumatized by the abuse. I'm not saying, of course, that abuse is a good thing, only that people differ in the damage they experience from potentially traumatic events. Abuse might affect your sexual taste and at the same time not drive your behavior. But taste doesn't require therapy; only behavior does.

Some gay men have told me that they liked parts of their childhood sexual abuse with adult men. They say, "This was my first sexual experience, and I enjoyed it." Early in my career, I was very surprised and in disbelief. I spent many years confronting my gay clients when they said this. I insisted that they couldn't have enjoyed it, because it was all bad and all abuse. Over time, I've learned from my clients and my training that there are parts of childhood sexual abuse that people sometimes enjoy, and I cannot take that away from them. So, I've moderated my response to my clients who say this, and I'm telling you, the therapist, because I want you to tell your clients not to feel ashamed if they reflect back on their childhood sexual abuse and say, "You know, there were parts of it I liked." Tell them, "That's normal. It's okay. It makes sense. It doesn't mean that you liked the abuse. It means that parts of the abuse were your first sexual experience."

The Case of Walt: A Gay Boy Abused

Walt, a gay man, was arrested for public indecency after flashing an undercover police officer in a public restroom. In therapy, he told me that he had been doing this throughout his adult life. He also disclosed that he wasn't happy with his partner.

Even though he was in a committed relationship, Walt had frequented rest areas and restrooms in malls and airports without his partner, Zack, knowing about it. Because he preferred cruising to spending time with Zack, he assumed their relationship was over.

Walt: Clinical Interpretation and Treatment

During our work together, I suggested that his sexual behavior in public might be the root of his problem, and his relationship with Zack might be salvageable. Despite his unhappiness, Walt defended his compulsive sexual behavior. He enjoyed the risk, as well as the novelty, of sex with the new men he met.

In exploring his childhood, Walt recalled his grandfather giving him a bath at the age of 6. The grandfather washed Walt's penis and scrotum for an unusually long time. Finally, Walt asked, "Why are you doing that?" His grandfather said his penis was dirty and needed extra attention. Walt dried off, dressed, and went downstairs to tell his grandmother, who dismissed the whole issue. Walt never tried to discuss the incident with his parents at all, but he knew something was wrong. His mother had never washed him that way. His grandfather had done something bad to him. Walt didn't know what it was called; at 6 years old, he didn't have the concepts or vocabulary to talk about being sexually groped. But what his grandfather had done bothered him at the time, until he "forgot" about it.

He was left without any resolution. He had needed validation: someone to tell him that what his grandfather had done wrong and that Walt had done the right thing when he told his grandmother about it. His grandfather should have felt fear, shame, and anxiety about what he had done. Instead, Walt took those emotions on himself and lived with them.

After he grew up, he frequented public bathrooms and rest areas. He jerked off with strangers and enjoyed oral sex through glory holes. Only quick, anonymous sex interested him. He didn't want to meet men online, in bars, or in clubs.

I helped him understand the connection: His grandfather had molested him in a bathroom. Now, his unconscious—having received no resolution to the trauma—was "telling about it" through his compulsive sexual behavior in bathrooms.

Walt eventually told Zack about his arrest and about what he had learned in therapy. Zack tried to help Walt by being creative. They put up a drywall "stall," drilled a glory hole, and engaged in oral sex. For a while, this private glory hole—and the legal charges hanging over his head—helped Walt resist his urge to cruise. He and Zack began to work on their relationship with me, while Walt explored his compulsive sexual behavior.

But he didn't want to look very closely at what his grandfather had done, other than to accept that it had happened and that it was linked to his public sexual behavior. He wanted to "move on." I strongly encouraged him to look at the abuse more closely to help resolve it.

I was running a group for men who'd been sexually abused and who were having problems with sex. Walt declined to join the group, saying that individual therapy and periodic couples therapy with Zack were enough. Walt had stopped seeking sex in public bathrooms, and he now felt that he had been "cured."

But after a while, the glory hole in his basement no longer gave him enough pleasure. After his legal hassles cleared, his urge for bathroom sex returned. He told me that despite the risk, he wanted to keep on cruising rest areas and bathrooms, because "it brings me joy."

When he finally agreed to join the group, Walt responded to my challenges and admitted he was in total relapse. He began working harder on his recovery and his relationship. Ultimately, he became internally motivated. He could take charge of his life without needing the external threat of possible legal consequences.

Is It OCSB or Something Else?

Clinicians need to know how to differentiate out-of-control sexual behavior from Stage 5 of coming out, when LGBTQ individuals date and experiment sexually. If Stage 5 persists for too long (more than 2 to 3 years), OCSB may be an issue. Sexual abuse can also prompt victims to reenact their abuse, and you must learn to recognize this as well. In some cases there may be overlap, causing a dual diagnosis of sexual abuse and OCSB, as well as Stage 5 behavior. And finally, heterosexually married gay men often are compulsively sexual, as they hide their orientation and try to keep it suppressed. Once they come out to their wives and integrate a gay identity, they no longer display sexually compulsive behavior.

Therapists can also explain to their clients that OCSB is not, in fact, about sex at all. It is about re-creating unresolved childhood trauma involving emotional, physical, or sexual abuse or neglect in the erotic arena. Compulsive sexual behavior is, by definition, behavior the client engages in despite not wanting to—just as trauma is something the child is forced into against his or her will. In other words, the acting out is a "return to the scene of the crime," and the psyche believes this time there can be resolution through sex.

Sometimes, clients speak with pride about their sexual escapades and affairs. Others need to talk about it in detail in every session to reduce the shame and allow you to help them. It is easy for clinicians to have negative reactions and judgments about such behavior, but the job of the clinician is to listen to the suffering under the sexual acting out and help clients get in touch with it themselves.

Bathhouses

Gay bathhouses are places gay men go to have anonymous sex. Bathhouses may contain gym equipment, swimming pools, and steam rooms, but they are hardly used for that. Mostly, gay men pay an admission price to get a locker or a private room; they then walk around wearing towels around their waists and cruising each other. Some sex acts occur in the open, some in groups, and others in the private rooms. Men in the rooms keep the door ajar so onlookers can look inside. If mutual interest exists, the man enters the room and they engage in sexual acts.

Going to the baths requires few to none of the social skills that flirting or forming an attached relationship necessitates. Within the baths or other areas where cruising is common, few rituals are predictable and expected.

Most interestingly from a cultural perspective, bathhouses are acknowledged and frequented in gay culture, yet there is a stigma attached to those who admit to or are seen as frequenting them. As openly acknowledged as going to bathhouses seems to be—even among straight people (singer Bette Midler admitted to having performed at bathhouses with Barry Manilow before they made it big)—it's impolite to talk about at parties, and when dating, many (if not most) gay men will never admit to going. I've heard both clients and friends tell me that they'd never date a man who goes to the baths, even though they may have gone themselves. Those who admit to going are generally judged as promiscuous and talked about in negative ways.

For this reason, most of your clients won't admit to going to bathhouses. But simply adding this to the list of questions you ask about their sexual history will help them relax and realize you're at least knowledgeable and willing to discuss it.

I encourage clinicians to withhold any negative judgments about the baths until they've gathered all the information. It may be a healthy, legal outlet for some gay men—particularly older ones—to express their sexual needs.

A Few Dos and Don'ts

When asking LGBTQ clients about their sexual practices, don't assume anything. This is a good rule to have with any clients, yet it can be difficult to do. Here are some of the dos and don'ts I recommend:

- Don't assume that there are sexual problems just because the client is coming to see you.

- Don't assume penetration exists for gay or lesbian couples. Don't assume it doesn't, either.
- Don't use language just to impress your clients. Use informed language to show them they can trust you and tell you things you might already understand.
- Don't assume that because there is a lot of sexual talk, particularly for gay men, that it is pathological. Remember that gay men lead with sexual interests, especially in the context of dating.
- Don't assume everything an LGBTQ client struggles with is related to covert cultural sexual abuse or homophobia. The client's issues could be issues that affect straight individuals and couples as well.

CHAPTER 10

Working With Today's Lesbian and Gay Couples

What does a lesbian bring on a second date? A U-Haul!
What does a gay man bring on a second date? What second date?
—Popular joke in the gay and lesbian community

This joke has much truth to it. But it also reflects the stereotypical behaviors of men and women in general. Women tend be more relational and men tend to be less so. In gay and lesbian relationships, there is a "doubling" of the qualities traditionally associated with that gender, making lesbian couples more likely to move quickly toward intimacy (Slater, 1995) and male couples likely to hold back romantically and not make themselves vulnerable to other males (Greenan & Tunnell, 2003).

Many therapists who work with gay and lesbian couples say that "a couple is a couple." These well-intended therapists are trying to say that they are not prejudiced toward these couples and would treat them like any other. But ignoring the impact of gender-role traits among gay and lesbian couples does a disservice to them and ignores the specific issues these couples need to work on. Believing that a couple is a couple is a covert form of homophobia and heterosexism as well as a microaggression, because it diminishes or disregards the unique issues—positive and negative—that gay and lesbian couples face.

At the same time, however, surprising similarities do exist between heterosexual and gay and lesbian couples. It's as important to keep these in mind as it is to remember what makes each of these relationships unique.

It is also important to remember that although gay men and lesbians face many of the same prejudices and challenges, there are critical differences between gay male relationships and lesbian relationships. This chapter debunks some common myths about gay and lesbian relationships and explores the common differences and similarities between straight, gay, and lesbian couples.

Common Myths

There are several common myths about gay and lesbian relationships that many people—including therapists and even gays and lesbians themselves—buy into. Conducting therapy without challenging these ideas can lead to problems.

Male/Female Roles

Although some lesbian couples maintain strict "butch/femme" relationships, most gay and lesbian couples do not. It is a myth that one person plays the "male" role and the other the "female" role. All couples—straight and lesbian and gay—tend to think of one person having traditional "female" energy and the other "male" energy. Today's straight couples are abandoning the need to be in traditional male and female roles; they are realizing that each person should do what he or she does best without worrying if it's masculine or feminine. In this way, they are catching up to what gay and lesbian couples have been doing all along.

Isolation

Many people assume that all gay and lesbian couples live in isolation from friends and family. But studies have shown that this assumption is a misconception. These studies showed that gay and lesbian couples "develop caring, supportive networks of family and friends" (Chernin & Johnson, 2003, p. 117). That said, there are places—especially areas that are more conservative or religious and where gay communities are mostly invisible—where this may not be the case. It is up to the clinician to assess how isolated the couple is or is not.

Today with social media outlets such as Facebook, Twitter, Instagram, and so many more, gay and lesbian couples are becoming increasingly visible. The legalization of gay marriage has brought much more attention to these couples, and many have chosen to be more public, ending much of the isolation.

What Makes Gay and Lesbian Couples Different From Heterosexual Couples

There are few, if any, differences reported in relationship satisfaction between heterosexual couples and lesbian and gay couples. Both heterosexual couples and lesbian and gay couples face a variety of common issues that can cause problems, including children, sex, money, communication, family of origin, conflict resolution, and balancing work with personal commitments. And like straight couples, lesbian and gay couples enter relationships with the initial infatuation stage of romantic love, go through the power struggle when the romance and honeymoon wear off, and then enter the final stage of real love.

What is unique to gay and lesbian couples is that LGBTQ people are taught throughout their lives that they will never be able to find a relationship, and that if they do, it will not endure. As a result, when gay men or lesbians find romance, they tend to cling to it more than heterosexuals do. When these couples experience differences and conflicts, they may interpret it as confirmation that society is right and that gay and lesbian relationships are doomed to fail. Unfortunately, many people leave their relationships prematurely based on this misinformation.

In a society that sees most relationships—gay and straight alike—as disposable, lesbian and gay relationships are seen and treated as even *more* disposable. Lesbian and gay couples are not often asked about their relationships, and if they are, the question is, "Are you still with that person?" The implication is that gay and lesbian relationships do not last. Lesbian and gay relationships *can* and *do* last, but as Berzon has written, "there is a tradition of failure among these couplings" that is expected both by outsiders as well as by the couples themselves (2004, p. 16).

Gay marriage is changing all of this. It is much less likely that someone will ask you if you are still with a married partner than if you were simply dating or even in a long-term unmarried relationship.

Relationship Satisfaction

For 40 years, John Gottman, a well-known marital psychologist, has worked with heterosexual couples and, in the last two decades, with gay and lesbian couples too. His work is research based; he brings couples to a "love lab"—essentially, a pleasant bed-and-breakfast—and videotapes them and monitors their heart rates and perspiration levels (measuring stress and anxiety) while they interact with one another.

In his work with Robert Levenson, Gottman showed that gay and lesbian couples have some advantages over their heterosexual counterparts (2004). To determine why relationships succeed or fail, Gottman and Levenson assessed 21 gay and 21 lesbian couples over 12 years, directly observing their expressions and tones of voice, conducting interviews and asking for self-reports, and videotaping the partners interacting. They compared these data to a "control" group of 42 straight couples. All the couples researched had been together at least 2 years.

Gottman and Levenson found that gay couples were comparable to heterosexual couples in the quality of relationships—reporting the same happiness and satisfaction. Interestingly, gay couples weren't as jealous as their straight counterparts. The study showed that two gay men can often admire another male and comment on how attractive he is with neither person taking it personally or feeling threatened. Both partners usually looked at the third man in appreciation rather than comparing him to themselves. Conversely, in my experience with heterosexual couples I've treated, women often feel as though their male partners, by commenting on another woman's good looks, have literally cheated on them.

Additionally, Gottman and Levenson found that same-gender couples were much better at talking openly and honestly about their sex lives. In an article by Mubarak Dahir (2001) in *The Windy City Times*, Gottman was quoted as saying that he had "no idea" what heterosexual couples were talking about when they discussed lovemaking. (I believe this distinction arises because the gay community is forced into focusing primarily on the sexual aspect of their lives.) When two people of the same gender are a couple, they have the same orgasmic reactions, timing, and sensations. Heterosexual couples, being opposite gendered, have less understanding of each other and function differently.

Gottman and Levenson also found that in the face of adversity, gay and lesbian couples were much more optimistic. When addressing conflicts between them, they used more humor and affection. In my own practice, I've noticed that lesbian couples generally hug each other before leaving my office at the end of a session. I've learned from that, and I encourage gay male couples to do the same. At the very least, one will crack a joke, and both will laugh—which can be just as effective. They leave in a connected way. I have not seen or been able to get heterosexual couples to do this after a heated session nearly as often.

Commonalities Between Lesbian and Gay Relationships

There are several commonalities between gay and lesbian relationships that set them apart from heterosexual relationships. Understanding these similarities will help you conduct more informed, effective therapy with your gay and lesbian couple clients.

Coming Out, Relationally

Both gay men and lesbians face new obstacles when they begin a relationship with someone of the same sex. It's easier to be gay and single than to be gay and partnered—particularly if you are not out or are in the early stages of the coming-out process. When partnered, gay men and lesbians must take a stand on how they feel about going forward toward another level of coming out—a relational one. Whatever they might have done to keep their homosexuality less visible now becomes more problematic, involving hiding or removing one's partner from important social situations. If they choose to be honest and overt about their relationships, they face more obstacles partnered than single. Families, friends, and colleagues experience the existence of a partner as evidence of the person's lesbianism or gayness, and it may make them uncomfortable. Knowing in an abstract way that someone is gay or lesbian is one thing; seeing evidence of it—the partner—is another. It is another level of coming out for both the family and the gay or lesbian family member. Gays' and lesbians' willingness and bravery to face all of this usually comes from being in the later stages of coming out and feeling more solid and secure with their sexual identity.

Coping With Holidays

Each year as the various holidays start to approach, I ask all of my couples what they plan to do. Most straight couples say they are going to one of the partner's parents' places, or are celebrating in their own home where families and friends will visit and blend together. Gay and lesbian couples, however, often have different scenarios. Often they decide to go separately to their respective families (a consequence of internalized homophobia, addressed in the next section).

Straight therapists may miss this as an important issue. However, if a married heterosexual couple stated the same thing—that they planned to spend the holidays separately with their own families—it would be a red flag.

Although some of the problems associated with holidays are external, due to family reactions and feelings, others cut deeper and are internal, as was the case with Lisa and Paula.

The Case of Lisa and Paula

Lisa and Paula had been together for 13 years and were in couples therapy with me. Their presenting problem was a growing distance between them over differences and conflicts they were unable to overcome. During our work together, as Thanksgiving was approaching, I asked them what they were doing for the holidays. Lisa told me she was going home to her family and Paula said she was going home to hers. I knew both had families locally and questioned why they were splitting up. They said this is what they usually did and that neither had a problem with it.

I questioned why they didn't do what most other couples do—take turns going to each other's families each year so they could spend the holidays together. Although some couples prefer to separate because they do not like the partner's family, this was not the case for Lisa or Paula. They were liked by each other's families and each enjoyed them as well.

However, although the couple was out to Lisa's family, they were not to Paula's family. In my early intake assessment I had asked them if Paula was out to her family, and she told me she thought her family knew she was lesbian and they were a couple but they had never declared it openly. She said, "We use the 'don't ask, don't tell' method." The couple suspected Paula's family knew but Paula felt it did not need to be stated overtly.

So each year they went separately for the holidays. They spent nonholiday times with their families together but felt that going together on the holidays was being "in their face." In addition, both of the families expected to see them on each holiday, and both women enjoyed helping their mothers cook and get things ready.

Then, however, Lisa spoke up and said it had bothered her that they went to their families separately. Her family always wanted Paula over for the holidays and wondered why Paula would not attend. Lisa had initially protested Paula's refusal to spend the holidays with her, but Paula was insistent, so she dropped it, deciding it was nothing to make a big deal about, as Paula seemed so troubled by it.

My questioning brought this issue back to the surface. Paula became angry toward me for "raising an issue that was not a problem" between them. But I disagreed. It was a covert form of internalized homophobia and I felt it needed to be addressed.

Paula started crying, saying that as the only daughter in an Italian Catholic family, she felt like a disappointment to her family, especially to her mother. She did not want to put her homosexuality in her mother's face. She knew it hurt Lisa but believed that Lisa could tolerate the hurt more than her mother could.

Lisa and Paula: Clinical Interpretation and Treatment

I educated both women about internalized homophobia among couples and explored whether this was an expression of that. Both denied that this was an issue and stated that it did not *harm* their relationship because they had both agreed for it to be this way. I stated that I believed it *did* harm the relationship in subtle ways. I told them that the message they were giving to themselves as a couple and to their families was that they were not "really" a couple and that they could operate as singles at will and not be affected. I asked them to imagine their heterosexually married relatives doing the same.

Lisa defended Paula, telling her that it was okay that they went their different ways over the holiday. I stated that although it *might* be okay, I was not so sure. I kept pressing the issue a bit more, especially after learning that Lisa was not okay with this arrangement from the beginning.

I gently asked them—particularly Paula—if I could pursue this holiday issue with them, as I was concerned it might be part of the distancing problem within the relationship. I stated that even if they separated only on holidays, their refusal to declare their relationship verbally and behaviorally would inevitably affect their relationship.

I then suggested to Paula that this might be more a question of individuation within her family. It turned out that Paula was still in a child role with her mother. I told Paula that I thought her loyalty was more toward her family of origin than toward her partner and explained how this would weaken the bonds of intimacy with Lisa. This angered Paula immensely, and she accused me of making a bigger problem out of this than it was. I told her I was trying to prevent it from becoming a bigger problem than it could be for her relationship. Over time it would degrade their bonds and intimacy by neglecting times where couples reromanticize and bond more deeply with family. I then turned to Lisa and addressed her codependency on the issue and identified how she enabled this detachment between them by not being consistent with her feelings about the holidays.

The issue that then came forward was that Paula *did* have internalized homophobia in terms of identifying herself overtly as a lesbian and in a lesbian relationship. This was connected to her developmental stage of identity and attachment issues with her mother. Paula knew her mother did not want to have to face her lesbianism in an overt way, so Paula remained quiet about it.

I educated both Lisa and Paula about the covert and negative ways in which their behavior harmed their relationship. Not identifying overtly as a couple minimizes the attachment to one's partner and keeps it from growing into a healthy adult relationship. For Paula, addressing this would mean bringing up the subject with her mother and tolerating her mother's disappointment and possible rejection—a developmental task of individuation that she had not completed. The reward would be going from child to adult and having a healthier relationship with her partner.

This delayed developmental task was Paula's to undertake. In the end, she did decide to sit down with her mother one-on-one and tell her that she was a lesbian and that she would be celebrating the holidays with Lisa from now on, which meant that they'd spend one year with one family, and the next year with the other family. They both cried. Paula's mother said she'd known this day would come. She had wanted to initiate it herself but thought that Paula did not want to discuss it. She thought that because Paula did not bring it up, it must be taboo. Paula was shocked, as she had thought the same with her mother.

As this case shows, initiating conversation about the holidays can be an effective way to tease out internalized homophobia within the couple.

Couples' Internalized Homophobia

In Chapter 2, I discussed how to identify internalized homophobia in LGBTQ individuals; here, I will talk about how it manifests in couples. Missing the internalized homophobia among same-sex couples can cause prolonged time in therapy or, at worst, remove any chance of success in helping the couples at all.

Most couples don't enter therapy saying that they need to work on their own internalized homophobia as a couple. It is your job as the therapist to identify it, assess it, and help them address it. The following list, adapted from Kleinberg and Zorn (1998), outlines how internalized homophobia manifests, sometimes in subtle ways, in gay and lesbian couples.

- Couples don't identify as gay or lesbian even after they've been in a committed same-sex relationship for years.
- Couples hide their relationship even when it's objectively safe to be out.
- Partners avoid public displays of affection even when it's safe to do so.
- Couples believe that others would never accept them as a couple.
- Couples don't announce their anniversary to close straight friends because they believe anniversaries aren't as "important" for gay and lesbian couples.
- Partners avoid taking their partner to family gatherings.
- Partners use the term "I" instead of "we" when discussing events attended with the partner.
- Couples fail to recognize their partnership as a family.
- Partners criticize their partner for looking too effeminate or butch.
- Partners take on too much personal responsibility for relationship problems, stemming from the belief that gay and lesbian relationships cannot survive.

The previously discussed case of Paula and Lisa illustrates several of the issues outlined in this list. Pinpointing these forms of internalized homophobia was crucial to helping Paula and Lisa address their presenting problem of a distant relationship.

It wasn't until Paula directly confronted her own hesitance to acknowledge her lesbianism that the couple's relationship began to improve.

Coming-Out Stage Discrepancy

A common situation therapists will see is a couple with one partner in the later stages of coming out and the other in earlier stages. This affects many aspects of the relationship, including what the individuals call each other and how they present themselves to their families.

Lesbians and gays, on the other hand, are left to create their own names for their partners. Terms such as *partner, lover, boyfriend, girlfriend, significant other, life partner*, and *spouse* will be used by your clients.

I have found that it is diagnostically and clinically valuable to hear how gay and lesbian partners refer to their significant others. You will be able to pick up on issues such as their internalized homophobia and early stages of the coming-out process and their level of commitment or experienced commitment from their partner. Although it is important to use your clients' terminology when working with them, it is also important to know when to challenge them. For example, when I see couples who have been together for 2 or more years, have combined their incomes, are living together, are citing each other in their wills, and still are calling each other "boyfriend" or "girlfriend," I challenge these terms. We explore internalized homophobia and their stages of coming out, because terms like *boyfriend* or *girlfriend* suggest that the relationship may not be as deep as the one they have actually created.

Couples may not have thought about why they use the terms of endearment they do. In some cases, internalized homophobia and coming-out stage discrepancy may not be the issue; the couple may simply be comfortable with the word "boyfriend" or "girlfriend" and in the habit of using it.

It's up to the therapist to raise the couple's consciousness around this issue. It is also important to explore the concept of internalized homophobia with the couple and help them present themselves and their partner as a family unit.

The Case of Patrick and James

Patrick and James, ages 30 and 32 respectively, came to see me because even after 3 years together, James still didn't want to call Patrick his "partner" in front of his parents; he referred to him as a "friend." James was not out to his friends or family, nor was he out at work. He was still in Stage 3 of coming out. He knew he was gay but was not comfortable telling others. Patrick was angry because he believed that

James was either ashamed of him or did not care about the relationship enough to identify him as his partner. What made Patrick angriest was that at family gatherings, James's family would ask and talk openly about James's ex-partner, Marty, whom the family really liked. Marty, however, had never been identified as a partner either, so the family was not tuned in to being sensitive to the new partner, Patrick. When the family talked about Marty, they did it under the assumption that he was simply a friend of James's.

"Have you met Marty yet?" James's parents asked Patrick at one family gathering. "He is the nicest guy." Then, turning to James, they said, "You seemed to have so much in common with him, and his family was so nice. Why don't you bring him around more than you have recently? Patrick would probably like him too."

James insisted the problem was that Patrick was being too sensitive, but the real problem was that James was not ready to come out to the degree Patrick wanted. James came from a conservative family and knew that they would have a problem with his being gay. He also knew it would cause problems at work, where he held a high-level corporate position. He did not want to jeopardize his job by coming out.

Complicating things further was the fact that James brought his best girl friend to office parties, introducing her as his girlfriend and referring to her in place of Patrick when talking about his weekend activities. This infuriated Patrick and hurt him deeply. Both James and Patrick cried in my office about the pain they were in and how this was affecting the relationship.

"I am not asking that you come out at work and risk your fiscal success," Patrick said to James. "I am only talking about my being out as your partner at your family gatherings so people will stop talking about your ex. I mean, they don't talk about your sister's ex-husband in front of her new boyfriend!"

Patrick went on to say that he wanted to live together soon and have each other's families meet. He also wanted invitations they received to parties and other events to have both their names together, and for gifts to be given to them as a couple rather than to two individuals. Patrick's request made sense, but it seemed too overwhelming to James.

Patrick and James: Clinical Interpretation and Treatment

James was still in the early stages of coming out. I wasn't sure he'd ever achieve Stage 6—some people remain in the earlier stages of coming out for years or even for most of their lives. Patrick was out in every area of his life and wanted an open, out life with James. James had met many men and knew Patrick was the ideal partner for him, but he was highly resistant to being pushed out of his comfort zone by telling his family.

I pointed out the partners' different stages of being out and assured them that many gay couples experience this discrepancy. James needed to explore how willing he was to move into the next stage of coming out, while Patrick needed to be patient and understand how difficult this was for James. James also had to consider whether his loyalty was going to be to his family or to Patrick. James became angry at me when I said this, accusing me of being a gay-pride-flag waver who was so out that I could not understand him and the difficulty of his situation.

I was ready for this negative transference, as I have had a lot of experience with this from gays and lesbians. Earlier in my practice, I would have looked at James's resistance as nothing more than internalized homophobia. However, I have learned over the years to consider many factors along with internalized homophobia and being stuck in the early coming-out process, such as individual developmental issues, family-of-origin issues, and covert cultural sexual abuse issues.

I responded to James by saying that even if he was right about my being so out that I couldn't understand him—which he was not—he was in a position of losing Patrick if he chose to ignore Patrick's request. I identified and validated his fears about what would happen with his family. I educated him about covert cultural sexual abuse, explaining that I thought he was suppressing and postponing his trauma of growing up gay by not telling his family in order to avoid the anxiety and depression that could become activated from making Patrick a priority. There was a reason that James had spent his lifetime not telling them, and we needed to discover what that reason was. I expressed curiosity about what James thought would happen if he came out to his family, and I wondered aloud about what could be so terrible that James would actually be willing to lose Patrick in order to avoid it.

Sometimes this is not about where someone is within the coming-out process, nor about internalized homophobia. It can be about someone's racial and religious identity superseding the willingness to tell. It is typical and nonpathological to never reveal one's sexual identity if revealing it will lead to rejection and ostracizing by one's family. (See Chapter 2 on intersectional identity and LGBTQ individuals from minority families.) This was not the case with James.

James's resistance prompted the next part of their therapy, which was exploring James's identity development within his childhood. His family taught traditional values where "boys needed to be boys and girls needed to be girls." Thinking outside the box was not allowed. Once, when he was caught playing with his sister's dolls, he was shamed profusely by both his mother and father. For James, his identity imprint was inflexible, and he was at risk of losing not only his partner but also his sense of self if he did not examine this issue more closely.

I told Patrick that he could decide to leave the relationship and find someone else, but that if he loved James and chose to stay, he needed to understand and be curious about James's struggle. At the same time, James needed to look at how his position could cost him his relationship. I asked him to ask himself whether this was worth it.

Both Patrick and James were going to need to make compromises in terms of moving forward. I had James talk at length about his concerns in front of Patrick. His concerns at work were real. Although to outsiders his company claimed to be gay friendly, it was not. James had known and seen others who were overlooked for opportunities and promotions simply for being gay. Believe it or not, this is still true today for many corporations at the upper-management level. He could not change jobs or press the issue at work. Patrick asked if he would at least be willing to stop bringing his female friend to office parties, but James was not willing to do this at the time.

It took James 6 months to finally be able to choose his relationship (and himself) over his family of origin. His parents took the news very hard, as James had worried, and asked that he stay away from them for a while. Much to his surprise, James felt good about telling them, and although he was hurt by their distancing from him, he felt like he had gone from a boy to a man. The intimacy between him and Patrick deepened. After almost a year, James's family told him they were willing to see him again, but it was conditional—he couldn't bring Patrick with him. James declined, telling them he would see them with his "partner" or not at all. Ultimately, the family acquiesced and invited Patrick as well.

Partners being at different stages in the coming-out process is a very common problem for gay and lesbian couples and is something heterosexual couples, obviously, never have to address. As the case of Patrick and James illustrates, this situation is stressful for *both* partners: The person who is fully out to family and friends may feel underappreciated, and the person who is not completely out may feel pressured and misunderstood.

As a therapist, it is important to assess the stage of each partner's outness and explore how discrepancies may be causing or fueling problems in the relationship. Clinicians need to help the couple navigate through this by highlighting their personal integrity as well as their relational integrity. You must educate the couple about the importance of pacing this according to the comfort of the partner who is struggling the most with his or her level of outness. It is essential for partners to be patient and express goodwill toward each other.

The different stages of outness can feel threatening to partners. The "less out" partner may feel forced by the other and experience a lack of sensitivity to his or her difficulty. The "more out" partner may feel that his or her partner is being disloyal for not wanting to be more out and open to others, thereby limiting their freedom to be a couple in public and preventing them from going certain places together. In other words, it can look like one's partner is simply going too slow or fighting the coming-out process for reasons that do not seem to make sense on the surface. Partners' empathy for one another can get lost in their attempt to remain a couple with these stage discrepancies. This is trauma work—even if it doesn't look like it. I recommend educating the couple about the effects of covert cultural sexual abuse on lesbians and gays, both as individuals and in their relationships. This may also help them both to understand on a deeper level what is happening.

Talking about each partner's childhood history in front of their partners and relating those experiences to their particular reasons for not being out is not only helpful for you as the clinician but also helps the clients better understand each other. Reframing is helpful here as well. For instance, if one partner wants to come out more and have more visibility as a couple, it can be reframed as an invitation to deepen the intimacy within the relationship rather than being seen as a threat.

Clinicians need to separately validate each partner in front of the couple during sessions. For instance, to the partner who is more out, you might say: "Waiting for James to come around must be frustrating and remind you of the time you were more closeted and how painful that was for you." To the more closeted partner, you might say, "It makes sense that you need some time and don't want to feel rushed— you probably feel anxious about losing the support of your family and friends, and then potentially losing your relationship with Patrick on top of that."

One thing to do next would be to help each partner validate where the other is in terms of being out and the comfort level around it. In other words, the more out partner might say, "It makes sense to me that you are not out given your fears—and the real possibility—of losing your friends and family." The more closeted partner might say, "It makes sense that you want me to be more out and open about our relationship and what you mean to me, as it hurts you to feel hidden and secretive." These kinds of validation help keep the partners more connected to each other and negotiate what to do.

Additionally, clinicians should educate clients about the realities of not being an "out" couple. This weighs heavily in a negative way on the couple. Ask them to imagine the stress that would be put on a marriage if a husband or wife refused to tell his or her family about the marriage. The bottom line is that if the couple wants to remain together, the more out partner may have to live with being closeted in the way the less out partner wants, and the more closeted partner may have to decide to come out more fully and risk rejection.

Couples cannot thrive if they remain at two different stages. It is like settling for a machine's operating on a lower performance level. I understand there are valid reasons to not be out to one's employer, family, and various friends. That said, the closetedness still affects the couple even on a subtle, covert level, and the couple needs to know this and prepare for this.

I explain this to couples, saying that although the relationship may endure, the level of satisfaction will be poor *in this area*. I do not believe it is healthy for the relationship, and the relationship will suffer even on a small scale in the long run. Every couple I have worked with and know who finally are as out as they can be have told me that, looking back, they see how their lives were negatively affected by being closeted, even if the reasons were valid.

The Case of Meghan

Sharon, a psychotherapist, came to me for supervision; she was concerned that she might not be working effectively with Meghan, one her clients. Sharon believed that Meghan's partner, Carla, was narcissistic and couldn't commit to the relationship. She was trying to direct Meghan away from the relationship.

For her part, Meghan was getting increasingly anxious and angry about Carla's behavior. Carla had been heterosexually married for 13 years and was a devoted mother of two children. Meghan and Carla had been friends for years; their sons played soccer together. Two years earlier, Carla confessed she was gay and in love with Meghan. They began an affair. Then, Carla decided she had to tell her husband and get a divorce so that she could move on to a more serious relationship with Meghan.

Meghan had dated many women; two relationships had ended because the other women cheated on her. Meghan knew that Carla was monogamous during her entire marriage (until they started their affair), which gave Meghan hope that Carla could be monogamous with her. She saw Carla as having the highest level of integrity.

Carla had recently begun going to the gym and working out. She felt good about how she looked in a way she never had before. When Carla's divorce became final she expressed interest in going to the lesbian bars. Meghan did not like socializing at bars and did not want to go, but Carla insisted and Meghan finally complied. When women at the bars approached Carla and began flirting with her, she flirted back.

When Meghan commented on this, Carla denied that she was flirting—she said she was just looking and having fun. She told Meghan she was being insecure and tried to reassure her that she was not interested in other women. But after a few months, Carla made friends with some of the women who frequented the bar, and she began going out regularly without Meghan. This created more conflict between them, and their fighting increased.

Supervision With Sharon for Meghan's Treatment

Carla was clearly in Stage 5 of coming out—she was showing identity pride, enjoying her new body and the opportunity to flirt with other women. Meghan was shocked by this, as she'd never known Carla to be narcissistic or to consider herself a "player." This confused Sharon. She felt that Carla had come out 2 years earlier, when she confessed her love to Meghan. "She was out to herself before coming out to Meghan," Sharon told me. This was true, but the relationship accelerated Carla's coming-out process, moving her from Stage 3 to Stage 5 (see Chapter 7 for the stages of coming out).

This rapid progression often occurs when gays or lesbians begin relationships. In fact, it is common knowledge among gays and lesbians that one should be wary of dating someone who is just coming out. There is an awareness that the person may not be stable precisely because he or she is caught up in a "gay adolescence" and needs to "play the field." This does not make the person a player or narcissistic; it simply means that the person behaves like a teenager for a time.

Sharon had to help Meghan decide if she could tolerate Carla's Stage 5 behavior, knowing it was probably temporary. The risk was that it would last longer than Meghan could tolerate. The other risk was that during that time Carla could meet someone else and lose interest in Meghan. Even though Carla insisted she was not interested in anyone else, the inevitable Stage 5 had its grip on her, and there were no guarantees.

Eventually Meghan decided to stay attached to Carla and see where the relationship was headed. It was painful for her, and she worried constantly that Carla would eventually end the relationship. Carla understood she was in Stage 5 and that this worried Meghan, and she did all she could do to make Meghan believe she was attached and committed to her yet needed to feel some of her freedom to flirt and be social.

After 2 years of this, Carla settled down and no longer felt the surge of power of Stage 5. She became tired of the bars and games of those she had been hanging around with. To Meghan's delight, they were able to nest and settle in and deepen their relationship as a couple. They made friends with other lesbian and gay couples, and although they occasionally went to the bars, it was not because Carla felt any urgency to go.

Differences Between Gay and Lesbian Couples: The Doubling Factor

Just as heterosexual couples are different from same-sex couples in critical ways, gay male relationships are often different from lesbian relationships in important ways. Using your experience treating gay male couples as a template for treating lesbian couples—or vice versa—will compromise your ability to conduct effective therapy. As said in the beginning of this chapter, the "doubling" factor of traditional gender characteristics both complicates and helps these relationships. Therapists need to be aware of the most common characteristics that manifest in male and female couples.

Common Lesbian Relationship Dynamics

As the joke in the epigraph of this chapter plays on, lesbians tend to commit to relationships quickly and move toward a high degree of intimacy and dependency. They also are more inclined to remain friends with their former partners after they've ended the relationship.

Fusion, Merging, and Enmeshment

Much of the literature about lesbian couples focuses on the tendency toward merging, fusion, and enmeshment (Biaggio, Coan, & Adams, 2002; Slater, 1995). In many lesbian relationships, female traits are "doubled up": Both partners may have strong dependency needs, both may be focused primarily on the relationship (having been conditioned to strive toward intimacy), both may be less sexual and more domestic, both may lack differentiation, both may place a premium on togetherness and emotional closeness, both may value romantic love and monogamy, and finally, both may give minimal importance to the partner's physical attractiveness.

Many lesbians say that the fusion between two women in lesbian relationships is the closest they can get to understanding how women relate outside the world of sexism and patriarchy. Indeed, some fusion may be a normative expression of what women want—a high level of closeness and intimacy that gay male and straight couples usually cannot experience (Biaggio et al., 2002).

But such a high degree of fusion can cause problems in a relationship. One problem of fusion can be that a partner's identity is overwhelmed by the other's. It is the concept of "You and I are one, and I'm the one," or "You and I are one, and you're the one"—depending on which partner is losing her identity. Another problem of fusion is the intolerance of differences between the two. Most couples have this struggle, where one partner insists that he or she is right and concludes that the other must therefore be wrong. However, this is magnified in fused lesbian couples, leading to strong feelings of anger and contempt. Fusion brings on a highly undifferentiated couple dynamic that can burn out and destroy the relationship. What starts as a healthy attempt at togetherness becomes a nightmare of enmeshment.

Working with these couples to help them differentiate can be challenging. I have often joked with lesbians that I need to get the "jaws of life" out to separate them and to help them see that two individuals can exist within a relationship and that both can be okay with that. Lesbian couples, like all couples, need to achieve a healthy balance of togetherness and separateness and understanding of "the other." I have found this work to be more difficult among lesbian couples.

The Case of Marilyn and Sheila

Together for 2 years, Marilyn, 40, and Sheila, 43, came to me complaining about their sex life. Marilyn was convinced that Sheila was not really "into" their relationship and would return to being with men.

Indeed, Sheila had a history of dating both genders. She had been heterosexually married but was now divorced; her two teenage children were living with her. Marilyn had been out since her adolescence and never dated men. Marilyn told me that when the couple started their relationship, she had been the one who "taught Sheila about lesbian sex." Sheila agreed, stating that she hadn't known the pleasures of receiving oral sex and being stimulated by a partner's fingers as well. However, Sheila still wanted penetration from dildos, and this often created friction between them.

Marilyn had been initiated into lesbian sex by an older, experienced lesbian who taught her that lesbian sexuality did *not* include using sex toys that resembled male genitalia. Marilyn believed that Sheila's interest in vibrators and dildos—particularly ones that resembled penises—was due to her "hanging on to her interest in men" and that she was rejecting lesbian sex. Sheila stated that she was not rejecting lesbian sex or Marilyn, but that she enjoyed that type of stimulation along with oral and digital sex.

For Marilyn, the last straw came when they purchased a strap-on; while Marilyn was wearing it, Sheila performed oral sex on the dildo as if it were a "real dick." Marilyn was enraged and hurt that Sheila might be fantasizing about being with a man rather than with her. She abruptly stopped the sex act, yelling and crying about how rejected she felt: "I don't get anything out of you doing that!" she said. "I don't feel a thing!"

Sheila stated that she had no interest in being with men again but did miss performing oral sex on them. Sucking a dildo as if it were real fulfilled her oral needs.

Marilyn continued to protest that this was not lesbian sex, explaining that lesbian sex is oral and manual. She also believed that if dildos were used, they shouldn't resemble penises. She stated that she'd been out longer than Sheila and accused Sheila of being naive.

Marilyn and Sheila: Clinical Interpretation and Treatment

It became clear to me that Marilyn was engaging in maintaining an enmeshed and undifferentiated relationship. Marilyn was blocking Sheila from having her own independent sexual interests and autonomous expressions; she was trying to force Sheila into what Marilyn called "lesbian sex." To me, that seemed like a way of controlling Sheila and making her more like Marilyn.

I educated Marilyn that lesbian sex could indeed involve penile-shaped dildos if this is what they decided as a couple. Although a segment of the lesbian community intentionally chooses to stay away from anything male—especially in sex play— Sheila had the right to choose what worked for *her*. The question was why Marilyn was so focused on rigid ways of being sexual with her partner.

I had both Marilyn and Sheila engage in basic safe dialogue, with one partner actively sending information about her point of view and the other actively listening and putting her own point of view aside momentarily. Called *intentional dialogue*, this type of communication comes from the imago relationship therapy (IRT) model, which I discuss at the end of this chapter. It blocks reactivity, interruption, and interpretation and allows for clear communication using the other's point of view. As Marilyn talked about this issue, it surfaced that she didn't feel involved emotionally and physically in the sex play because the dildo was not part of her body and she could not feel it. This revelation helped Sheila reframe Marilyn's resistance to using the dildo as a reflection of her desire to be connected to Sheila rather than as a rejection of her needs.

Another tenet of IRT is to have both partners talk about what childhood experiences the issue reminds them of. Marilyn said she felt that she was being ignored— which was a childhood issue for her. As a young girl, Marilyn assumed that her receiving love depended on how she dressed and behaved—and that was now showing up in the bedroom as well.

Once made aware of this, Marilyn was able to settle down and understand that Sheila's sexuality was a statement about Sheila's sexuality; it wasn't meant as a personal statement about Marilyn. Marilyn began working on her childhood issues around receiving love, and also on allowing her partner more sexual independence.

Former Partners

It is common for lesbians to remain friends with their partners after the relationship ends. Lesbians often become such good friends with their partners that the friendship endures even if the romance and sexual part of their relationship doesn't. Additionally, lesbians frequently bond with and create primary friendships with other lesbians. Some gay men are able to do this, but it is much more commonplace for lesbians. I believe this is primarily due to gender; if men were more relational, perhaps gay male couples (and straight couples) would also be able to remain friends after the romantic love has gone. Slater postulated that "perhaps heterosexuals as a group limit this intimacy in order to avoid the jealousies, competitions, and likely threats to their couple relationships" (1995, p. 138).

After the breakup of a lesbian relationship, there is often a period of distancing so that the ex-partners can grieve. After a while they pick up the friendship and even become friends with each other's new partners. Lesbian comics joke about this phenomenon as part of being a lesbian. Kate Clinton, a popular lesbian comic, jokes about how she has a pushpin system on a wall in her home to keep track of her friends' "shifting relationships." This joke always gets the mostly lesbian crowd roaring with laughter, as they immediately recognize themselves in it. However, for partners new to being out and still coming from a heterosexist mindset, this lesbian tradition may not be so funny, as the following case illustrates.

The Case of Christine

Christine, just recently out at the age of 33, told her therapist, Carol, she was uncomfortable with a new relationship she was having. When she went out with Bernie, her partner, Bernie would sit close to her friends, put her arm around them, and kiss them hello and goodbye. Some of these friends, including Bernie's best friend, were also Bernie's ex-partners, which bothered Christine even more.

Christine found this threatening and insulting. She compared it to her past heterosexual relationships, saying that her boyfriends were never affectionate with past girlfriends in front of her and would not have tolerated her doing this with other men, either. Carol, who was straight, agreed with her that it was disrespectful. This made Christine even angrier. She went back to Bernie and told her what her Carol had said, which prompted an argument. Bernie told her that it was commonplace for lesbians to be friends—even best friends—with ex-partners, and she gave Christine some books by lesbian authors to underscore her point. Christine went back to Carol with this information, suggesting that she read the material.

Several months later Bernie went out to dinner with her most recent ex-partner, with whom she had broken up 2 years ago. When Christine discovered this, she was devastated. She became angry with Bernie and told her that she would have to stop her relationships with her ex-partners if she wanted their relationship to continue. Bernie stated that her friendships with her former partners were deep and meaningful for her. She told Christine that although she loved her deeply and wanted to continue their relationship, if it came down to choosing between her or her former partners she would choose the latter.

"I know this is a typical lesbian thing, but I don't think I can get used to it," Christine told Carol. She knew in her heart it was nothing personal—she had met other lesbians who were also friends with their ex-partners—yet she still couldn't get used to it.

Christine: Clinical Interpretation and Treatment

Carol called me for supervision, saying that she believed her countertransference was getting in the way of helping Christine. "If the guys I dated or my ex-husband had done anything like that, I would have felt insulted and provoked," she said. I told her that it made sense that she would feel this way because in the heterosexual community it is not the norm to become friends with an ex. However, for lesbians this is extremely common because of the strong relational bonds they form while together. Carol dealt with her feelings about her ex-boyfriends and ex-husband. "I would have liked to stay friends with a couple of them, actually, but they became jerks when I suggested it."

I told Carol to go back to the assessment she took of Christine and look into her childhood for signs about why she was having such a difficult time. It was likely that her distress was being caused by more than just the situation with Bernie's former partners.

When Carol asked Christine about her childhood, Christine reported that she was the oldest of five children and felt the most alienated. She did not feel liked by her mother, who fussed over Christine's more feminine sisters. Her father appreciated Christine's interest in sports but was more involved with his sons, who were just as athletic as Christine. Within minutes of beginning to tell Carol about her family, Christine was in tears.

This conversation helped Christine see that she was transferring her childhood feelings of abandonment onto Bernie. If Carol hadn't addressed her countertransference and educated herself about lesbian dynamics, she never would have identified the underlying source of Christine's pain. As she worked with Christine on her family-of-origin issues, Christine's reactivity about Bernie's friendships with former girlfriends gradually abated.

Common Gay Male Relationship Dynamics

The stereotypical gay man is thought to be sensitive, kind, emotive, expressive, and loving—more so than straight men. Women often say things like, "I wish my husband was as easy to talk with as gay men are." So it is natural for clinicians to think of gay men as more emotionally available and open. Although this may be true in terms of gay men's relationships with their family and with women in their lives, it does not tend to be the case in their romantic relationships with each other. Unlike lesbians, gay men often have difficulty showing strong emotions toward each other in committed relationships.

When two males enter into a relationship, they both bring their gender roles and socialization traits along with them. This translates into a lack—or even absence—of relational skills toward each other, as they have been socialized to disengage emotionally from other men.

Terrence Real, author of *I Don't Want To Talk About It*, said it well when he wrote about how boys are "pressured to yield attributes of dependency, expressiveness, affiliation—all the self-concepts and skills that belong to the relational, emotive world" (1997, p. 130). He went on to say that the price of traditional socialization for boys is "diminished connection to aspects of the self, and diminished connection to others" (p. 137). Given all of this, male couples have to be taught how to develop interpersonal skills, dependency, intimacy, and expressiveness.

Males—both gay and straight—are socialized to be the breadwinners and taught to be sexual predators whose conquests are cause for pride and status. Strong emotions are discouraged. This makes it difficult for men to express anger, hurt, and vulnerability in healthy ways. Consequently, conflicts in gay relationships frequently involve money, jobs, sex, jealousy, and emotional closeness.

I often feel when working with male couples like the woman in a heterosexual relationship, who has to remind her husband about the relationship and to nurture it. Of course, this is a sweeping generalization, but I find it to be true that men need to be coached on how to be in a relationship, whereas women have a head start in this area. Males don't necessarily know how to do it naturally—or at all—with each other.

The Case of Will and Richard

Will and Richard had been together for 8 years. They came to me after Will's employer offered him a job out of state. Will wanted to take the job, as it offered a large salary and the opportunity to live in a warmer and more gay-friendly environment.

Over the past 5 years Will had been offered several promotions, and his status and income went up as well. Will had always made considerably more money than Richard did, which often left Richard feeling inferior and self-conscious, despite the fact that Will did not feel this way and never gave him the impression that it was a problem.

Richard had felt awkward about the salary discrepancy throughout their relationship. Even though Richard made a six-figure income, their friends often talked more about Will's job and status and assumed the couple's homes and cars were the result of Will's job and not Richard's. Richard felt hurt each time this happened, and he would remind his friends that his money was used to pay for much of what they owned, too.

Now the couple's relationship was at a turning point: Was Will going to take this job and move out of state? If Richard moved with him, he would have to give up his job. They talked about whether Richard should stay back in case Will's new job did not work out, or if they should take the risk together as a couple.

I noticed while they talked about this in my office that they expressed little emotion and affect both toward each other and for themselves—it was as if they were going over a business deal. I commented on this, which prompted Will to cry. He turned to face Richard.

"I don't want you to feel pressured to come with me. I know you make a lot of money and enjoy your job too," Will stated.

Richard was more constrained emotionally and said, "Even though I have a good-paying job, I feel like my place is supposed to be going with you. But I want to have both. I love you and don't want to lose you or my job." After a pause, he continued, "It also bothers me that people will see me as 'the woman' in this relationship if I follow you. I know that sounds weird, but it's how I feel—especially because people are always viewing you as the breadwinner and not me, too."

"I'll let you decide whichever way you want to go with this, Richard," Will said.

Will and Richard: Clinical Interpretation and Treatment

I asked Will why he was not taking more of a stand with Richard about wanting him to come with him. I was concerned that perhaps unconsciously he did not want Richard to come. But this turned out not to be the case. "I don't want to pressure him," Will said. "I want him to come because he wants to, not because he has to."

"But Will, you have to let him know where you stand and that you really want him to come so he can make a decision with informed consent. If you don't, he may not realize how much you want him to come. If he feels pressured, that is his issue, not yours," I responded.

I asked Will to turn to Richard and tell him how he felt. Will did this, explaining to Richard that he really wanted him to join him and that he did not want to go alone. They wept together and held each other for the first time in the six visits I'd had with them. They were finally learning to open up more emotionally to themselves and each other. By having these difficult discussions about the pros and cons of all the options, they were pushing their relationship forward in a relationally mature way.

Monogamy Versus Nonmonogamy

Perhaps one of the most controversial issues for couples is whether they choose monogamy or nonmonogamy. (By nonmonogamy, I am not talking about cheating, affairs, secrets, and lies, but rather about a mutual and ethical decision on the part of the couple to have an open relationship.) This is especially an agreement for gay male relationships. Male couples are more apt to have open sexual relationships than female couples. In fact, studies show that 50% of gay male couples become nonmonogamous after passing their 5-year mark (Nimmons, 2002; McWhirter & Mattison, 1984; LaSala, 2010). Nonmonogamy is not, however, restricted only to male couples. As sociologist Helen Fisher (2004) has illustrated, as humans we are not wired for monogamy. It's a choice, as is nonmonogamy.

Many therapists assume that those in polyamorous relationships and swingers and those in sexually open relationships have some kind of attachment disorder or problem that keeps them from enjoying full intimacy; monoganormativity is seen as the top of the hierarchy in terms of a good, healthy relationship. I used to believe this as well. But after more than 30 years as a therapist, I have seen all sorts of couples able to make that arrangement work without creating problems in their relationships. Many have even become *closer* as a result of opening their relationship. Therapists must be careful not to advocate or condone monogamy or nonmonogamy; the question is what works for the couple, not what anyone else believes should or shouldn't work. That said, it's imperative to discuss the issue, as it is something your clients may face.

When you initiate the conversation about monogamy versus nonmonogamy, make sure you understand how your clients define these terms. I once had a couple who told me during the initial consultation session that they were monogamous. Several months later, they mentioned that they'd recently had a three-way. When I asked if they had they changed from monogamy, they assured me they hadn't.

I was confused. Hadn't I gotten the correct information in our initial consultation? "I thought you told me you were monogamous," I told them.

"We are," they said.

Now I was *really* confused! "But you just told me that you had a three-way."

"We did. But we only have three-ways together, and we always play together, never separately from each other." I asked what they meant by "play" and they said they only engage in sex with other people *together*—as a couple.

I slowly began to get it. Like many couples with open relationships, these men made a sharp distinction between *emotional* fidelity and *sexual* fidelity. In other words, they were emotionally monogamous but sexually open. For other couples, monogamy may mean having no sexual partners other than each other. Again, it's crucial to ask the couple to define their terms. You may discover that they don't have a mutual understanding, which is in itself diagnostic. You can then explore this issue with them.

I routinely ask couples, gay or straight, to explain their contract around sex and commitment. Do they have an assumed contract or an explicit one? I don't jump to the conclusion that every couple or individual who comes in for therapy is in an open or closed relationship, nor do I assume that they have—or haven't—talked about it.

I have found from the trainings and talks I've conducted that those who have the most negative reactions to nonmonogamy are women and single gay men. Both tend to be very judgmental about the subject. I surmise that women tend to be more relational and, therefore, function more smoothly in a monogamous relationship. This is especially true of lesbian relationships, although younger lesbians are engaging in polyamorous relationships more and more. Over the years, I've found that gay men who are not partnered or find themselves in new relationships are the most judgmental of their nonmonogamous peers. They strive to maintain the ideal of monogamy because they've been taught they should want it. But after a couple has been together for a while, many agree to open their relationship to include others.

In some cases, this may mean deciding to have three-ways; other times it might mean playing separately from each other. Some couples combine the two modes. I've also seen many gay male couples switch back and forth between monogamy and nonmonogamy; there don't seem to be any consistent patterns concerning when, how often, or for how long they do so. Whatever the couple's agreement is, responsible nonmonogamous relationships do exist, and to ignore or pathologize them with heterosexist standards across the board does clients a disservice. Watching your own countertransference and checking your own biases is crucial.

Problems can arise, however, if secrecy is involved. Nonmonogamous relationships require extra dialogue, communication, and trust. That trust is broken if cheating occurs—if an agreed-upon contract changes without one partner telling the other. I tell clients, "If you and your partner choose to have ethical nonmonogamy"—or responsible monogamy—"it's imperative that you maintain effective communication. Healthy, open, and effective communication is like an antivirus program on a computer. Without it, you risk ruining your relationship." My questions for these couples include:

- Do you sexually play separately or together?
- Define *monogamy*. What does monogamy mean to each of you?
- Is this really what you *both* want or is one of you acquiescing to keep the relationship together?
- How does it make the relationship work? Are there times when it doesn't work?

I do think, however, that there are times when couples with open relationships should be monogamous, if only temporarily. Following are a few situations in which it might be counterproductive for the relationship to be open.

- *If the partners enter therapy as a couple.* Clients who seek therapy as a couple typically have suffered some rupture in their connection, so I recommend that they remain monogamous until their issues are resolved. I always emphasize to them that nonmonogamy may *not* be the problem, but that therapy is about ruling out all possible causes of the distress. (Additionally, abstaining from outside sexual contact eliminates distractions.) Couples' reactions to this recommendation also tell me whether the subject should become an issue for treatment. For example, if they react negatively in a strong way and say something like, "We are not doing that—it is not the problem, and don't try to make it one," then I might further explore the issue with them, making sure they understand that I am not biased toward monogamy.
- *If out-of-control sexual behaviors are an issue.* Sometimes both the partner who is sexually acting out and the other partner are struggling over what constitutes sexual acting out and what doesn't. Until they figure this out, I usually recommend that they maintain monogamy until the OCSB is resolved.
- *If a couple is in the first 3 to 5 years of their relationship.* It takes that long for partners to bond to each other and establish a sense of safety, trust, and attachment. If, after the 5th year, they still want to try a nonmonogamous relationship, I

recommend that they discuss it then. This said, there are many younger couples these days, gay and straight, who are opening up their relationships within the first 2 years successfully. These couples report that they knew they wanted an open relationship from the beginning and are making it work.

Younger Gay Couples

Lowen and Spears's "The Couples Study" (2016a) notes a prevalence of nonmonogamy among gay male couples. However, a second study, "New Trends in Gay Male Relationships: The Choices Study" (Lowen & Spears, 2016b), focuses on younger men (18–20 years old) and comes to somewhat different conclusions. (See their book [Lowen & Spears, 2016c] for a summary of both studies.)

The Choices Study shows a prevalence of monogamy among young gay male couples, but the authors believe that there is no convincing data that they choose to be monogamous out of internalized homophobia. Many of the younger gay men interviewed preferred monogamy as a rational choice that would be best for their relationships. Also, younger gay couples feel that being monogamous is a socially viable option for them. Factors include marriage, children, and mainstream acceptance. It is a "choice," not an "expectation" imposed on them by the mainstream society.

Lowen and Spears speculate that younger gay people have much less internalized homophobia than older gays. Younger gay people come out earlier—many come out in high school—and they generally do not spend agonizing years in the closet. They have experienced much more acceptance from their straight peers. Thus, they are not so influenced in their choices by homophobia.

The authors draw a contrast with older gay people, for whom having multiple sex partners has been a "gay-positive" expression, defying mainstream expectations and values. They claim that mainstream expectations and internalized homophobia have more greatly influenced older gay choices in relationships.

However, the authors do not claim that younger gay couples are all committed to monogamy. They note that couples who start out monogamous may decide to be open after an average of around 7 years have passed. They also note that while younger gay couples want to avoid completely open relationships, they are willing to experiment or develop their own rules. The term *monogamish* has been coined to reflect this "mostly monogamous" philosophy.

I'm not as convinced as Lowen and Spears that younger gays are so much less influenced by internalized homophobia than older gays, but as they themselves admit, it is difficult to get definitive and convincing data on such a complex psychological and sociological topic as monogamy.

Ethical Nonmonogamy

When both partners consent to a mutually open relationship, they are practicing ethical, responsible nonmonogamy. They are emotionally exclusive and sexually open. Here, each agrees to open the relationship in ways satisfactory to both. Some partners prefer not to know about their partner's sexual behavior outside the relationship; others insist on knowing. Rules are all-important here. I've heard gay male couples say, "We only do it on vacation" or "only with people we don't know." Working this out *in advance* is imperative.

Following are guidelines for establishing rules regarding nonmonogamy:

- *Play safely.* Outside their relationships, gay men should be very cautious about STDs, and they should use condoms. Assume that everyone else is HIV positive and act accordingly. It's inappropriate and unrealistic to hope the person you're with is telling you the truth about his status—or about how recently he's been tested. Play safely, no matter what.
- *Maintain emotional fidelity.* Gay couples often report that what works best for them is to engage in encounters based on sexual attraction only, not on emotions or affection. In other words, it's about "no-strings sex and nothing more." They avoid getting to know their temporary partners on any deeper level. In this way, any sex brought into the relationship is simply behavioral in nature, not relational.
- *Maintain an open dialogue.* Effective dialogue is the best thing couples can do to ensure safety, respect, and trust.
- *Be aware of problems that can occur with nonmonogamy.* Jealousy is bound to arise at some point. I've heard partners, gay and straight, express their anxiety that their partner liked another person more, preferred sexual behavior from that other person, and so on. Resolving these problems, again, requires dialogue and safety between partners. It is our job as therapists to educate clients about these possible issues. Knowing the kinds of conflicts that an open relationship can present may help prevent some of them in the first place.
- A lot of single gay men fear they'll never find someone who wants to be monogamous because the gay community is into open relationships. Therapist Michael LaSala (2010) did research showing that 50% of gay male relationships are open. But 50% open means 50% closed. The feeling that you'll never find a monogamous gay partner is a heterosexist prejudice.
- On the other hand, the belief that all relationships *should* be monogamous is also a heterosexist prejudice. If you're judgmental about it, which a lot of single gay men are, I ask you to look at your own internalized homophobia. What's wrong with

people choosing to have open relationships? It may not be what *you* want, but if you condemn it for everyone, then that says more about you than the gay community. (I talk more about monogamy versus nonmonogamy in Chapter 6 of my book *10 Smart Things Gay Men Can Do to Find Real Love* [Kort, 2003]. See also *Opening Up: A Guide to Creating and Sustaining Open Relationships* [Taormino, 2008].)

Alan and Brad: A Story About Open Gay Relationships

As you read the following story, check out how you feel. See if you have a strong reaction, a strong tendency to take sides.

Alan and Brad were married and monogamous for 7 years, and then they decided to open it up. They created a contract between themselves that specified the rules they would follow, including a rule about falling in love. If either detected anything like love happening with anyone else, he was supposed to stop playing with that person. In an open relationship, even though the two parties are having sex with other people, it isn't "cheating" if they're following their rules.

Soon, Alan and Brad were both spending a lot of time having casual sex with random partners. After a few years, Alan became very attached to one man, Carl, and Brad felt that Alan was in love with him. Brad confronted Alan: "Our rule was to stop everything once you started to fall in love." But Alan didn't think he was in love. "It's just sex," he told Brad, "and I'm not going to stop seeing Carl."

Their disagreement over Carl festered for a while, and then they came to see me. Brad said, "I can't go on. I'm going to end our relationship if Alan doesn't end this affair with Carl." Alan protested. "I'm not having an affair. I'm not in love." Alan seemed sincere, but soon it became obvious to me as a therapist that Brad was right. Still, Alan wasn't convinced.

I worked with them for several months, and finally Alan told a story in therapy that I thought I could use to help him see what was going on. Alan had bought a gift for Carl, and he'd told Brad about it. I said to Alan, "If you and Brad were a straight couple, and you were the husband, and you were telling your wife that you bought a gift for Carla and made a special trip to surprise her with it, would you think that your wife would say, 'That's so cool. What did you get for her? What was the look on her face when you gave it to her? Was she surprised?'"

Alan said, "No, that would be preposterous."

"But that's the very thing you seemed to expect from Brad when you told him about the gift you got for Carl."

And suddenly Alan saw the light. He understood, and he agreed to end his relationship with Carl.

I always recommend a guideline for open relationships: Once there's a breach of the contract, then close the relationship so that you can repair it. Then, later, if you want to, you can reopen it, but close it for a while just to bring back the connection. Also, I recommend that if one person in the partnership feels there's been a breach, then there's a breach. They need to push the pause button to talk about it.

The story of Alan and Brad continues. In therapy with me, they dealt with Brad's feelings of hurt and betrayal over the affair. After a year, they felt okay with each other again. Their trust was restored.

Besides the particulars of the affair, while their relationship was open, they had stopped having sex with each other. They were having sex only with other people. This is one of the dangers of having an open relationship, especially between gay men. If that's a decision you've made in your relationship, that's fine. It's not pathological in and of itself. It's pathological when one (or both) of the men in the couple misses having sex with the other.

Alan and Brad decided to open up the relationship again. They were coming to see me monthly, and everything was fine between them.

This story has a striking ending. One day, Alan came home and told Brad, "I had really hot sex with this guy, Dave." Alan showed Brad Dave's picture on Grindr, and Brad said, "Oh my god, I was with that guy last month. And he *was* hot." Brad told Alan about his experience with Dave. Then, they both said almost at the same time to each other, "Wouldn't Dave be great for our friend Phil?" So they contacted Dave and set him up with Phil, who was single. And now they're all best friends, and they go on trips together.

I always say when I do training for straight therapists: "How many straight therapists in this room, and how many women, could imagine themselves in this story?" Everyone laughs, because they all know how rare it would be for a heterosexual story of open relationships to end up like this, with two happy couples going on vacation together.

I like this story, because it illustrates the rich range of possibility in open relationships. An open relationship has benefits and difficulties not found in a closed relationship, and the difficulties don't mean the relationship is over or even the openness of the relationship is over.

I started this section asking you to check out how you feel as you're reading this story. Gay men with a lot of internalized homophobia tend to have a strong negative reaction: "See, this is what happens when you open a relationship. Gay men can't control themselves, and there is always trouble." And if that's what you found yourself thinking, I want you to catch yourself.

We gay men need to depathologize our sexuality. Check your homophobia. Be open to opportunities. It's okay if you don't care for open relationships. It's another thing if you have a strong negative visceral reaction: "This is wrong for everybody!" Likely 90% of that kind of visceral revulsion is about your negative conditioning, not about whether the challenges of open relationships are worthwhile or not.

Treatment Approaches With Gay and Lesbian Couples: The Imago Relationship Model

I have found that imago relationship therapy (IRT; Hendrix, 2001) is an excellent tool in working with same-sex (and straight) couples. Most relationship models focus on differences between males and females. IRT, on the other hand, emphasizes the individual and not the gender, making this model perfect for gay and lesbian relationships.

Imago is the Latin word for "image." According to IRT, each of us assembles an imago from both the positive and negative traits of our mother, father, and any other primary caretaker we had growing up. The imago is the blueprint of the person we want in a committed, intimate relationship. Consciously or otherwise, we project this composite template onto prospective partners to see if they fit.

When working with straight couples, some therapists focus on how the wife might be projecting her issues about men onto her husband (particularly those related to her father) and how the husband might be projecting his issues about women onto his wife (particularly those related to his mother). However, IRT recognizes that it is the more dominant negative parent that is projected onto a partner, and the gender is secondary.

It is the negative traits of the dominant parent—the one who affected the client most—that begin to interfere with the relationship. I teach my clients—both gay and straight—that they'll find themselves seeking to resolve issues from their child-hood now, in their current relationship.

Another thing I like about IRT, especially when working with lesbian and gay couples, is that it turns conflicts that seem negative and hopeless into something promising, positive, and hopeful. Differences between partners on various issues can be very threatening to all couples, gay and straight alike, but particularly to the gay or lesbian couple.

Our society treats gays and lesbians badly for being "different" than the norm. This can make gays and lesbians resistant to change—they don't want to have to conform for anyone ever again. So when differences surface in gay and lesbian rela-tionships and partners ask for change, they are met with a high level of sensitivity and suspiciousness. The partner's request can feel invalidating to the other partner, who hears, "You don't like me the way I am, just like no one liked me the way I was in my childhood." Additionally, when these differences and conflicts arise, it can feel like confirmation that society's attitude is correct and that gay and lesbian relationships are doomed to fail.

Validating a partner's reality, especially when it is different from your own, can feel threatening. To lesbian and gay couples the threat is more profound. IRT helps ease this by teaching the partners to validate and empathize with each other's realities. It is about respecting and honoring the differences and not invalidating either reality.

IRT helps couples see that behavior change requests help you grow as a couple and an individual. The concept in IRT is that we hire our partners to be our greatest teachers and then we go kicking and screaming into the classroom! The reframe here is that the behavior change request is for our own good as well as that of our partner. This helps clients be less reactive.

IRT also normalizes the tension and difficulty that all couples go through, calling it the "power struggle" and defining it as a necessary stage for growth of the individual and the relationship. This creates yet another anchor for lesbians and gays to stay in the relationship and work things out. Many gay relationships do not have family support and other factors that cause heterosexuals to pause and reconsider whether divorce is truly the right answer.

Finally, another aspect of IRT that is extremely helpful to lesbian and gay couples is turning to face each other rather than sitting side-by-side. Sitting face-to-face with the therapist off to the side reminds couples that they are in charge and taking ownership of the relationship rather than passing that over to the therapist. It engages the couple to focus on each other as active partners without the therapist's being in charge.

Growing up gay and lesbian imprints the impulse to run from each other, turn away, and refrain from looking at one's desired love object. Making couples look into each other's eyes while doing their therapy work allows for safety and underscores the fact that looking at and being with each other is normative and good.

Treatment Guidelines for Lesbian Relationships and Gay Relationships

The following lists outline treatment guidelines for lesbian and gay relationships, based on the separate issues typically involved in each. For lesbian relationships:

- Help them view differences as valuable rather than threatening.
- Help them develop more autonomy as individuals within the relationship.
- Challenge their pseudomutuality as much as possible, helping them individuate and allow for differences.
- Teach them how to directly express their individual wants and needs in the relationship.
- Help them be more assertive in the relationship.
- Educate them about how to more fully enjoy the purely physical aspects of sex.
- Help them express anger in healthy, productive ways.

For gay male relationships:

- Teach them interdependence, as well as how to express a range of emotions.
- Teach them how to be more comfortable being vulnerable with each other.
- Emphasize cooperativeness over competitiveness.
- Emphasize emotional relatedness over physical attractiveness.
- Educate them about how to get greater enjoyment out of the emotional aspects of sex.
- Ensure that both partners have agreed to a contract about monogamy or lack thereof.

CHAPTER 11

The New Mixed Marriage or Relationship: One LGBTQ Spouse and One Straight

"Listen up straight people. If you let us
marry each other we will stop marrying you."
—Jason Stuart, gay comic

"Mixed marriage" usually refers to marriages between people of different races or religions. However, the *mixed-orientation* marriage (MOM) or the mixed-orientation relationship (MOR)—one LGBTQ spouse and one straight—has been around just as long and is becoming increasingly visible. The Straight Spouse Network (www. ssnetwk.org) claims that there are more than 2 million mixed-orientation couples, where one spouse is gay, lesbian, bisexual, or transgender. As already addressed in previous chapters, most LGBTQ individuals seek self-esteem from outside validation. They often don't know they are LGBTQ, as they were raised like everyone else to have permission only to explore a heterosexual orientation and a cisgender identity. These are the main reasons why they heterosexually marry—not because they are selfish or self-centered, as many people assume.

Amity Pierce Buxton started the conversation about these marriages for straight partners in 1994 in her book *The Other Side of the Closet: The Coming-Out Crisis for Straight Spouses*. Carol Grever added to it in her book, *My husband is gay: A woman's guide to surviving the crisis*". As Buxton explained, not all LGBTQ–straight marriages follow the same path after the disclosure that one of the partners is LGBTQ. She described three trajectories:

- A third of the couples break up quickly.
- A third stay together for 2 or 3 years to sort out alternatives but ultimately decide to separate.
- A third commit themselves to redefining the marriage so that they can stay together. Of these, about half determine after about 3 years that separation is best for them, while the remaining half stay married with different arrangements for the marriage.

This research is now quite dated, and there are researchers today working to update these statistics. Jennifer A. Vencill and Sarah J. Wiljamaa (2016) have done research on mixed-orientation couples, both married and not, wherein either partner might be LGBTQ and sexually fluid or heterosexual. In their article "From MOM to MORE: Emerging Research on Mixed Orientation Relationships," they state that the existing information is mostly based on:

- Married couples where one is straight and the other is LGB
- Couples *not* already out to one another nor intentionally partnering
- Limited to one straight spouse, usually female, and one LGB spouse rather than two people whose sexual orientations do not match

The current thought is that many more mixed-orientation couples are choosing to stay together, but accurate statistics are difficult to obtain because many live in the closet out of fear of being judged negatively. Also, some people criticize the LGBTQ partner for "wanting his cake and eating it too," especially if the relationship is non-monogamous (whether the partner is unfaithful or not).

In a rush of countertransference, therapists often coach the LGBTQ spouse to come out and the straight spouse to move on with his or her life and find a straight partner. But this isn't always the best option for the couple.

As LGBTQ issues becomes more accepted by our society, more LGBTQ individuals will feel comfortable coming out in their heterosexual marriages. But often the people involved in these relationships lack the information they need to move forward with their lives. Both partners have their own coming-out process to undergo, but they can negotiate this process together as a couple. In fact, often they need to go through this process together. Therapists must remember this.

Clinicians must also remember that there are many men and women who know they are homosexual, bisexual, or transgender but choose not to self-identify as LGBTQ. Many of these people heterosexually marry, as the following case illustrates.

The Case of Barry

Barry admitted to his clinician that he married at the recommendation of psycho-therapists and doctors. During the 1970s, when he was in his 20s, he lived a "gay lifestyle" but found gay culture to be too sexual and promiscuous. He never could find a man with whom to settle down and have the ongoing monogamous relation-ship, including having children, he longed for.

After meeting a woman at work, Barry gave up trying to find a man to settle down with. He and his coworker fell in love, married, and had three children. Although Barry's wife knew of his sexual interest in men before they married, he assured her that he would not act on what he called his "sexual impulses" and denied having a true gay identity.

After 20 years of marriage, with the kids grown and out of the house, Barry was struggling with his sexual urges. He began experiencing depression and anxiety symptoms and went into therapy. He told the therapist that he had never acted on his sexual impulses in all the years of his marriage, but now, thanks to the Internet, these urges were more difficult to manage. It was easy to find pornography, which Barry often used to satisfy his sexual urges, and to initiate contact through chat rooms with men who wanted to have sex with other men.

Barry's therapist, who was gay affirmative and considered herself nonhomopho-bic, believed that Barry's use of pornography was akin to adultery and advised him to stop using it. She also urged Barry to consider coming out of the closet and leav-ing his marriage to pursue a gay lifestyle. However, Barry still did not see himself as gay and did not want to leave his wife. He loved her, believed they had a good life together, and did not see anything positive about living a gay life.

Ultimately, though, Barry did talk to his wife. Neither of them wanted to separate or divorce. Barry's therapist was not supportive of their decision to stay married and told him that it would inevitably lead to a life of depression for him and resentment on the part of both partners.

Barry: Clinical Interpretation and Treatment

Barry's case is more common than you might imagine. That's why clinicians need to know how to address the issue without inserting their personal biases, as Barry's ther-apist did when she urged the couple to separate. In this case, the therapist was acting on her own countertransference; she wasn't thinking of what was best for Barry.

Although Barry might have benefited from coming out as a gay man and finding a male partner had he tried it, from his point of view this would never work, and his clinician needed to honor this. Barry and his wife were already in their late 50s; deciding to stay together made the most sense for *them*. And in Barry's case, he *was* out of the closet. He was simply choosing what to do with his sexuality now that he and his wife knew.

A more informed and attuned therapist would have helped Barry and his wife explore other options in addition to the possibility of leaving the marriage and moving on. For example, a more respectful and informed therapeutic intervention would have been to help Barry learn to avoid exposing himself to chat rooms that stimulated his homosexual urges and desire for contact. The therapist's negative stance on Barry's using pornography was also misguided. Barry's wife did not have a problem with his looking at pornography—she believed that as long as it helped him manage his sexual urges so that he didn't act on them with other men, she could live with that.

This is a good example of how a therapist's biases can derail effective therapy. In an attempt to be gay affirmative and nonhomophobic, the clinician, instead of following her clients' lead, pointed them in the wrong direction for their particular situation. Supporting clients who wish to stay married should *never*, however, involve using the methods of reparative therapy (discussed in Chapter 1).

Therapists' Biases

Clinicians who treat mixed-orientation couples need to understand that a partner coming out doesn't mean that the couple stops loving each other. In fact, I've found that uncovering one partner's homosexuality or bisexuality can actually strengthen a marriage—but only if both people in the marriage find the help they need. Most often, the person who has just come out is the one who seeks therapy, usually as a prelude to the couple's splitting up. But some mixed-orientation couples can make their marriages work, albeit in new ways, as I explain later.

Often, the dilemma is centered not around sex but around love. Many of the heterosexually married LGBTQ partners I've counseled have been married for 10 years or more. Most have children, have built good lives together, and feel a deep and abiding love for each other. Neither has fallen out of love. The prospect of separating and divorcing is devastating, not only for them but for their children as well.

With all couples—straight, same-sex, and mixed orientation alike—the work is about *shared* responsibility. When the woman in a relationship is pregnant, *they* are pregnant. When one partner has an affair, they both share the burden of how it evolved and how to resolve it. When one partner has an addiction, they are an addicted couple. Given this, the therapist must explore the needs and desires of *both* the gay and the straight spouse in mixed-orientation marriages.

There are several types of countertransference that may surface during work with clients in mixed-orientation marriages:

- Your feelings about infidelity
- Your feelings about nonmonogamy
- Your feelings about divorce—especially if children are involved
- Your homophobic feelings toward the LGBTQ or straight spouses
- Your interest in helping the straight spouses move on even if they don't want to or aren't ready to
- Your investment in keeping the straight spouse a victim and the gay spouse a perpetrator
- Your own unconscious homoerotic interests

As you read this chapter, pay close attention to your countertransference. The subject of mixed-orientation marriages and relationships is provocative for many people. Pay attention to what you dislike, or to your sense that you would have handled a particular case differently. Notice if you have overly strong reactions to what these couples do and what therapists—including me—have done to help them. This very well could be your negative countertransference. Better to clear it up here than in the room with your clients!

Why Do Gays and Lesbians Heterosexually Marry?

This is probably the most common question asked of LGBTQ people who heterosexually marry. When Caitlyn Jenner came out as transgender and admitted she knew she was trans early on in the marriage, I heard people accusing her of misleading her wife, Kris Jenner. This is a complete misunderstanding of what happens for those who are LGBTQ.

Part of the answer, already discussed in other chapters of this book, is that our culture doesn't permit young people to explore anything but heterosexuality. Married LGBTQ individuals are a hidden population—even to themselves. Often they do not identify their homosexual interests as an LGBTQ identity. They might have an interest in same-sex fantasies and behaviors and wonder about their gender identity, but more often than not they do not *know* they are truly LGBTQ. They are in the early stages of denial in the coming-out process (see Chapter 7 for further discussion of the stages). Those with conscious homosexual urges and desires are urged to marry heterosexually in the hope that everything will "work itself out." This is particularly common among gay men, who are usually more conscious than women are of their homosexual and bisexual tendencies. Lesbians are often genuinely unaware that they're attracted to other women in homosexual ways.

The following sections identify some other reasons why LGBTQ individuals may heterosexually marry.

Hetero-Emotional, Homosexual

As addressed in Chapter 16 on sexual fluidity, some men and women are hetero-emotional but homosexual. They are not interested in anything more than sexual activity with members of the same gender. Some hetero-emotional men and women are married to the other gender and might (or might not) have sex with them. Many do have very satisfying sex with their other-gender partners, while also sometimes fantasizing about same-sex attractions and behaviors. Yet they enjoy a life that's full of love and family, even though they might (or might not) decide to be sexual outside the marriage. Their "home" and feelings of belonging are in the heterosexual world and nowhere else.

In fact, studies on sexual fluidity show that romantic love isn't limited by a person's sexual orientation. Chapter 16 on sexual fluidity discusses the work of Lisa Diamond, a University of Utah psychology professor who studied the distinctions between romantic love and sexual desire. Diamond wrote that "it seems that individuals are capable of developing intense, enduring, preoccupying affections for one another regardless of either partner's sexual attractiveness or arousal (2004, p. 116). Diamond based her model on the notion of romantic love evolving from the attachment bond formed between infant and caregiver. After reviewing work by other love researchers and delving into accounts of love and friendship across cultures, Diamond distinguished love and sexual desire. In her model, sexual desire and romantic love are functionally independent, and romantic love is not intrinsically oriented to same-gender or other-gender partners.

In an article published in *Psychological Review*, Diamond stated: "While the goal of sexual desire is sexual union for the purpose of reproduction, romantic love is governed by the attachment or pair-bonding system, with its goal of maintaining an enduring bond between two individuals" (2003, p. 174). And because romantic love, as she hypothesized, is an outgrowth of infant–caregiver attachment, there is no way to "code" romantic love for gender. Diamond also argued that the links between love and desire are bidirectional, because sexual desire can facilitate affectional bonding, and affectional bonding can facilitate sexual desire.

According to Diamond's model, it's possible for someone who is heterosexual to fall in love with someone of the same gender, and for someone who is homosexual to fall in love with someone of a different gender. But gays and lesbians who fall in love heterosexually often cannot sustain a heterosexual lifestyle. In time, their defenses against their sexual identity begin to crumble and their true orientation, which is now in conflict with their chosen love attachment, surfaces. Many people suffer depression as a result of suppressing their sexuality. They also find that as their true sexuality surfaces, they can no longer hide it or fight it, and they lose sexual interest in their opposite-gender partner. See Chapter 7 for more on this.

Over the years, however, I've met and treated hetero-emotional, homosexual men and women who do decide to live heterosexually. When treating these men and women, I don't focus on trying to help them suppress their orientation; rather, I help them acknowledge it and move in the direction of their stated goal of choosing to live a heterosexual life—which sometimes includes *not* acting on their homosexual desires. They don't change their orientation; they simply choose how they want to live. Having weighed every consideration carefully, many live happy lives with their opposite-gender partner.

We talked about intersectionality in Chapter 2, and this is a good place to reflect on the fact that for some people another part of their identity supersedes evolving their LGBTQ identity.

Family-of-Origin Conditioning

To better understand your LGBTQ clients who marry heterosexually, you need to explore their family-of-origin issues. All LGBTQ individuals who heterosexually marry have, along with social and personality traits, family-of-origin factors that led them to stay closeted and get married in the first place. Simply chalking it up only to homophobia, microaggressions, and a heterosexist society is not enough of an explanation.

For example, LGBTQ individuals may have been conditioned to be conflict avoidant, obedient, conforming, appeasing, and people pleasing. They may have been sexually or physically abused, or have suffered other forms of neglect and abuse, causing their defenses and adaptations to manifest by conforming to the "authority," just as children who are abused learn to adapt by conforming to what the perpetrator demands. Later, as adults, they reenact their early abuse by conforming to other figures or societal "authorities." Not LGBTQ individuals who suppress their sexual and gender identity grow up to eventually marry, but covert cultural sexual abuse and other covert *and* overt factors can push them in that direction.

Some LGBTQ people marry the other gender in order to be taken care of, to bond with a parental figure, as a cover or "beard" for their LGBTQ activities, or in the hope that straight sex will "cure" their desire for the same gender (or at least keep that desire strictly sexual). The latter is more common among men than among women.

Guilt and Shame

For many LGBTQ individuals who are coming out of the closet, the journey is solely about themselves and their family of origin. They may feel shame and guilt about the disruption their coming out engenders, but they know that both they and their families must just get past it. For heterosexually married LGBTQ individuals, however, the shame and guilt are compounded, and they inevitably feel 100% responsible for hurting their spouses and children. It takes them years to get through feeling that they've ruined everyone's lives, including their own. "How could I have done this to my spouse, to my kids?" is the mantra I hear in my office. "My spouse didn't know this about me when he married me! This isn't fair to him. It's all my fault, and I should suffer!" Everything negative that happens in their children's and straight spouse's lives is seen as related to their coming out.

Sexual Abuse

Some LGBTQ individuals are out of touch with their sexuality because they were sexually abused as children or teenagers. This confuses their sexual identity. Based on this confusion, people often believe their same-sex attractions come from the abuse and that they are naturally heterosexual. They then ignore their same-sex attractions and don't attribute them to an LGBTQ identity. Also, as discussed in Chapter 4, covert cultural sexual abuse causes confusion over identity for most LGBTQ individuals, even if overt sexual abuse did not occur. Because of the compulsory heterosexism that exists in society, it is the norm for these sexual abuse survivors to consider themselves heterosexual and attribute any homosexual feelings and thoughts to their sexual abuse. If a male is abused by another male, he might view his sexual feelings toward men as stemming from his abuse. If a woman is abused by a male perpetrator, she might consider her feelings for women a result of her turning away from men. Many therapists support this kind of thinking, as do many books.

The research and clinical literature on sexual abuse show that those who have been sexually abused—whether heterosexual or not—have difficulty accessing and expressing their own genuine sexual orientation and desires. From a developmental perspective, the perpetrators of the sexual abuse contaminate their victims' arousal templates. So it makes sense that given their confusion, LGBTQ individuals choose heterosexuality, banking on the fact that it is inherently who they are. Trans folks choose a cisgender identity, also banking on the fact that it is inherently who they are.

Therapists need to explore the history of the LGBTQ spouse to determine whether sexual abuse affected his or her choice to marry heterosexually, as well as help the LGBTQ spouse and straight spouse understand why the LGBTQ spouse chose heterosexuality.

Keeping a Straight Face

A gay client of mine once said that for him married life was like "heterosexual prison." Sadly, he thought of himself as many inmates do: He had sex with his wife simply to relieve his sexual urges. He was sexually attracted to her, just not to other women. Out of his love for her, he was able to be sexual and romantic with her. Other gay and lesbian clients I've had over the years agree that they live imprisoned within the structures and boundaries of heterosexism—and that, like the incarcerated, they do what they must to survive by depriving themselves of a same-sex outlet.

You will see in your practices among these couples that the 40-year-old and over gay or lesbian spouse loses complete interest in having sex with the straight spouse after coming out of "heterosexual prison." I have noticed that those 40 and younger do not lose interest in their straight partners and can continue to have sexual relationships that are pleasurable even during and after their coming-out process. I don't fully understand why those in the over-40 group find it difficult to continue engaging in sex and those under 40 do not. The older lesbians tell me that after they accept their sexual orientation, vaginal sex becomes painful. The older gay men say they have a complete lack of interest in being sexual with their female partners, even though up until then they enjoyed it. Like straight prisoners who engage in homosexual sex during incarceration, once released, these older gays and lesbians no longer want to engage in heterosexual behaviors.

Many of these survival strategies are dysfunctional, causing long-term harm to both the gay or lesbian individual and the straight spouse, as well as to their children. The following sections describe several of these dysfunctional coping mechanisms.

Addictions

Some gay or lesbian spouses act out in addictive ways to avoid dealing with their gay identities: They drink too much, have promiscuous sex, do drugs, or overeat. Like any other time-consuming addiction, this is a way of burning off extra energy and avoiding introspection. Other addictions can be less obvious. People may distract themselves by spending too much time at work or committing themselves to sports or hobbies that suppress their unwanted impulses; they may also become flatly asexual, as was addressed in Chapter 3.

Often these people have no one to confide in. They find it difficult to seek comfort in organized religion or through support groups like Alcoholics Anonymous (AA). With no one to help them articulate their innermost feelings, they bottle up these inchoate feelings and fears, which slows the coming-out process (Corley & Kort, 2006).

Infidelity

Extramarital affairs, whether the couple is straight or gay, result from one or both partners' inability to get their needs met. These needs might have nothing to do with the marriage, or they might be about the marriage. The partners might be able to articulate their needs to each other or not. Although these factors affect many heterosexual marriages, the gay or lesbian spouse's predominant motive for "straying" is to find and reveal his or her true identity. Lesbians and gay men typically cheat or act out because they're repressing part of themselves. Therapists need to remind their clients that because society grants little to no permission to explore anything other than heterosexuality, it makes sense that homosexuals marry heterosexually and explore their homosexuality later. Of course, this exploration should have been allowed during their earlier adolescent and young adult years. The process is backward.

When the conflict does erupt years later, it is about their "identity," not about their ability to love and bond with their partner. Nor is it the result of marital problems. Marital problems might exist in addition to the issue of straying to explore sexual orientation, but they are often not the main reason.

Therapists need to understand this important distinction. They can help the gay or lesbian spouse understand that although he or she may be acting out of integrity by going outside the relationship, the infidelity is often caused by unresolved sexual identity issues—it isn't because the marriage is poor or because he or she is a bad person.

Typically, straight spouses feel as though *they* did something to cause their gay or lesbian spouse to seek affairs with the same gender. Therapists can also help straight spouses stop blaming themselves for their partner's wanderings and encourage them to avoid concluding that there was something wrong with the marriage itself. In truth, the mixed-orientation couples I have seen have had some of the best marriages and have been the best of friends.

Renaming Behaviors and Feelings

Some men who have sex with men and women who have sex with women do not see themselves as gay or lesbian or even bisexual. This is discussed in both Chapter 7 (on coming out) and Chapter 16 (on sexual fluidity). Men may tell themselves that their wives won't perform a certain sexual act they desire, such as oral stimulation, and then give themselves permission to find oral release from another man, never thinking of it as gay or as cheating on their wives because it was from a man. Women may have sex with other women and tell themselves that it is for their male partners who enjoy watching them with another woman. They won't label it as lesbianism at all.

Therapists need to know that there *are* men and women who are not gay and for whom these situations are true. As the above-mentioned chapters show, sexual behavior does not always reflect sexual orientation. Although some clients who engage in homosexual behavior might be in denial about being gay or lesbian, others truly might just enjoy the behavior and not be. It's your job to find out which is the case, with the client leading the way and you helping them with the right questions.

It is also important to help the straight spouse understand that most gay and lesbian spouses really did not know that they were gay before getting married. Although popular wisdom has it that LGBTQ individuals always know, this is only partially correct. LGBTQ individuals may say, "Looking back, I can see that what I was feeling was something gay or lesbian," but in the early stages they were truly not conscious of their LGBTQ identities.

Going on the Down Low

We talk more at length about this in Chapter 16. Going "on the down low"—a man's engaging in sex with other men and not telling his wife—is a consequence of not coming out to himself and to his marriage partner (King, 2004; Boykin, 2005). Psychological fallout from this uneasy dynamic includes depression and low self-esteem, plus many other dysfunctional behaviors I often see in my practice: suicide attempts, affairs (from cybersex to in-person meetings), and unprotected sex. This is because men on the down low don't admit to themselves that they are sexually interested in other men: If they were to use condoms, they would have to admit to themselves that they are gay. They would also have to address their urges as meaningful rather than dismissing them as simply a sexual release. To stay in denial, these men have random, anonymous sex and suppress the knowledge of what this might mean even from themselves.

Closed-Loop Groups

Some gay and bisexual men belong to closed-loop groups—underground clubs frequented by heterosexually married men who want a boyfriend (also heterosexually married) on the side. The men remain "monogamous" to both their wives and their boyfriends. Each man knows of the other's secret life, but their wives don't. This is often an example of gay men wanting to have their cake and eat it too, believing they can keep a spouse *and* a boyfriend while not being up-front about the latter. Accordingly, they change the definition of what they're doing from cheating to "not wanting to hurt her."

Historically I have not supported these arrangements for many reasons. My chief objection wasn't moral but one of personal integrity—I believed we need to be congruent with ourselves from the inside out. An even bigger issue is that of the straight spouse's lack of awareness. If a couple mutually agrees to this arrangement openly and honestly—on the "up high"—then I completely support their decision.

I still feel this way today. However, I have a new therapeutic lens through which I look: protecting my clients from me. In other words, it doesn't necessarily matter what I think about integrity or what I think should happen for the couple or for the individuals in the relationship. I respect the couple's self-determination when they come to therapy. I feel it is important to support them where *they* want to go rather than where I think they should go. It is difficult, of course, when your personal and professional values are bumping against those of your clients. However, it is their life and their decision. I still talk to them about their own personal integrity. I help them look at how things might play out if they decide to engage in behaviors outside the relationship. However, in the end, it is completely up to them.

I will work with couples of all orientations in the following way. I see the couple together for the first appointment, and then I see each of them individually once, and then back together again. I will also see partners individually while I work with couples. I have the following guideline I use (with their consent): "If I see you individually and you tell me something you don't want the other to know, I won't tell. The exception is if one of you tells me something that is putting the other at risk for STIs or legal problems or something that will jeopardize the health or welfare of a partner. Then, I will insist that you tell your partner or I won't work with you. Otherwise, you are free to tell me things and trust I won't share them with your partner."

Often in couples therapy training, we therapists are taught not to keep secrets, but I see it as keeping confidences. How will they tell me things they are struggling with if they believe it will be betrayed? I do have a caveat: If I am holding a confidence but it becomes problematic in working with the couple, I will meet with the individual with the private issue and begin addressing the need to disclose. If they refuse, I reserve the right to stop working with the couple. This gives the partners with the private information a chance to choose what they want to do with the information. This can be awkward, but I find that it works. If I see a couple together and separately, and it seems that a triangulation occurs or feels like it is occurring to anyone involved, I refer them out individually to avoid problems in the couples therapy.

The Case of Noah and Brittney: A Closeted Spouse

Noah, age 40, and Brittney, age 38, had been married for 12 years. They rarely had sex and came to see me because of my sex therapy training. Brittney was frustrated because she wanted sex more than Noah. Noah was unhappy with the frequency as well, but the problem was on his side. In general, Brittney had been the initiator of sex in their marriage. (There usually is one partner in a marriage who is the initiator of sex.) She never felt Noah's desire or attraction to her, but he said that he did, in fact, feel both for her. He said that he had been sexually abused as a child, and that was preventing him from feeling sexual and engaging in sexual relations with Brittney. She suspected he was gay and asked Noah repeatedly if this was true, but Noah denied it vehemently. Brittney told Noah that she would respect him if he were gay and do nothing to prevent him from seeing his kids or parenting them. However, if he were gay, she would want to end the marriage to find a partner from whom she felt desire. She said that if his reluctance to have sex with her was only about sexual abuse, she would feel more hopeful for the marriage than if she were married to a closeted gay man.

Noah and Brittney were devout Catholics with two small children. Noah said that he had been sexually abused by a priest as a preteen and had been in therapy for it for quite a while. Brittney said she could be patient and understood that while he was going through the healing process, being sexual would bring out memories of his childhood abuse. This is common for both men and women going through sexual abuse healing work.

I saw them both privately, and Noah confessed to me that he was "homosexual." He told me that because of his religious beliefs, he would never act on it, nor would he tell his wife. However, he knew it was part of what was wrong with his showing desire for his wife. He saw nothing affirmative about being gay, which is why he used word *homosexual*. He felt terrible about not telling his wife, but he knew she would leave him if she knew.

We talked about the differences between privacy and secrecy, and Noah said he understood he was keeping a secret but that he did not want to lose his wife and children. He knew that Brittney was correct when she said he did not desire her, but he didn't want to let her go and believed he could learn to want and desire her.

Brittney revealed to me that she had been sexual with men outside her marriage. She felt horrible about it and told me that she would never have done this had Noah been willing to be sexual with her. She was willing to engage in mutual masturbation and other forms of sexual stimulation and that it did not have to be intercourse, but Noah's response was always no. She told me she loved Noah and did not love any other man. She said that her sexual infidelities were strictly to receive sexual satisfaction. She felt great guilt over this due to her own integrity and religious beliefs and had a great deal of shame. She did not want to divorce and break up her family over Noah's sexual-abuse issues.

Noah: Clinical Interpretations and Treatment

In working with Noah individually, we sorted out whether his homosexual feelings might have come from being sexually abused in childhood, which can sometimes occur as a response to the trauma. I talk about this at length in my book *Is My Husband Gay, Straight, or Bi?: A Guide for Women Concerned About Their Men* (Kort & Morgan, 2014). Noah had been in ongoing individual therapy for his sexual abuse for 5 years, which included eye movement desensitization and reprocessing (EMDR) and group therapy with other abused men (with another therapist).

Noah wished his same-sex feelings were a result of the abuse, but in his heart of hearts he knew he was homosexual. He spoke at length about the inner conflicts he felt about dealing with his religious beliefs and his sexual orientation. He felt that his religious beliefs were more important to him than coming out as a gay man. He had no plans to act on his desires, nor had he ever.

I implemented sex therapy interventions with Noah and Brittney, such as sensate focus, and I encouraged sexual conversations between them to see if they could start moving in the direction of a sexual relationship, but none of this was effective.

During the couples therapy, Brittney would often cry and say she just wanted to be released from the marriage if Noah were gay, and that it would make sense to her and she could move on, but Noah would not budge nor tell her. She discovered gay porn on his computer at one point, but Noah explained this was part of his "trauma reenactment" from having been sexually abused by the priest.

It became increasingly difficult for me to work with this couple, given that I knew of Noah's sexual orientation, and that if Brittney knew, she could leave the marriage and move on to a life with a partner she felt desired by. Over time, I no longer felt comfortable working with them.

I told the couple that I felt we had gone as far as we could and that I would need to refer them to someone else. I told Noah I was going to do this before I announced it to both of them, and I told him that the reason for my decision was that the real issue was his sexual orientation and not his sexual abuse. When I announced to the couple I could no longer go forward, Brittney asked me if this was because of something I knew that I could not disclose. I could not reveal this, but I knew that Brittney knew I had information that was blocking our ability to go forward in therapy.

I have to admit I felt terrible about their situation and the fact that Brittney didn't know. I wanted Brittney to know the truth, but that was not my call. I completely understood why Noah did not want to share information that he was never going to act on. He had hope that he could become sexual and desiring of Brittney. I worked with Noah a great deal in alleviating gay shame and internalized homophobia from his religion and other sources. But it became clear that Noah's loyalty and allegiance to his religion superseded everything else in his life.

Disclosure: From the Down Low to in the Know

Many therapists believe that *all* affairs or encounters should be disclosed, but therapists need to understand the need for selective disclosure. Just because a spouse has had sexual encounters and affairs during the marriage doesn't mean that he or she has to tell the partner about these experiences. Just as Step 9 of AA declares, "Make amends whenever possible except when to do so would injure them or others."

When affairs or encounters *are* disclosed, it has to be done with discretion, by which I mean in a manner that causes the least possible harm to both partners and the children. Therapists need to help their clients achieve this. Success often depends on the personality and emotional stability of the spouse.

Disclosing to a straight spouse that one is LGBTQ can be difficult for many reasons. If children are involved, the first thing to address with clients, however, is the practical issue of state laws concerning visitation and custody of children. In many court systems, a gay spouse's infidelity or homosexual partnering can be cause for limiting visitation or requiring supervised visits.

Here it is best for heterosexually married LGBTQ clients to consider for themselves what feels right for them and for their children. If they know that telling could cause their straight spouse to try to keep the kids from them, they should not tell. Many of my clients do not like this option, but I remind them it is for the children—it is not fair to them if the straight spouse, in his or her anger stage, forces supervised or limited visits.

If children are not involved, gay and lesbian spouses should carefully consider how much information about their extramarital affairs or sexual encounters their spouse really needs to know.

The Case of Betty

Betty, 32, was married and the mother of three children, ages 9, 6, and 3. She realized she was lesbian after she met Donna, a lesbian in her knitting group. They fell in love and began a secret relationship. Betty was in therapy and told the therapist about the situation. She finally realized she wanted to leave her husband and make a life with Donna. The therapist encouraged her to tell her husband the truth so they could have a healthy dialogue about how to move forward.

Betty's husband was outraged. He felt humiliated and betrayed by Betty's deception. He promised her that she would never see the kids again. He hired an attorney and outed Betty as a homosexual and adulterer. Betty became suicidal and was hospitalized. This only further injured her case in keeping her children.

In the end Betty was only allowed supervised afternoon visits with her children, and she had to come alone—she couldn't bring Donna. Betty's appeal for shared custody was denied. After 2 years fighting in court, Betty was granted rights to see her children without supervision and eventually was allowed overnight visitation. Even then, however, her partner was ordered not to be at home when the children slept over.

Betty: Clinical Interpretation and Treatment

Betty's therapist should have warned Betty about these legal ramifications before Betty revealed her sexual orientation to her husband. The legal system is often biased against the gay spouse. Withholding one's homosexuality during a divorce is a way to protect the children.

Many gay or lesbian parents can't imagine that their straight spouses would react vindictively, especially about the children. But spouses may react in unexpected ways out of anger and feelings of betrayal. Therapists should advise clients like Betty to contact the Straight Spouse support group in their area or to find such a group online. This would have armed Betty with more information about how to proceed so that she could make a more informed decision. Therapists can also recommend to their clients that a gay or lesbian attorney informed about these types of problems be present in the courtroom when custody is discussed.

The Bisexual Spouse

When a spouse comes out bisexual, it is important that therapists understand that this is a true sexual orientation. (See Chapter 15 on bisexuality.) However, if the spouse comes in questioning himself or herself, it is important for the clinician to do an assessment to ensure the client is, in fact, bisexual. What's the difference between a straight man acting on a trauma-induced compulsion to have sex with men, a gay man, and a bisexual man whose identity requires acknowledgement? To an outside, superficial observer, their behaviors may look the same, but—and this is the core of the insight needed to understand what's going on here—*the roots of the behavior and its drivers are different.*

A bisexual man or woman might not need to have relations with both genders for their whole life. I've treated bisexuals who've explored both sides of their sexuality before they got married and that was enough. "Yep. I'm bisexual. Those were great times. Loved it. I don't need to do it anymore." Other bisexuals find they want to have relations with both genders all their lives.

A period of exploration for gay men before they settle down, the so-called gay adolescence, is well recognized. Less discussed is this "bisexual adolescence," but the same developmental process seems to be operating.

My bisexual friends and associates want me to make sure to say here that many bisexuals can make a choice to be monogamous. Like anybody else, personal factors for bisexuals are part of the equation in how people manage their life choices. Bisexuals can choose to be monogamous, but Saul seemed to need at least a period of sexual exploration.

The Case of Saul

Saul came to see me. "I'm bisexual," he told me. "I always knew I was a little bi, but I didn't think I would ever have to act on it. I never told my wife, and now I just feel like I have to go out and meet some men."

Saul: Clinical Interpretation and Treatment

I saw Saul for several months before I could confirm that he was bisexual. What made his case tricky was that he had never had any sexual experiences with men, only women. I had to rule out childhood abuse and other issues that might lead a straight man to feel he needed to have sex with men. But Saul didn't feel compelled.

He wasn't curious. He wasn't responding to a whim. He was truly sexually turned on by men as well as women.

He wanted to enter into the local LGBTQ community and socialize, but he didn't want to do this behind his wife's back. We discussed his options, and he decided he would just tell her everything. However, he wanted to start in my office.

Karen came with him to his next session, and Saul stammered out the story of his bisexuality, how he had wanted to be monogamous, but now he needed to "meet" some men. Could she agree to let him do this?

Karen was calm but confused. She wanted to know exactly what he wanted to do. She was especially concerned about STIs and AIDS. She wanted to know if he might leave her for a man. Having started this discussion in my office, they continued it on their own for weeks. Saul confirmed his commitment to Karen. He promised he wasn't gay, he'd be careful, he'd make sure no one who knew them would be involved, and so on.

Saul told Karen that he didn't want to leave her but he had to have this, and eventually she agreed. Saul could look for men to connect with. She didn't want him doing anonymous one-night stands, and Saul was okay with that.

He learned to use Grindr and other "gay-finding apps." He used Craigslist. He met men for coffee, just as someone dating would, although he refused to call what he was doing dating, because romance wasn't on the table. On the other hand, he was bi, and he wanted at least some thrill of gay sexual excitement. He found a few men he wanted to see again. He offered to introduce them to Karen, but she didn't feel she needed to get that close to what he was doing.

Saul wanted to be faithful to Karen, and his need to explore his bisexuality lasted less than a year. He enjoyed being part of a couple. He was more comfortable monogamous than exploring. It's not that Saul wasn't really bi, or that all bi men need just a year of sex with men. Saul is bisexual. It is a core part of his identity. However, having a relatively brief period for "identity confirmation" was enough for him.

Saul's case is not unusual. I've counseled several men in this situation. They need to explore the unexplored side of their bisexuality, and then they can choose to be monogamous. It is a sort of adolescence, delayed into adulthood because society doesn't encourage gay/lesbian/bi adolescence for teens. It is not a counterexample to the general fact that bisexuals can be monogamous. The key to dealing with an emerging bi coming out/adolescence is not to panic but to work out an honest plan to facilitate controlled exploration with contingencies allowed for as needed.

I don't want to imply that Saul and Karen's story is typical of all bisexual–straight mixed-orientation marriages. It's just one way things can go. On the other hand, in my experience, when a spouse is bisexual, there is a better chance for the mixed-orientation marriage or mixed-orientation relationship to go forward than when the spouse is gay or lesbian. That said, every couple is different, and it would be irresponsible to overgeneralize.

The Lesbian Spouse

In my experience, when a lesbian comes out in a heterosexual marriage or relationship, the husband or boyfriend is intrigued at first, but only as long as it stays a sexual interest or fetish of some kind. Once a woman says she truly feels that she is lesbian and wants to date and romantically connect with another woman, the male partner often ends the relationship and does not try to work things out. This is very different from the gay male partner who comes out to his female partner. While the straight partner of a gay man usually says she is going to leave immediately and not stay in a mixed-orientation marriage, many decide to stay and make it work. For straight men married to lesbians, and even bisexual women, who have emotional interests in other women, the window is much shorter in terms of how long he chooses to stay or not. Most leave within 6 months or less.

Straight Spouses Who Marry Gays and Lesbians

When I talk to straight spouses in mixed-orientation marriages, I often discover that personal issues played an important role in their deciding to get married. Although straight spouses may not have consciously known that their partners were gay, it usually wasn't an accident that they married people who couldn't completely commit or be as intimate and available to them as a straight spouse would have been (Kort, 2005a).

In some cases, a straight spouse is unconsciously drawn to a partner who might betray him or her. Perhaps this spouse suffered childhood traumas such as emotional boundary violations that remained unresolved; this could prompt the spouse to unconsciously seek a "familiar" partner who violates his or her trust all over again. Other times, straight spouses believe that they are attractive or skilled enough to "convert" an unavailable partner.

Some straight spouses marry LGBTQ partners out of unconscious codependency and a desire to control or micromanage a "flawed" partner. A common partnering in this situation is a caretaking women married to a gay man—especially a gay man who wants to be taken care of. Often the gay man had problems in his family of origin: He may have been raised in a large or neglectful family that overlooked his emotional needs or lost a caregiver at an early age. The caretaking wife, in turn, may have come from a disempowered role in her own family and feel a need to be in charge in order not to feel vulnerable.

Also, gay men are open to letting their female partners influence them, whereas research shows that straight men are less open to letting their wives and girlfriends influence them. Women will often tell me they could tell something was different about their male partner and that they could tell immediately. Some do not connect it to the possibility that he is gay, but others do. Still others know simply because the man told them he had "gay tendencies" prior to marriage.

Family-of-origin issues are always involved in any person's attraction to a mate. For example, suppose a woman grew up with a sexually abusive father. She may decide—consciously or not—to avoid future abuse by marrying a man whose sexual power is distant or who has problems with impotence. Or she may marry a gay man struggling to squelch his homosexual impulses. This can be a way of protecting herself from straight men's sexual aggression. Gay men make women like this feel safe, especially if sex is kept to a minimum.

Much less is written and known about the men who marry lesbians. I suspect they are attracted to lesbians for similar reasons that women are attracted to gay men—they unconsciously want to marry someone who is distant and cannot be fully available in the marriage emotionally and sexually. What I have seen in my practice over the years is that some men like that their wives occasionally enjoy sex with women. They find it erotic and do not equate it with lesbianism. To them, their wives are helping them with their erotic fantasies of watching and being sexual with two women.

Therapists must remember that straight spouses aren't usually without some accountability for the mixed-orientation union—there is usually a reason why they married someone who had limited emotional or sexual availability. Ignoring the psychological process that is at work for the straight spouse does both clients a disservice. It is also extremely important for the therapist to tell gay and lesbian spouses that they are not 100% to blame for this situation. They need to consider why their partners married a gay spouse—consciously or unconsciously.

Straight Spouse Reactions to Disclosure

Often LGBTQ spouses say they know how their straight spouses will react when in fact they don't. Some straight spouses manage to remain supportive and understanding, but many become angry and behave unpredictably, particularly around their own homophobia as well as in response to the threat of losing their spouse. Clients need to be prepared for the worst.

Many straight spouses react to the news that their partner is LGBTQ by going into the very closet their LGBTQ spouse is in the process of leaving. Once they acknowledge that they knew or suspected, on some level, that their spouse was LGBTQ, they have to deal with their own denial or, in some cases, their unconscious homophobia. Other straight spouses feel embarrassed, cheated, or fooled. They worry about being judged by others. They're not sure how to move forward—whom to tell, how to tell them, and when. Some straight spouses grow so enraged and bitter that they quickly divorce, never examining themselves and the situation from any point of view other than their own. They may try to turn their kids against their gay ex and refuse to reconcile.

Often straight spouses struggle with feeling that they weren't "man enough" or "woman enough" to keep the marriage together. They need to hear from a therapist that this isn't the issue—that the split-up has nothing to do with their performance as a spouse. They also need to understand that their gay partner's sexuality has absolutely nothing to do with *them*. They simply married a partner with sexual conflicts.

Victim Mentality: Oppressing From the Victim Position

Some straight spouses want to stay married, even if they feel embittered and betrayed. Often this only perpetuates a bad situation. Women who cling to their negative feelings unwittingly betray their loyalty to the very men who have inflicted pain. Their motives for having stayed married—and now, their inability to move forward in life—reveal their underlying need to be attached to a man. Whether or not he can be there for her, she clings to her desire to remain part of a social unit. As one betrayed socialite defiantly declared, "I am *still* Mrs. Smith, and I intend to remain so!" Frozen in time, these women cultivate their humiliation because they enjoy the sympathy they receive as a "victim."

Some straight spouses, however, feel relieved. They may have blamed themselves for the problems in their marriage—especially sexual problems—only to now realize that they were not at fault. Others are happy to feel released from having a sexual relationship with their spouse and grateful to enjoy a continuing emotional relationship.

Straight spouses' reactions also depend on their feelings about the opposite gender in general. A woman who has negative impressions of men may use her husband as the nearest target. When one woman with whom I worked discovered that her mate was gay, she exclaimed, "This proves my point—men are pigs! Even when I tried to marry one who I didn't think was, he turns out to be one. Just like the rest—liars and cheats."

Unfortunately, society typically supports the "betrayed" ex-wife and blames gay men for marrying in the first place. In cases like this, the woman is rewarded for staying indignant and angry, thus keeping her a victim. Sadly, some therapists also take this position. A better strategy would be to approach a woman in this situation as someone who made a decision that didn't work out.

For men, learning their wives are lesbian can feel like a slight to their manhood. They are not only humiliated by their inability to fix the problem but also worry that others will see them as "less of a man" for having married a lesbian.

Coming Out as a Couple

Mixed-orientation couples come out in several typical ways. William Wedin, director of Bisexual Psychological Services in New York City, has identified four stages: humiliation, honeymoon, rage, and resolution (Ball, 2004). Just like the stages of the grieving process, these stages are not rigid or the same for everyone; individuals approach the crisis differently according to the context of their lives.

Stage 1: Humiliation

Both spouses may feel a significant amount of humiliation surrounding the coming-out process. The gay or lesbian spouse feels humiliated about being gay. Straight spouses feel humiliated that they weren't man or woman enough to keep their mate interested. They may question whether they can trust anything that seemed real in the past regarding the marriage or their partner.

One wife said to her husband, "Is it because I repulse you and am fat?" Another husband asked his wife if she used him to have children. Others agonize over what they did wrong or why they did not see that their spouse was gay before this. During this stage, many report that they had no idea that their partner was gay.

Stage 2: The Honeymoon

Here the LGBTQ spouse may have ventured into the LGBTQ community and be in Stage 3 of the coming-out process. They cannot find others they can relate to, nor find a "home" in which they belong, and never find other LGBTQ individuals whom they can relate to. These LGBTQ spouses come back to their straight spouses and are so grateful to their partners for still unconditionally loving and accepting them that they want to stay married. The more the straight spouse has genuine loving feelings and empathizes with what the LGBTQ spouse is going through, the more the LGBTQ spouse will be drawn to the straight spouse, due to the LGBTQ spouse's attachment need for closeness and comfort. Often, they also feel overwhelmed by the evidence that the straight spouse might want to stay. The emotional distress softens them for a period of time, and both will have some hope for the marriage. Feelings of shame often diminish; both think that perhaps things will go back to the way they were before the disclosure.

Stage 3: Rage

Eventually, however, both partners realize that things will never be the same: The gay husband or wife can't retreat back into the closet and typically goes back out into the LGBTQ community to find their place and others with whom they can relate. The straight spouse can't deny the distance between them. Straight spouses often begin to interpret every negative feeling as a sign that their partner is unhappy with them, and gay spouses often respond to their partner's inquiries by being avoidant or overly emotional. The distance that was present in the marriage before the disclosure returns, and the straight spouse or both spouses turn to anger and rage as a distraction from the intense pain of the loss they feel. The LGBTQ spouse continues on their psychological trajectory of coming out, which puts increasing distance between themselves and their straight partners.

Stage 4: Resolution

Once both partners understand that the coming out is about issues of identity, not dissatisfaction with the straight spouse or the marriage, mutual blame ends. The straight spouse can stop interpreting the sexual or romantic acting out as a personal affront, and the LGBTQ spouse can begin treating the straight spouse as a partner rather than as an adversary. They can then begin to deal with the impact on their relationship.

During this stage, each partner determines whether he or she wants to stay together or transition to another type of relationship. They take into account various factors such as children, social considerations, belief systems and personalities, and the degree of openness between them. If they stay together, they must negotiate and often compromise about how homosexuality will play a role in the marriage. Boundaries regarding sexual behaviors and coming out to others have to be determined. Decisions need to be made about what homosocial activities are acceptable to both, and what to tell children, extended family, and friends.

Does Coming Out Have to Mean Getting Out?

Once the disclosure is made, the relationship undergoes rapid changes. Again, this is a rough transition; as a clinician, you need to smooth it. The first step is educating clients about their options. They can:

- Divorce and lead separate lives
- Wait to divorce until the kids leave home
- Decide on an in-house separation (usually a temporary solution)
- Divorce or separate but remain best friends
- Continue to live together as friends, or live close by
- Stay married but find new partners for the gay spouse, the straight spouse, or both
- Practice responsible nonmonogamy (being sexually open to others but remaining emotionally monogamous to one's spouse)
- Allow the gay spouse to become "homosocial" (live as an LGBTQ person in the LGBTQ community but never have sex outside of the marriage)
- Stay together and renegotiate the terms of the marriage in other ways
- Choose not to act on sexual feelings and recommit to the marriage

It's very important to support couples who decide to stay together. Many therapists erroneously see divorce as the only option. To them, an arrangement to stay together constitutes an intimacy disorder. They evaluate the LGBTQ spouse as a person who needs to come out of the closet fully and lead an LGBTQ lifestyle. Other times, the therapist will advise the LGBTQ partner to remain in the closet and be the spouse and parent he or she promised to be; in short, these therapists ask the LGBTQ spouse to rewrite history. Both of these approaches ignore society's heterosexism and homophobia and hold the LGBTQ spouse accountable as the only responsible party.

As a couples therapist, I take the position that it's not for the clinician to decide whether a couple should stay together. The final decision is *theirs*. Our job as therapists is simply to make our clients aware of their options and the possible ramifications of their decisions. The rest is up to them. We support them in what works for *them*, not us.

Before deciding on any course of action, a couple must clarify what is important to each of them personally and jointly. They can then begin to figure out what arrangement will work best for them. This can be, of course, an arduous process—such arrangements are often unorthodox, and there are precious few role models for what a healthy mixed-orientation relationship can be.

Staying Together

When mixed-orientation couples decide to stay together, they need to establish ground rules for what the new relationship will be. For example, they can practice responsible nonmonogamy, with clearly defined rules about what that means for both partners. Some couples allow the gay partner to explore gay porn, as Barry (discussed at the beginning of this chapter) did.

Many see this as potentially addictive or even pathological, but I don't agree. I believe that couples should define healthy sexual and emotional fidelity for *themselves*. Part of this involves identifying healthy aspects of their old relationship—components they feel are worth preserving in their new marriage. The couple also needs to establish limits and boundaries. For example, they need to know when unhealthy nonmonogamy may develop into affairs or lead one of them into sexual addiction.

Splitting Up

If the couple does decide to split up, it's important to explore how this will affect them and their family. As a therapist, you can help ease the hurt as much as possible, knowing that pain will inevitably be a part of the picture. Prepare gay spouses for the anger and misunderstanding that will come their way from straight spouses, children, family, and friends, and educate them on how to protect themselves against potential injury.

Many therapists—and nontherapists—dishonor LGBTQ partners who leave marriages and kids, and this fuels the LGBTQ spouse's guilt for marrying in the first place. The cultural and therapeutic mindset is that gay men or lesbians show more integrity by staying with their spouse and children than by leaving them, as they "made their choice" and should "live with it." But those who hold these views forget what brought the LGBTQ spouse to heterosexually marry in the first place.

Many LGBTQ spouses never fully recover after a divorce. They say things like, "I never stopped loving him. The divorce was not about no longer loving or liking each other." They know inside that they are truly gay or lesbian, but they regret leaving a person they loved and splitting their families apart.

More men than women tell me that they never found a same-sex partner who was able to fulfill their emotional needs the way their ex-spouse did. In other words, they miss the relational part of their old relationship, an aspect that for most gay men—or men in general, for that matter—is often not very well-developed.

Many gay women who come out in their heterosexual marriage are upset when the role of sex in their lesbian relationships diminishes. They ask themselves why they left a relationship that was not sexually satisfying only to find themselves in another that is mostly sexless.

As therapists, we must help these clients understand that they need to work on the new relationship so that it includes both sex and relational closeness.

CHAPTER 12

Gay Affirmative Therapy Principles in Clinical Practice: Establishing a Differential Diagnosis

Nothing is ever settled until it is settled right.
—Rudyard Kipling

Many LGBTQ individuals can appear to have mental health disorders when instead they are suffering the effects of suppressing their sexual identity or going through the coming-out process. Depression and anxiety are basic components of suppressing one's sexual orientation and coming out. A lifetime of psychological splitting and compartmentalization may produce behaviors typical of personality disorders. The LGBTQ child hears the message, "We will love you unconditionally as long as you are straight and cisgender or pretend that you are." This promotes splitting, which "consists of compartmentalization of opposite and conflicting affect states; subjects may be aware of their contradictory, ambivalent attitudes but fail to recognize that they spring from their own internal conflicts" (Campbell, 1988, p. 622). Splitting, of course, is the essential ingredient in personality disorders, but with LGBTQ individuals, this splitting is often caused not by a personality disorder but rather by an attempt to fit into a world that doesn't accept them for who they are.

Mental Health Disorders That Mimic the Effects of Covert Cultural Sexual Abuse

Long-term closetedness can lead a person to become overly rigid, judgmental, and difficult to work with (not just in therapy); have difficult friendships and tenuous romances; and have low self-esteem or grandiosity and narcissism that ultimately move from being a psychological defense to being part of the client's character. During the coming-out process, particularly during Stage 5, clients may appear bipolar, self-absorbed, narcissistic, and potentially exhibit out-of-control sexual behavior. However, once this stage of the coming-out process ends, these clients no longer display any psychological problems.

Therapists need to differentiate between the stigma or minority stress of growing up LGBTQ and true psychopathology on the part of the client. Are clients reacting to the stigma of being LGBTQ, the life of having been closeted, the difficulty of the coming-out process? Or is psychopathology operating in addition to, or separate from, the stigma and stress of growing up LGBTQ? As author and psychotherapist Kristine Falco (1996) wrote:

> Misdiagnosis is occasionally possible in cases where a patient in a sexual identity crisis, or coming-out crisis, responds with mood swings, hyperactivity, and impulsive behaviors reminiscent of hypomania. Resolution of the sexual-affectional issue may alleviate symptoms and can help clarify the diagnosis. (p. 407)

As discussed in Chapter 6, developmental delays are often the real cause of apparent psychopathology and personality disorders.

Common mental health disorders that mimic the effects of covert cultural sexual abuse are:

- Borderline personality disorder
- Avoidant personality disorder
- Narcissistic personality disorder
- Depression disorders
- Anxiety disorders
- Bipolar/hypomanic disorders
- Addictions
- Obsessive-compulsive personality disorder

Common types of characterological-appearing overlays I have found in my practice and heard from those I have supervised are borderline-appearing personality traits, endogenous/chronic depression (dysthymia) and reactive depression (adjustment disorders), and narcissistic-appearing characterological overlay, which is often confused with narcissistic personality disorders in LGBTQ clients. Although some clients are truly characterological, others may appear to be but are not—their symptoms are defenses and more neurotic than characterological.

According to Gonsiorek, if an overlay remains a part of a person's functioning for a prolonged period of time, it "may begin to set down increasingly deep roots and begin to dwarf the preexisting personality structure" (1982, p. 19). He went on to say that "some victims may be scarred psychologically with the marks of social oppression of homosexuality as indelibly as some concentration camp victims retain their tattooed numbers."

Borderline Personality Disorder

The diagnosis of borderline personality disorder (BPD) is overused with lesbians, as it is for women in general (Falco, 1991). A quick look at the *DSM-V* criteria (2013) for a BPD diagnosis reveals a striking similarity between such symptoms and the behaviors typical of gays and lesbians, especially those in the coming-out process. For example, LGBTQ clients may exhibit the following (Ritter & Terndrup, 2002):

- Efforts to avoid real or imagined abandonment
- Unstable and intense relationships
- An unstable self-image or sense of self
- Impulsivity in areas that are potentially self-damaging
- Suicidal behavior, gestures, or threats
- Affect instability
- Feelings of emptiness
- Intense anger or difficulty controlling anger
- Transient, stress-related paranoid ideation

For LGBTQ individuals, these behaviors may be completely normative. It isn't surprising, for instance, that a lesbian who has spent her entire life suppressing her natural identity in an attempt to gain the acceptance of others might suffer from an unstable sense of self—or for a gay man who has felt invisible his whole life to suffer from feelings of emptiness. "Intense anger" is an appropriate reaction to years of oppression; self-harm is predictable when a person is feeling damaged and unworthy, and paranoid ideation is completely understandable if one is at risk of losing one's job. You can see how all of these "symptoms" may not be indicative of BPD in LGBTQ clients.

The Case of Shane and Fran

Shane, age 52, was the head physician of a local hospital. He contacted Rhonda for counseling with his wife, Fran. Shane was afraid Fran was going to divorce him, and he wanted to try to save the marriage.

Five years prior to Shane's making the appointment, Fran had found gay pornography on his computer, as well as chats of a sexual nature between Shane and other men. Fran confronted Shane, and he promised to stop looking at porn on the Internet and to discontinue all contact with gay men.

Three years later, however, Fran again found sexual emails on Shane's computer, and he admitted to more sexual hookups with men. This time he said he was deeply depressed, which he believed drove him to return to the behaviors, and he entered individual therapy and began taking antidepressants, which helped his mood considerably. After 6 months, however, he stopped therapy, and soon thereafter, without telling Fran, he stopped his antidepressants as well. His depression returned.

A year and a half later, Fran found more gay porn and cell phone text messages from men Shane had met up with. Fran demanded they enter couples therapy and threatened to leave the relationship. Shane threatened suicide if she left.

Shane and Fran entered therapy with Rhonda, a straight clinician, and liked her immediately. Shane commented on her professionalism and noted aloud that she had a PhD. Although Rhonda told Shane he could call her by her first name, he insisted on calling her Doctor. "You're the best and the only one I think can help me," Shane told her.

Shane admitted that he enjoyed looking at gay porn but said that it meant nothing other than a sexual release. "Sometimes I think I might be gay, and other times I think I might be bisexual because I am so attracted sexually to you," Shane said to Fran. When Fran asked about his sexual hookups, he said it was out of curiosity and nothing more. Fran felt betrayed, and Shane was not able to validate or see *her* reality at all. He promised her he would stop again, but Fran said she no longer trusted him. Shane responded by saying that she was overreacting, and he blamed his acting out on their constant arguing. "I had these fantasies throughout our whole marriage, but when you started up attacking me about my hours and the way I run my career, that pushed me toward acting out with other men."

During the therapy Shane would switch back and forth between blaming Fran and blaming himself for his homosexual acting out. He could not accept any form of sexual identity, as he felt that nothing fit. He did not feel straight, as his sexual urges had always been toward men, and yet he enjoyed sex with his wife and looked forward to it.

Shane was unusually open about his past sexual escapades in front of Fran. "I am already busted, so I might as well confess everything," he said. He reported that he had met men through gay Internet sites and apps, had safe sex, and engaged in nothing more in terms of relationships. He was truly confused by Fran's negative reaction. "If you would give me more sex with you, Fran, I would not feel like I have to get it elsewhere. Be thankful that I don't get it from other women!"

Shane did reduce his work hours considerably during the couple's therapy, and Fran was grateful. They began having sex again on a more frequent basis. However, Shane eventually started canceling appointments due to work hours. Rhonda offered him other times, none of which worked for him. One of the cancellations was less than 24 hours before the appointment, causing a missed appointment charge that Shane said he would not pay.

When the couple finally was able to come to another appointment, Shane challenged Rhonda's high fees and told her he had done some research and found therapists who would slide their fee scale for him. Fran colluded with Shane and said they wondered about Rhonda's commitment to them given what they called her "lack of flexibility."

Shane then asked Rhonda about her life and whether she was straight or gay. Rhonda's approach was to provide little information about herself, but she was willing to disclose that she was straight. Shane asked her personal questions about her marriage, to which she responded that it was not appropriate to answer but found it therapeutic to explore with him what he thought. This angered Shane, and he told her, "I feel very exposed in here with you. Can't you just tell me some things to balance it out?" Rhonda declined, telling Shane it was not therapeutic. Upset, Shane told her that her approach was unfair.

Before the next session, Shane called Rhonda and left a message telling her in confidence that he had met a man through the Internet and swallowed the man's ejaculate. He did not want Rhonda to mention it in the couple's session. Rhonda had made it clear to Shane and Fran that she was seeing them as a couple and that if one person told her something through a phone conversation, she would not keep it a secret. She called Shane back and told him this, which made him extremely angry.

In the next session, Rhonda urged Shane to admit to having unsafe sex. He did so, and then also disclosed that he'd had unsafe sex all along. "That explains the yeast infections I've gotten over these past years!" Fran screamed.

In the next appointment, Shane came in with personal information about where Rhonda lived, her age, and her husband's name, all of which he'd gotten from the Internet. At this point Rhonda became fearful of Shane and sought supervision with me.

Shane and Fran: Clinical Interpretation and Treatment

Rhonda had diagnosed Shane as borderline personality disordered with depressed mood. She based this on his initial overidealization of her and then his negative transference toward her, his angry outbursts about her payment structure and schedule, and his intrusiveness in looking her information up on the Internet. She also noted the splitting he was trying to do between his wife and her around his sexual acting out and the attempted secrecy. In fact, the whole issue of his sexual identity seemed to support a BPD diagnosis in that he was unable to experience a consistent identity.

Rhonda saw Shane's workaholism and unsafe-sex practices as confirming a BPD diagnosis because of their impulsivity. It did appear that Shane was characterological, but before confirming this I wanted to have Rhonda use some GAT interventions.

Rhonda said that Shane came from a strong Catholic family with rigid rules and that sexuality was never talked about. It was a matriarchal family: His mother and grandmother ruled with an iron first, whereas his father was passive and spent most of his time out of the house either working or drinking.

In addition, he had an uncle who had molested a male cousin and who was referred to as the "uncle who queered the cousin." Shane had learned that this was homosexuality when, in fact, it was pedophilia.

As he had grown up with a strict mother, a rigid family style, and a homophobic message that gays are pedophiles, it was likely that Shane learned that to get his needs met, he had to go underground and do it secretly. Surely this would have provided the groundwork for him splitting part of his personality off.

Rhonda was focusing more on the marital problems because the couple insisted on dealing with "the here and now." I urged Rhonda to be stronger with them in the office in terms of keeping them focused on the underlying problems and not on the symptoms. If Shane were truly BPD, he would not be able to tolerate the insight and accept the feedback about himself, and we would have support that he was characterological.

I asked Rhonda to translate Shane's sexual acting-out behaviors as the initial stages of coming out and normalize his unsafe sexual practices as typical of Stage 5 behaviors of the coming-out process. Of course, we needed to keep in mind the fact that he hid them from Fran and put her at risk. I suggested that this might be due to his projecting his hostility toward his mother onto Fran. I thought his negative transference toward Rhonda was about his mother, too, and urged her to explore this with him.

Rhonda did all of this and Shane, caught off guard, started crying. He began admitting to having had more than just sexual contact with men. In fact, he dated and had fallen in love with a man, but the relationship had not worked out. However, he did not want to lose Fran and was willing to do whatever it took to keep the marriage.

I talked with Rhonda about interpreting his anger and depression as signs that he was keeping his sexuality closeted. I had Rhonda interpret Shane's overworking as his way of not facing his sexual desires. Rhonda started translating Shane's behaviors from the normative framework of a developing gay identity, and over time Shane accepted this. However, he and Fran had to now face what would happen to their marriage.

As they ventured into the marital work with Shane coming out as a gay man, he went to gay support groups, no longer had an issue with Rhonda's fees, and stopped canceling appointments. His anger subsided and he was able to do the real work of facing his identity and his marriage.

Avoidant Personality Disorder

In the first three stages of coming out, many LGBTQ individuals display traits of an avoidant personality disorder. They may be reluctant to venture into the LGBTQ community and simultaneously withdraw from the straight community. The more they recognize they are LGBTQ, the less likely they are to want to socialize with their straight friends out of fear of being discovered.

The fear of developing close relationships may be conscious or unconscious, but either way it becomes a way of life. What these clients are really doing is keeping the covert cultural sexual abuse at bay so they can avoid dealing with the trauma. With the help of GAT and group experiences, they can overcome this avoidant style. If the avoidance persists despite such treatment, it would be appropriate to start exploring personality dynamics and mood-related disorders.

Narcissistic Personality Disorder

It has long been a stereotype that gay men and lesbians are self-centered, narcissistic, and pleasure seeking. Historically, it was believed that homosexuality was a form of sexual perversion in which the individual takes himself as a sexual object. Psychoanalysts saw a close connection between homosexuality and narcissism stemming from the view that homosexuality is a more primitive condition than heterosexuality, with impoverished object relations. The diagnosis of narcissistic personality disorder (NPD) was commonly used among psychotherapists for gay men and some lesbians. It was concluded that one's narcissistic tendencies caused a homosexual acting out, as lesbians and gay men looked for the ideal self in a member of their own gender.

Some historic studies exploring personality disorders in gay male subjects primarily administered psychological projective tests such as Rorschach inkblots (Reiss, 1980). These studies showed that gay men were more prone to narcissism (Exner, 1969; Raychaudhuri & Mukerji, 1971).

GAT understands that the narcissism found in these projective tests are a defense rather than a personality disorder. A study done by Alexander and Nunno (1996) found that the narcissistic responses were a result of the gay men having high levels of introspection and turning inward. Alexander (1997) believed, and I agree, that a gay man's outward, inflated sense of self masks an underlying rage and depression associated with an inadequate and fragmented sense of self that stems from a lifelong self-hatred.

It makes sense, then, that seeing these traits in a therapy room, a clinician would make an assessment of narcissism. Narcissism usually requires constant admiration and attention from others in order to undo feelings of inferiority. To mask shame—a negative view of the self—narcissism is used as a defense to represent a positive view of self. This is exactly what clinicians will see in their clients.

However, clinicians need to be aware of the underlying feelings of shame, guilt, and depression in LGBTQ clients, which are often masked—a behavior called the *narcissism defense*—by demonstrating the very opposite feelings and behaviors in interpersonal relations. The narcissism defense is used to keep others from getting too close and from doing additional harm to an already fragile sense of self. From a gay affirmative approach, narcissism is seen as a healthy defense—a natural process of growing up gay and a vital part of healthy adaptation, which helped clients get through childhood.

Depression Disorders

Sometimes what can look like a chronic depression can simply be the result of being treated as invisible throughout your life. Once clients progress through the stages of coming out, the depression lifts.

Sometimes, however, clients remain depressed even after they have come out of the closet, gotten involved in lesbian and gay social situations, and begun to feel positively about their identity. In these cases, a clinician might be tempted to give a diagnosis of dysthymia or major depression. However, before making such diagnoses, clinicians must address the client's loss of heterosexual privilege and the grief surrounding it. There may also be tremendous losses from telling long-term friends and family members. In some cases, changes in how family or friends relate to the client contribute to the depression.

If such factors are addressed and clients remain depressed for more than 6 to 8 months afterward, a diagnosis of depression should be considered. An excellent resource on depression for LGBTQ individuals is the book *Queer Blues: The Lesbian and Gay Guide to Overcoming Depression* (Hardin & Hall, 2001).

Anxiety Disorders

As I have already discussed, lesbian and gay children typically grow up in a state of constant hypervigilance, worrying that they will be discovered and humiliated. It is a severe threat to one's psychological and sometimes physical well-being to keep such a secret and then to reveal it to others. Adult clients may find it difficult to control or stop their worrying. Ruminating about what will happen when they come out is common, as is excessive worry, feeling on edge, and muscle tension and sleep disturbance. All of this will usually abate after clients successfully pass their identity crisis and accept their gay or lesbian orientation.

Bipolar/Hypomanic Disorders

Research shows that there is no difference between gays or lesbians and heterosexuals in terms of the frequency of bipolar disorders (National Institute of Mental Health, 1987). The coming-out process—especially Stage 5—can look hypomanic or bipolar. Clients may do many things that resemble the symptoms of hypomania and then plummet into depression when things don't work out as they hoped.

The Case of Jonathon

Jonathon was a 38-year-old married man with two children ages 7 and 9. His wife was pregnant with their third child. Jonathon reported that his marriage was happy and he did not want to leave his wife even though he had secretive sexual fantasies about men. "They're just sexual kinks that I can take care of online," he said.

One night, however, Jonathon was online in a chat room and started a conversation with Dave, who lived in another state. They stayed up until 6 a.m. talking.

The next night, the same thing happened. This continued for weeks, and Jonathon, once the quintessential devoted father and loyal husband, began missing work and neglecting his responsibilities as a parent and spouse.

Realizing that he was developing romantic feelings for Dave, Jonathon decided to arrange to meet him. He told his wife it was a business trip and left her to care for their children alone. The relationship soon became more serious, and Jonathon fell in love, spending countless nights online, on the phone, and traveling to visit Dave—all during his wife's pregnancy. Convinced he was having an affair, his wife confronted him, but Jonathon denied everything.

Jonathon ran up credit card bills, missed payments on other bills, and was completely focused on nothing but Dave. He started using party drugs and traveling to attend circuit parties across the country. He was scarcely available for his wife's doctor appointments around her pregnancy.

When his wife complained and expressed her anger, Jonathon told her, "Everything has always been about you" throughout their marriage and that "now it was time for me." He denied that his behaviors were affecting her or the family in the ways she said they were. As he put it, he was just finally creating a "slice of life" for himself.

Eventually Dave told Jonathon that he had met someone else. Jonathon was devastated. Angry with Dave for "leading [him] on and then dumping [him]," Jonathon fell into a deep despair. His wife was about to have their baby and he had never been more depressed.

Jonathon now realized how much he had put at risk. His job was in jeopardy because of his absences; his marriage and his relationship with his children had suffered immeasurably. He found himself hopeless and helpless and crashed into a deep depression.

Jonathon: Clinical Interpretation and Treatment

Jonathon's therapist was not aware that Jonathon had been looking at online gay porn, and she was under the impression that he had never previously experienced sexual feelings for men: He had told her that he met Dave through work and that it was "a fluke" that he felt this way for another man. She diagnosed him as having undergone a hypomanic episode, explaining that he met all the criteria: inflated self-esteem and grandiosity while not thinking about the effects on his wife and children, decreased need for sleep, and excessive involvement in pleasurable activities with a high potential for negative consequences.

The problem with this diagnosis was that Jonathon had never experienced an episode like this before, nor had anyone his family. Jonathon was not hypomanic; he was in Stage 5 of coming out and had fallen in love.

Like with any new relationship, Jonathon had a different experience with Dave. For years Jonathon had experienced sexual hookups that were meaningless in terms of emotion. Each man served as a physical release and nothing more. Dave, on the other hand, brought out an emotional side that Jonathon did not know he had. The more contact he had with Dave, the more he wanted to see him. Just like anyone who falls in love, Jonathon needed less sleep, became consumed with the object of his affection, and felt euphoric, making him appear to have an inflated self-esteem.

While this was happening, Jonathon was also coming out. So in addition to experiencing all the symptoms of romantic love, he entered his gay adolescence and abandoned all responsibilities. From this perspective, it made sense that Jonathon behaved in the way he did. Dave's breaking off the relationship jolted Jonathon back to reality, and he finally realized what had happened to his life.

Addictions

As discussed in earlier chapters, clients going through an LGBTQ adolescence may seem to exhibit addictive behavior. They often act out with drugs and alcohol and sexually experiment with numerous partners. When we watch young adults on a college campus, we might easily diagnose them as alcoholics, drug addicts, or people with problematic sexual behaviors, including unsafe sex. Their behaviors and lives appear this way. But when they leave college and start settling down, their profiles begin to look very different. The same is true for LGBTQ people—the difference being that they experience this period when they come out, which may not happen until well into adulthood.

If addictive behaviors persist 2 to 3 years after the client has gone through all of the stages of the coming-out process, a diagnosis may be appropriate. Some LGBTQ individuals do go on to become addicts trapped in the disease and unable to pull themselves out, as I discuss later in this chapter.

Obsessive-Compulsive Personality Disorder

Some of your LGBTQ clients may be obsessed with orderliness, perfectionism, and control. They may be overly conscientious and inflexible about matters of morality, ethics, and values. Those who are struggling with whether or not to come out may be able to cite verse after verse of religious doctrine. All of this is typical of obsessive-compulsive personality disorder (OCD). The reality, however, is that many of these clients engage in these behaviors as a way to keep their sexual identity suppressed, and all of the symptoms fall away after they come out of the closet.

Establishing a Differential Diagnosis

Establishing a differential diagnosis is essential in working with any client, but it is especially important when working with LGBTQ clients. Although the effects of covert cultural sexual abuse may mimic mental-health-disorder symptoms in many cases, there *are* times when an LGBTQ client does suffer from a true mental health disorder that is independent from the trauma of covert cultural sexual abuse.

In working with LGBTQ clients, you must determine whether the symptoms are the result of covert cultural sexual abuse or indicate a true mental health disorder. If you always assume that the symptoms are the result of the trauma of growing up LGBTQ and only later consider other possibilities, you may not effectively help the client. Conversely, if you begin by only considering mental health disorders and pursue GAT later, you will probably miss important issues that need to be addressed. Striking a balance can be difficult; excellent data-gathering and history-taking skills are essential.

When clients are unresponsive to gay affirmative interventions, it is important to examine other factors that may be stalling therapy. This was the case with Ben.

The Case of Ben

Ben, a 35-year-old gay male, came to me after a breakup. Ben told me he was deeply in love with his ex and could not understand what had made his partner leave him. Their relationship had lasted a total of 3 months. In fact, Ben had never sustained a relationship beyond 6 months, which bothered him. He was frustrated with the gay community and told me that he wished he had been born straight, as women would be more interested in him and what he had to offer than gay men seemed to be. He was referring to his professional and financial success.

Ben was likeable and charismatic. He told me that in relationships he was generous—perhaps to a fault. He said he "wined and dined" the men he dated and enjoyed being able to provide for any man he could meet. He also told me he did the same for friends and even some strangers. He took pride in his generosity.

As I took a background history, Ben explained that his parents were Mormon and unaccepting of homosexuality. He remembered his father telling the family, "No son of mine is ever going to be a queer," after seeing Ben playing with Barbie dolls. When

Ben came out at the age of 19, his father kicked him out of the house. His mother sent him money, however, as Ben was in school and could not support himself.

When Ben was 24, his father reconciled with him and their relationship became closer, even though his father still did not accept his homosexuality. They agreed to disagree. Ben never brought up his homosexuality, and they never asked.

Ben's mother continued to send him money, which now paid the mortgage on his house. When I asked him why she continued to give him money and he continued to accept it despite the fact that he had a well-paying job, Ben said, "That is the least she can do for having married my father, with all he has done to me in my life as gay man." Ben frequently began his sessions with me by asking if his clothes and haircuts looked expensive. "This is what people wear and how they look in New York," he explained. He told me he shopped at the finest places, getting everything tailored to his body. He worked out five times a week and often talked about how he had to resize his clothes because he was growing out of them from bulking up. When people made fun of his clothes, he saw them as being envious.

Ben's family did not take an interest in his work, his financial success, or his physical build. Instead, his mother would tell him he looked "overweight" and physically unusual, and his brothers would tease him about his "girly" designer haircuts and shoes. Ben cried as he told me that this type of abuse had occurred throughout his entire life.

Ben: Clinical Interpretation and Treatment

It was difficult for me to determine whether Ben was truly narcissistic, was reacting to family-of-origin dynamics, or was suffering from the trauma of covert cultural sexual abuse. He seemed to have inflated self-esteem, a grandiose sense of importance, and a sense of entitlement. He required excessive admiration by me and thought that others envied—or should envy—him. In working with Ben, I kept the NPD diagnosis in mind but saw his need for constant affirmation and admiration as the result of the rejection he experienced by his family. I used the trauma framework of covert cultural sexual abuse regarding the rejection he experienced in childhood about his atypical gender expression as well as the spiritual abuse by the Mormon religion in which he was raised.

I decided that group therapy might help Ben explore and heal his relational wounds, and I discussed this with him. I knew I was taking a risk because if he did suffer from true NPD, he would not do very well in group therapy. Ben agreed to attend the group therapy, telling me he wanted to stop repeating the relationship patterns he had.

Ben came to the group sessions dressed in provocative clothing that showed off his muscular arms, legs, and torso. Even during the winter months, he wore shorts and tank tops. He talked about how he was able to find a "bargain" and shared the cost of the clothes, which were high priced even with the discount. He asked for time in group each week and if he did not get it, he would complain the following week that the group was "too big in terms of the number of gay men" and that the time was not divided right by me as the facilitator.

Despite Ben's grandiosity, the group liked him and related well to him initially. They gently gave him feedback about his consistent need for attention and "showiness." Their interest was to help him drop his false sense of self and "get real" in the group. He told them they must be jealous of how much he had achieved. This was not the case, of course, and the group members told him how attractive he looked and how they enjoyed his sense of fashion. What they did not like was his leading with that. Ben also talked openly about how his mother made his house payments, and the group confronted him on his sense of entitlement. Ben felt increasingly rejected by the members of the group, just as he had felt in his family.

After several weeks, Ben started missing some group sessions. When asked why he was not coming, he said he had to travel to New York to purchase the latest clothing by the fashion designers. When the group and I challenged his reasons for missing sessions, he interpreted it again as jealousy.

One night Ben came to group and informed everyone that he felt it was time to move on and receive a "different style of therapy." He said that neither the group nor I were meeting his needs and that he was leaving to see a "better-trained" therapist.

The group responded angrily to this. Some called Ben a "bitchy queen" and said they expected more from him. Others felt dismissed and used by him. As the facilitator, I used these responses as a way for the other gay men to address what Ben was bringing up for them. I asked them to explore that instead of attacking Ben. Ben, however, interpreted my attempt to protect him as a desire to take the focus off of him. When I tried to explain that I wanted him to hear their responses but in a nonattacking way, he became angry and stormed out of the group before it ended.

I never heard from Ben again, despite my attempts to contact him. In retrospect, I realize that he truly had a narcissistic personality disorder. Had I worked with him longer in individual therapy, I would have probably seen more of this and not placed him in group therapy. However, the group therapy highlighted his narcissism in a way that might not have been as evident in individual therapy.

The Case of Lynn

Lynn sought therapy after a breakup with her partner, Andrea, of 7 years. Lynn was 30 and Andrea was her first love. According to Lynn, the breakup had "come out of nowhere." They were living together, planning on having children, and supported by each other's families. Lynn never suspected that Andrea was considering leaving.

One day Andrea came home and told Lynn she had fallen in love with another woman. Lynn was devastated. She begged Andrea to go to couples therapy, but Andrea refused. In less than a week Andrea moved her belongings out and moved in with her new love. Lynn sank into a deep depression and went into individual therapy with a straight therapist.

During her therapy, Lynn began taking antidepressants and engaged in weekly sessions. Over the next 8 months she cycled between getting better and then relapsing back into her depression whenever she received a call or e-mail from Andrea. She was suffering from sleep problems and weight loss. She would regularly drive by Andrea's new home with the hope of getting whatever glimpse of Andrea she could.

Lynn's depression was triggered whenever she was reminded of Andrea—whenever a piece of mail was not forwarded to Andrea or when one of her friends mentioned something about Andrea and her new partner. Lynn asked her friends to stop talking about Andrea, and she asked Andrea to stop contacting her, but she still found herself reminded of her and would regress back into depression.

As Lynn started dating again, she found numerous dysfunctional women and blamed the lesbian community for being so "messed up." She lamented lesbians' "serial monogamy" and inability to commit. She talked about how single lesbians made moves on partnered lesbians and didn't value others' relationships.

Lynn's therapist explored the possibility of covert cultural sexual abuse and PTSD expressed through internalized homophobia, which Lynn insisted she did not have. She explored Lynn's growing-up years around being lesbian, but Lynn reported no dysfunction within her family. She said she felt loved and close to both of her parents. When she came out to her family, they were accepting and loving and just wanted her to be happy. When she partnered with Andrea, her mother embraced their relationship and developed a close relationship with Andrea.

Sadly, Lynn's mother had died from an aggressive return of breast cancer a year before the breakup with Andrea. Lynn was devastated but at least had Andrea at her side. Now she had lost Andrea, too, and the therapist worked with her around the grief of losing the two most important people in her life.

After 2 years, however, Lynn still was not improving. Her therapist now began to wonder whether Lynn's inability to move on from the breakup was due to growing up lesbian, even though Lynn had said her family had always been supportive. She began using a trauma-based framework in her treatment. But this didn't work either, so she sought supervision with me.

Lynn: Clinical Interpretation and Treatment

When the therapist talked about Lynn's mother's death, I asked for more information about Lynn's relationship with her mother. The therapist explained that they truly were close and that Lynn felt loved, supported, and affirmed by her mother throughout her life.

Lynn's mother had been diagnosed with breast cancer when Lynn was 5. It was treated and stayed in remission throughout Lynn's childhood, but the family nonetheless remained fearful that it would return.

I asked the therapist to talk more about this with Lynn. When she did, Lynn said that she had been frightened most of her life that her mother would die. This turned out to be the real issue: Lynn was struggling with symptoms of trauma not from growing up lesbian or losing her partner but rather from the anticipated loss of her mother throughout her entire childhood. When the therapist started talking about this with Lynn, everything clicked and seemed to make sense to her. It explained why Lynn could not let go of Andrea and held on longer than expected. It helped her understand that she was reenacting what she did with her mother—which was to stay close and not let her mother out of her sight for fear of losing her.

Lynn gradually began to improve. Each time she had an episode of depression triggered by learning something about Andrea, she recognized it as related to her past and was able to talk herself through it.

To make accurate diagnoses, you need to look at the whole picture and rule out as much as possible. As you help clients through their problems and symptoms, the bigger picture will become clearer, and you will be more able to assess whether your clients have a mental health disorder or whether they just appeared to have one because of their situation as gay or lesbian.

Dual Diagnosis

In general, GAT explores the trauma, shame, alienation, isolation, and neglect that gays and lesbians grow up with. Important as this is, therapists need to recognize that LGBTQ clients who seek treatment may have other issues as well. Because of the historical pattern of pathologizing homosexuality (discussed in Chapter 1), GAT has tended to minimize assessing and diagnosing *any* pathology and has deemphasized emotional disorders that are not related to growing up lesbian and gay.

There can sometimes be too much emphasis, however, on the trauma of growing up LGBTQ and the coming-out process, leading therapists to overlook or mistreat problems that are not directly related to the client's sexual orientation. GAT clinicians must remember that LGBTQ individuals suffer from the same mental health disorders that straight clients do.

Some clients have emotional and personality disorders that, I believe, result from a lifetime of closeted dissociation, adapting to the sexual and romantic orientation that others expect. Others have personality disorders that would have been present regardless of the client's sexual orientation. In some cases, the suppression of one's sexual identity also suppresses other problems, which do not surface until the identity does.

In cases of true dual diagnosis, treatment in addition to GAT may be needed. This is sometimes the case even when the mental health disorder has been triggered by the trauma of growing up LGBTQ, as patterns of behavior can become entrenched over the years and extend to areas of clients' lives that have little to do with their sexual identity. For example, a client whose depression was triggered in response to a hostile school environment may find that his depression returns every September long after he has finished school and begun his adult professional life. For this client, antidepressant medication in addition to GAT may be the best solution.

The same is often true in cases of chemical dependency. While clients are in the closet, they are vulnerable to developing chemical dependencies or patterns of chemical abuse. In the early stages of coming out, they may keep their gay identities suppressed by drinking too much or using marijuana. During the socialization process, most LGBTQ individuals frequent bars, where they are vulnerable to drinking too much to avoid their anxiety.

Sometimes chemical abuse is simply a stage and naturally tapers off with the passing of Stage 5 of the coming-out process. Other times, however, it may develop into alcoholism and has to be treated as such.

The Case of Esther

Esther, a 45-year-old single woman, came to me with the recognition that she was lesbian and wanted to come out. She had never married or acted on any of her feelings toward women. She was now ready to come out and live as a lesbian.

Esther's childhood was riddled with shame from both her parents and her brothers. Teased for not being "feminine" enough, she was a tomboy at heart. She always thought it was from having four older brothers and trying to keep up. Her father and mother wanted her to be more feminine and forced her to wear dresses and have her hair done at the beauty shop with her mother. She rebelled against this as a little girl until one day she saw the contempt and anger in her mother's eyes. She remembered this vividly, and from that day forward she decided conform to whatever her mother wanted, to get the love she so desperately needed from her. She wore the dresses her mother picked out for her, started using makeup, and stopped playing sports. She told me that at points she even fooled herself into thinking that this was who she was—a girly girl just like her mother wanted.

After finishing a PhD in education, Esther decided to become a nun. She was in the convent for 5 years and during this time recognized that this was not the life for her. She left on bad terms with the Church and returned to live at home with her parents at the age of 35. She became a teacher in a local school district and was much happier in that profession.

During college and her time in the convent, Esther began drinking. Even after she returned home, her drinking increased to the point that she was experiencing blackouts and passing out. She received her first drunk-driving charge at the age of 40 and went to classes mandated by the court. Drinking was "all [she] had left" to make her own choices around, Esther told me. She said her drinking had subsided, that she was able to control it, and that she no longer experienced blackouts.

During therapy we explored Esther's childhood, and she was able to address the covert cultural sexual abuse she suffered at the hands of her mother. She recognized that the reason she became a nun was to keep her lesbianism at bay and suppress her sexual urges. During therapy with me she began going to lesbian bars and events and enjoyed her experiences. Over the next year she came out to her family and friends. Although her mother was disappointed, she ultimately accepted Esther as a lesbian.

Esther denied that she was an alcoholic and explained that she had started drinking heavily again from being at lesbian events. She told me that the lesbian community also drank heavily, particularly those who played baseball with her during the summer.

I asked Esther about her family patterns surrounding chemical use. She reported no family history of drinking or drug abuse. She said she drank heavily during college but was able to stop for long periods of time. She also said she was able to recreationally drink when she "wanted to" but admitted that she could drink a fifth of vodka herself in a night out with her friends.

Esther refused to go for chemical dependency treatment, believing her drinking was a stage of the coming-out process and that after she stabilized and settled down as a lesbian her drinking would subside. I was not so sure and challenged her thinking, but this made her angry, so I agreed to work with her and see how it went.

The following year Esther received another drunk-driving charge. Now she finally had to face the fact that although the drinking was initially about suppressing her lesbian tendencies and masking her core self, she now had a real problem. Esther was an alcoholic.

Esther: Clinical Interpretation and Treatment

Mandated by the court, Esther went for treatment at an intensive outpatient program at a local chemical dependency center. We agreed she would finish chemical dependency therapy there and then return to therapy with me. The staff advised her to stay closeted—that the other patients would not take kindly to having a lesbian in their group. Their intention was to protect her, but instead Esther was insulted. She did come out in the group, and she received much criticism from the other patients, just as the staff had warned her. The staff did not protect her, and Esther called me, sobbing, to ask what she should do.

I advised her to confront the staff and to sign a release for me to talk to them, but she was determined not to return. She feared she would relapse if she complied with my advice. I recommended that she return to therapy with me and also attend LGBTQ AA meetings. I gave her a list of AA locations, and she followed through on going.

During the next year, Esther was able to stay sober and go to meetings. Recognizing that suppressing her lesbianism had contributed to her alcoholism, Esther hoped that resolving this would prevent her from becoming a problem drinker again, and she started drinking once again. Within 3 months she was back to abusing alcohol.

This time, however, Esther had begun dating a woman who was also in AA, and the woman told her that if she did not stop, she would leave her. Faced with the loss of this relationship, Esther finally accepted that regardless of how her drinking began, she truly was an alcoholic and could not return to social drinking.

Working With Lesbian, Gay, Bisexual, Transgender, and Questioning Clients

In this book I have illustrated the various presenting problems and concerns typical of LGBTQ clients. Although I have tried to be as thorough as possible, there are many issues and treatment approaches I did not cover. Ethnic and minority issues, for example, may intersect with LGBTQ identity issues in myriad ways that are beyond the scope of this book.

What I hope to have conveyed here is the importance of not assuming that LGBTQ individuals suffer problems simply *because* they are LGBTQ but rather to consider these issues as stemming from the trauma involved in being invisible, neglected, and ignored in a predominately heterosexist world. Many of the issues facing LGBTQ individuals are connected in some way to covert cultural sexual abuse and the trauma of growing up LGBTQ. That said, there are also many clients who have suffered covert cultural sexual abuse but did not experience it as the type of trauma I have addressed throughout this book. These clients are much like those individuals who were sexually, physically, and verbally abused but seem to have the resilience to get past it and not have it contaminate their lives.

The most important thing we can do as clinicians is learn as much as we can about the clients we are sitting across from. You now have the framework and tools to conduct GAT. Deciding whether GAT is enough or if there are other issues that need to be addressed is something you will have to feel out on your own with each client.

Clients will help you know what direction to pursue as you continue checking in with them. It is important that they feel they can be honest with you even if it means telling you your style or approach is not for them. This may mean you need to refine your skills, or it may mean you are not the right therapist. My goal in writing this book is to let you, the therapist, know that you *can* be enough for your LGBTQ clients, as long as you remain educated about the particular issues they face.

CHAPTER 13

Working With Today's LGBTQ Teen

I believe in a world where hope outshines fear.
—It Gets Better Project

Doing therapy with teens has special challenges, as any therapist knows. The client may be dealing with any of the psychiatric problems that would come up for an adult, but because the client is a teen, there are additional issues, things to look out for, things to expect.

But what if the client is also LGBTQ? Then there is a third axis of considerations. First, an LGBTQ teen has had an LGBTQ childhood, so all the considerations discussed in Chapters 3, 4, 5, and 6 apply. The teen has grown up LGBTQ and suffered from the potential trauma of covert cultural sexual abuse (see Chapter 4), having to suppress and repress his or her sexual and gender identity, and also "minority stress," having to live as a member of a hated few in a hostile environment. This trauma must be assessed and addressed. Second, LGBTQ teens typically overlook many concerns about safely coming out. After they achieve the victory of coming out to themselves, they will impulsively want to tell everyone everywhere: parents, family members, teachers, fellow students, and everyone else they know. They may have concerns about rejection before they are ready to come out, but once they are ready, they will throw caution to the wind. It is the job of the therapist to help guide them to think through the consequences of coming out to different individuals and groups. Third, even an "out" teen will be lonely and typically have few resources to connect with others. While a heterosexual teen generally has many opportunities for friendship and dating, an LGBTQ teen may have very few. The social, legal, and religious context of the teen's life will be significant to treatment strategies. If coming out will have serious consequences, the therapist should not thoughtlessly advocate it.

Let me note that I will not consider transgender teens in this chapter except in passing. See Chapter 14 for a discussion of the transgender client.

Although adolescent behavior issues may draw attention from the parents or the clients themselves, the therapist cannot take the position that "a teen is a teen" and proceed without considering the LGBTQ issues. At the same time, adolescent behavior cannot be ignored. Both parts need to be considered at the same time. An LGBTQ teen is simultaneously LGBTQ and teen.

LGBTQ youth face some daunting challenges. The suicide rate among LGB teens is 30 percent. Self-harm (e.g., cutting) is common. LGBTQ teens are twice as likely to use alcohol or drugs as their heterosexual peers and half as likely to report that they are happy (Human Rights Campaign, 2012). They are more likely to report eating disorders, self-harm, and depression. These all can be viewed as the result of minority stress. In the first study to look at the consequences of antigay prejudice for mortality, researchers at the Mailman School of Public Health at Columbia University found that LGBTQ individuals who lived in communities with high levels of antigay prejudice have life expectancies that are 12 years shorter on average compared with their peers in the least prejudiced communities. Each episode of LGBTQ victimization, such as physical or verbal harassment or abuse, increases the likelihood of self-harming behavior by 2.5 times on average. Suicide attempts by LGBTQ youth and questioning youth are 4 to 6 times more likely to result in injury, poisoning, or overdose that requires treatment from a doctor or nurse, compared to their straight peers (Maza & Krehely, 2010).

"Sexual minority youth, or teens that identify themselves as gay, lesbian or bisexual, are bullied two to three times more than heterosexuals," and "almost all transgender students have been verbally harassed [e.g., called names or threatened] in the past year at school because of their sexual orientation (89%) and gender expression (89%)," as reported in GLSEN's *Harsh Realities, The Experiences of Transgender Youth in Our Nation's Schools* (Greytak, Kosciw, & Diaz, 2009, page xi).

Thus, as therapists engage with LGBTQ teens, issues of safety should be never far from their minds. Suicide, self-harm, bullying, sexual harassment and assault—all are much more significant factors for LGBTQ youth than for straight teens.

I should note here another point. These days, LGBTQ teens do not always come in to talk about their sexual identity. Many are coming in just like any other teen with relationship issues, parent issues, and other issues of daily living. Don't focus on LGBTQ identity unless either the client tells you it is a problem or you assess that it is more of a problem than the client thinks it is.

A Teen Walks Into Your Office . . .

When an LGBTQ teenager walks into a therapist's office, the therapist needs to keep certain basic truths in mind. Even though things are getting better for LGBTQ adults in our culture, they are not necessarily better for teens or children before they come out.

Loneliness and Social Isolation

We're all socialized only to be heterosexual, and so LGBTQ teens miss the experience of a sense of belonging. Belonging is an important developmental task for teens, and most teens are able to have some version of it at school. They have their cliques. They have their niches. LGBTQ teens do not have a sense of belonging at school unless there is a gay-straight alliance or some other such organization. The loneliness and isolation can be crushing. That's why it can be so important to find opportunities away from school, like at LGBTQ community centers or online. There are now summer camps for LGBTQ teens (often specialized to L or G or B or T) and in appropriate age categories such as 13–15 or 15–18. One of my teen clients was very enthusiastic about her camp experience. "I've been born again," she told me.

I advise parents to check out clubs at school—for instance, a gay-straight alliance. I suggest the parents take the teen to the gay community center, if available. Sometimes that means traveling an hour or an hour and a half, but it's crucial to give the kid some outlet and a sense of belonging. Often, a teen has already established his or her own community online, but face-to-face contact is still important. (See the section below, "Breaking the Wall of Isolation.")

Even in the very best situation—the teen is out at school and to his or her family, people know and they're accepting, the teen has friends—the question we have to think about is: How many other people in school are LGBTQ? And of those others, how many are out and would the teen even get along with or want to hang out with? The numbers are going to be small, even if the kid is out. So it's unlikely that he or she would have the same social experience that a straight teen would have: a large pool of fellow teens to be friends with and to date. The opposite gender is available to a straight teen to date—generally about 50% of the school population—where it is not for the LGBTQ teen. So for an LGBTQ teen, lifting social isolation would require the school to go out of its way, or the parents to go out of their way, or someone to go out of their way to get that kid with other LGBTQ teens. And it's usually not going to be at the school, because LGBTQ individuals are a small minority, and a lot of those aren't out. (Note: For linguistic simplicity, I will often write "LGBTQ teen," realizing that sometimes different groups of individuals—be they gay male, lesbian, bi, transgender, or questioning—might require their own accommodation, and one size often does not fit all. For example, transgender teens may want and need their own support group. Again, for simplicity, sometimes I will gloss over this important point in order that the text not be overburdened with cumbersome language.)

Feeling Endangered and the Risk of Suicide

Dan Savage and his husband created the It Gets Better Project as a direct response to LGBTQ teen suicides. (The Trevor Project was also motivated by this issue.) I support that initiative, but I would say this: It's *not* better for a teen before he or she comes out. It's just not. When you talk to teens before they come out and before they're ready, it's like the '70s all over again. It's like the '50s. They don't *know* it's safe, even if they're in the most supportive possible environment. I've treated gay teens who felt terribly unsafe, anxious, and depressed, even though they had a gay older brother or a gay father. Their experience, their perception is: I'm not safe, and I could be brutalized in some emotional, physical, or verbal way, no matter what you say. Their minority stress is profound. This can be the result of prejudice and brutality in the family, but it certainly is the result of covert cultural sexual abuse. Gay teens have lived their whole lives protecting their secret. Now, telling people, exposing themselves, being vulnerable—they don't know what might happen.

In 2010, the media focused on six LGBTQ youth who committed suicide in a span of weeks. It started with the story of Tyler Clementi, an 18-year-old Rutgers freshman. His roommate set up webcams in his room and streamed him live making love with another man. He was exposed and humiliated, when he wasn't even ready to be out. As a result, Tyler killed himself by jumping off a bridge. His case alerted the media to be more aware of LGBTQ teen suicides, and they noted five more, all in a short period of time. Of course, there were many before and many after, but the media chose to focus only on those six. Remember, adolescence is a very vulnerable time of life. When you're a teen, your identity is not yet formed in every way—not just around LGBTQ issues. You're learning how to be a young adult, and you're self-conscious. You have adolescence to deal with, but you're dealing with sexuality as well.

I want therapists to hear that it's not "better" for their teen clients until they come out. You must make an assessment of how endangered these teens feel and how they are experiencing the world. The suicide assessment is critical. I can't emphasize that enough.

An LGBTQ teen feels a special sense of isolation and a special sense of threat. If he tells you he feels endangered, you need to take that very seriously. It would be very easy for a therapist to disagree, to try to argue, "No, no. Don't worry. There's no threat. It's all in your mind." Don't do that, no matter how good things seem to be.

Further, a well-intentioned therapist, in trying to be affirmative and supportive of an LGBTQ teen coming out, might not see all the potential problems the teen actually will face. I've talked with some therapists who were surprised that a kid would feel endangered even with a reassuring circle around him or her. Think about it. When the kid was 5, he or she saw video clips of ISIS throwing gay people off buildings. A child doesn't think, "That's a thousand miles away." An LGBTQ 5-year-old sees it and thinks, "That could happen to me right here." The kid's priest or rabbi is saying homosexuality is an abomination, and that also becomes a part of the kid's worldview. A child doesn't know, "Oh, that's just the stupid bigoted prejudices of an idiot who thinks that he knows everything."

A parent of a lesbian child who didn't have a clue the child was lesbian once said in her hearing, "The fags will go to hell." Another client remembers being 10 and his father pointing at a gay bar they were passing and saying, "That's where all the queers go to meet." You take such things very seriously because you're a child. You know you're the very thing that your parents said something bad about. So, now, even though they're telling you they're okay with it, are they really? The child may not know consciously that he or she is LGBTQ at the time the homophobic messages are received; however, the messages are stored in the child's memory, and once the child realizes he or she is LGBTQ, the messages are recalled and work to keep the child ashamed, threatened, and in the closet.

One of my clients was a child in the 1950s and 1960s in the Deep South. He is white, but the atmosphere of racial violence was traumatizing. Being white didn't make him feel safe. He was just overwhelmed by the brutality going on around him. He absorbed the atmosphere of threat at a nonrational level. Covert cultural sexual abuse works the same way for an LGBTQ child. These were his intersectional identities, as discussed in Chapter 2.

No Gay Planet: Why Coming Out Is the Key

LGBTQ teens didn't land here from some gay planet when they reached puberty. They were here all along—they were babies, they were toddlers, they were little kids, they were tweens—but they were invisible, and things were happening around them that nobody was helping them make sense of. Nobody was talking to them about sexual identity and homophobia because nobody knew they were LGBTQ. And so the LGBTQ children make their own sense of it, and the sense they make is, "I'm not safe."

LGBTQ kids are traumatized by having something so emotionally charged inside them with no way to express it. There is no downloading it. So they are living in fear and are hypervigilant. Like a sexual abuse survivor, they're living with a horrible sexual secret. This is the fundamental unavoidable trauma of growing up LGBTQ in a homophobic society. You have had to hide who you really were growing up, even from your own family. Now you're grown. You have an adult's more balanced perspective, but the effects of the trauma remain.

Children and teens feel this sense of threat, but after they come out, it can be partly lifted. Therapy can address the trauma, while positive reactions to their coming out can help them begin to feel safer in their families and their communities.

LGBTQ Children Have a Child's Sexuality

I should note here, as I have before, that being gay (or L or B or T) does not imply an adult sexuality. A gay child has a child's sexuality but with a gay orientation.

When my first nephew was born, we passed him around to share our wishes for his future. One person hoped he would become a doctor. Another saw a nice Jewish girl and beautiful children in his future. When he came into my arms, I wished that he might meet a nice Jewish boy and live happily ever after. My wish received looks of horror and outrage.

"How could you wish something sexual on him?" my uncle said.

He took my hopes for a happy LGBTQ future as something sexual and dirty. He had superimposed an adult sexuality on my baby nephew. But the wishes for a happy heterosexual future didn't get that reaction. This oversexualization of gayness is a misrepresentation of our humanity. All of us have an age-appropriate sexual-selfhood, and there's nothing wrong with that. Some of my straight colleagues have had trouble with this concept, but it is very important. Think about crushes. Little children have crushes that reflect their sexual orientation. Yes, little straight boys blush and stammer over a pretty woman 20 years older, but little gay boys do the same for an attractive man.

Sexual orientation emerges in various ways for children. When I was 8 years old, I was a Cub Scout. We all got naked to go to the showers before we went in the pool, and I was mesmerized by all the naked bodies and penises I was looking at. I didn't know what was going on or why I felt that way, but I knew that I was overwhelmed by it and very stimulated in a positive way.

The Case of Josh

Josh was 15. His original presenting problem was depression. His parents had taken him to another therapist, but then they had discovered gay porn on his computer. They asked him if he was gay, and he equivocated. "I don't know," he said, not denying but not wanting to come out to them, suddenly, after being caught. The therapist said that since Josh was unsure about his identity, he should see someone who specialized in LGBTQ issues and "identity confusion." To soothe his anxiety about being outed, his parents told him, "Okay, looking at gay porn doesn't make you gay, but you've said you were uncertain, so we'd at least like you to talk with a gay therapist."

He was a big guy, perhaps as you would expect of a high school football player. He had heavy stubble and looked at least college age. He was also remarkably mature and self-confident for a boy of 15. "I *am* depressed," he told me, "but I'm also gay. I just can't . . . I'm not ready to tell everybody." He looked down, perhaps embarrassed. "I'm not sure how people will respond. I go to a parochial school . . ."

He opened up to me quickly, in the first session, perhaps because I'm gay.

As we began, I was immediately assessing him for suicidality; 30% of LGBTQ teens attempt suicide. His parents were concerned about that, too. They'd heard that same statistic. Josh told me he didn't intend to harm himself, but he had thought about it. He told me calmly that he would hang himself if things became unbearable, but they weren't unbearable yet.

"I don't have a problem about being gay," he said. "I just worry about the people around me."

I asked him what he expected in terms of coming out. "I'm not sure. Everybody says it's okay to be gay, but that's what you're supposed to say, isn't it?" He wasn't sure about his parents or the people at school, teachers or students or fellow football players. One bright spot: He felt pretty confident that his female friends would be okay with it. Still, he was very frightened to come out at school. And in general, coming out is a frightening thing to do. He was particularly worried about the other football players. "They're macho guys, and they go after anyone who acts weak. I'm not sure they'll let me be."

"Sometimes I feel like a fake," he told me. "I get all As, and I'm on the football team. Everybody thinks I'm great. But if they knew about me being gay, that's all they would see about me. I'd just be 'that fag.'"

Josh: Clinical Interpretation and Treatment

At first, as he was seeing me, his depression worsened. The conflict was now building with regard to his being gay, and whether or not to come out. In general, gay teens feel better after they come out, but he had been prematurely outed. He hadn't been ready to come out when his parents discovered his porn. Being prematurely outed was causing him to be more depressed. The decision to come out had been taken out of his hands. We know that in the coming-out stages, people have to go at their own pace, or they will experience trauma and high amounts of anxiety. (See Chapter 7 for more on stages of coming out.)

Josh's parents were wealthy and came from privileged backgrounds. They were politically conservative and sending him to a Christian school, but they were not stereotypically prejudiced. They wanted what was best for their child. They had taken pains to assure him that if he was gay, they would still love and care for him.

Josh's story illustrates the power of covert cultural sexual abuse and its trauma. Despite his parents' assurances and support, Josh's worldview was: I'm not safe, the world is unsafe. Even if political correctness kept people silent, maybe in their hearts they were burning up with prejudice and hate.

Josh and I worked on his depression, and I kept an eye out for signs that he might hurt himself. As I helped him feel safer, I taught him about the stages of coming out. When I met Josh, he was at Stage 4 of the six stages: He accepted that he was gay. By helping him understand the stages, I was helping him prepare to transition toward being a fully integrated out gay adult.

As his depression lifted and he began to feel safer, he wanted to begin by coming out to his parents. In a family therapy session, Josh came out to his parents in my office. That went well. His parents were accepting and encouraging; they really were okay with his gayness.

After Josh established his safety at home, he began to feel an intense need to tell everyone. He was moving into Stage 5 of coming out. This is the stage where a gay person wants to tell the world.

One day, in a family therapy session, Josh told me and his parents, "I have a tweet scheduled to go out tonight while I'm sleeping. When I wake up tomorrow, everyone will know I am gay. Isn't that awesome?"

I wanted him to wait on the tweet until he considered all the consequences, but I didn't want him to think I was an old-fashioned gay guy who was too scared to come fully out. And if you're a straight clinician, you risk being judged as ignorant of gay life if you caution too strongly a teen who's caught in the enthusiasm of Stage 5.

I first focused on his strengths as a newly out gay young man.

"This is wonderful," I told Josh. "You're out and proud. You've come a long way from that depressed guy, thinking about suicide, who first came to see me. I'm happy for you and proud of you. Let's consider all the positives of this tweet, and we also need to consider the negatives, too. Are you willing to do that?"

Josh agreed.

First, I validated him. I said, "Yes, you want to tweet. It makes sense. It's appropriate in this stage of coming out to want to tell everyone." Then I asked him if he'd be willing to control the impulse for a while and really think about what that would look like the next day at school. The football team. His teachers.

His father expressed concern about Josh coming out. He was particularly worried that Josh would harm his opportunities in what is, after all, a straight society. "You're up-and-coming, and you know you like football. Sports culture can be homophobic. And you might want to go into business like me one day, and, well, whatever goes out on the Internet tomorrow will be there years from now when you're looking for a job."

In some ways, Josh didn't care. "What are you telling me?" he said to both me and his dad. "You're both older, and you don't understand the world today." In Stage 5 of coming out, the world is divided between straight and gay, and every straight person is seen as antigay. But then, Josh was also a teen, and for a teen the world is divided between adult and teen. So he had two things going on at the same time: *You're old. You don't understand*; and to me, *Even you're an old gay; you don't understand what it's like to be gay like me.* But I did understand. When I was his age, I tweeted myself "out" as soon as I knew I was gay, except that my twitter was a dial telephone and the phone book, and I called everybody.

In other ways, though, Josh was listening. "Okay, you're right," he told us. "I don't want to ruin my career. I don't want to go to school tomorrow and lose my heterosexual privileges." (I had taught him about heterosexual privilege; losing it can be one of the costs of coming out.)

I was strongly supportive of his wanting to be out to the world, but I also said, "Let's think this through all the way, think about all the different reactions you might get."

So ultimately he listened, and he didn't tweet—yet.

In our next individual session, I started strategizing with him. "Who do you think might be a problem at school?" He mentioned some teachers and of course the team. So we talked it over. We finally agreed that he would tell selectively, starting with people he felt would be supportive.

He started with the circle of girls that he hung out with at school, and they were totally fine with it. I suggested he seek the advice of the people he came out to. What did they think about the school situation? Did they think that it was safe to come out more?

He decided not to tweet it but told selectively until so many people at school knew he was gay that essentially everybody knew. And his gayness was completely accepted by his teachers and even by the football team.

I referred him the local gay community center, and his parents were willing to make the long drive to help him connect with other teens there. I suggested he check out some gay teen websites such as Gay Teen Chat Rooms (www.gayteenchatrooms .net) and TrevorSpace (www.trevorspace.org). They are monitored and seem to be a relatively safe option for teens, unlike adult sex apps such as Grindr. I also suggested he check out Tumblr, which gay teens use to connect. (See the section "Internet Options for Gay Teens," below.)

I should note that Josh was a kid in an upper-middle-class family in an upper-middle-class neighborhood. Coming-out stories don't always go like this. One size does not fit all. A therapist needs to be aware of not pushing a teen too hard, but not holding him back, either.

Helping the Parents of an LGBTQ Teen

A big part of the job of the therapist with an LGBTQ teen client is to help the parents and the family accept the reality of what the child is telling them. It is especially important for the parents not to withdraw their love and support, whatever their reactions and disagreements. We know that LGBTQ teens who feel rejected by their parents are likely to attempt suicide. Bringing the family around is a critical part of the therapy.

If the family is rigid in insisting that the child is not LGBTQ or the rejection is even more harsh—"If you're a fag, then you're no son of mine"—then the child is going to be pushed toward self-harm or even suicide. Many LGBTQ teens have been driven out of their family homes, and their situation can be dire. See "Detroit Mom Accused of Beating Gay Daughter Due to Her Sexual Orientation" (Dalbey, 2016).

A therapist should be empathetic to the parents and validate their feelings toward their child. Acknowledge their fears about social acceptance, about physical danger, about future opportunities for marriage, children, and a place in the community.

Educate them about what negative consequences really could result from their teen coming out and what feared consequences are not realistic. It is generally a reasonable concern that the child could face discrimination. It's often not realistic that the child will be facing imminent danger and violence. Of course, this depends on where they live. Birmingham, Alabama, might present one level of danger, and Birmingham, Michigan, another.

The parents' reactions may be rooted in their own time and their own generation. "Oh my god, she's going to go to school and everybody is going to bully her." Part of the therapist's job is to help the client's parents get in touch with what their child's sexual identity is bringing up for *them*: their own sexual issues, their own family history, their own hopes and dreams for their child.

Some form of family therapy is almost always helpful. The parents and the child should be urged not to shut down communication and connection with each other, even if there are strong feelings and disagreements. Tell the parents, "It's okay to have your own perspective, but hear your child's perspective, too." Emphasize that it's okay to disagree without making one person wrong. If family therapy isn't possible, then at least you can teach the parents how to go back to the child and have helpful discussions. This is what real differentiation looks like in a family, where people can disagree and still stay connected. Here, therapists can rely on their family therapy skills. This isn't just about LGBTQ; it's about family differences.

Conservative parents may believe that their teen child shouldn't have sex at all and they may insist that the child's therapist report to them any sexual thoughts or activity their child has (or might have, say, if they're going to gay gathering places, either physically or on the Internet). When you inform your teen client the rules you're operating under, he or she will most likely stop talking to you about sex and go his or her own way. This may leave the child without any functional adult guidance about sex at all. You might want to help the parents understand that this way of working with the teen could have very negative consequences. The truth is that most teens are going to experiment with sex whether you tell them they can or not. The only issue is secrecy.

One final note: Teens are often changeable in their tastes and opinions. That can happen with sexual orientation and even gender orientation, too. The child announces she's lesbian and then the following month she says she's bisexual or pansexual or queer or nonbinary, and the family can be confused, upset, even angry at this lack of consistency. What's going on? What is he or she talking about? As soon as the family's gotten used to the shock that their daughter is lesbian, they have to deal with her new status as bisexual, and so on.

The therapist should tell the parents not to be surprised if there is this kind of exploration, fluidity, and confusion. Offer them the suggestion, to the extent that they can, to "go with the flow" and not overreact. Often, the thing to do is nothing, and that can be hard, because parents are wondering, "What am I supposed to do now?" They feel helpless and confused. And that's okay, because that's how their child is feeling, too: going through all these different identities, with no idea what is happening.

Assessing the Family, School, and Community Environment

A therapist must judge how supportive the family, school, and community will be for a coming-out LGBTQ teen. Coming out is difficult, and there are always consequences that need to be considered ahead of time.

Even if the parents are supportive, the school or community may be a problem. If the client begins to selectively share (at school or at church), and he or she starts getting homophobic reactions—or maybe not that extreme, but negative reactions—you, the therapist, will have to deal with that. And note: Often, the teachers or the coaches can be more of a problem than the students. These days, students tend to be accepting, but teachers and other adults can be hostile.

In a significantly homophobic community: (1) You should advise the client to be very selective in coming out, and (2) you need to have a strategy for dealing with negative reactions. I've had clients so badly bullied in the locker room that they had to drop out of school. Schools can be abysmally inept, if not hostile, in handling bullying. Even with the "zero tolerance" program for bullying in schools, bullying still goes on. What I hear most often is that no effective action is taken, sometimes with a "blame the victim" attitude on the part of school authorities.

You have to know your community's level of homophobia or find out. A gay community newsletter and the gay community center can be good resources. If you're going to work with LGBTQ teens, you can't stay isolated in your office. You're going to have to develop some relationship with the gay community, even if it is just receiving information on what is happening locally.

In extreme environments, a therapist might advise a teen not to come out to anyone but his parents. Even then, I've known kids who've been thrown out of the house by homophobic parents. I've literally been told, "I'd rather have my son be a murderer than find out he's gay."

What's Happening Now

It used to be believed by clinicians that adolescence was a second chance for a person to mature into a heterosexual identity. That was a heterosexist, heteronormative mindset, and it's no longer a valid professional opinion. It's completely understood today that people who are gay, lesbian, or bisexual aren't stuck in "immaturity." That it is their natural identity.

In the 2000s, teen clients were coming in for therapy and saying, "I'm bi." Now, they've picked up a whole new sexual-identity vocabulary: "I'm genderqueer." "I'm sexually fluid." "I'm asexual." And many therapists are confused; they don't know what to do. Is what these teens are saying literally true? It might just feel good to say. It might just be a fad. My suggestion to therapists is to take the clients at their word but then ask them to tell you more. "Okay, you're sexually fluid. Let's talk about that. What does that mean to you?" You don't say, "Well, come on, that's just a fad. You're not really . . ." or "Are you sure?" Accept their label at face value. Don't put yourself at odds with them or their label. Validate them. "I hear you. What does it mean to you?" I do think it's important to hear what they say.

Teenagers today have something we of the older generation didn't have when we were their age—permission to explore their sexual and gender identities openly. This is a stark difference with being allowed to explore only a heterosexual sexual identity or only a cisgender gender identity. My hope is that this tolerant attitude will extend into childhood, so that people can grow up with minimal confusion about their sexual and gender identity.

Breaking the Wall of Isolation

Dating and hookup apps for gay men—like Grindr, Scruff, Adam for Adam, and many others—work like this: Commonly, the app is downloaded to a smartphone, although it can also be used from any Internet-enabled device. These apps require that users be adults (18 years old or older), although the apps do not check this in any way. A user registers with the app and includes a photograph. Using geolocation technology, the app can tell a man if there are any other men nearby who are looking to connect and shows their photos. If one man likes another's photo and personal information, he can send a text expressing interest. A return text can lead to a meeting. In some urban locations, it is expected that "dates" will be very nearby, feet away rather than blocks away, and men can use the app to meet almost immediately. Although some men specify "friends only," the apps are generally used for sexual hookups.

A gay teen may seek to lift his isolation and find people who accept him by meeting men on Grindr (or a similar adult site). However, it is illegal for an underage teen to have sex with an adult, although the specific rules about ages will differ from legal jurisdiction to jurisdiction. I warn my adult clients to know the law and insist their sexual contacts show them ID. I warn my teen clients about the dangers of seeking sex with adults, but teens don't always listen to good advice.

Gay teenagers making contact with gay men is not new. The adult hookup apps just make it easier to connect. Historically, gay teens went to gay bookstores, looked for phone numbers on bathroom walls, hung out in mall bathrooms, and they would find sex. And note here that sex is not just sex. Under these circumstances, sex is the way a teenager meets his need for gay contact, for connection, for affirmation. ("You're a good kid. There's nothing wrong with you.") The teen may want sex, but even more he wants to end his isolation, to find a "place" where others think he's okay. On the boy's mind, perhaps, he's just looking for sex, but really there's a lot more than that going on.

The Therapist's Dilemma

Whenever I do LGBTQ trainings for therapists, I make sure to raise the issue of the ethical and legal decisions that will come up for a therapist when he or she learns that an underage teen client is having sex with adults. If a client is meeting men on Grindr, then it is likely that he is having sex with men, so the same ethical and legal issues will come up, even if the client has not explicitly said he is having sex.

Whether we adults think teens should be having sex or not, many of them are doing it. Our only choice is to decide how we deal with what's coming our way. We therapists need to be aware and discuss and decide on a case-by-case basis what to do.

A teen client needs to be told very clearly that a therapist is a "mandatory reporter," that you must report to the authorities if he or she is being harmed or doing harm. And then to make it absolutely clear, you might say, "And someone having sex with you (or trying to have sex with you) if you're underage and they're not is automatically considered 'harm.'" However, the details of the law (for example, the age of sexual consent) vary from state to state and even from county to county, so it's important for the therapist to be up on the law. Also, laws around sex and the Internet can be especially byzantine. Get the facts.

You have to be really clear with a teen, because they might not understand from a general "disclaimer" that you're talking about, say, the "crime" of an 18-year-old giving a 17-year-old a blow job. (Many teens don't even consider oral sex to be "sex.")

So, getting back to the gay apps specifically, the teen tells his therapist, "I met this guy on this app . . ." And the therapist should ask, "What app?" and the kid says Grindr. You, the therapist, know that Grindr is for 18-year-olds and older. Your 15-year-old client is telling you he meets up at the mall with guys he has connected with on Grindr. He makes friends that way, and some of the guys are older. And right here the therapist feels a conflict.

First, you're delighted your client is breaking the wall of depression and isolation that gay teens tend to feel. The teen is less likely to commit suicide—and remember, the statistic is that 30% of gay teens attempt suicide. So all that is good. But, second, if he's having sex with "older men," even if they're only college students, then that might not be so good. It might not even be legal.

I guess I need to go on the record here: Whether you (the therapist) believe that teens should have sex or not, some of them are doing it. In particular, a typical teenage boy if he can have sex will have sex, whether he's using Grindr or not. And no, you generally can't get him to stop by telling him to stop. You—and their parents and the authorities—are going to have to deal with this reality.

When I do LGBTQ trainings, we always talk about these ethical and legal decisions that may come up. Reporting a teen for having sex with an adult immediately outs them in many ways—especially to their families. Many of the families of gay teens are unaccepting and would put their child on the streets or send them to treatment centers to make them straight. Others may physically and verbally abuse their child. Given this, some therapists feel that they have to play some version of "don't ask, don't tell." This is inevitable when the needs of a client come up against the requirements of the law. The therapist might say, "If you're having sex, don't tell me. I'll have to report you." Or, "Don't give me any specifics. Even if I have to report, I don't want to have anything actionable to say." You see, already this is tricky. If you tell any client you're going to break his confidentiality, he's going to shut up. Especially a teen. Then you won't be able to protect him from predators, and you won't be helping him in any other way either. In fact, you might be placing him at even greater risk, given the consequences of his being outed.

But suppose your teen client goes ahead and tells you he had sex with a college student. Now you're sitting on reportable information. So here are some other things to consider. The kid telling you this may be from a family that will kick him out if you report. But maybe that's not the most important thing to a therapist. I've had therapists tell me, "I'd rather have this kid struggle with getting put on the street than ruin my licensure. I already can't help this kid. If I lose my license, then I can't help the next kid."

But some therapists don't feel that way at all. They feel that's too rigid. So you have to decide. Are you going to report? Are you going to expose him to his family? Some therapists decide, "I'll talk to the kid until he's ready to tell his parents, but with a time limit."

But what if it's a violently homophobic family? When they learn he's gay, they may pull him from therapy with you and put him in reparative therapy (conversion therapy), which still exists under different names in this country.

Realistically, it's unlikely in most cases for a teen meeting men on Grindr not to be having sex. He's a teenager. He wants to at least experiment with his sexuality. However, you (the therapist) might decide to coach him to be discreet in what he tells you. "I'm meeting people. We're friends," and leave it at that, without any other details.

I realize many therapists are going to condemn a therapist's willingness to negotiate "don't ask, don't tell" with a client and say that's condoning the client having sex with older men, which is nothing less than sexual abuse. Rigidity here is not always in the client's best interest. The details matter.

Some therapists say, "don't ask, don't tell," but it's not that simple. The less detail a therapist knows, the less he will be able to say if he decides to report. The truth is that child protective services (CPS) often won't do anything because the teen will often not know the real name or address of their sexual partner. CPS might take the teenager's name and number, and then he's prematurely outed.

You want to know enough, so that you can help do "harm reduction" and "damage control" and really arm this kid with protective tools. You do want a general sense of what's going on. That's where the "don't ask, don't tell" gets tricky—if the teen tells you something you're legally required to call protective services or the police about.

However, keep this in mind. Suppose you've encouraged the teen client not to tell you too much, but you know he's on Grindr. Should you tell his parents? Are you ethically obliged to tell them? Most parents would want to know, but once you tell them, they may take actions that are not in the best interests of the client. On the other hand, they might help the client stay out of harm's way.

There are definitely risks when a teen is on Grindr. He could meet someone who assaults, robs, or even kills him. Even if everything is fine between the teen and his contact, the older guy he meets faces possible legal consequences. I advise my adult clients who like youthful-looking sexual partners (in gay slang, they're sometimes called "bois" or "twinks") to demand to see ID. I say, "If the contact won't show you his driver's license, you should have nothing to do with him."

Let me make this absolutely clear. Most gay men are not sexual predators. They are not pedophiles or ephebophiles. They do not want to have sex with children. If a kid gets on Grindr and says he's 14, nobody's going to have anything to do with him. But the problem comes when he says he's of age. That's why I tell men to ask for ID.

Therapists should help their teen clients break the wall of social isolation without using adult hookup apps—say, through gay community centers, gay-straight alliances at school, and teen-oriented websites and apps. However, some of your teen clients will inevitably try adult apps like Grindr. When you're counseling teens, you have to let them know that you're a mandatory reporter and that if they don't limit what they tell you, then you have a duty to report what they say to Family Services or the police. Many teens are unaware of how rigid and severe the law can be. If an 18-year-old has sex with a 17-year-old, the 18-year-old is a sex criminal in many jurisdictions and may face prison time and a lifetime on the sex offenders list.

Of course, the teen client needs to understand that there are adult predators on Grindr who are looking for underage boys. I know of one case in which a teen's teacher was on Grindr, and then the teacher approached the teen. He knew the boy was underage, and he ended up in jail. So being preyed upon is a danger.

I'm not advocating the specific choices a therapist should make. I'm just pointing out that we therapists need to think about these things. Not every therapist will take the same approach.

I have heard some therapists say that they would want to explore the psychological reasons why the gay teen would get on Grindr to begin with. They say they would do the same with a straight male teen or straight female teen. However, my response is that straight teens have a plethora of people of the other gender to date in their own grade and the grades above and below them. Gay teens do not. They are mostly isolated until after high school.

The Case of Travis

Travis, 14 years old, was being teased, taunted, and bullied in school because he was effeminate. He had told his parents, and they had gone to the school to see what could be done, but the school was not equipped to deal with what was happening to him. The assistant principal's attitude was that Travis was bringing it on himself. "Can't you tell him to stop acting that way?" he told the parents.

But Travis didn't want to change the way he was acting. He was being himself. He was a gender-nonconforming kid. He didn't think he should have to act differently.

His parents took him to a psychiatrist, who put him on antidepressants and Xanax. Travis continued getting bullied at school. He was traumatized and had nowhere to go. Even though his parents were sympathetic, they were of no help.

Travis found solace in Grindr, where he could touch base with other guys, people who enjoyed him and enjoyed talking to him, at least online. He hadn't met anyone yet face-to-face.

Travis was seeing a psychiatrist and also a psychologist, but he was getting increasingly depressed. He started abusing the drugs that the psychiatrist was giving him, taking more and more because he was getting more and more desperate. His parents started to focus on his substance abuse. They didn't know he was gay. Travis had never come out to them. Even with the bullying, he'd never said, "I'm gay." His family was conservative and religious, and it never occurred to Travis's parents that he might be gay. But the idea that he might be abusing drugs really got their attention.

In the meantime, he'd started meeting some of the guys he'd connected with on Grindr. He didn't tell his therapist or his parents. He began having sex. He was enjoying himself. But, because of the drug use, his parents decided to look in his phone to see what was going on. They discovered he was on Grindr. They confronted him, but he didn't want to talk about it.

They pressed him to see if he was having sex with adults. "Is anyone abusing you? Who have you met?" He wasn't sure how old the men he'd been meeting were, but some were in college and others had full-time jobs, and it was pretty obvious that they were mostly not teens. His parents went to the psychologist with this, and she said, "I have to call Protective Services, because he's been with adult men. This is a criminal act."

Travis was horrified, but he didn't know what he could do. He talked to Protective Services, but he wouldn't give any specifics. Protective Services couldn't do anything because he wouldn't tell them whom he'd met. He remembered Protective Services being very frustrated with him. "We're just trying to keep kids like you safe on the Internet," they told him. "Why won't you help us help you?"

Now his mother felt like she had to call the police, and Travis ended up at a police station. This was a disaster for him. The police made fun of him because he was effeminate, called him "pansy" and "queer," and blamed him for getting into trouble, telling him that he had brought this on himself. They made him show them his Grindr picture, and they made fun of it. They were angry because he wouldn't give them names and contact information. Then, they turned on him about the drug use. They threatened him and mocked him. They told him in crude terms what would happen to him in prison. Travis was terrified but stubborn, and eventually they let him go.

After that, Travis was increasingly depressed. He made a suicide attempt and was psychiatrically hospitalized. No one at the hospital asked him about his sexuality or his sexual orientation. They kept him in the hospital for one week, assessing suicidality and prescribing more psychotropic medications. He wouldn't talk with his parents, and he refused to say whether he was gay or not. Finally, his psychologist said, "I can't treat your son. I think he should be handled by a specialist who's gay." That is how he was referred to me.

Travis: Clinical Interpretation and Treatment

Travis was already 16 when he came to see me. I explained to him the stages of coming out. I worked on his depression and was alert to signs of any further suicide attempts. We addressed his trauma, which were not just from growing up gay but from overt forms of homophobia by the school, Protective Services, and the police. I convinced his parents that the medications weren't helping, so he stopping seeing the psychiatrist. They had already blocked him from using Grindr.

But Travis's case had a major difference from Josh's case—it involved bullying—and so we spent a good deal of time on that. I validated the fact that he was being bullied and that it was not his fault. "Just because you are who you are, you're not a bad person. You shouldn't have to change yourself to keep people from harassing you." No one had told him this before! I told him that I, too, had been bullied horribly in my own childhood, and I talked about how I'd made it through. This was comforting to him.

His parents, he, and I met for some family therapy sessions. He was very angry with his parents. Even though they had tried to help him, they had trouble understanding what their son was going through. They had been "big man on campus" and "big woman on campus" in their school days. They had never experienced bullying. "Can't you just go back to school and tough it out until graduation?" his father asked him. His father had no idea how vicious and relentless and destructive bullying can be. His parents didn't understand Travis's integrity either. Travis felt he shouldn't have to change. He refused to be intimidated, although what he faced at school was more and more nasty. I urged them to find him another school. They dithered on that, but they did agree to take him to an LGBTQ community center. We continued to meet in family therapy, and he continued to be very angry with them for not protecting him and for forcing him to give up his one consolation, Grindr and his Grindr friends. I suggested they join PFLAG, and they did attend some meetings.

I made one mistake with my approach to therapy with Travis. He had said, "I don't know why they're bullying me," and I had replied, "You are an effeminate gay guy. The more gender nonconforming we are and the more we can't pass as straight, the more we get bullied and teased and tortured like this."

After I said that, I tried to explain to him that it had happened to me, but it didn't matter. This really hurt him. He was very mad at me because I had called him "effeminate."

"You're blaming me?" he said, standing, shouting. "This is my fault?"

"That's not what I'm saying," I replied. "I just want you to understand that kids target kids like you, and like the kid I used to be, and it's not our fault at all."

But he didn't take it that way, and he told me he wasn't going to come back. "What kind of a therapist are you? You're just as bad as everyone else."

I understood his reaction as negative transference, but it was also my mistake. I felt terrible. We ended up texting each other, and I had an opportunity to say, "I'm sorry. I didn't mean to hurt your feelings."

He did come back eventually. "While I hated what you said," he told me, "I know it's true, and I'm not going to change who I am. I'm not going to change how I act, but I also need you to tell me how I can protect myself."

"I want you to own it and be proud of it," I told him. "I also want you to understand that there are people in this world who are not okay with it, but that is their problem, not yours. I want you to learn some coping skills for dealing with those people."

I did a lot of work with him to build back his trust. His situation at school was impossible, and I finally was able to convince his parents to let him move to a small charter school that was more humane in its overall philosophy than the public school. He was 16 years old and partway through 11th grade when he transferred.

I did EMDR with him to help him get past the worst of the trauma, and I worked on helping him come out. He told me he felt good about being gay. The only problem had been what was being done to him.

He graduated and went to college. I continued to work with him. He became less and less haunted by his high school experiences, but it took time. He was 25 when I saw him last.

Travis, like Josh, was outed by his parents when he wasn't ready to come out. But, unlike Josh, the trauma of school for Travis was enormously damaging, while Josh was dealing only with covert cultural sexual abuse. Travis turned to Grindr, as many teens do, to lift the burden of his isolation. His parents had already taken Grindr out of the picture before he came to see me, although I believe he began using it again as soon as he got to college. Protective Services, the police, and the psychiatrist were not helpful. Medications and the law are powerful, blunt instruments that are rarely useful in handling the vulnerable issues of an LGBTQ teen. The school also was ineffective; bullying remains a problem that schools do not address effectively. His parents had tried to be helpful, but Travis was introducing them to things that were far beyond their experience.

Internet Options for Gay Teens

There are ways for gay teens to connect with other gay teens. Aside from Gay/Straight Alliances at school and LGBTQ community centers, there are teen-oriented gay web sites that claim to be "safe sites," meaning, they claim to be monitored or moderated or to have parental controls. You should check these sites out yourself to see if those claims are accurate before you recommend them to any patients.

Distinc.tt is a web site promoting itself as a way for gay people to connect socially. It was awarded "12+" iTunes approval, which indicates that it is suitable for children 12 years old and older.

Gay Teen Chat Rooms (http://www.gayteenchatrooms.net/) promotes itself as a free, moderated, safe way for LGBTQ teens to chat.

TrevorSpace is a social networking site for LGBTQ youth ages 13 through 24 and their friends and allies. (www.trevorspace.org) It claims to be monitored by administrators to ensure content is age appropriate, youth-friendly and factual. TrevorSpace links members to The Trevor Project's home page, where information about The Trevor Lifeline (a suicide prevention hotline), "Dear Trevor," and other resources is available.

Many gay teens use the website Tumblr to connect. It is a microblogging and social networking website owned by Yahoo! The service allows users to post multimedia and other content to a short-form blog, and users can follow other users' blogs. Bloggers can also make their blogs private. As of January 2016, the website had 555 million monthly visitors.

Therapy for Teens: Questioning, Queer, Fluid

Therapists can be very concerned about knowing the right terminology when issues of sexual identity or gender identity come up. They don't want to make a mistake, especially when working with a teen. I advise: Stop fretting about whether you will say the right words. Ask the client not just how they self-identify but also, "What does that mean to you?" Sexual-identity definitions and gender-identity definitions are in flux these days; it's impossible to know what a client's words mean unless you ask.

A woman in one of my talks said she was "queer."

I said, "Can you tell me what you mean by 'queer'? That means a lot of different things to different people."

She said, "It means I'm not straight."

"Okay," I said, "so tell me more about what 'not straight' means, because that means a lot of different things to people, too."

"It means," she said, "I have sex with my wife, but I'm still attracted to men."

So her *queer* was a variation on "bisexual." I got more information by asking her again and again what it meant to her. It's important to press a client like this.

It's a golden rule of sex therapy: Even if you know what the words are supposed to mean, you've still got to ask, because the clients may have their own meaning for them.

I've had therapists of teens tell me they think that when their teen clients come in with different labels for themselves from session to session that the clients are "making it up." I say to them, "It doesn't matter." Appreciate the fact that they're exploring. We didn't have permission back in the day. You didn't. I didn't. It's brand-new that kids have permission to explore across the sexual-identity and gender-identity spectrum. Even today most kids are given permission to explore only heterosexuality and cisgender. So it's a blessing that they can come in and say, "Hey, I think I'm a bunch of things and not just straight."

The Case of Nancy

Sherry, a psychotherapist, came to me for supervision; she was concerned that she might not be working effectively with Nancy, one her clients. Nancy was 14 years old, and she'd told her parents that she was polyamorous and pansexual. She was attracted to females and males, more to females, but also to trans males and gay men. And she was in a relationship with a girl from her school and (simultaneously, in the spirit of polyamory) in an online relationship with a trans male in another state. Nancy's parents were upset. They told Sherry that Nancy was "attention seeking." They thought she was "playing games," purposely trying to upset them. They were worried that Nancy would be bullied at school. They believed she was "confused." They were certainly confused themselves, as well as concerned.

Sherry met with Nancy and her parents. Her parents were worried but didn't know what to do. They wanted Sherry to fix Nancy or figure her out or help her figure herself out. Then Sherry met with Nancy individually.

Sherry asked Nancy about herself, while assessing her for, and ruling out, suicidality and self-harm behaviors. Nancy seems to be okay, but Sherry wasn't sure what was needed. She asked Nancy about bullying or other trouble in school, but Nancy said she wasn't having any problems. Sherry was not sure she understood Nancy and was worried she might be missing something that a therapist should spot.

Nancy: Clinical Interpretation and Treatment

I reminded Sherry to ask Nancy, "What does polyamorous mean to you? What does pansexual mean to you? What does trans male mean to you? When did you first notice that you were attracted to males and females?" I suggested she look for signs of depression and self-harm, but Sherry was already aware of the need to look for such things. The key insight here was that Nancy had no apparent therapeutic issues. She was not complaining. She was not suffering. She knew who she was and what she wanted.

Nancy was in Stage 5 of coming out; namely, she was out and proud and wanted to tell everyone. As Sherry had already confirmed, Nancy was not in the least "confused." The main therapeutic task here was to help the parents get on board.

So the emphasis for this case had to be on family therapy to help Nancy's parents learn to accept her. They were blue-collar, not antagonistic but very confused and naive. I suggested that Sherry use the statistic for LGBTQ teen suicides (30%) with the number one reason for suicide being lack of parental support. (The number two reason is bullying.) I told Sherry to tell them unambiguously, "This girl may become suicidal if you don't give her the support she needs."

I pointed out that "support" includes learning the language. "Take her for who she tells you she is. If she's telling you she's a polyamorous pansexual, then she is. Understand her from her point of view. Go to PFLAG if you want; you don't have to. But the less you try to understand her, the more you're going to antagonize her and make her feel invalidated and misunderstood."

I told Sherry that Nancy's parents could certainly put limits on the time she was online, but they shouldn't try to take her offline entirely. One rule of thumb I like for young teens is that they can't spend more time online than they spend with the family. I suggested the parents get to know her friends, look over her shoulder and talk on Skype and meet the trans male she was talking to. And if she wanted to meet people, it could be at the mall to meet one of her friends.

Sherry also had to deal with the parents' concerns about *their* friends. "What are people going to think?" Sherry reminded them that the family had the option of keeping Nancy's business private. "You don't have to share anything you don't want to share. If someone asks about Nancy's boyfriends? She's 14. You can just say she doesn't have one."

The Case of Alyssa

"You tell her she's not a lesbian," were the first words out of Alyssa's mother's mouth, when the three of us first met in my office.

Alyssa, 16, sat looking down. She was wearing a black dress and silver chains, Doc Martens, and goth eye makeup. Her hair was dyed blue. She glanced up at me and flashed me an embarrassed smile, then looked down again.

Alyssa's mother gave every impression of being a formidable woman. She was large and dressed formally in a beige dress, wearing pearls and heels, and she spoke in a loud, indignant voice. "I found it on her phone. All this love talk. I thought she had a boyfriend. Then it turned out to be a girl! So I gave her a talking-to, and she just out and said she was . . . one of those."

After listening to her mother for 10 minutes, I suggested that Alyssa and I should talk one-on-one for a while. When we were alone together, I asked Alyssa what she wanted to talk about.

She grinned. "Could you say something to my mother that would get her to chill?"

"Maybe," I said, "but she's concerned about what she found on your phone."

"Oh, I'm a lesbian," Alyssa said. "She got that right."

"What does being a lesbian mean to you?"

"Don't you know what a lesbian is?"

"People don't always mean the same thing when they use self-identifying labels. I'd just like to know what it means to *you*."

"I've got a girlfriend," Alyssa said. "I love her, and she loves me."

We talked a while. Alyssa told me she "made out" with her girlfriend.

"Mother insisted I come here," she told me. "She thinks I'm crazy or a sinner, depending on her mood."

We talked more about when she discovered she was a lesbian. I asked her what messages she heard within her family, her community, and her church about being not straight.

"Would you like to come back and talk about things some more?" I asked her.

"Whatever will get my mother off my back," Alyssa agreed.

To the three of them, I suggested that Alyssa see me for some individual sessions, so that I could "clarify her case." Her mother agreed.

I spent the next few sessions with Alyssa educating her on aspects of sexual orientation, taking a family history, gently probing for conflicts or abuse at home. Alyssa's mother definitely insisted that she was straight. She couldn't bear anything else.

Three weeks after we first met, Alyssa told me she had a boyfriend.

"Okay, great," I said. "Tell me about that."

"I'm bisexual," she said. "I still love Kayla. But Ethan's cool. He's not like other boys. I love him, too."

My work with Alyssa focused on her mother and her environment. Alyssa told me she got "hassled" some at school for not being gender conforming. "Teachers hassle me the worst," she said. "The kids are mostly all right, but I've got a couple of mean teachers."

A few sessions later, Alyssa told me she was taking a rest from Ethan and going with someone named Ty, who was genderqueer. "I'm not into the binary anymore," she told me.

"Oh, that's great," I said. "How interesting. Tell me more about that. What does that mean to you?"

She explained that she didn't want to be burdened with "gender-limited expectations." We talked a bit about labels. She told me she wanted to be called "Ali," which she felt was less gendered than Alyssa. I asked if she wanted me to use a different pronoun.

"I'm okay with 'she,'" she told me. "Ty wants to be 'they,' but I still like 'she.'"

Alyssa: Clinical Interpretation and Treatment

When I first met with Alyssa's mother without Alyssa, I suggested that her daughter was "exploring" and that was what kids were doing these days. Her mother didn't understand. She wanted me to tell her that her daughter was straight. She wanted her daughter to tell her she was straight. She was terrified of labels like *lesbian, bisexual,* and anything else that didn't seem "normal." She worried about what the extended family would think if her daughter didn't go to prom "in a normal dress with a boy in a tuxedo like a normal girl." She worried if her friends at church would blame her for having a deviant daughter. I reminded her that she didn't have to give her friends details about her daughter's personal life.

I didn't see Alyssa for a month, and then her mother called to tell me Alyssa had made a suicide attempt with some of her mother's medications. Luckily, the "cocktail" hadn't been lethal, but the trip to the hospital and the aftermath had been sobering.

"Just tell me what to do," her mother pleaded when she came to my office.

I told her to go to PFLAG. She said she was too embarrassed, so she looked online to find support for parents of nonstraight teens.

"You can see," I told her, "that without your support, Alyssa is getting more depressed. She needs to know that you support her. Even if you don't agree, she needs to know you're trying to understand her. The number one reason LGBTQ teens attempt suicide is lack of family support."

Of course, I agreed to see Alyssa as soon as possible.

"I just felt so bad," Alyssa told me. "I don't know what I am. And my mother just can't stop talking about it. I should just tell her what she wants to hear. Maybe I am straight. Maybe I don't really love anybody. Who knows?"

It isn't that uncommon for an adolescent to be questioning her sexual orientation, but Alyssa's mother wasn't helping by insisting that Alyssa was straight. Despite my warnings, Alyssa's mother just did not seem to be able to listen to her daughter or offer her even nominal support.

I continued to do psychotherapy with Alyssa. We began to be able to explore her family history in more and more detail. It took us a while to discover it, but Alyssa had been sexually abused as a child. A neighbor, one of her playmate's fathers, had cornered her several times when she was 8 and forced her to give him oral sex. She stopped going to play at her friend's house, and the abuse stopped. Alyssa didn't tell anybody about it. She didn't know what to tell.

After we discovered this, I worked with her to let her voice her 8-year-old's feelings and to explore whatever posttrauma issues might be present.

Alyssa's mother was triumphant when she found out. "That explains everything," she told us in a family therapy session. "Now you can make her normal."

Alyssa was confused and even more questioning. She was even more unsure of herself. She didn't know which of her feelings she should trust. I told her and her mother that the results of the abuse were unclear and not necessarily the whole story of Alyssa's apparently varying sexual orientation. I agreed that Alyssa and I could do therapy around the abuse, but I told them that I thought her lesbian/bisexual/ nonbinary interests might not be a result of trauma. "Alyssa will need time to sort out her sexuality. In the meantime, we need to give her support and let her discover who she is."

Alyssa was very confused by this new uncertainty, by the childhood abuse. We spent some sessions with her voicing her fear of her friend's father, and in some sessions I mainly explored her thoughts and feelings around sexual orientation, bisexuality, and sexual fluidity, trying to help her look at her sexuality without moral restraints and lessening the influences from the negative messages she was hearing. "Your sexual orientation is something you're born with," I reminded her. "Sometimes childhood abuse leads to confusion about orientation, but we can deal with that in therapy. However, whatever you are inside is okay. You don't have to be straight to be a good person."

Sometimes, a therapist can become disoriented when a teen client exhibits sexual fluidity, as Alyssa did at first, claiming to be lesbian, then bisexual, then nonbinary, then questioning. I always advise therapists to work with a client as they present themselves in the moment, to let the client lead and tell you where they're at with their sexual identity and their gender identity. Ask them to tell you more. Be curious, but not skeptical. If a client is comes in one day and says he's David, then he's David. If the next time he sees you, he says he's Barbara, then you know to call him Barbara. You just use the names, and genders, and pronouns they're using on that day. And the same for sexual identity. If they say they're lesbian, they're lesbian, and if later they're bisexual, accept it, go with it. Don't try to enforce consistency. Don't expect consistency. Alyssa's mother was not helping Alyssa by insisting she was straight.

I'm always concerned about suicide with my sexually questioning or gender-questioning clients, especially teen clients, especially when the family is not supportive—and unfortunately Alyssa's mother was not. I became doubly vigilant after Alyssa's attempt, making sure she knew whom to call if she felt like harming herself. A local LGBTQ community center had a suicide hotline, and I made sure Alyssa and her mother knew about it. Although Alyssa had become "questioning," it wasn't reasonable to decide for her that she was straight or any other sexual identity. She would have to decide herself. Until then, I had to accept her as questioning in the context of LGBTQ.

Alyssa made some outward concessions to her mother. She let a boy take her to prom, and she stopped talking about her orientation at home. She continued to talk about it with me in session and online with her friends. However, having to be in the closet at home was very difficult for her. In my office, she cried and she grieved. She really felt like she had lost her mother. I told her and her mother in a family therapy session that it was important to keep talking about Alyssa's orientation even if they disagreed. The research shows that not talking can cause psychological problems and more family dysfunction. My providing her a space to explore all her gender and sexual identities was the relief that she needed to keep herself together.

She continued to be questioning until she went to college. We stopped her regular sessions after that, but she called me a year later to tell me that she was "mostly lesbian but a little queer." She still hadn't told her mother.

When a parent brings a teen in for therapy, raising questions about the nature of their child's sexuality:

1. Make sure the teen's okay. Go through your depression and self-harm assessment tools.
2. Try to get the family on board in terms of support, and coach the family about things like PFLAG and how to handle the neighbors. The family will sometimes be very supportive, especially when they consider that their child might attempt suicide, but some resist mightily, like Alyssa's mother.
3. Don't expect consistency of the teen. It's not unusual for teens to be questioning and to present as sexually fluid. This can be very frustrating for a therapist. Just respond in therapy to what teens present you with each day they come to see you. Stay in the moment. Ask, "What's happening?" and follow that up with "Tell me more."

4. As the teen gets older and is more "out," it may be more difficult for the family to keep things private. Advise the family to share first with the people closest to them, but don't let it become a toxic secret. A family can keep the nature of their child's sexuality secret when the child is 14, but as time passes, they're going to have to tell people because the child is going to tell people. If the family won't acknowledge something so fundamental about their child, the child is going to feel invalidated.

Chapter Summary: Treatment Approaches With LGBTQ Teens

LGBTQ teens were LGBTQ children first, and therefore they have lived with covert cultural sexual abuse and its associated trauma. The teen client must be simultaneously treated for (a) potential trauma from growing up LGBTQ; (b) teen-related issues like loneliness and group acceptance at school and in the community, exacerbated by being LGBTQ; and (c) "ordinary" trauma and family issues.

An LGBTQ teen must be educated in the stages of the coming-out process and must be helped to come out to himself or herself, to the family, at school, and in the community, if this can be done safely. The therapist must be aware of homophobia in the community and in the school and guide the teen wisely in coming out and other aspects of growth.

No matter how "safe" the teens' immediate environment, they will be suffering from vicarious trauma and anti-LGBTQ microaggressions. They will have issues with giving up heterosexual privilege in the coming-out process. The most healthy outcome for them is to enlist the support of their families to be out and not have the families makes excuses to "cover for" their gayness with the extended family or the community at large.

LGBTQ youth who come from highly rejecting families are 8.4 times as likely to have attempted suicide as LGBTQ peers who reported no or low levels of family rejection. Thus, bringing a client's family on board is a major therapy goal. Its importance cannot be underemphasized. PFLAG can be a significant resource and educational tool for the parents of LGBTQ teens.

The safety of the LGBTQ teen client is a very serious issue. Suicide is much more common for LGBTQ teens than others. Bullying at school can be fierce. Finding support at school via gay-straight alliances and other such organizations, as well as gay community centers, should be strongly recommended. Where appropriate, safe sex practices should be explained.

Finally, the therapist must help the client find resources to combat the social isolation and loneliness. This is beyond safety. This is about belonging. School resources and community resources, and, yes, even resources online should be recommended, as well as projects like It Gets Better and The Trevor Project.

Treating an LGBTQ youth is not simple. It is an exercise in multitasking. Everything must be considered and dealt with. You may find support from colleagues and appropriate supervision from specialists to be especially useful. The rewards, however, are great. You can literally help set a life on a healthy track, when the alternatives are brutal.

CHAPTER 14

The Transgender Client

Sexual identity is who I go to bed with.
Gender identity is who I go to bed as.
—Amy Ellis Nutt, *Becoming Nicole:*
The Transformation of an American Family

It wasn't about the water fountains in the '60s,
and it's not about the bathrooms today.
—Christopher Turner,
protesting the North Carolina anti-trans bill

The only way I will rest in peace is if one day transgender people aren't treated the way I was, they're treated like humans, with valid feelings and human rights. Gender needs to be taught about in schools, the earlier the better. My death needs to mean something.
—Leelah Alcorn, teen suicide, transgender martyr

My Journey Toward Working With Transgender People

This chapter only touches on the basics of working with transgender individuals. Therapists who plan to work with transgender clients will need a good deal of specialized training and continued education, which is beyond the scope of a single chapter. My intention here is to introduce the clinical issues that come up when a therapist is working with gender-nonconforming and transgender clients and provide an overview for a foundation in working with these individuals.

I am still in a learning mode, and I imagine that many of the readers of this chapter may be also. The therapeutic community's understanding of the subtleties of gender and gender expression is evolving, in terms of both language and conceptual frameworks. Some therapists and advocates have strong opinions about how to discuss gender as well as what lenses might be appropriate to use to explore it. I want to steer us away from politics or dogmatic opinions. This chapter is entirely focused on helping clients in the therapy room. What we understand, and how we understand it, is changing rapidly. We will do best by keeping an open mind and (above all) listening to what our clients are telling us.

In the therapy room, all that matters is being there with the client the way the client needs you to be. While you're there, you're in the trenches. You don't have to be a researcher, a theoretician, or a partisan. You listen and try to figure out what to do to help your client during each session.

The Case of Joanna

My new client looked like the epitome of a middle-aged businessman: three-piece suit, hair cut short and graying at the edges, leg crossed ankle on knee. However, on the completed intake form, the client had checked "transgender," so I began the session by asking what name and pronoun I should use.

"Joanna, and I'm a she/her/hers," she said, smiling, noticeably soothed that I'd asked. (The issue of name and pronoun can be very important to a transgender client, and I recommend asking on your intake form and again when you are face-to-face.)

Joanna told me that she was an executive at a very conservative insurance company and only a few years from retirement. She was trying to "hold out" until then, but she didn't think she was going to be able to make it.

"I can't live like this," she said. "If I don't transition soon, I'm going to die. I'll kill myself."

I asked her what she meant by "transition," and she told me she wanted hormone therapy and gender confirmation surgery.

"I'd be fired in an instant if they find out at work," she assured me, "and I'll lose the pension I've spent the last 20 years of my life earning."

The only person who knew her plight was her wife, who was sympathetic. Together, they worried about Joanna's job, their children, their friends, and their elderly parents. "We'll end up with no money and nobody who will talk to us," Joanna told me.

I spent most of that session speaking calmly to Joanna and assuring her that others had faced the same issues and worked out better lives for themselves. "It just takes time," I told her, "and I'll help you through the whole process."

She was not actively suicidal, but she let me know she thought about it a lot, especially if she didn't transition.

The next session, she was calm enough to move forward.

"My wife has known, more or less, for years," Joanna told me, "but we've only talked about it recently. I don't think she'll insist on a divorce, and I love her for that."

I didn't interrupt, but I made a mental note that we'd have to come back to consider Joanna's marriage more carefully. Sometimes, a person coming out LGBTQ doesn't anticipate the full impact on a spouse.

She went on, "I hate having to wear this suit and pretend I'm a man. I don't think I can continue doing it. But they would fire me if they found out at work. They've known me for 20 years, but they'd throw me out in an instant . . ."

Joanna was depressed and miserable. I was empathic and validated her feelings, and we talked about two things she could do immediately to make her life more manageable: First, because of her suicidal ideation, I strongly recommended that she consult with a psychiatrist who was knowledgeable in gender-identity issues, and see if antidepressants (and perhaps antianxiety medications) would help her manage her affect during the delay in her transition. Once a trans person comes out, it is very challenging to keep living in a gender-incongruent manner. Second, we talked about coming out in baby steps that would not require that she reveal her gender identity at work or to her friends and family.

She liked the idea of starting to wear women's underwear and other women's apparel under her suit at work. She decided that she could easily hide a bra and a camisole. However, she worried that this wouldn't be enough to make a difference in how she felt. We talked about it, and she decided to give it a try.

She did and reported, to her surprise, that it did seem to comfort her and make her feel a little less desperate. I pointed out that she was coming out to herself and that this was an important step. The clothes functioned as a little reminder all day long of who she really was, even though only she knew.

She did go on antidepressants, which were helpful. Generally, strong feelings of depression, body dysphoria, and suicidal ideation can arise when a transgender person begins to come out. Issues related to employment, finances, and family life can seem overwhelming.

"Once you start taking hormones," I suggested, "you can probably go off the antidepressants. But for right now, I'm glad you're taking them."

We talked about other baby steps concerning clothing and body hair that she could hide at work and socially. I brought up the idea of shaving her legs. "But I socialize in a boating community," she objected. "People will notice." This is an example of a relatively small decision that trans people have to deal with: Be true to myself or follow societal ideals. It takes a lot of courage to choose yourself, but once a person begins, it gets easier.

We went over a number of other similar ideas. She took some and postponed others. She decided that she could start getting electrolysis for her facial hair. Men shave their faces, so she could probably do that without being outed at work.

Joanna: Clinical Interpretation and Treatment

It's important to help trans clients in the early stages of coming out meet their trans needs and at the same time balance their needs within their existing public gender expression. Joanna worried that if she went for electrolysis, the beauticians would laugh about her behind her back or gossip about her. She felt like "damaged goods," and being "witnessed" would make her feel even worse. She was terrified she'd be recognized and outed.

I educated her about internalized transphobia, which is common in trans people. (Internalized transphobia is similar to internalized homophobia; see Chapter 2.) We talked about how this might be coming up for her and how to deal with it.

Joanna was a woman, and finally she just couldn't stand her "act," pretending to be a man. "I can't wear this suit and tie anymore," she told me more than once. "I can't handle it, but I have to because it's the uniform of my job, and I can't afford to give up my retirement."

The more Joanna talked about transitioning, the more she wanted to go further and come out. She decided to start hormones sooner rather than later. If she had to, she would take early retirement and use her savings to "make do" financially. Therefore, after a few months, I wrote a letter that her health insurance and physician required for her to begin medical treatments.

Letters from therapists to the medical and insurance communities used to be universally required, but now the rules are less consistent and uniform. Some doctors don't require referral letters at all, though most insurances still require them. Many therapists have their own standards and require a certain amount of therapy before they will write clients letters. Often a therapist will urge a client with mental or emotional issues to delay medical procedures until the client is more mentally stable. I write letters when they are requested by doctors, insurances, and the client, although ultimately it is the doctors (and the insurance companies) who decide what they are going to do.

In the course of my work with Joanna, we did several sessions with her wife to help her through Joanna's transition. Her wife seemed more uncomfortable than Joanna had led me to believe (but I wasn't surprised). I encouraged Joanna's wife to engage in her own therapy, but she declined. We discussed many aspects of how Joanna's transition was affecting her. When and how to tell the children. When to tell Joanna's and her wife's parents. Some trans women decide to still wear men's clothing when they visit their parents until hormone therapy and gender confirmation surgery make that impossible. This is obviously the client's choice.

The Language of Gender Dysphoria and Gender Nonconformity

The World Professional Association for Transgender Health Standards of Care (WPATH SOC, page 5, 2001) uses *gender dysphoria* to refer to "discomfort or distress that is caused by a discrepancy between a person's gender identity and that person's sex assigned at birth (and the associated gender role and/or primary and secondary sex characteristics)." Some individuals address their gender dysphoria with medical interventions (e.g., hormones or surgery), but the WPATH emphasizes that treatment for gender dysphoria is individualized, and there is no one "right" way to address it.

The WPATH SOC uses the term *gender nonconformity* to refer to "the extent to which a person's gender identity, role, or expression differs from the cultural norms prescribed for people of a particular sex." Generally speaking, gender-nonconforming people do not follow cultural stereotypes about how they should look or act based on their natal sex. The term *genderqueer* is often used as a synonym for gender nonconforming.

Note that the WPATH SOC is mainly concerned with the psychological and medical treatment of gender dysphoria.

The opposite of transgender is *cisgender*. You are cisgender if your sense of yourself as a male or a female matches your body's biology and the gender you were assigned at birth.

Transgender people may choose not to be gender nonconforming (perhaps because they live in dangerous environments or for other reasons), and many gender-nonconforming individuals are not transgender. For example, a genderqueer person or a cross-dresser may not feel that their gender identity is different from the gender they were assigned at birth. (I will discuss cross-dressers later in this chapter.)

From my training with WPATH and from my clients, I have learned reasonable definitions of some of the standard terms that fall under the umbrella of gender nonconforming, but please understand that there is much disagreement in this area. There is no term that someone doesn't find disrespectful or offensive, and no general agreement about what these terms mean.

Those who self-identify as "genderqueer" individuals tell me they have a settled sense of themselves as a third gender, both male and female. That is, they are not "confused" or "questioning." How they express this or enact it will vary from individual to individual. As an illustrative example, consider: I met a natal male at a conference wearing butterfly earrings, nail polish, and a three-piece suit. I asked him how he self-identified, male or female, and the reply was, "My pronoun is 'they,' and yes! I'm experiencing myself as both male and female. I'm not identifying with the male-female binary currently. I see myself moving toward identifying as female." A genderqueer client may tell you they consider themselves both male and female genders—or neither.

Gender Fluidity

I've most often heard *gender-fluid* used to refer to a person who identifies as either male or female but varies from one to the other. The following is from https://nonbinary.miraheze.org/wiki/Genderfluid.

> Genderfluid people often feel a need to change their gender expression to match whatever their current gender has become. This may mean having groups of different kinds of clothing in their closet, so they can dress as a woman, man, or otherwise, depending on how they feel that day. It can also mean temporarily changing their body shape by using binding, packing, breast prostheses, or tucking. However, in some situations, changing gender expression isn't possible. This could be because the changes happen more than once a day, . . . or because they don't feel safe in society if they were to present a certain way.
>
> Gender dysphoria . . . isn't a requirement in order to be genderfluid. Each person is different, experiencing gender fluidity in their own way. Some genderfluid people experience gender dysphoria at times or all the time. Some want to change their bodies . . . which may include hormones or surgery. Others don't choose to transition because any change they make to their body would only feel right to them when they were in a certain gender and would feel wrong in others.
>
> Some genderfluid people ask to be called by a different name and pronouns depending on what gender they feel at a certain time. For people who switch between only two genders, this can mean switching between two names. . . . They may also take a gender-neutral name that works for them at any time. (paras. 12–15)

As a clinician, it will be most productive to follow the lead of your gender-fluid client. Each time they come to see you, address them as they refer to themselves at that moment. There is no need—nor is it helpful—to try to impose "consistency." The client needs permission and support to explore all aspects of their gender identities. Also, you need not assume they have come to therapy to work on gender issues. The well-intended impulse of many clinicians is to pathologize gender-fluid clients and insist on exploring gender dysphoria or other mental health issues. It is simpler and more useful to let the client tell you what they want to work on.

To summarize, the term *gender-fluid* may refer to people who think of themselves as (a) being a third sex—both male and female, (b) moving back and forth between genders, or (c) falling completely outside the gender binary as genderless—nonbinary (NB) or agender. *Genderqueer* is sometimes used as a synonym for gender-fluid. *Cross-dressing* can be considered a form of gender fluidity; more on cross-dressing below. It should be obvious that these terms do not have precise or universally agreed-upon meanings, and not all gender-nonconforming behaviors are easy to categorize.

What Should Therapists Do If They Don't Know the Meaning of an Identity?

Many therapists worry about offending their clients by not knowing the definition of each new label clients enter therapy self-identifying as. I have the same concerns.

What I have found is that it is perfectly acceptable for a therapist to ask clients what *they* mean if they use such terms. Although I've had clients get upset when I've asked them to define their terms, I simply explain that not everyone uses these terms in the same way, and I want to respect the terms' meanings, so I'll know exactly what my clients are telling me.

More on Terminology

I should note that sometimes *transgender* and *genderqueer* are used as synonyms for gender nonconforming or to refer to any gender identity other than cisgender female or cisgender male. All such definitions are currently in a state of flux. Not everybody agrees on them, and I often hear "gender-fluid," "genderqueer," "gender nonconforming," and others used interchangeably.

Also note that "gender identity" is connected to, but not dependent on, "sexual identity" (also called *sexual orientation*). Sexual identity more or less means "whom you are attracted to," whereas gender identity refers to what gender you identify as (if any). We now understand that orientation and gender cannot be reduced to the simple binaries that used to represent mainstream thinking.

What Terms Are Offensive to Transgender People, and Why Ever Use These Terms?

The term *transsexual* is not necessarily offensive, but it is to some extent becoming out-of-date. Older clients may use the term. If the client uses it, then I use it, because I use the same terminology my clients use.

The labels *drag queen* and *drag king* do not refer to trans people. A drag queen is a man or woman who is impersonating a hyperfeminine woman for entertainment. In the past, these impersonations have been enjoyed for the skill of the entertainer and for the thrill of the forbidden in crossing gender lines. "Female impersonators" can still be found in the entertainment world, often at campy gay performance venues. Drag bingo has become very popular around the country, bringing in mostly straight women, often with their bridal parties. The less common *drag king* refers to a man or woman impersonating a hypermasculine man for entertainment, such as an Elvis impersonator.

Shemale and *tranny* are definitely offensive terms used to describe transgender individuals, but therapists should be aware that many straight men are into porn featuring trans women, and this porn goes by the labels "shemale porn" or "tranny porn" or "chicks with dicks porn." It's not called "transsexual porn."

Cross-dressing and *cross-dresser* are commonly used terms that some people consider derogatory and others do not.

The *DSM-V* still lists "transvestic disorder" as one of a number of paraphilic disorders. As with all paraphilias, the behavior is a "disorder" only if the individual is distressed by it.

The term *transvestite* is completely out-of-date. I often say it belongs with the movie *The Rocky Horror Picture Show*, and it should never be used as a label for transgender individuals.

Also, just as some black people under some circumstances will refer to themselves or others using the N-word, some trans people will call themselves "tranny." This can be ironic or used in an attempt to reclaim the word in a positive way. I wouldn't use it, even if a client does.

Also note that we refer to a *transgender* person, not a *transgendered* person. They are not a verb and do not like to be referred to this way.

Someone can be *intersex*, which means they have genitals of both sexes. (Or more properly, a combination of chromosomes, gonads, hormones, internal sex organs, and genitals of both sexes.) The formerly used term *hermaphrodite* is now generally considered offensive.

My colleague Nick is intersex and very open about it. He was assigned female at birth and raised female, had a vagina, menstruated, had normal female breast development in puberty. Nick was always attracted to girls but never felt like a lesbian, because he never felt female. When Nick was 33 years old, his testosterone kicked in. He masculinized over a period of months. His doctors were very concerned. They ran some tests and decided that Nick needed a hysterectomy, but inside they found undescended testicles. They performed the hysterectomy, and Nick transitioned to male. He started male hormones, had top surgery, fell in love with a woman, and adopted a child. Nick is now living as a man, and this feels more right to him than living as a woman.

Transphobia: Prejudices, Slanders, and Microaggressions

Even though we call ourselves the LGBTQ community, in many ways we are not a community at all. I have already talked in this book about how lesbians, gays, and bisexuals do not always mix well with one another. (Happily, this is changing among younger people.) Similarly, transgender individuals are often not very welcome in the LGB community. It's important for a therapist working with trans clients to know this. I encourage people to challenge nontrans LGB people about their transphobia and trans-erasure, and for the therapist to be aware of the grief their trans clients may feel about being so isolated.

Note that while bisexual people are to some extent also outcasts to the lesbian and gay community, trans people are more so. The difference is that bisexuals are understandable to lesbians and gays, because they are distinguished from other people by the nature of their sexual orientation and attraction—that is, their *sexual* identity. Transgender is about *gender* identity. A lot of LGB people feel they're completely different from trans people, that the *T* in LGBTQ shouldn't be there. "It's mixing apples and oranges," they will say.

I don't agree. We should all be united as a community, even while honoring our differences, because there is in fact a lot of overlap. Also, we can be united as a community on the issue of discrimination. The arguments used to justify discrimination against trans people are exactly the same as those that have been used against LGB people and also people of color. An excellent article on this is "Two Consonants Walk Into a Bar" (Bruno, 2017).

The number one argument to support transphobia is: "What about the children?" In other words, "Can you imagine *those people* raising healthy children?" This is a ridiculous point of view. What's going to happen to the children? As if having a trans mother or father would be worse than child abuse, worse than sexual abuse, worse than domestic violence. The argument against LGB parents used to be, "Those children are going to grow up gay (or lesbian or bi)!" There's no evidence that children's sexual or gender orientation is determined by who raises them. And there's no evidence that having loving parents who are LGBTQ is anything but healthy (Stacey & Biblarz, 2001). As recently as the 1960s, pundits and "experts" were decrying the tragic fate of the children of interracial marriages. In the Supreme Court decision *Loving v. Virginia* (1967), a Virginia judge is quoted:

> Almighty God created the races white, black, yellow, malay, and red, and he placed them on separate continents. And, but for the interference with his arrangement, there would be no cause for such marriage. The fact that he separated the races shows that he did not intend for the races to mix.

Further references to Virginia law in the same Supreme Court decision note that the purpose of Virginia's law is to avoid "a mongrel breed of citizens." This legal material illustrates that bigots often evoke both God and children to justify themselves.

A therapist should have these "arguments" in mind when treating trans clients. Your clients will have had these very hurtful slanders cast at them either directly or as microaggressions. "What about your children?" and some version of "You are an abomination in the sight of God." As ridiculous as these slights are, your clients may well be battered by their constant repetition. It contributes to their minority stress.

All the microaggressions trans people experience are harmful. Laws that prohibit transgender people from using bathrooms of the gender they identify with are based on the slander that trans women are really child molesters—that they're men pretending to be women so they can molest little girls. The bigots don't seem to be worried about trans men molesting little boys. Which I think is very telling. If they were really worried about children, then they would be worried about the boys, too.

But who can figure out the mind of a bigot? The point is, they're sexualizing ordinary behavior and superimposing a pathological interpretation on something that's natural and normal and not particularly sexual: going to the bathroom.

Transgender people are dealing with the grief of their outcast status within the LGBTQ community and their persecution by society at large, both of which they have often unknowingly internalized as self-hatred—that is, *internalized transphobia*. Not surprisingly, it is common for trans people to have problems with alcohol and drugs and other addictions, as well as a high incidence of suicide attempts.

Statistics on Transgender People and Suicide

Haas, Rodgers, and Herman (2014) reported that "the prevalence of suicide attempts among [transgender people] is 41 percent, which vastly exceeds the 4.6 percent of the overall U.S. population . . . and is also higher than the 10-20 percent of lesbian, gay and bisexual adults who report ever attempting suicide."

This survey found increased percentages of suicide attempts for different groups of transgender individuals, as follows:

- 57% had family who chose not to speak to or spend time with them
- 50%–54% were harassed or bullied at school (any level)
- 50%–59% experienced discrimination or harassment at work
- 60% experienced a doctor or health care provider refusing to treat them
- 64%–65% suffered physical or sexual violence at work
- 63%–78% suffered physical or sexual violence at school (any level)
- 57%–61% were disrespected or harassed by law enforcement officers
- 60%–70% suffered physical or sexual violence by law enforcement officers
- 69% were homeless

Transitioning for Trans Men and Trans Women

Material in this and later sections is informed by *The Lives of Transgender People* by Genny Beemyn and Susan Rankin (2011). I appreciate the insights they've shared in their excellent book.

Transgender clients are generally presenting one of the following three situations:

- The client is a trans woman, a natal male who identifies as female and wishes to express themselves as female and to be accepted in society as female. Abbreviated as MtF.
- The client is a trans man, a natal female who identifies as male and wishes to express themselves as male and be accepted in society as male. Abbreviated as FtM.
- The client is a trans man or trans woman. They are a natal intersex individual who has been raised one gender but identifies as the other.

Before we consider some of the details of "transitioning" gender, let's clarify a few key points. First, trans women and trans men do not have any choice about what gender they are. They are strongly gendered male or female, whatever their biological sex. This gendering is in the brain, and for trans people, their true gender is not their assigned gender at birth. In particular, they have usually been assigned one gender at birth and raised that gender, but at some point in their lives they realize that they are living as the wrong gender.

Second, there are various ways of transitioning a body from one gender to another through surgery and hormones. Not all trans people make the same medical choices around transitioning. Some have no surgery and do not take hormones. (It's expensive; it carries medical risks; some simply don't want it.) How a trans person transitions is individual and personal. Some are content (or must be content) with only changing their dress and other elements of expression.

Although the word *transitioning* is often taken to mean surgery and hormones, here we'll call any systematic change of one gender expression to another "transitioning" and call people who have transitioned in any way trans men or trans women. However, be careful not to assume that someone who is gender nonconforming is a transitioning trans man or trans woman. Being transgender is a self-identified state, and transitioning is a self-ascribed mental and/or physical process.

Third, it is physically much more difficult to transition from male to female than from female to male. Once a body has been subjected to male levels of testosterone, it is permanently "masculinized" (facial hair, bone structure, Adam's apple, deeper voice, etc.), and the effects cannot be completely undone even with surgery and hormones. This is why the parents of young adolescent trans females may want to arrange for injections of hormone blockers to delay puberty and the effects of testosterone, so that if their child is going to grow up to be a trans woman, the transition will be easier. (I will talk about hormone blockers later in this chapter.) Due to rigid societal standards about masculinity and femininity, trans females have a harder time socially than trans males as children. Transgender girls are much more likely to be bullied, rejected, and ostracized. Trans women are much less likely to "pass" as women if puberty suppressors are not used early in adolescence. In contrast, FtM behavior is more acceptable pre-puberty than MtF ("tomboy" as opposed to "sissy"), and FtM expression in adulthood is much less socially controversial than MtF. (People think a woman dressed as a man is cute; a man dressed as a woman is scorned.) Trans men can often easily pass as male even before hormone treatments.

Gender confirmation surgery—formerly known as gender reassignment surgery—is the term commonly used by medical professionals to refer to a group of surgical options that alter a person's biological sex. In most cases, one or multiple surgeries are required to achieve legal recognition that a person's gender has changed. Some people refer to "top surgery" and "bottom surgery" to distinguish between different procedures without needing to be more explicit.

Trans women often choose to have hormone treatments—both androgen suppressants and estrogen—and these must continue for the rest of their lives. Estrogen can be taken in pill form, via skin patches, or by injection. Androgen suppressants lessen the effects of male hormones such as testosterone. (The trans woman may choose to have her testicles surgically removed, after which she will no longer need to take androgen suppressants, but she will continue to need to take estrogen.) These treatments cause an onset of "physical puberty," including breast tissue increase, body hair decrease, a redistribution of body fat from a male to a female pattern, and a decrease in libido. Some trans women experience increased emotionality or "a greater emotional range" (Lee, 2016, paragraph 11). Hormones do not thin the thickened male vocal cords, so the voice does not automatically become more "feminine." Instead, voice training can be useful.

Many trans women elect to have facial feminization surgery and tracheal shave (to reduce the prominence of the Adam's apple). Commonly, they have electrolysis or laser hair removal. (Many trans women have expressed to me their frustration that this hair removal must be repeated periodically for the rest of their lives.) Breast forms can be used, as well as devices (called *gaffs* at trans and crossdressing specialty stores) to tuck male genitalia in place to make the area appear more female.

Trans men also need to have lifelong hormone treatments—in this case, with testosterone. While trans women need to take testosterone blockers (or have their testicles removed), trans men do not have to take estrogen blockers. Testosterone overpowers estrogen and causes the ovaries to shut down. Here, the onset of "puberty" results in a variety of changes: an increase in body and facial hair, male-pattern baldness, body fat redistribution to a male pattern, a deeper voice, and an increased libido. Many trans men also experience clitoral enlargement. Some trans men report increased anger issues and more difficulty expressing emotions.

Hormone treatments carry medical risks. Testosterone can damage the liver. Estrogen can increase blood pressure, increase blood glucose levels, and interfere with blood clotting. Androgen suppressants can lower blood pressure, disturb electrolytes, and dehydrate the body. A person with health difficulties or conditions (e.g., obesity, diabetes) may be discouraged from undergoing hormone treatments or surgical procedures until their BMI is within range (Vanderbilt University School of Medicine, 2017).

Transitioning and Sexual Orientation Changes

There have also been reports of trans people who begin hormones and then experience a sexual orientation change. If they're trans female and they have historically been attracted to men, suddenly they're attracted to women, and vice versa. Some report bisexual or fluid sexual attractions; others report a permanent change of orientation. However, some experts dispute whether there has been a "change" at all. Mizock and Hopwood (2016) noted in their publication that hormones do not change the gender to whom one is attracted, but some trans people may have pre-existing sexual attractions that were not explored for many reasons (including fear of sexual objectification in a body that was not congruent with one's gender identity).

A therapist should be aware of the link between starting to take hormones and experiencing a sexual orientation change and forewarn a transitioning client that they might experience it and that it is normal.

Psychotherapy for the Gender-Variant Adult

Although I've cited the WPATH SOC (2001) above, opinions vary greatly on transgender standards of care, and not just among therapists. The medical community, the insurance community, and the legal community can be voices that need to be considered.

Working as a Team

Medical doctors often require that patients provide letters certifying that they have been examined and "cleared" by a mental health clinician before the doctors will begin any medical intervention. This is often their way of making sure that everyone is working together and on the same page in giving clients what they need and what they want. Sometimes, two referral letters from two different clinicians are required. Medical insurance companies also typically require such letters. Therapists sometimes impose various requirements before they will write referral letters. There are basically two issues: (1) Is the patient getting effective treatment for any mental health conditions he or she has? (2) Is the patient a reasonable candidate for transgender medical treatments? That is, is it reasonable that this particular person change their physical gender?

Letters

Most therapists agree that issue 1 is reasonable to consider, and they will be hesitant to write letters for an emotionally or mentally ill client who is not being effectively treated. In fact, these letters describe any preexisting mental health conditions (depression, anxiety, psychotic disorders) and certify that (if they exist) they are being managed through therapy and medication. Moreover, it is very helpful for a person to be psychologically stable before taking hormones, which tend to intensify feelings.

On the other hand, therapists are not necessarily in agreement on how to address issue 2. In the past, it was a standard requirement that a client live as the opposite gender and be in therapy for at least a year before beginning hormones and live another year on hormones before any surgery. However, the current WPATH SOC makes it clear that therapists are no longer required (within the ethos of the psychological community) to approve transitions. You, as a therapist, if you are asked to write referral letters, will need to decide what makes sense to you.

The basic principles for treating transgender clients are:

- Gender variance is normal, not pathological, and gender is not assumed to be binary.
- Mental health practitioners are not gatekeepers for treatment; the client decides what treatment options to pursue. In particular, the decisions for hormones and surgery involve a negotiation between the patient, the doctors, and the patient's medical insurance company. A therapist is involved only as an adviser.
- Often, when transgender people begin transitioning, their mental health issues begin to abate.

The main things to include in letters requested by doctors and insurance companies are:

- An evaluation of the client's level of stress and its persistence
- A consideration of how "consistent, insistent, and persistent" the client has been in not being aligned with his or her gender
- An evaluation of gender incongruence and gender dysphoria
- A statement by the therapist supporting hormone therapy and gender transition surgery

I counsel my associates that they should explain their own transgender SOC to new clients and note that other therapists may have different SOC. For example, my associate, Nick Zielke, requires that a trans client meet with him for 12 sessions before he will write referral letters. However, he also tells his clients that some other therapists don't require so many sessions. This lets them know that Nick's SOC are not a universal standard and that clients may have other alternatives if they work with someone else.

Problems that might need to be addressed before a client proceeds with hormones or surgery include: (a) health concerns; (b) psychiatric or substance abuse problems; (c) depression, anxiety, suicidal ideation, and other mental health disorders. Note also that problems can emerge during transition. I've seen this with gay clients, too. When gay people come out of the closet, they think they're going to automatically feel better, but often they don't, because now other issues they've never dealt with emerge that were in that same closet as their orientation.

Some people believe a therapist shouldn't raise sexual issues with a transgender client unless the client raises them first. It is true that trans clients can be very sensitive about discussions around sex and their genitals. However, when a new client comes in, I routinely ask them about their emotional health and their sexual health, and I don't make an exception for transgender clients.

On Language and Terminology

The most fundamental rule is to ask clients to clarify what they mean by the terms they use, even if you think you know.

At my Center for Relationship and Sexual Health (CRSH) in Royal Oak, Michigan, we ask on our intake form: "How do you self-identify?" And we offer options: straight, gay, bi, queer, fluid, questioning. The form also asks, "How do you gender identify?" with possible choices being male, female, gender-fluid, genderqueer, transgender, nonbinary. When the client comes in, I'll say, "Okay, you checked [the boxes they checked]. Now I'd like you to tell me in your own words: How do you self-identify in terms of your sexual orientation, and how do you *gender* identify?" Then, no matter what they tell me, I'll ask, "What does that mean to you? I don't want to assume that because you tell me you're queer [or genderqueer, or whatever], I know exactly what it means to you."

It is not uncommon for a client to resist this question and respond with something like, "You should know." (I noted this kind of response above, with the client who identified as "queer" and resisted clarifying what she meant.) If the client reacts this way, I reply, "These days everybody's identifying in different ways using different definitions. So I never assume, because I'd rather not offend by assuming. I'd rather you tell me what it means to you."

If the client has not made it clear in the first session what name they want to be called by and what pronoun they want to be referred to by, then you should ask. I have a natal male client transitioning to female. This client wants the "he" pronoun but a female name. The therapist should also be clear that the client is not required to be consistent. Clients can change their minds and ask the therapist to use a different name or pronoun, and this is not uncommon in the course of therapy.

Many therapists worry about saying the wrong thing or using the wrong terminology. It's okay to mess up; just make sure you apologize and correct yourself, and go on. You don't have to be perfect. In fact, when you make a mistake, it may be a therapeutic opportunity, an opening to explore your client's negative transference. Don't get lost in your own shame or countertransference or the clients' negative transference toward you for making the mistake. Ask the clients what it means to them that you messed up. "What other person in your life doesn't get it right? How does that make you feel?"

A Client Who Identifies as a "Cross-Dresser"

Joanna's case (described at the beginning of this chapter) was fairly straightforward. She presented herself as a transgender person, a trans female. Joanna was suffering from *gender dysphoria*, in that her assigned gender (male) was the opposite of the gender she knew herself to be (female). My job as a therapist was to witness and validate Joanna's reality, to help her with her anxiety and depression and her internalized transphobia, to help her plan her transition from male to female and negotiate the family and social implications of her transition. I also consulted with the medical doctors who were involved in her physical transition.

If a man comes to you for help because he is, in his words, "a cross-dresser," the case may not be so straightforward as Joanna's. Several different things may be going on (separately or together). (a) The man may be sexually aroused by dressing like a woman, but he has no sense that he *is* a woman. (b) The man may be transgender and in a transitional phase of self-discovery. He may evolve (like Joanna) to the knowledge that he is actually a woman. (c) Third, and more subtly, the man may be dressing up not for sexual arousal but for comfort and a reduction in anxiety. When he dresses in women's clothing, his anxiety and depression subside.

Although I realize some believe the term "cross-dresser" to be derogatory, clients and others continue to use the term, and I will use it here to avoid confusing circumlocutions.

Consider the basic concept of a fetish or paraphilia. A man might come to see you with a shoe fetish. He tells you, "I'm turned on by high-heeled shoes. I rub my penis against a shoe, and I get erect, and then I ejaculate." This is how a "standard" fetishist expresses himself. But now compare this: What if the client tells you, "I just like to keep a high-heeled shoe near me." Or maybe, "I wear a pair of high-heeled shoes. It makes me feel better and calms me down, but I don't get an erection. I don't ejaculate. It's not anticipatory for me in a sexual way. The shoes just make me feel good, calm, less anxious, more myself." Now the client is not describing a classical fetish. It is something more like a transgender experience. Since the client is wearing women's shoes, some therapists might classify him as a cross-dresser. Whether this term is appropriate or not, he seems clearly on the transgender spectrum rather than a spectrum of fetishes or paraphilias, given that cross-dressing is not a sexually arousing experience for him.

Now, treating a cross-dresser depends on the diagnosis. Suppose a cross-dresser is believed to be suffering from a paraphilia. A standard treatment is to address the depression and compulsion that he feels, perhaps in his struggle to avoid cross-dressing. (Most cross-dressers who seek treatment are heterosexual men; for simplicity, I will use the masculine pronoun.) The cycle usually is that he dresses up as a woman to "feel" like a woman, not because he feels he *is* a woman. He often checks into a hotel or dresses like a woman when his wife is out of town, takes pictures of himself and even goes to a gay bar to be seen as a woman. He may also dance with other men and even have sex with another man to feel like a woman. After, he often feels tremendous shame and will throw out all the paraphernalia that went into dressing as a woman, only to go and buy again everything he threw out when the urge to cross-dress returns.

In these cases, a typical treatment often is the prescription of an SSRI, which both addresses his depression and lowers his libido, so he can reduce his sense of loss of control over his sexual behavior. This gives the client a chance to get some relief from depression and compulsive behavior and helps him talk about his cross-dressing with less shame. Medication is not a long-term solution but merely a short-term intervention as he and the therapist sort through what is happening for him. Ultimately, we want the man to be in control of his sexual behavior, not to be controlled by it. The therapist's job here is to help him embrace his fetish by accepting that this turns him on and not fight it or shame himself. In so doing, a client can become free of the depression and shame around the cross-dressing. The clinical intent is not to eradicate the paraphilia but rather to help the client manage it.

However, the treatment suggested for the "cross-dressing for comfort" client is different. This man is neither at odds with the experience nor ashamed. He does not go through a cycle of buying clothes and throwing them out. Here, the hypothesis is that the same variations in the brain associated with transgender identity are associated with the cross-dressing, perhaps not to the degree that they cause the client to feel that he is a woman, but to the extent that some cross-gender expression helps him feel more calm and reduces anxiety. This man may have difficulty stopping his cross-gender expression not because he is compulsive but because he is expressing a gender variance that is rooted in his brain. Stopping the cross-dressing feels like a denial of an important part of who he is. For this "partially transgender" person (in the terminology of Milrod, 2013), anecdotal evidence is suggesting that a clinical intervention might include treatment with (small doses of) estrogen, which is analogous to the standard hormone treatment for trans women. This treatment may help him become less depressed and anxious.

A therapist who is counseling a client concerned about cross-dressing should be aware of the possible links to transgender issues as well as paraphilias. As always, each individual case is unique and needs to be considered on its own merits.

In her book *My Husband Betty: Love, Sex, and Life With a Crossdresser*, Helen Boyd (2003) tended to identify her husband's cross-dressing more toward the transgender spectrum than as a paraphilia. The challenge for a wife, Boyd suggested, is that she might be able to be sexually interested in a man who likes to cross-dress, but not in a woman. If her husband transitions toward being a trans woman, then at some point will he "cross the line," so that he can no longer function as her husband? With this question in mind, some trans women have held off on bottom surgery to maintain their marriages. Boyd examines many aspects of "cross-dressing husbands" in this book and its sequel, *She's Not the Man I Married: My Life With a Transgender Husband* (2007).

One final note on the phrase "cross-dressing": Although it may be outdated or even derogatory, a man who is struggling with the paraphilia of cross-dressing may very well use that term when he consults with a therapist and have no other way to describe what he is dealing with. A man with a cross-dressing paraphilia is most likely not going to self-identify as gender-fluid, genderqueer, or transgender.

The Case of Carlton/Cary

This case illustrates the many different ways that gender identity and cross-dressing can manifest in one person.

When Carlton came to see me, he was in his mid-50s, happily married with three children. He was seeking therapy because he had had a series of major moments of self-awareness over the past several months that made him wonder if he might be transgender. He was confused. He didn't "think [he] was a woman," and when he was little, he'd never thought he was a girl. He couldn't figure out what was happening.

I told him we should start at the beginning, and he should tell me his story. As always, I wanted to develop a family history and a sexual history. And I asked him his gender identity and what name and pronoun he wanted me to use. A little uncertainly, he told me he was male, his name was Carlton, and he wanted me to use masculine pronouns.

He told me the overshadowing situation in his childhood was that his mother had been disappointed that he was born a boy. She had had two boys by the time she was pregnant with Carlton, and she wanted this third child to be a girl. So he was a disappointment to her. His two older brothers and his father knew that she felt this way. The entire extended family knew. She was uninhibited in expressing her disappointment and bitterness throughout his childhood.

Of course, this was an issue for Carlton as a boy. It bothered him. He really wished he could please his mother, and he knew he couldn't. He didn't personally feel that he wished to be a girl. But he wanted it for his mother.

As a young teen, he developed a fetish for women's panties. He started compulsively stealing them from clotheslines and clothing stores and his mother's clean and dirty laundry. He would wear them, smell them, masturbate to them. It because a fully ritualized sexual fetish for him.

His fetish continued into his early 20s, and he was bothered by it. He wanted it to go away. So he consulted a therapist. The therapist told him that he'd developed his fetish because of his mother. "This was your way of satisfying your mother's wish fulfillment," the therapist told him. "This part of you isn't something you were born with. It has a psychological origin."

They worked together for 2 years to eliminate the fetish. Carlton did gain a better understanding of it. It was imposed on him because of his mother's need. It was about her, not about him. He worked through his grief at not being able to please his mother. But the fetish didn't go away.

He continued to wear panties throughout his 20s. He wore them every day under his masculine clothes. But there was one change. He told me, "I had been using the panties for masturbation, but then I discovered in addition to that, I liked wearing them for comfort."

Then he confessed to me an element of his sexual fantasies he had never told anyone about. His core erotic fantasy was "forced feminization," a (common) fantasy of dominance and submission where a woman (or a man) humiliates a man by forcing him to dress as a woman. In Carlton's case, he just wanted a woman to feminize and humiliate him.

Carlton had always been unambiguously heterosexual. When he was 30, he fell in love with a woman, and they married. She was okay with his wearing panties. She understood it as something caused by his mother that he couldn't control. She accepted it as a harmless quirk and nothing more. There was nothing "kinky" or unusual about their relationship. He didn't tell her about the forced-feminization fantasy, although he continued to use it for masturbation.

I should note that he did not relate wearing the panties to his fantasy. He thought of them as two separate things. He was wearing women's clothing, and in his sexual fantasy he was forced to wear women's clothing. In therapy, he'd talked about the cross-dressing and the fantasy, and he and his therapist agreed they both came from the same cause, but he still thought of the "comfort" of the panties as separate from his erotic fantasies.

Carlton said his married sex was great until he and his wife started having children. Then, because of the kids, his wife was less available to him, and he began to hire female sex workers to enact his forced-feminization fantasy with him. (He didn't have sexual contact with them, but he did masturbate during the scenes.) He traveled for his very successful business, and it was during these travel times that he met the sex workers.

He still loved his wife, was very happy with his family and very ashamed of his sexual fantasy. But he'd found a way to express it that was fulfilling to him.

As he moved into his 40s, he no longer wanted just to wear panties. He was now wearing camisoles, too. They too felt "comforting" to him, not sexual. He was disturbed by his need to cross-dress and tried many times to stop wearing the camisoles and panties, but when he did, he found himself overcome with anxiety. So he didn't stop.

He had ongoing arrangements with the women he met in the various cities he traveled to, but they weren't relationships. The sex workers knew what he wanted, and he hired them to do it. Humiliation, domination, forced feminization.

The compulsion of the fantasy was with him every day. He acted it out with these sex workers regularly when he could. He discovered pornography for this fantasy, in the more edgy men's magazines and later on the Internet, and the porn was very much a turn-on for him. As time went on, he became less conflicted about his cross-dressing and his sexual fantasy. He accepted that they were important to him.

When he was in his early 20s, he would buy whole outfits of women's clothes. He would dress up as a girl, masturbate to the forced-feminization fantasy, pretending that a woman was forcing him, and then he'd be overcome with shame. He'd throw all the clothes and cross-dressing porn away to affirm his determination not to do it anymore. Later, he'd go back, buy more clothes, and do it all again. Many cross-dressers who are struggling against it go through this kind of cycle, which is called *purging*.

Later, when he was meeting sex workers to act out his fantasy, they would keep his women's clothes for him. He'd split his fantasy off from the rest of his life. He'd found a way to contain and enjoy it.

And during all this time—through his 20s and 30s and 40s—it never occurred to him to identify with transgender people. He saw himself as a cross-dressing man, not a woman. (The mainstream cultural awareness of transgender individuals grew toward the end of the 20th century, but transgender people were still not generally acknowledged the way they are today.)

But in his 40s, a development occurred for Carlton. He told me he "started feeling sexy while wearing the panties and camisoles, as well as comforted."

And then, in the first decade of the 21st century, when he was in his mid-50s, Carlton experienced three major events within a short period of time that confronted him with the possibility that he might be trans. Here is how he described these three events to me in therapy.

"Right before my father died, he told me that his father, my grandfather, was a cross-dresser and wore women's clothing every weekend. It was a powerful shock to hear that my grandfather had the same inclinations I did. My father had no idea about my cross-dressing—or, anyway, I assume he didn't. I never told him.

"By this time, I was doing the same thing as my grandfather, wearing women's clothing every weekend. And I always kept my toenails painted. I was vacuuming barefooted. When the vacuum passed in front of my red-painted nails, I had this epiphany, and said to myself, 'Fuck, Mom, you got your girl, didn't you?' And I fell on the floor and started sobbing."

Right about then, he and his wife had a trip to Europe planned. He didn't want to take his panties and camisoles. He was afraid he'd get in trouble going through customs, especially in homophobic countries like Russia. So he left them all at home and did without them for 3 weeks.

"This was the first time I had not at least worn panties and a camisole under my clothes in years. The first week wasn't too bad. However, each day I became more and more anxious. By the time we were ready to come home, I wanted to claw my eyes out."

He returned to America. He put on the panties and camisole and was flooded with emotion, not in a sexual way but in a "this is right" way. It was more than just comfort. It was more than just a sexual turn-on. In his words, "I realized that this is who I am. I'm a girl!"

Within a month of this realization, he came to see me.

Carlton/Cary: Clinical Interpretation and Treatment

Carlton did not think he was trans initially, because he imagined that a trans woman has a clear sense of being "a woman in a man's body." He didn't identify with this. However, as he told me his story, I realized that what he was telling me fit some new understandings of cross-dressing. I told him about the theory that "cross-dressing for comfort" was an indication that a person might be transgender. And this made immediate sense to him.

Now in our work together, he has begun a transgender coming-out process. Carlton now self-identifies as Cary. The gender she identifies with is female; the pronouns she wants are she/her/hers. She has told her wife and children and a few select friends.

She remembered something that she realized had a new significance for her. "About 15 years ago," she told me, "I decided I didn't like my body hair. It felt absolutely gross and icky to me." So she had it all permanently removed. Then she incorporated her lack of hair into her forced-feminization fantasy. The sex workers would humiliate her, laugh at her about how she was hairless like a woman. She used the fantasy to "explain" having her hair removed, but now she has a different way of looking at it. "Being disgusted by my body hair," she told me, "I can see that makes sense, since I'm a trans woman."

She's kept her job. She goes to work as a man, comes home and immediately puts on makeup and women's clothing. Her wife continues to be supportive, while her children are still adapting to the change. She goes out sometimes as a woman but has to be careful. Her story continues very like the case of Joanna that begins this chapter. We've discussed hormones and surgery, but she's not ready for that. She's still in the early stages of transition.

Perhaps surprisingly, she still enjoys the forced-feminization fantasy. So both exist side-by-side: She identifies as a woman, and she finds erotic a sexual fantasy about a male's forced feminization. Some might expect that the fantasy would go away now that she's in transition, but deeply embedded sexual fantasies don't just go away. And like dreams and the unconscious mind, they have their own logic.

The moral of the story is: See how complicated all this is? This is an example of a case that hinges on issues of erotic orientation as well as sexual orientation and gender orientation. It really involves all three.

Cary was transgender all her life but couldn't know it because of our culture, because of uninformed therapy, and because of her mother. Her first therapist wasn't completely wrong. Cary most likely did eroticize her mother's rejection and disapproval; the forced-feminization fantasy most likely comes from that. It is well established that we eroticize pain in the form of sexual fantasies and fetishes so that we can change from victim into victor. (This is discussed further in Chapter 9.) The way little boy Carlton could handle his mother's disapproval of his masculinity was to encode her negativity into this fantasy that could be acted out and played with later. That kind of erotic imprinting doesn't go away. It's important for a therapist to know that you can't give somebody an eroticectomy. This fantasy will always be a part of Cary's erotic orientation.

At the same time that Cary had to deal with her mother's scorn, she had to deal with society's scorn for anyone who is trans. Children (usually) are not allowed to have any other gender identity or sexual identity than cisgender and heterosexual. Trans children experience covert cultural sexual abuse, like all LGBTQ children; they are often forced to go underground and hide themselves. Cary was engaged in a coming-out process as a transgender woman, but there was no way for her to know this. The "knowing" began when she put on women's underwear after her trip to Europe and experienced the flood of "rightness."

If she hadn't been pressured by her mother and hadn't been pressured by society, she might not have had to protect herself with a fantasy. She might have simply discovered that she was trans. Of course, the forced-feminization fantasy and the eroticization of women's underwear obscured what was going on and made helping Cary that much more difficult for herself and her therapists.

Both Testosterone and Estrogen Affect Moods and Feelings

There's a myth that testosterone makes you angry and raging, and you may end up being physically abusive to your partner. That's a myth. However, such hormones do tend to amplify how you're feeling. Any hormone does, even estrogen. I don't want to overgeneralize, but I have noticed differences in how trans men just beginning to take testosterone, and trans women just beginning to take estrogen, handle their feelings.

If a trans man is feeling anger, resentment, sadness, grief, loss, or frustration, it may first come out as anger, and I have to help him work to get at how he's really feeling. I also counsel trans men that people may think they're angry because their voices are deeper and they tend to speak more loudly than before.

The "new" trans woman may tend to cry more or be more likely to call someone to vent. My trans women clients are often shocked at how strongly they are now reacting to other people.

There will be emotional changes for both trans men and trans women, but it's difficult to anticipate them all specifically.

Do Trans People Need to Present Their Gender Publicly?

The old rule for a transitioning transgender person was to live as the gender they want to transition to for one full year before starting hormones or having surgery. While this is generally a good idea, it's not always feasible, practical, or safe, and a therapist needs to be sensitive to these considerations when counseling a client.

A trans person's job or family connections or social connections might be in jeopardy as soon as people realize they are transitioning. And, of course, they could be attacked by trans bigots. The murder rate for trans women (especially trans women of color) is significantly higher than for ciswomen (Schmider, 2017). So sometimes trans people need to plan their coming-out carefully, as illustrated by the case of Joanna. She was comforted by coming out in little ways that wouldn't be noticed by other people but were still significant in that they allowed her to claim her identity. Some trans women begin hormones before they are "out" at work or in the community or even to family. Generally, they have a timeline for transitioning that allows them to begin in stealth mode for a while until their bodies make it impossible to hide their gender. They can extend their time undercover, for example, by binding to hide their developing breasts. As they begin to show themselves in their new gender expression, they might need to think about finding safe neighborhoods and places to go.

Trans people may also start saving more money or start downsizing, so they can live on a lower income and survive being fired. It's not just about therapy and hormones and surgery. It's about their whole lives.

Hormone-Induced Puberty and Second Adolescence

When a trans person decides to live their gender and begins to take hormones, it's not uncommon for them to go through a second adolescence, just like gay, lesbian, and bisexual people sometimes do after they come out.

I've seen trans guys go out and get a skateboard to do tricks on, because they've always wanted to do that. And several trans women I've treated, even though in their 40s or 50s, chose to wear clothes that society norms deem are what a teenager might wear. They didn't realize, or didn't care, that they weren't being age-appropriate to our society, and I didn't bring it up with them. They told me that other therapists they'd seen focused on that, and they stopped going to those therapists, because they didn't want to be told what to do. They wanted to go through this phase. And I was okay with that, and I support therapists being okay with it, too.

I did try to make sure that they were being safe. You can get hurt both with skateboards and with outfits that may draw unwanted attention. Trans women are particularly vulnerable. It can be more difficult for them to pass, and the irrational anger they induce in others can be cruel and violent. This needs to be explored with the client.

I remember one client in particular who seemed to have little sense of this. One day she came to show me an outfit.

"I really like my nipples showing through this blouse," she told me. "Isn't it cute?"

But I knew her body hadn't changed enough for society to see her as female. So I asked her, "Well, where do you wear that shirt?"

"I wear it everywhere," she said.

"Do you feel safe," I asked her, "when you're at the mall?"

I wanted her to think about it. I worked with her to try to bring it out, instead of just telling her. There was a real danger she'd get defensive and not come back.

I've had clients react that way: "You're judging me. You're telling me what I can and can't do." They have to identify safety as a problem before they're going to want help with it. I had one client who was 60 years old in transition, and she didn't live in a safe neighborhood at all. I told her, "Maybe that dress . . . if you love that dress, maybe it might be safe to wear in your apartment, or if you drive yourself somewhere, a safer area, you could change in a restroom." I wanted to raise the issue of safety without her feeling criticized or judged. I didn't want her to take my comments as my personal appraisal of her gender-expression choices.

On the Issue of "Overdoing It"

Coming-out lesbian, gay, or bi people can experience their second (or delayed) adolescence by "oversexualizing." Trans people undergoing second adolescence will sometimes "overgenderize." They will try too hard to be "one of the boys" or "one of the girls." Just as presentation can be too young or overdone, body and verbal mannerisms can be too much. For example, a trans man might be with a group of cisgender guys and feel he needs to talk sexually about women, even if it doesn't feel right or natural to him. Common sense will help curb the excesses, but of course, adolescents don't have much common sense when they're trying to fit in.

I've had long-term clients tell me that they *now* realize they "overdid it" when they were first coming out, in the sense that their gender expression was unnecessarily provocative or aggressive or their "take me or leave me" arguments with family and friends were unnecessarily confrontational.

One trans woman told me she told her children, "Either accept me or I'm going to cut you out of my life," and as a consequence, she lost contact with her children.

While she meant it at the time because she was in an adolescent coming-out stage, she regretted it later and had to work to mend fences.

Several trans men and women clients told me they had embarrassed themselves (in retrospect) by overdoing their gender expression, overgenderizing via clothing or behavior. What they thought at the time were "typical" male or female behaviors (these clients later decided) were "too much." Of course, it is common for adolescents to express themselves this way for a few years.

On the other hand, a therapist must remain vigilant about the dangers of responding inappropriately to a client's transitioning gender expression.

On Countertransference With Transgender Clients

I think it's really important that therapists check their own countertransference, especially when working with a trans client who is first coming out. Therapists shouldn't let their own reactions to clients' gender expression interfere with their role as therapist. Therapists might have judgments or reactions that reflect their own issues about gender expression (or political beliefs or opinions about rich people or poor people or pretty women or showoff men). In this mode of countertransference, a therapist might be inclined to say something like, "Ooh, do you think that's too much?" or "Isn't that skirt a little too short?" which would be justified only in the context of safety (if at all). Clients will choose their own mode of gender expression, and it's usually not the therapist's job to critique it.

Therapists should always be clear with themselves about what the issue is. If you're counseling about safety, you should be clear with yourself and the client that that's what you're counseling about. This is tricky. You may feel that the transitioning trans woman doesn't look very much like a woman and shouldn't dress really feminine. That kind of reaction can get very close to being transphobic.

In the case of Troy, my own countertransference with a trans client became an issue in the therapy.

The Case of Troy

Troy was a young adult trans man. As I worked with him, I found myself being surprised that, although he self-identified as male, he kept a feminine gender expression. He had a very feminine face, and his hair was long and styled in a way more typical of women than men in our society. He did wear oversized clothes that obscured the contours of his body, but he assured me he had no problem with his body—for example, with his very full breasts. He kept telling me that he was presenting male, and I always wanted to ask, "Why aren't you expressing your gender in a more masculine way?" But I never said it, because I didn't want to make him upset.

So one day he came in and he was furious with his mother. I asked him what was wrong, and he said, "You're not going to believe what she asked me."

And I said, "What?"

"My mother said to me, 'You're telling me that you're male, so why don't you look more like a male?'"

And I replied, "Oh my god, I can't believe she said that," even though that was exactly what I had been thinking. "What did you say to her?"

"'Mom, this is how a male presents himself. This is how *this* male presents himself.'"

It was the best possible answer. That's it. There's nothing more to say.

Eventually, he chose to get hormone therapy and to have top surgery. He went out of town over the summer and came back with a really deep voice, deeper than mine, and he did start presenting more male. By that I mean more traditionally male in societal terms. To him, his transitioning had always been going in the right direction. Every little piece was just enough for him at the time.

Family Considerations

One of my trans clients told me, "I can deal with the fact that a lot of people don't see me as female out in the world. What I can't handle is that my family doesn't."

Rejection by family is the number one cause of suicide attempts by trans people. Acceptance means so much. It is, of course, a shock when the trans child (or parent) discloses that their gender is different from what the family thinks. The family has to go through a process of being upset, of negotiating ("Can't you just be gay?"), and finally of finding a new equilibrium with this new reality. (See Arlene Lev [2004] on the stages a trans person's family goes through.) The loss the family feels is deep and painful, and a therapist for a trans person will no doubt need to counsel relatives as well as the client. The web TV series *Transparent* (Amazon, 2014) shows a family in which the father is transitioning. The family members' extreme reactions are played for comedy but reflect reality.

Parents, particularly of trans children, will worry about the physical effects of puberty blockers and hormones and of surgery. So many choices are effectively irreversible. So many medical issues have not yet been resolved, especially the long-term effects of blockers and hormones. Parents will worry about social acceptance, for themselves and their children. And of course, there is the specter of prejudice and bullying and hate crimes. The world is much more unsafe for a trans person than for anyone cisgender. A therapist can offer support, can counsel for medical and social safety, can witness and encourage clients in their choices. It is a hard road the trans client must take, under the best of circumstances.

Boutique Identity

All clients have their own personal identity. We love to classify—*kinds* of sexual identity, *types* of gender identity, and so on—but when clients are sitting in front of you, they tell you whatever "irrational" mixture of kinds and types make sense to them, and somehow it adds up to their unique "boutique identity." When Troy says, "This is how *this* male presents himself," he is staking his claim to his own identity. He's calling it "male," but really it's "Troy." He was bold and courageous to claim himself that way.

Your clients come in. They tell you who they are and why they're there, and you ask them to tell you more, and you listen, and over time you discover their personal boutique identities. You're not classifying; you're listening. It's a great lens to look through.

Psychotherapy for the Gender-Variant Child and Adolescent

Children as young as 4 can express strong claims to be the other gender. If little William wants to be called Julia, wear a dress, and play with dolls, the current thinking among gender-affirming psychotherapists is to let it happen. It may be a short-term whim or a change that will last a lifetime, but the child can lead the way. Of course, I realize this is not always convenient for the family, but we can all learn to be a little more flexible, a little less grim and more playful.

One point is that William may want to be Julia only at home or only sometimes, and generally William/Julia can sort that out for him/herself.

Of course, a gender affirmative therapist will be aware that people are going to have reactions to children who want to be gender flexible. These reactions may limit or determine options, and the parents may have to run interference for their child or put protective limitations on the child's behavior. Still, it should be clear to the child, as well as to everyone else, that the child is not doing anything wrong. It is other people who are the problem.

In this section, we will look at various aspects of helping gender-variant children and their parents navigate the sometimes-stormy waters of gender nonconformity.

The Very Young Trans Child

People who are transgender are born that way. It happens in utero during the first trimester, and some children know at a very young age. One (loose) rule of thumb is that the child is probably trans if he or she is "consistent, persistent, and insistent" in claiming the other gender. However, we don't have to decide that when the child is very young. The first step for prepubertal children who claim to be the other gender is to let them explore. Let the child decide how they will dress, what name they want to be called and by what pronoun (he, she, they), and what gender bathroom they will use outside the home. (They can be coached in discretion.) The child should be supported in being "inconsistent," changing from feminine to masculine to combinations of both, as much as they feel they want to. Medical interventions (hormones, blockers, surgery) are rarely considered until the onset of puberty.

A 5-year-old natal male consistently insists he's a girl, so his parents bring him to me. "What should we do?"

In my office, I would ask the child, "What name would you prefer that your parents and I call you?" If the answer is "Elizabeth," I'd say, "Okay. From now on, we'll call you Elizabeth."

If Elizabeth wants to dress as a girl, then she should be allowed to do that when possible. And the parents may have to deal with other people's reactions within the family and elsewhere.

And at this point, while Elizabeth is 5, we don't know what her future will be, exactly. She should have the right to explore her gender, changing if she wants, and changing again, and not be forced into an unnatural consistency.

If as Elizabeth grows older, she persists in her transgender identity, then the societal and family issues will become more and more complicated.

A therapist could recommend that the parents interview schools before they place their child. If Elizabeth is going to a day school connected to a kindergarten connected to an elementary school, she might potentially be there for a long time. The parents and the therapist could go talk to the administrators. They should tell the story in a straightforward way: "My child now identifies as a girl. Her name is Elizabeth. She's going to use the girls' restroom. We will teach her to use a stall. No one should be concerned about her genitals. There's no reason to be."

So prepubertal children should be supported in their gender exploration. The therapist will need to work with the parents, the family, the schools, and society to allow it to happen.

The Case of Brian

I had a trans male child client, Brian, whose school contacted his mother and told her that another mother had called and said that her son was uncomfortable sharing the bathroom with a trans male.

Brian's mother called me. She felt very intimidated. She asked me, "What should I do?"

And so together we called a trans hotline. They said that my client's mother needed to contact the school and say, "Tell that other mother that if her son is uncomfortable with Brian in the bathroom, then perhaps her son should use a different bathroom."

And that was the end of the story. The school never said another word.

Puberty and Discovering If You Are Gay, Lesbian, or Trans

At a WPATH conference I attended, one speaker taught that many prepubertal children who express gender dysphoria grow up to be gay (or straight or bi). However, if the child's claim to be a nonnatal gender continues to be "insistent, persistent, and consistent" as he or she enters into puberty, then the child is much more likely to be trans. Note that not all trans children have the temperament to be "insistent" and "persistent." For example, Darlene Tando (2017) argued that parents must be sensitive to the fact that their children may be influenced by assumptions about their assigned gender and therefore hesitate to be "insistent" or "persistent," most especially if they are timid or docile by nature or if their parents are intolerant of gender-nonconforming behavior. And of course, it is possible that parents will overact to their child's gender-nonconforming behavior and assume they are trans when they are not (Olson & Durwood, 2016). Therefore, a common-sense caution about jumping to conclusions is reasonable. Thus, a possibly trans child can be supported in many important ways before medical interventions are required.

Adolescence is a difficult time for everyone, but it is especially brutal for trans children (most especially for MtF). All gay, lesbian, and trans children may experience gender dysphoria as little children. Little boys may want to dress up as glamorous women. (Cher was the icon when I was a child.) Little girls may dress like "tomboys." One rule of thumb is that gay little boys will say, "I feel like a girl," while trans (MtF) little boys will say, "I *am* a girl." (Or for girls, "I feel like a boy" versus "I *am* a boy.") Sometimes, the distinction is very clear, and sometimes it is not. The real clarification comes at puberty.

When puberty hits, the gay boys and lesbian girls, say, "Whoa, I'm not a girl. I'm not a boy. I'm just attracted to people of my gender." The trans child will say, "Yikes, this is a nightmare." His or her hormones are kicking in, and their gender dysphoria gets worse—that is, they have the sense that their bodies are getting more and more ugly and wrong. We see many suicide attempts (and suicides) in trans teens.

Issues that would be appropriate to address for trans teens in therapy are:

- Rejection by parents, school, peers, community
- Bullying
- Comorbid conditions (depression, anxiety, suicidal ideation)
- Apparent "suddenness" of condition. Often, the prepubertal child will have hidden their feelings, even from themselves, or the parents will minimize signs of gender dysphoria.
- Impatience: "I want to transition right now. Where are my hormones? Where's my surgery?"
- Finding support groups/networks

Bigotry at all levels tears at the spirit of a trans child. By far the most damage results from rejection by parents. It's devastating for these children, many of whom end up committing suicide. If there is significant bigotry at the schools and in the community, then the parents may have to consider moving. It's unfair to turn the family into refugees because William wants to live as Julia, but many communities are willing to be cruel about gender. (There are also many supportive communities.) Ultimately, the therapist is there to add clarity, support, and acceptance, but the parents will have to decide what to do.

A Parents' Dilemma

When a gender-nonconforming child is entering puberty, the parents have to decide whether to begin puberty blockers. These delay the onset of puberty and, in particular, prevent the hormone-induced biological changes that can be especially distressing to children who are gender nonconforming or transgender. The main benefit is that later "cross hormone therapy is even more effective at achieving the desired physical appearance in gender transition" (Selva, 2016).

But what if the children change their minds later? Perhaps they turn out to be gay. Will getting blockers confuse them about their orientation, or will there be other permanent changes? Anecdotal evidence suggests that merely delaying puberty will not cause permanent changes, but giving blockers to children is a fairly recent medical practice, and scientific longitudinal studies have not been completed. There is evidence that it can cause bone-density problems, so doctors prescribe an increase in calcium. There is also some discussion about how it might affect children's fertility later on in life. The immediate evidence is that when blockers are stopped, normal development proceeds.

On the other hand, once hormones (estrogen and testosterone) begin, either out of normal development or as a part of hormone therapy, then the resulting physical changes—for example, vocal cord changes, the development of breast tissue, changes in facial structure—can be only partially reversed, and this often only with surgery. (Note that estrogen as well as testosterone has irreversible effects, although MtF transition is generally considered more difficult than FtM.) A therapist counseling parents or children can help them understand the difference between blockers and hormones and the implications of using each. In particular, a therapist can help them understand the permanence of the changes brought about by hormones. Of course, questions about whether and when to begin treatment need to be discussed with an endocrinologist, who is the ultimate authority.

Responding to the high rate of suicide attempts among trans adolescents and young adults, some therapists and parents have concluded that it is better to allow medical transition for a consistent, persistent, and insistent adolescent than risk suicide. If the child decides later that transitioning was a mistake, they are alive to reverse the transition, even if this reversal will not be perfect. Keeping them safe is the most important thing.

Psychotherapy With Transgender Teens

Teenage clients like to challenge the therapist. They will talk about things they know the therapist doesn't know and then act shocked or offended or both when the therapist will have to ask for clarification. They like to bring up all the friends they've made on Facebook, Tumblr, Reddit, and similar social media sites—and their friends are genderqueer, or gender-fluid, or go by "they"—and the therapist is expected to remember everything.

They mention Margaret, so you might ask, "Who's Margaret?"

And they say, "Yeah, I told you about them before. Last week they identified as Ryan, and now they're Margaret."

But you're supposed to know that.

"You're the gender therapist. You're supposed to know things."

You have to remember that the client is 14, and this is their negative transference. When a trans teen does this, a therapist should deal with it the same way as for any teenage client's negative transference.

The Case of Adam: Transgender Sexual Fluidity

I have a trans male client. Adam is 18, and I've been seeing him for 2 years. He identifies as straight, and he likes girls. He has lots of dates with lots of girls, which he always tells me about with gleeful enthusiasm, but one day he was a little more guarded.

"I had a date," he told me, looking down.

He didn't say "a date with a girl," the way he always did before, so right away I guessed the date was with someone other than a girl. But I didn't want to push him. I asked him how the girl he had told me about in his last session was doing.

"Oh, she's playing games with me," he said. "She's going back with her girlfriend."

"Do you have any other love interests?" I asked him.

"I had a date with somebody."

"Well, how was that?"

"I really don't want to talk about it."

So we talked about his excitement around going on to college after high school, and then I asked, "Is the person that you went on a date with going to the same college?"

He said, "No, I don't know what's going on. Hold on a minute. I have to go to the bathroom."

When he came back from the bathroom, he said, "You know what. I went on a date with a guy."

I said, "That's awesome. Tell me about it. How is he?"

His reluctance to talk to me about dating a boy was probably related to the idea that he ought to be consistent in his gender orientation. He had told me he was straight. He had told me about dating girls. And now he was letting me down by changing. I reminded him that sexual orientation can be fluid for a trans teen. The *Q* in LGBTQ is there for a reason.

"Just go with it," I told him. "As long as you're happy and you're true to yourself, it's okay."

And he just lit up and told me all about the guy.

My strategy with gender-questioning clients is to make sure they feel safe to talk about whatever they want to talk about. I don't say things like, "What do you think this says about your sexual orientation?" Because I know he's already questioning it.

Adam is a natal female who had approached me originally at 16 wanting to start hormones. He told me he identified as straight. "I only date girls," he said, "and I've always identified as a boy since I was little." And his dad was there and said, "Oh yeah, he's very masculine." And now he's legally male. So he felt inconsistent when he wanted to date a guy.

In my experience this is not uncommon. Transgender men, once they start testosterone, may explore being with people of different genders. A lot of transgender men come out as gay or bisexual, even if they dated only women before hormones. In my work with these clients, we have to consider their confusion from internalized homophobia as well as transphobia. When we get past that, they are freer to be themselves.

Summary: Children and Adolescents

The general principle is we support the child in terms of names and pronouns and clothing and gender expression but hold off on medical interventions at least until puberty. Gender and sexual orientation for a teen can be fluid. Just go with it. I encourage children and teens to explore gender in whatever way feels right to them. And at some point in the transition through puberty, it is normative for apparently trans children to discover they are gay, lesbian, bi, or gender nonconforming but not trans. We adults don't have to control the process. At every moment, we just support the child.

Summary and Conclusions

A mother of a young adult trans child came to see me for counseling, and she shared with me the letter her child had sent her to come out. It is not only a moving document but also a good summary of many of the points we have considered in this chapter. Therefore, I reproduce it essentially verbatim below (but, like the other letters reproduced in the book, with a few identifying details changed).

A Trans Daughter Comes Out to Her Parents

Dear Mom and Dad,

I want to start this off by saying that I love you and although I sometimes have trouble showing it, I appreciate everything you have done for me over the years. It has not gone unnoticed and I am very lucky to have you as my parents. That is not why I am writing you though.

I am writing you because I have something to say, something that is immensely important to me and has been a part of my life for as long as I can remember, but it is something that may come as quite a shock, so brace yourself. Instead of doing it in person or over the phone, I decided to write you because I have a lot to say and any past attempt to bring any of it up to you in person ended before it even began. I was scared. I still am scared. Scared of how you would react, scared of disappointing you, and scared of losing you. But my feelings have gotten strong to the point where I cannot take it anymore. I need to get this off my chest.

I have been suffering from a medical condition called gender dysphoria for my entire life. What this means is that I am transgender; although my sex is male, my gender (or my brain, or my soul, or my subconscious sense of self, whatever you want to call it) is female. Inside I have always felt that I was female, but this used to scare me beyond belief. I tried hiding it away and not thinking about it. I tried forcing it out of my brain, and I tried to pray to God to make it go away. I would pray every night hoping that God would one day make me feel normal, but all of this was to no avail. In fact, the feeling of disassociation between my mind and my body got worse and worse as I got older. I stopped caring about my health, it became very difficult to focus on school, and it started to drive a wedge in my relationships with both friends and family.

It wasn't until after high school that I realized I needed to do something about this. I started doing research online and found, for the first time in my life, that I was not alone. My journey from that point on has been trying to undo the years of guilt and shame I had put upon myself. After moving down south, I tried to be honest with myself and talk to somebody about it. Up to this point, I had only ever dealt with it in my own head. I had nobody to talk to, and it was literally eating me alive. Although coming out to all my friends was the hardest and scariest thing I have ever done, their support and unconditional love has been amazing! I expected before this to lose a couple of friends along the way, but so far every person I have told has been completely accepting and kind, and we have only grown closer since. This transition that I spent my whole life fearing has been a beautiful and eye-opening experience. It completely changed my point of view. In spite of some added stress and financial issues, I have never been happier.

After coming out I decided to seek professional help. I have been seeing a therapist semi-regularly for half a year, which has been an immeasurable help for my self-esteem and anxiety levels. I have also been seeing a doctor about this. We have been doing tests to monitor my hormone levels and overall health, and she, along with my therapist, has helped me start transitioning. She started me Hormone Therapy by prescribing female hormones, which I have been taking for a month and a half. These pills over the course of the next year or two will change my outward appearance to better match the person I am inside by reducing the amount of testosterone my body produces, softening my skin, redistributing my fat, shrinking my genitals, widening my hips, and growing my breasts. I know that probably sounds crazy to someone who is comfortable with his or her assigned gender, but to someone like me, it makes them happier than anything! You don't have to understand it, it is very difficult to understand, but I am hoping you can accept it.

I am not a gay man; I am not a cross-dresser; I am not a transvestite. I am not a man pretending to be a woman.

This has nothing to do with my sexual orientation. This is not something I jumped into lightly. This is not a phase I am going through. This is a real medical condition. It has been known for a while that male and female brains are different, so when a mismatch happens during the fetal stage of child development, and mismatches do happen, it will cause confusion, depression, and discomfort. HRT is the only known cure. This is not your fault, and there is nothing you could have done differently while raising me to change this. It is simply the way I was born.

I understand that this is a lot to take in. I want to assure you that I am still the same person you know and love. My hopes and dreams, my sense of humor, my love of movies, and just about everything else about me is exactly the same. I am still a human being, and I am still your child. I am, and always have been, your daughter. You just could not see it before. I love you so much, but I have felt that our relationship has been strained over the years because of this unacknowledged elephant in the room. I was scared of rejection, so I subconsciously pushed you guys away, and I am sorry.

Within maybe six months or so, I plan on living as a woman completely. This has not been, and will continue not to be, cheap or easy. I have been working day and night to be able to pay for the therapy, the doctor bills, the prescriptions, and a complete change of wardrobe. I am constantly scared of discrimination and isolation. I understand that I am giving up some privi-leges and that I may be off-putting to some people because of my transition, but all of that is well worth it, if I can finally live comfortably as myself.

I've had years and years to process all this information, so take your time with it and mull it over, but please try and keep an open mind. And if you have any questions, anything whatsoever, do not hesitate to ask me. Now that this is on the table, I have nothing left to hide. I love and miss you more than you know, and I hope you are doing well. I look forward to talking to you once you have had time to digest this. If you want to answer by text or e-mail at first that is fine, too. I understand this is a hard subject to broach, and even I still have difficulty discussing it sometimes. This will not be an easy journey, but I hope I can count on you guys to always be on my side.

Final Thoughts

When I went to my first therapist as a teenager, decades ago, and told him I was gay, the first words out of his mouth were, "No, you're not." He didn't believe I was old enough to know I was gay, or even to be gay. I'm not sure what he was thinking, but a therapist should never do this.

Transgender people exist. If someone comes in your office, if they're 5 or if they're 50, and they tell you they are a gender different from their natal gender, it is your first and most important duty to affirm their sense of themselves. "Tell me more," not "No, you're not."

You can explore with your clients the broad and flexible map of gender variance (and sexual variance, too, if that comes up). Some people are questioning. They should be allowed to try things and change their minds and then change their minds again. Some people are dealing with gender dysphoria; others are not. Gender-nonconforming people may be transgender; many are not. Eventually, the individual clients will decide what they need and what they want.

CHAPTER 15

The Bisexual Client

I'm bisexual. I'm attracted to both straight and gay men.
—A gay stand-up comic

> I call myself bisexual because I acknowledge that I have in myself the potential to be attracted—romantically and/or sexually—to people of more than one sex and/or gender, not necessarily at the same time, not necessarily in the same way, and not necessarily to the same degree.
> —Robin Ochs

Bisexuality has no fixed, commonly recognized and understood definition. That's why the most important thing a therapist should know to do when a client identifies himself or herself as bisexual is to ask, "Tell me what bisexuality means for you." It's okay to ask, even if the client is a little ruffled by the question. You certainly should honor the client's self-identification. But if you assume you know what the client means, you're inevitably starting out with misconceptions.

What Should a Therapist Know About Bisexuality?

"Bisexual" is a true sexual orientation, but it is mocked and denied by some members of both the straight and the lesbian and gay communities. There are myths and prejudices about bisexuality, which are discussed below. The individual bisexual client will have preferences and behaviors not shared by all bisexuals.

You need to start by asking your clients, "How do you self-identify?" They might say, "I'm sexually fluid," or "mostly straight" or "mostly gay," even though their description of what they like and what they do aligns with your experience of bisexuals. However, don't correct them and tell them they are truly bisexual. The therapist in general should try to understand what the clients' self-identification means to them and not try to impose what they think on the clients. There are so many different ways of being bisexual, so many different ways of being sexually fluid, and there's overlap. Someone might say, "I'm sexually fluid. I'm attracted to both men and women." Is that bisexual? Well, not to them. But another guy might have the same preferences and behaviors and say, "I'm bisexual." (Chapter 16 focuses on sexual fluidity.)

In general, the difference between someone who is bisexual and someone who is sexually fluid is that the bisexual person is attracted to both genders sexually or romantically, whereas someone sexually fluid is often only attracted to one gender but willing to be sexual with someone of the other gender in the right circumstances.

So, two different clients come to see a therapist, and one says, "I'm bisexual," and the other says, "I'm sexually fluid," and they both go on to describe the same issues and questions. It really doesn't matter what their "correct" orientations are. Because in both cases, the therapist responds the same way: "Tell me more about what being bisexual/sexually fluid means to you."

Therapists can be overly concerned about what they "ought to" know when a client self-identifies in a certain way. We all want to do the right thing and care about not misunderstanding our clients. I say to therapists, "Don't be overly worried about knowing all these definitions. How can you know?" Some clients believe they've never "had sex" because they've only done oral or mutual masturbation and never had vaginal or anal intercourse.

So when a client says, "I'm bisexual," you have to ask, "What does bisexual mean to you?" And sometimes clients do get upset, as I've noted in Chapter 13, and you, the therapist, might feel ashamed if your client challenges you this way, but you shouldn't. Often, the clients who are so hypersensitive are adolescents (or in the adolescent stage of bisexuality). Another possibility is that they may have a personality disorder. In any case, I have to emphasize, as I've done before, it's not wrong for the therapist to ask this question. It's the question that must be asked.

These days, even those who self-identify as gay or lesbian, or even straight, often don't mean it in an orthodox way. Don't assume that just because someone identifies as gay, lesbian, or straight that they haven't had sex with the other gender or that they would never want to. My younger clients sometimes identify as "heteroflexible" or "homoflexible." They're straight, gay, or lesbian, but they episodically have sex with the other gender just because they want to.

Despite the fact that a therapist should ask, "What do you mean by bisexual?" it's good to have a sense of the factors that come up when considering bisexuality. In my experience, the way people connect sexually and romantically are the major elements that define bisexuality:

- *Sexual attraction.* Who are you attracted to? This is often summarized by the "beach test": When you're on a beach, whom do you notice? The men, the women, both, neither?
- *Romantic connection.* How do your romantic connections work? Are you romantic with one gender or both, or does it depend on the circumstances?
  - Many of my bisexual clients have been men who were attracted to men and women *sexually* but only to women *romantically*. However, all "combinations" of sexual and romantic attraction can occur. I should note that a bisexual orientation tends to be stable, not changing.
- *Identity.* Bisexual is an identity. If clients tell you they're bisexual, they're telling you who they are psychologically, socially, spiritually, emotionally, and sexually.

There's a culture war going on around sexual orientation and identity, both within the LGBTQ communities and between those communities and the straight dominant culture. People are arguing what it means (and should mean) to be gay, lesbian, bisexual, and queer. So you're going to have clients coming in bashed and confused and disoriented by the cultural controversies and prejudicial laws, and your job will be to help them find their own sexual selves through their own lens, not through a political lens, and not through your lens either.

The Case of Jane: The Loss of Gay and Lesbian Privilege

Jane was about 50 years old, and she told me that she'd identified as lesbian throughout her entire life. She was attracted to women, always had relationships with women, had always been sexual with women. "I was with women all the time," she told me. "I was going to lesbian events, and I felt that lesbians were my people."

Then the roof fell in.

"I found Jim," she said, "and I realized I'm really bisexual. Not just because of Jim, but because I realized I had always been attracted to men, just not as strongly as to women. But it's always been there, enough so that I can claim the identity.

"I was so unprepared for what happened next. I was so naive. I came out bisexual to my friends in the lesbian community—people I've known for years and who have been my best friends in the world—and they turned on me immediately. They called me a traitor. They said I was just wanting to keep a foot in the door of heterosexual privilege. They said, 'We're done with you.'"

She was crying while telling me this. "I love the lesbian community. I used to go to all the events. It was my family. Now that's all changed. I've been told to stay away. I've been disinvited to the parties I was always invited to, and even unfriended on Facebook.

"I tried to bring my boyfriend into the community, because he wanted to meet my friends. He was open to it. He's straight, but it didn't matter to him. Well, now I realize what a mistake *that* was. My lesbian friends were even more offended. They didn't want to have anything to do with my man. I just couldn't believe it. He's such a sweet guy!"

Jane: Clinical Interpretation and Treatment

There is a lot of talk in the media right now about male privilege, white privilege, cisgender privilege, and straight privilege—each of these is important to recognize and address. However, there is another privilege that isn't addressed: gay and lesbian privilege used against bisexuals and transgender individuals. Jane had lost her lesbian privilege, her right to be accepted, to be welcomed and cherished.

I focused at first on Jane's grief and her sense of loss. I validated her. I let her know that I understood the depth of what she was going through, the disenfranchisement, the rejection. The depression. The blow to her self-confidence and her self-acceptance. I told her I could see she was feeling all the rejection of being disinherited from her family, of being cast out of her community into the wilderness.

After some sessions, she asked me for practical advice. What were her options? What could she do?

I noted that she could try to stay connected to her old friends, to brave the snubs and sneers and try to connect with anyone who would still connect with her. Some people would keep treating her as a "traitor," but others might be more tolerant. I told her it was unlikely that the "most political" of her old friends would "forgive" her. Even though being bisexual wasn't her fault—after all, she was born that way—the primitive tribalism generated in the pressure cooker of antigay, antilesbian prejudice in our society would be hard to overcome for anyone whose reaction to her was "traitor!"

However, on a more positive note, I suggested that she try to make new friends among younger lesbians, who in my experience tend to be less rigid about sexual orientation boundaries.

The option I felt the most optimistic about was that she could enter into the bisexual community. She could organize her own group or join one. If she wanted it to be face-to-face, I suggested that the local LGBTQ community center would help her. Also, there are many opportunities online.

If she gathered together her own community, she would discover lesbians and gay men who would be totally okay with her being bisexual. The group would be inclusive by design. The people who didn't want to be with her wouldn't join, but the LGBTQ community center would appreciate an inclusive group and try to help her. The center would try to cultivate a different kind of attitude. If she wanted to become an activist for bi inclusion, they would support her.

I had already asked Jane the question I ask everybody who comes to talk with me about issues of identity. I had asked her what she meant when she identified herself as bisexual. "I'm lesbian, but some men turn me on, and I love my Jim," is in essence what she told me. She wanted to be socially lesbian but sexual and romantic with men (monogamous with Jim), but in the past she had found it natural to be sexually and romantically lesbian. She told me she was living a heterosexual life with her boyfriend, but she was unhappy because that was "not who [she] fully was." She was lonely and missed her lesbian community.

She wanted her old lesbian social life back, just this time with her boyfriend. I had to help her see that that was unlikely for the lesbian women of her generation. I told her she needed to grieve the loss of what once was. The kinship and community she had been so supported by in the past was gone. She wasn't going to be able to get it back. Again, I noted the possibility of new friends among younger lesbians.

I worked with Jane on self-acceptance and on her grief, on depression and anxiety. I wanted her to feel that she could enter into a community again, if not with her old circle of friends, then with some new ones. She came to me with deep depression and very low self-esteem, with the sadness of enormous loss.

We worked together on her loss and inclusion issues, and I encouraged her to look for what in her past might have sensitized her to the sense of not belonging. We discovered several important times in her life when her sense of inclusion was wounded.

Her mother had died when she was 5. Her father remarried a woman with two children older than Jane. Her stepmother tended to favor her own children and ignored Jane. She never made friends with her half sister and half brother. Her father was away too often to offer much comfort.

The distant suburb she grew up in was one of those that had never been developed as planned. Only half of the houses were occupied, and there were few neighborhood children. Her family moved closer to town the summer before she entered sixth grade, but that didn't lead to much improvement for Jane. She started middle school knowing no one and was identified early as a potential victim by the mean girls who like to torment the defenseless. They identified her as wounded and tried to wound her more. She maintained a defensive isolation and made no friends, but as she entered high school she began to connect with others through the gay-straight alliance. This was her first experience of peer acceptance. She discovered in herself a capacity for leadership, and she attained the previously unthinkable: She was "popular."

Nobody had advocated for her at home, and nobody had advocated for her at school until she had connected with the lesbian community. She was never "one of the girls" until issues of sexual orientation helped her find friends and energized her to the cause of lesbian rights.

Now her past feelings of isolation and rejection informed her current grief and sense of loss. She had been so blindsided by her lesbian friends' extreme reactions. It was like her mother's unexpected death.

Jane and I worked on her issues in several years of psychotherapy. She recovered somewhat from her debilitating depression, which was replaced by anger and determination. She decided to take me up on the idea of being an "activist" for bi inclusion.

She was able to reclaim her self-respect and make new friends as she learned more about bisexuality and met others who were advocating for bisexual rights. I don't know if she was ever able to reconnect with any of her old lesbian friends, but she did find lesbian activists who would work with her on bisexual inclusion. They focused especially within the gay and lesbian communities on understanding and tolerance.

On Gay and Lesbian Privilege

Jane's case is in no way unusual. I had been running a gay men's group for a number of years when I brought in a man who identified as bisexual. The group was very hard on him, insisting that he had to be gay or straight, one or the other. Their biphobia shocked me. They were doing to him the same thing that many heterosexuals do to LGBTQ people—shunning him and making him an outcast.

JoAnn Loulan's story is similar to Jane's. A psychotherapist and author of several significant books on lesbian sexuality, Loulan had a large and enthusiastic lesbian following, but after she married a man, she lost her "lesbian credibility." According to Ted Gideonse (1997),

> [Loulan] rejects the term bisexual because she fell for this particular man, not men in general. But that's hard to get across. "I understand they're upset and don't want me to have the privileges of being a lesbian and having heterosexual privileges at the same time," Loulan says. "But I'm proud of myself for telling the truth."

Loulan self-identifies as lesbian, not bisexual, and I respect that. However, portions of the lesbian community are less flexible and less understanding of how variations of sexual attraction, romantic interest, and sexual identification can coexist.

It's important as a therapist for you to recognize that we LGBTQ people are not really a community. We say we are, but we're not. Bisexuals, in particular, are scorned by some gays and lesbians for not wanting to give up their "heterosexual privilege." It's a controversy grounded in the politics of our culture wars.

Chapter 7 considers heterosexual privilege and the loss of it after coming out. If people identify as heterosexual, they are accepted in the majority culture and celebrated in songs and movies. Anywhere they go they can hold hands or kiss, and no one gives them a second look. They are not feared as a threat or scorned as an abomination. They are not at risk of being arrested or harassed. They have heterosexual privilege.

When we come out as gay or lesbian, we lose that heterosexual privilege. Rejected and vilified by family, friends, and the culture at large, we seek out accepting communities, look for people who will understand and welcome us. We find a label, an identity: We're gays or lesbians united against the rest of the world. As minorities, we become a political force fighting against discrimination. We feel power and pride.

Then a person comes along who does not identify as gay or straight and declares that they are comfortable sexually with either gender. Suddenly, the house of identity we've built is rocked by winds of change and seems less solid, more vulnerable than we imagined. We feel fear, and we cling to our foundation, arguing that there must only be a binary identity—either/or—and unconsciously protect our hard-won identity by rejecting this person, mentally casting them out of our community and withdrawing our love and support. We point our collective finger, not realizing we are giving in to the same sort of prejudice society has imposed on us.

This bisexual is a "traitor." Gone are the invitations to bars, parties, and tea dances. Lesbians and gays become angry toward the person, and say he or she is guilty of keeping a foot in the door of heterosexual privilege, betraying the cause. Just ask JoAnn Loulan what it feels like to lose your "lesbian privilege."

We do to each other what was done to us, and that's been very painful for bisexuals and transgender individuals. This biphobia and transphobia within the gay and lesbian community, as well as within the straight community, will be evident to any therapist treating LGBTQ clients.

Myths and Prejudices About Bisexuals

Myth 1: Can't Commit

Bisexuals can't commit. Everybody knows it. Actually, that's not true, but it's a myth that follows bisexuals everywhere they go, especially male bisexuals. In seminars where I have spoken, I have asked for a show of hands of women who would marry a bisexual man, and I've been stunned to see no more than one or two hands in the air. I have counseled many men who remain secretive about their bisexuality because they don't want to lose the woman they love to the misinterpretation that they are unable to commit to her.

Just like gays and lesbians, bisexuals are oversexualized in the imaginations of straight people. This "can't commit" myth comes from the idea that bisexuals are out-of-control sex machines. These myths all go together: bisexuals can't commit, can't be monogamous, can't make up their minds. The truth is, bisexuals are just as able (or unable) to commit as anyone else. We're all momentarily sexually attracted to passing strangers. That doesn't mean we're going to run off with them. Claiming that bisexuals can't be monogamous is like saying that a person attracted to both redheads and brunettes can't be monogamous. If they marry a brunette, they will inevitably sneak out to be with a redhead. That's just as ridiculous as it sounds.

Will straight men date bisexual women? Often, they will, when they think of the woman's bisexuality only as something erotic and they imagine watching or participating. But if a man is dating a bisexual woman and she tells him she has the propensity to have romantic feelings, in addition to sexual feelings, for women, the man may feel threatened by that possibility and back away. I've also counseled straight male clients who *unknowingly* dated and fell in love with bisexual women and then found out and ended the relationships out of fear of competition with women.

Myth 2: Really Gay

The other myth about bisexuals that I hear all the time: It's just a stage. They're really gay. "Bi now, gay later" is the saying.

The grain of truth here is that many gay and lesbian people identify as bisexual during their coming-out process. Then, as they continue to come out, they realize they're really gay or lesbian. And that's what gay men and lesbians sometimes can't get past when they meet a bisexual. They project onto the bisexual person their own experience of having identified as bisexual before they recognized they were truly gay or lesbian.

Bisexuals themselves typically struggle before coming out, or during coming out, with whether they really have a bisexual identity. "Is my bisexuality real? Or am I really gay or lesbian?" A therapist can help a struggling person gain clarity and discover the truth of their own identity.

Once past understanding that they are not gay or lesbian, a bisexual person will often agonize over the shape of their bisexuality. "I'm bi, but what kind of bi am I? Where can I go to find people like me?" The client struggling with these questions will often benefit from support groups, many of which are online.

Myth 3: More Common Among Women Than Men

This myth may come from the greater pressure on bisexual men to deny their bisexuality. In general, women do not feel strong societal disdain for being bisexual, nor are they particularly shunned by men they might wish to date. The opposite is true for men. They do fear strong societal repercussions (ostracism, firing, ridicule, physical violence), and they fear that potential partners will shun them.

> Dr. Eric Schrimshaw at Columbia University's Mailman School of Public Health recently conducted a qualitative study with 203 closeted bisexual men to further explore the reasons why so many bisexual men are afraid of coming out to their female partner, to family, and to friends . . .
>
> Schrimshaw found that many men aren't "confused" about their (bi)sexuality. That's not the reason for their non-disclosure to their female partners. They know they are attracted to both men and women; however, they aren't open about their (bi)sexuality because they fear stigma, ridicule, and being outed to others. They also fear judgement and being left by their female partners because of their previous same-sex sexual actions. (Bisexual.org, paragraph 6, 2016)

Myth 4: Bisexuals Can't Make Up Their Minds

Bisexuals are not confused about their sexual orientation once they can sort through the sexual disorientation created by our heteronormative culture. Just like gays and lesbians, bisexuals have their own coming-out process to integrate their identities.

Defining Bisexuality

There have been a number of attempts to place bisexuality in a theoretical framework. Alfred Kinsey (1948), when his team interviewed people about their sexuality, asked interviewees to self-identify from a choice of seven sexual orientations including: exclusively heterosexual; predominantly heterosexual; only incidentally homosexual; predominantly heterosexual, but more than incidentally homosexual; equally heterosexual and homosexual; bisexual; predominantly homosexual, but more than incidentally heterosexual; predominantly homosexual; only incidentally heterosexual; and exclusively homosexual.

This list is often referred to as the Kinsey scale. We see that already in 1948, Kinsey was questioning the "binary" of "straight or gay" and even the "trilogy" of "straight, bisexual, or gay."

Fritz Klein (1993) adopted Kinsey's idea of seven "levels" but extended it in two ways. Klein asked his interviewees to consider not just "sexual preference or desire," but seven categories of sexual preference, and in addition the interviewees were asked to score these categories for three time frames: the past, the present, and "ideal," this latter category being a prediction for the future.

Klein included sexual attraction, sexual behavior, sexual fantasies, emotional preference, social preferences, which lifestyle one identifies with including heterosexuality, gay, lesbian or bisexual, and finally self identification meaning how do you self identify.

The seven choices for categories A–E are: other sex only, other sex mostly, other sex somewhat more, both sexes, same sex somewhat more, same sex mostly, and same sex only; while the choices for categories F and G are: heterosexual only, heterosexual mostly, heterosexual somewhat more, heterosexual/homosexual equally, homosexual somewhat more, homosexual mostly, and homosexual only. The Klein Sexual Orientation Grid (KSOG) uses values of 1–7, rather than the 0–6 of the Kinsey scale, to describe a continuum from exclusively opposite-sex to exclusively same-sex attraction.

Since Klein offers seven choices in seven categories in three time frames, there are a total of 147 different kinds of bisexuals in Klein's view. Compare this to two kinds for the straight/gay binary and seven kinds for Kinsey's classification of sexual orientations.

Klein's grid, when used as an interviewing tool, provides intriguing insights into different interpretations of sexual orientation, and studies have been done to analyze how answers tend to "cluster" to see if some higher-level (and easier-to-understand) patterns emerge. The analysis reported by Weinrich, Klein, McCutchan, Grant, & the HNRC

Group (2014) is complicated, although the most significant categories for clustering are reported to be (A) sexual attraction, (B) sexual behavior, and (G) self-identification. An intriguing additional result is that women were much more variable in their sexual fantasies (C) than men; in other words, women's fantasies do not correlate with the other three important variables, whereas men's fantasies seem to correlate with them.

Note that in my experience categories A, D (interpreted as emotional or romantic preference), and G have seemed most significant to my clients. Thus, emotional preference (D) is more often cited than sexual behavior (B), which might mean that for my clients A and B are so correlated, clients do not make a point of distinguishing them. I should emphasize that Klein's concept is complicated, and so far no statistical study tells us how to "boil it down" to a uniformly simpler framework.

Dr. Charles Moser (2016 defined sexual orientation to be a person's "most intense sexual interest." He also considered identity, behavior, and less intense sexual interests. Moser discussed some fine distinctions such as lust versus desire: "I want to have an orgasm" versus "I want a hot man (or woman)," respectively. He postulated that BDSM or foot partialism might qualify as orientations for some people. Thus, he decoupled genital configuration from orientation in some cases.

If a client identifies as bisexual, there's really nothing to do but ask him or her to tell you more. Some unexpected choices might emerge. I focus on Klein's categories A and D, and most importantly G—that is, sexual attraction, romantic attraction, and self-identity—because these have emerged most often when I'm talking about sexual orientation and sexual behavior with a client. Sometimes, a person's choices in the straight–gay continuum for Klein's categories seem to be very consistent, sometimes not. Sometimes we see stability or fixedness over time, sometimes not. Sometimes what people imagine as their ideal (perhaps in the future) is consistent with their present and past, sometimes not. With this understanding and this handful of concepts and vocabulary, we don't even imagine we have all the answers. We just commit to carefully considering what our clients bring us.

Bisexual Issues That Come Up in Therapy

Bisexual Erasure

She came into my office. "It's as if I don't exist," she told me. She was bisexual, but she said that gays and lesbians always insisted she must be mistaken. She must be a confused lesbian. A straight person might have the same reaction. "You must be gay." "You must be lesbian." Bisexuals get very tired of hearing this.

Bisexual erasure or bi-erasure is the tendency to act as if bisexuals don't exist. In its most extreme form, bi-erasure can include literally denying that bisexuality exists. This was overt a few decades ago in the gay and lesbian communities; now it's often more implicit, not talked about, just assumed. Either way, bisexuals suffer from bi-erasure. They're wounded by it. They feel invalidated.

I myself have been accused of bi-erasure because I talk about straight men who have sex with men. But straight men who have sex with men really are straight and are not bisexual. I explain this in detail in Chapters 1 and 2 of my book *Is My Husband Gay, Straight, or Bi?* (Kort & Morgan, 2014) as well as in numerous articles I have written for *Psychology Today* (www.psychologytoday.com) and *The Huffington Post* (www.huffingtonpost.com). Defining bisexuality can be complex, so defining straight men who have sex with men can be equally complex. Briefly, straight men who have sex with men are not attracted to men but are either responding to circumstances of the moment (no women available is a common reason) or are responding to a psychological state called *trauma reenactment*, in which the unconscious mind is forcing someone to act out a script from the past. We will look at this further in Chapter 16 on sexual fluidity.

Bisexuals are hypervigilant about lack of inclusion. When gays and lesbians are being discussed, bisexuals don't want to be ignored.

Should Bisexuals Tell Their Partners They're Bisexual?

Bisexuals can be monogamous, but sometimes it's not so simple as just making a commitment. We consider two cases.

The Case of Jamie

Jamie came to see me because he wanted to know if he should tell his girlfriend that he was bisexual. "I mostly like women," he said, "but I'm also sexually attracted to men." He told me he'd been meeting men through Grindr and Craigslist and having sex with them, but then he started dating Zoe and became monogamous with her. "I'm in love with her. I want to propose to her."

His dilemma was that he wanted to be honest.

"Every time I tell a woman I'm bisexual," Jamie said, "she breaks it off. She won't even date me." Jamie looked frustrated. "They all think I'm gay. They tell me, 'Maybe you don't even know yourself. Maybe you're just fooling yourself.' The same old crap I always get."

He'd come into therapy because he was struggling with his own integrity. "Do I have to tell her? What's the point of that?"

Jamie: Clinical Interpretation and Treatment

Jamie's main therapy issues were worry and anxiety, not depression (although depression might have come up if Zoe had discovered his secret and left him). He was feeling isolation and loneliness; there was no one he could tell about his sexual orientation.

He had tried to tell his gay friend, Josh but Josh just couldn't get past his own experience of coming out. "I thought I was bi, too," Josh had told Jamie. "I really did, for the longest time." Josh was trying to be helpful, but he couldn't accept Jamie's word that he was bi. "I respect the fact that you don't believe you're gay right now, but think how devastated Zoe will be when you come all the way out, and you just don't feel in love with her anymore."

How does a guy know if he's bisexual or coming out gay? Many men have sought counseling with me on this issue. There are many bi variations; that is part of what is confusing. Jamie was sexually interested in men and women, but romantically interested only in women. (A number of bi men I've treated have had that set of inclinations.) A completely gay man is not really sexually attracted to women in general. He may have had the experience of being in love with (and sexual with) one woman, but he's not quite sure what's attractive about women in general. "She's very pretty," he might tell me. On the other hand, he might see a man and think, "He's smoking hot!" That's the logic of the "beach test," which is particularly effective for completely straight or completely gay men. A gay man on the beach will see the men and ignore the women; a straight man, the other way around.

Of course, we know there are other elements to sexuality, such as romance and fantasy. Jamie was not romantically attracted to men. He couldn't imagine "keeping house" with a guy. A hot hookup was fine, but he was totally not interested in dating men. And his masturbation fantasies were entirely heterosexual.

After a few sessions with Jamie, I was convinced he wasn't gay. Which of course is what he had told me in the first place. "I just want Zoe to give me a chance," he told me. His plan was to be monogamous, faithful to his wife. Yes, he was sexually turned on by men, but straight men are turned on by other woman, and their wives believe they can be faithful. Ideally, his woman would understand him, and he could be open and honest . . . but he just didn't want to risk it.

Not only might he lose Zoe, but they traveled in each other's social circles, and he was afraid she might out him to their mutual friends and, in particular, to his business acquaintances. He was the successful CEO of a medical equipment company. He had over 500 employees. He and Zoe socialized with doctors, hospital administrators, and other executives. His business could suffer from the "scandal" of his bisexuality.

He told me he was strong-willed. He was sure he could keep his secret from Zoe. But he knew that holding back an important part of himself would be lonely and dishonest. "I can be monogamous," he told me many times. "I can be gay celibate." But he felt that if he didn't tell her now, he'd never be able to tell her.

In the end, Jamie decided on a half-truth. He told Zoe that he had "experimented" a bit when he was in college. He told her "it wasn't a big deal." I pointed out that he wasn't really being open with her, but he felt he'd done what he needed to do. They married.

He touched base with me a few years later. I asked him how he was doing around monogamy. He said he had "the usual temptations," but everything was "under control." And that was the last I heard from him.

Internalized Biphobia

This self-doubt, or in extreme forms self-hate, manifests itself in accepting the negative myths about bisexuals, even when the bisexual individual should know they aren't true. Lesbians and gays experience internalized homophobia. Both biphobia and homophobia are natural responses to cultural prejudice. See Chapter 2 for more on internalized homophobia.

Bisexual Coming Out and Bisexual Adolescence

Many models for bisexual coming out have been proposed, including separate models for men and women. (See, e.g., Brown, 2002.) However, none of these models have been as validated or accepted as the Cass model for lesbian and gay coming out (see Chapter 7). The Cass model doesn't seem to work as well for bisexuals (or sexually fluid individuals) because it looks only at monosexual coming out, whereas bisexual coming out is nonbinary and more complex.

Patrick Richards Fink (2014) paraphrased Bilodeau & Renn (2005), saying that using a monosexual (gay, lesbian, or straight) like Cass's model can be potentially harmful to bisexuals because their development is frequently nonlinear.

Richards Fink's article did a fine job of explaining task models of bisexual identity development compared to stage models.

He offered one possible task-based model of bisexual identity development with these elements:

1. exiting monosexuality
2. developing a private bisexual description
3. developing a public bisexual description
4. becoming a bisexual offspring
5. exploring fluidity of attraction and behavior, and
6. engaging with bisexual community.

As part of their coming-out process, bisexuals (like lesbians and gays) can undergo a late adolescence. In their adolescent phase, bisexuals see the world as divided into an "us versus them" dichotomy; in other words, there are bisexuals and there are monosexuals. And monosexuals are really bisexual; they just don't know it. During their delayed adolescence, bisexuals can go through a period of hypersexuality, just like gays and lesbians. They may feel a need to have different sexual encounters, maybe different boyfriends and girlfriends. That can last up to 2 or 3 years and then typically will become less urgent. A third element of bisexual adolescence is that they will become passionate advocates and activists for bisexual rights. Very "in your face." Very passionate and determined. All this adolescent behavior will typically settle down over time, although many bisexuals maintain their committed advocacy of bisexual rights.

The case of Saul and Karen in Chapter 11 illustrates how this bisexual adolescence can come up in a bisexual–straight mixed-orientation marriage and how in one case it was resolved. As noted in Chapter 11, an emerging bi coming-out and adolescence can be dealt with calmly, with a plan to allow the bisexual to explore but with agreements and boundaries specified, depending on the needs of the particular case.

Final Thoughts

Some bisexual clients will come into your office, and bisexuality won't be their issue. Then, you will simply find out what they want to work on and proceed from there. We all have a sexual orientation; it isn't always what we need to talk about.

Some bisexual clients will want to deal with their depression, anger, and grief over their bisexual issues: isolation, finding community, dealing with bi-erasure or dealing with social issues connected to bisexual coming out. Suicidal ideation is not uncommon. Here, the standard tools of psychotherapy will be most useful.

A bisexual client is typically feeling a lot of self-doubt. Men will especially be doubting their orientation. They will ask you to help them discover if they are actually gay. And like Tom, some will be agonizing about "coming out" to those they love and fear losing. All you can do is help them clarify their own reality, come out to themselves—gay if they are gay; and if they are bisexual, to better understand what "bisexual" means for them. What choices they should make with other people is something ultimately they will have to decide for themselves.

CHAPTER 16

Sexual Fluidity

*Fluidity represents a capacity to respond erotically
in unexpected ways due to particular situations or relationships.*
—Lisa Diamond, author of *Sexual Fluidity:
Understanding Women's Love and Desire*

Stan came to my office.

"I thought I was straight," he told me, too embarrassed to make eye contact. "I still think I'm straight, but the other night I had sex with a guy." Then he did look up. His tone was pleading. "I wasn't that drunk. I didn't get pressured or anything. We kind of *noticed* each other at this party. I went up and we said a few things. I don't remember what. We found an empty bedroom upstairs and just went at it.

"When it was all over, we just kind of sat there for a while. I told him I was straight. He shrugged and grinned and said he was straight, too. I didn't know what the hell to do next. We ended up saying goodbye and getting out of there. I don't even know his name. I've never done anything like that before.

"What's going on? Does this mean I'm gay or at least bi? Am I going to come out and don't even know it?"

I worked with Stan in therapy, as described below, to help him clarify his orientation. The point right now is that the old idea that a single sexual episode reveals someone's sexual orientation is completely false. From this one encounter, we can't tell if Stan is straight, gay, or bi. Or he might be straight but fluid. This chapter is about the concept of sexual fluidity, and it can be a confusing idea to understand.

Some people are sexually fluid; some are not fluid at all. It is a characteristic of sexuality that runs parallel to sexual orientation but is not itself a sexual orientation. There are also many modes of sexual fluidity. Fluidity can be expressed through one-time sexual encounters like Stan's, but it can also lead to long-term connections and even relationships. Also, many variations of sexual hazing, sexual experimentation, and sex in special circumstances might be labeled as sexual fluidity. We consider what's going on in all these different situations in this chapter.

It is particularly subtle and difficult to distinguish a straight fluid person or a gay fluid person from a bi person (who might or might not also be fluid). For this reason, in the first part of this chapter I will mainly focus on individuals who are straight or gay. Later, we will specifically consider bisexuality.

First, let us review a clinical issue that comes up often in my office. Clients come to me saying they thought they were straight but now aren't sure.

How Do You Help Clients Decide If They Are Straight or Not?

In a course of therapy that can take months (or in some cases, years), I can help a person better understand his or her sexual orientation. But there isn't any absolute rule or test for straightness or gayness. The idea that identity is objectively determined by sexual behavior is outdated and incorrect. Whatever therapy and expert opinion a person receives, in the end each individual must decide his or her own sexual identity (or decide not to claim a sexual identity). However, I have found the following guidelines helpful.

First, I'll focus on men.

- *The beach test.* Gay men notice the men on a beach and don't notice the women. "That man is hot!" a gay man might say. In my experience, straight men, even those who have sex with men, don't notice the men; they notice the women. Bisexual men notice both, sometimes one more than the other.
- *Youthful noticing.* This is the children's version of the beach test. Before puberty, gay boys notice with a kind of giggling delight other boys, just as straight boys do girls. This is a perfectly natural expression of prepubescent identity that straight boys in our society typically get to share out loud with their peers and gay boys typically do not. Gay men often report to me memories of youthful noticing of boys; straight men never do. Gay men will often say they didn't know what it meant at the time but that they recall being strongly drawn to another boy their age or preoccupied with another male on television. Only

looking back can these gay men understand that their interest was romantic and sexual.

- *Waking up or coming home.* Who do you want to wake up next to—or come home to—a man or a woman? Some straight guys will kiss and hug other men and so forth, but they still don't want to wake up next to nor come home to a man. There's just something "off-putting" to a straight guy about the morning light on a face full of stubble. Home for straight men is with a woman, whereas home for a gay man is with another man.

- *Falling in love.* No matter how much quick or anonymous sex a gay man might have engaged in, he loves everything about other men: their faces, their chest hair, their deep voices, their humor, their penises. A straight man who has sex with other men (or has fantasies about it or watches gay porn) is most often compulsively focused on certain male body parts or on certain sex acts or sexual scenarios. A gay man yearns for an entire man, not just parts of a man. Gay men can—and often do—fall in romantic love with other men; straight men rarely do.

- *Romantic hopes and dreams with a male partner.* After a period of promiscuous "gay adolescence," which will occur typically for a few years after a gay man comes out, he will tend to mature beyond a frantic need to express his newfound sexual freedom and yearn to "settle down" with a loving male partner.

- *Gay sex not degrading.* Out gay men don't feel degraded by their sexuality. Straight men sometimes interpret gay sex as humiliating. For some religious moralists, the core of their objection to homosexuality is a repugnance for dehumanizing acts. However, gay and bisexual men find gay sex fundamentally joyful, not degrading.

- *Homophobia.* Gay men unconscious of their gayness are much more homophobic than are straight men who have sex with men. Straight men who are confused and questioning come to my office and say, "I don't think I'm gay, but I might be. If I'm gay, help me just go ahead and come out and be gay." These men are tortured by the thought that they might be fighting the coming-out process. If a gay man is repressing his gay identity, he is often extremely negative about gay people and "the gay lifestyle." He might complain that gay life is oversexualized, gays are too effeminate, and gay men never have successful relationships. In therapy, these homophobic gay men hope the therapist will make them straight, not help them come out as gay.

These guidelines work best for men who are strongly oriented to gayness or strongly oriented to straightness. (Let us say, men scoring 0 or 6 on the Kinsey scale.) Men whose orientations are more bisexual or more fluid are less easy to characterize.

When a woman comes to me to discuss the possibility that she might be lesbian, some of these guidelines seem to be more relevant than others. For example, many lesbians report "youthful noticing." Since women's sexuality tends to be less strongly linked to their vision system than men's, the beach test is less determining. Since women have more societal permission to touch and be affectionate with each other than men do, a more nuanced examination of their past sexual behavior is required to pin down orientation. The women who have come to me most concerned about their orientations have been older, politically active lesbians who have been shaken by discovering they have some unexpected sexual interest in men. (I've never had a lesbian under 40 raise this with me as a concern.)

Also, my experience is with a clinical population. I am sure that there are plenty of younger heterosexuals these days who have sexually fluid encounters, are not concerned about them, do not feel conflicted about their orientations because of them, and never consult with therapists about them.

Stan: Clinical Interpretation and Treatment

I asked Stan about his sexual interests and did a basic family and sexual history. He noted no particular sexual interest in men, and his history had no obvious incidents or situations that would lead me to consider trauma reenactment. (See section below on "Special Situations.") I asked him whom he noticed on the beach; he focused on the women. He recalled zero youthful noticing. He wanted to wake up next to a woman. He'd never fallen in love or had any romantic feelings for men. He didn't believe gay sex was degrading. He wasn't homophobic at all. He knew I was gay. Most gay men who are in the closet won't even come to see me because I'm too gay for them.

Stan and I met for several sessions, but he seemed simply to be a straight man. Sometimes straight guys, under special circumstances, will spontaneously be drawn to sex with another man. Stan's encounter was a typical incident of sexual fluidity and said nothing about his orientation or his sexual interests in general. This kind of encounter might never happen for him again, or it might, but even if it does, that wouldn't necessarily imply anything about his sexual orientation.

What Is Sexual Fluidity?

Sexual fluidity is the understanding that sexual preferences can change over a lifetime and be dependent on different situations. It is a person's ability to engage in sexual behaviors and interest in members of both genders independent of their sexual orientation.

Each person has a sexual realm. When people stray outside the boundaries of that realm, they are being sexually fluid. So a straight man who, to his surprise, wants to have sex with a man he meets at a party is being sexually fluid, as in the case of Stan. A straight woman may have a similar "surprising" encounter with another woman.

Sexual fluidity is not an orientation. Sexual orientation can be someone who self-identifies as straight, gay, lesbian, bisexual, pansexual, and asexual to name a few. Sexual fluidity is a separate variable that can go side by side with sexual orientation. Some people are highly fluid and others are less so (Selterman, 2014). Thus, sexual fluidity expresses the degree to which an oriented person will tend to circumstantially deviate from their orientation.

Some straight people cannot function at all with a same-sex partner (even when they want to). For others, this is fairly easy, and occasional gay encounters are no big deal. Thus, we talk about people being "not fluid at all" or "very fluid," and of course various levels of fluidity in between (usually meaning that the fluid encounters require very special circumstances that rarely occur). Similarly, a gay person can be fluid, in that they are open to occasional opposite-sex sexual encounters, or not at all fluid, or somewhat fluid.

One Delicious Moment or a Long-Term Connection?

There are two common types of sexual fluidity: (1) The first type is a spontaneous or "circumstantial" encounter that leads to sex. A typical case is like that of Stan: He's straight. He meets a guy at a party, or an out-of-town meeting, or a school reunion. "Lightning strikes," and for no reason they understand, they decide to have sex with each other. They might never see each other again, or they might have more encounters, but the sense of their connection is sexual, not relational. This sort of unexpected circumstantial encounter can also happen to women. (2) The second type of fluidity is a spontaneous connection that becomes relational or romantic and continues over some extended period of time. In my experience, type 1 is more common for men, type 2 for women, but there are exceptions. Also, it's good to remember that not everyone who has a sexually fluid encounter goes to see a therapist about it!

To be sexually fluid, an encounter (short-term or long-term) has to have an element of surprise or an uncommon circumstance. If you're a straight man looking for a sex with a woman and you find it, that's not sexual fluidity. To be sexually fluid, the encounter should be *out of orientation*—that is, not ordinary for the person's orientation or identity. Finding love with a woman is not out of orientation for a straight man, but it could be considered sexually fluid for a gay man.

What Aspects of Sexual Fluidity Should a Therapist Be Particularly Aware Of?

As in the case of Stan, a therapist may be asked to help a client who has had a "surprising" sexual encounter decide if he or she is gay, straight, or bi. Men, in my experience, are more intensely concerned about pinning down their orientation than women are. Aside from a routine family and sexual history, a therapist may use the seven guidelines listed above.

Therapy should proceed to differentiate sexual fluidity from orientation (in particular, bisexuality) and also from the situations listed in "Special Situations" below. In any case, the "surprised" client should be educated about sexual fluidity, as well as orientation.

Another situation that brings a client to seek therapeutic counseling is the committed relationship that comes under stress because of orientation-compatibility issues, such as in the following case of Helen and Joanne.

The Case of Helen and Joanne

Helen came to see me distressed because her long-term relationship was falling apart. She and Joanne had met and fallen in love 20 years before. They legally married in Massachusetts and set up a home. They had four children.

Helen knew all along that she was straight, but things had never worked out for her with men. She had had a troubled relationship with her father, and the men she dated had all turned out to be "losers." Then she met Joanne at a party, and to Helen's surprise, she had an immediate attraction to her. Joanne was openly gay, but Helen wasn't particularly influenced by that one way or the other. They formed a deep friendship, which turned into a romance, which turned sexual. Helen felt increasingly comfortable with Joanne in ways Helen had never felt with any man.

Helen told Joanne she was straight from the beginning, but Joanne wasn't concerned. Helen seemed comfortable enough in the lesbian community when she was with Joanne. And anyway, they were in love. Joanne was active in the lesbian community and the gay political scene. Helen was not attracted to other women. She never felt like a lesbian herself, and she never felt like she fit in the lesbian community. But she loved Joanne and for a long time that made everything all right.

By the time Helen came to see me, she wanted to return to dating men. She didn't want a divorce; she wanted an open marriage with Joanne. She did not identify as bisexual. She was clear with me that she was straight—a straight woman who had fallen deeply in love with another woman.

Joanne resisted the idea of an open marriage. She didn't want to share Helen. In fact, Joanne was feeling very betrayed. She told Helen: "You will either be sexual only with me, or we get a divorce. I'm not opening up our marriage for you to be with men." And that's why Helen came to consult with me.

You might be wondering: Why after 20 years did Helen need to have other partners? Married people generally accept monogamy as a condition of marriage. The truth is, I don't know. I just know I've seen this a great deal in my practice. A "happily married" mixed-orientation couple is suddenly confronted with one partner needing to express his or her true sexual orientation. Helen told me that she had started to feel attracted to some of the men that she met at work. She didn't want to be unfaithful, but she didn't want to have to hold back either. She told me she didn't actually need to set up a life with a man because she loved her wife and wanted their family to continue.

Helen and Joanne: Clinical Interpretation and Treatment

I started by educating Helen about sexual fluidity and bisexuality, helping her get clear with her own identity. We also worked on her grief about the potential loss of the life she'd created over so many years, her love for Joanne and their four children.

As always with a case involving marital difficulties, I urged Helen to do couples therapy with Joanne. Joanne agreed, but with a different therapist. Which is fine. It's often good to keep a person's individual therapy completely separate from the couples work. Obviously, Helen and Joanne needed to have some complicated discussions whether they separated or not.

In individual therapy, I helped Helen look at her family history and ended up focusing on her strained relationship with her father, and how it had affected her relationships with men. She had a pattern of meeting men who were like her father, who was patriarchal and controlling and not very female affirming. This had led to her being open to a relationship with a woman.

Still, she told me she never felt like or self-identified as lesbian. "I never felt comfortable in the lesbian community. I was always attracted to men. I would think about men when I was having sex with Joanne, but I could also be very present and very much enjoyed and loved her, and we had great sex." The key to understanding that Helen was not bisexual was that she wasn't attracted to any other women, just Joanne.

Neither wanted a divorce, but Joanne wasn't willing for the marriage to be open and Helen needed it to be. They ended up having a very bitter divorce because Joanne felt so betrayed.

Let's note in passing the romance between the straight actress Anne Heche and gay comedian and talk-show host Ellen DeGeneres. Anne was not looking for a gay partner, but she fell in love with Ellen. They were a couple for over 3 years and then parted. All of Anne's other romantic interests have been with men, and after Ellen, Anne made it plain that she was still straight. The public didn't believe her for a while, but eventually they let it go. When a straight man has a fling with another man, the public goes crazy with "He must be gay." Sexual fluidity is still less accepted for men than women in our homophobic society.

Male Versus Female Sexual Fluidity

We saw in the case of Stan (and the list of special cases, below) that straight men circumstantially have sex with each other, often quick anonymous sex, for a variety of reasons and in a variety of circumstances.

One straight male client of mine, Terry, uses Craigslist to set up special sexual encounters for himself with another man (a different man each time).

"Every once in a while I have a guy come over," Terry told me. "We don't touch, and we don't have sex. He pulls out his dick. I pull out mine. We watch straight porn. We drink beer."

Together we labeled this under sexual fluidity, but it is really also a form of male bonding. Our society doesn't allow many ways for males to connect except through sports and a few other special situations. By culture and biology, men are pushed into limited modes of sexual and tenderness expression. Straight women can touch, hold hands, kiss in greeting, even lie in each other's arms without being vilified or (for the most part) misconstrued as lesbian or bisexual. By contrast, little boys are rigidly de-feminized and discouraged from being affectionate with each other from the time they are about 8 years old. In essence, men, under threat of physical violence and ridicule, learn to compartmentalize tenderness, sex, and love. So the need for a man to bond with other men sometimes comes out erotically.

I should note that there was for Terry no particular therapeutic issue. In particular, he was seeing me about another problem and told me about his fluid experiences in passing without expressing any unhappiness about them. In my experience, such sexual male bonding usually seems to be harmless.

When Lisa Diamond, professor of psychology and gender studies at the University of Utah, published her breakthrough book *Sexual Fluidity* (2008), she focused on women who had sex with other women. She distinguished between these women and women who identify as bisexual. It is still generally accepted that women are "more flexible" than men. In Fugere (2016), they discuss that women's sexuality is more fluid and flexible than for men and that women's sexual attraction can shift more than men. The social science researcher Jamie Budnick (2016) noted that for women, same-gender experiences are common in all socioeconomic backgrounds. Also, "it's not binary: Women don't kiss each other only for the attention of men, or on their way to a proud bisexual or lesbian identity. There is a lot of rich meaning in the middle."

However, in the past few years, evidence has suggested men's sexuality is more fluid than we thought. Lisa Diamond presented a convincing amount of data to this effect in her 2013 lecture at Cornell University (Kort, 2016). Ritch Savin-Williams is doing his own research on "mostly straight" males at Cornell University, studying men who score 1 on the Kinsey scale (Mustanski, 2013).

But male and female sexual fluidity is expressed in ways that may not yet be showing up in psychological studies. If a guy marks a box on a survey indicating, "Yes, I've been attracted to another man," or, "Yes, I've had sex with another man in the past year," it may not mean at all the same thing as when a woman checks the same box. There's a big difference between a 5-minute bathroom glory-hole adventure and sex with an emotional bond.

To best understand how complicated this is, we need to be able to differentiate four terms that are often confused: *sexual orientation, sexual preference, sexual fantasies*, and *sexual behavior*. Contrary to common usage, they aren't always in alignment.

Sexual orientation encompasses one's sexual and romantic identity, in which thoughts, fantasies, and behaviors work together. It's the alignment of affectional, romantic, psychological, spiritual, and sexual feelings and desires for those of the same or opposite sex. Sexual orientation doesn't change over time; it is fixed. One's sexual behaviors and preferences might change, but like temperament, orientation remains mostly stable. Orientation also refers to how someone self-identifies, not how others may categorize him or her. Some people self-identify as straight, while others self-identify as gay or lesbian, bisexual, or questioning. It's important to ask clients how they self-identify, regardless of whom they have sex with.

Sexual preferences refer to sexual acts, positions, and erotic scenarios that someone prefers and finds erotic. The term takes into account what individuals like to do and get into sexually (for example, BDSM), not necessarily with whom they like to do it. Sexual preferences and erotic interests can change over time, as one becomes more open or closed to certain thoughts and behaviors.

Sexual fantasies are any thoughts that one finds arousing. They can encompass anything—sexual positions, romantic encounters, body parts, clothing and shoe fetishes, even rape fantasies. Sexual fantasies aren't necessarily acted out. In fact, in many cases they aren't. Straight men and women sometimes fantasize about having sex with members of the same sex; they sometimes find gay porn arousing. Some lesbians report that they enjoy watching gay male porn. They say it is not about the men in the porn but about the mutual and externalized sexual desire and power balance that exists between the male porn actors, which is not usually seen in heterosexual erotica (Bernstein, 2010).

Sexual behaviors are not necessarily aligned with sexual orientation. For example, gay men have sex with women all the time, and this behavior doesn't change their orientation. Men who are imprisoned engage in sexual behaviors with other men, but they do so out of sexual necessity, not because of erotic interest in other men. They desire the sexual release it achieves, and the gender of the partner is secondary.

Men and women tend to be sexually fluid in different ways. For guys, expressions of sexual fluidity tend to focus on sexual release. It's not about the other guy; it's about the sex act. This is true even when the men touch each other. It's still more of an objectification than a connection. It may be satisfying a need for male bonding, but it isn't about connecting with a particular man. It's not a relationship.

When women are fluid, their connection is often relational. There's an emotional component to it, and it can sometimes lead to a long-term romantic relationship (most often, in my experience, between a straight woman and a gay woman, as in the case of Helen and Joanne above). They might even set up house together, live openly as a couple, adopt children. To the community at large, they would appear to be a lesbian couple, but one or both are straight. Men tend not to do this. The norm for men is quick, impersonal sex. It could be long-term in the sense of every Wednesday afternoon, but it's still just sex. It's not romance.

The only exception I've encountered in my practice I discuss below. My straight client Jason was driven by his "father hunger" to fall in love with a man.

The Case of Jason: Father Hunger

Jason was minding his own business at the gym, and Andrew came on to him in the sauna.

"I'm really into you," Andrew said, but Jason gave him a firm reply.

"I'm not into you. I'm straight. I'm married."

Andrew wouldn't be put off. "Well, that's fine," he said. "Maybe we could just be friends."

Through series of meetings, not sexual, Jason fell in love with Andrew. Jason felt confused and upset but excited at the same time. They were on the phone for hours. They spent time in bed, spooning, kissing. Then, they tried to have sex, and Jason couldn't get an erection. He was completely sexually turned off, and he felt horrible about it because he'd disappointed Andrew and Jason really liked him.

Jason was baffled. He'd never had ED and he was feeling romantic toward Andrew, but he wasn't able to perform. They made multiple tries, and it never worked.

In spite of that, Jason was in full-blown love with Andrew. He couldn't stop thinking about him. He would write his name over and over on his notepad when he was supposed to be working. He counted the hours until they could talk on the phone or meet.

Jason came to see me. "What's going on? I'm scared. I'm frightened. How can this be happening when I'm a happily married straight guy? Does this somehow mean I'm gay?"

Jason: Clinical Interpretation and Treatment

After a few sessions with Jason, Jason and I were convinced that he wasn't gay, but as we talked about his childhood, his issues with his father quickly emerged.

His father was very narcissistic: grandiose, selfish, always out for himself, with no nurturing instincts at all. He spent as much time away from home as possible, and he had nothing to offer Jason in the way of fathering. After we started working together, Jason sought confirmation from his mother of his father's abandonment, and she confirmed it. (By then Jason's mother and father were divorced.)

Jason grew up with a longing for male mentoring. He sought out male coaches and male bosses and always hungered for male attention and affirmation. He never thought anything about it. He didn't worry about possibly being gay and never made a connection between his hunger for male validation and his dad. In his therapy, we started making these connections. By happenstance, Andrew looked like Jason's father. He talked like him, dressed like him, even walked like him. When Andrew was eager to connect with Jason and affirm his worth, Jason couldn't resist. This despite the fact that Andrew was gay and Jason was straight.

When a boy is sexually abused by a man (a coach, a priest, his father) in childhood, the boy often grows up to compulsively seek sex with men, even if he's straight. This is an example of trauma reenactment, and I've treated many cases. But when the boy suffers neglect and abandonment by his father, he sometimes feels an intense need for male connection after he grows up.

This "father hunger" is a kind of displaced love for the parent. Often, such a need is sexualized because we tend to eroticize our childhood losses, our hungers, our needs. But for some reason, sex didn't work for Jason with Andrew. The erotic element was transformed into a romantic attraction, maybe because of Jason's rigid straight orientation. He was not sexually fluid at all; being romantic was as far as he could go. Yet his longing to connect was powerful. They were tender and loving with each other, but it wasn't sexual for Jason. (It was for Andrew.)

We probably shouldn't classify the case of Jason under sexual fluidity. However, a therapist should be aware of the possibility of such a romantic connection between two men who are not (both) gay.

The treatment for Jason followed a standard course of therapy for a man suffering from childhood neglect. I coached him eventually to go to his father face-to-face, to talk about the abandonment. Jason needed to tell his father about the neglect and his longing. "Dad, you weren't there for me." His father continued not to be there for him, even in this, but after being prepared in therapy, it was helpful for Jason to confront his father, whatever his father's reaction. Jason finally understood why he had been so ready to fall into Andrew's arms. Jason as a little boy had romanticized his love for his father, and that had turbocharged his feelings for Andrew.

I also helped Jason deal with his grief and guilt at disappointing Andrew, and his sense of having been unfaithful to his wife. Eventually, the relationship between Jason and Andrew did resolve into a friendship, and as far as I know, Jason's marriage was not affected.

I should note that I've had cases where—unlike in Jason's case—a straight man and a gay man started out being sexual and then the connection evolved into more of a relationship. (In the cases I'm thinking of, the straight guy was not confused about his identity and was up-front about it with the gay guy.) For the gay man, it is a romantic and sexual partnership. It is not romantic for the straight man; he goes along with it because he likes the sex, he likes the attention, and he likes the guy.

Typically, over time the sex goes away. They might maintain a friendship because they're both getting something out of their connection, but the gay partner will inevitably feel that he has lost what he really wanted: a romantic and sexual partner. I work with these gay men to help them with grief issues, their longing, and their internalized homophobia. I tell them that they cannot have the relationships they want with straight men, and we consider why they are looking for unavailable men, men who can't attach back to them.

Because of their ability to be impersonal (or inability to be personal), guys are more often drawn to various kinks and fetishized body parts. They are able to relate sexually with little personal connection. Research has shown a 20:1 ratio between men and women in terms of fetishes and paraphilias.

Look no further than the ads on the gay app Grindr for affirmation of this tendency. These ads display a nice direct, unsentimental appeal to raw sexuality between two gay men who understand each other:

"Come worship my huge 9-inch . . ."

"Hairy thick-bearded bear bottom, prepared to take a pounding . . ."

Once, I was teaching a sexual orientation course for straight therapists and talking about gay male ads for dating and sexual hookup partners. I asked how many women would answer an ad like one of the above. Almost immediately, a straight female therapist said, "I'd never answer an ad bragging about some body part!" Almost every woman in the class agreed. Yes, it's anecdotal, but it does speak to the more relational aspect of women's sexual fluidity.

There are videos online that show straight men being asked to comment on gay dating app posts. A typical reaction is, "I am in awe of the directness of these guys around sex." This directness may be one reason a man with an exclusively heterosexual orientation might seek out sex with another man (or, for that matter, a female prostitute). He responds to a type of language that is incomprehensible or hurtful to his wife or girlfriend. He seeks to fulfill his fantasies in an arena where they are welcome.

I'm not trying to say men cannot have a personal romantic attachment that is sexual. But male sexual attraction or activity doesn't necessarily lead to attachment, and often the language men use to express their attraction is different from that used by women; take, for example, the recent trend of giving a name to any sexual or affectionate relationship between straight men. If a guy has a new friend, he has a bromance. If he has a strong admiration for a male celebrity or sports figure, it's a man crush. If he only digs guys when he's stoned, it's highsexualism.

In contrast, women don't have all these categories for themselves. Why would they? Society doesn't misread affection between women in the same way.

Sexual Fluidity and Porn

Some lesbians enjoy gay male porn, some gay men enjoy watching straight porn, and some straight men watch gay male porn. A study (Downing, Schrimshaw, Scheinmann, Antebi-Gruszka, & Hirshfield, 2016) reported that 21% of heterosexual men said they had watched man-on-man porn in the past 6 months, compared to 98.3% of gay men and 96% of bi men. Also, 55% of gay guys reported watching man-on-woman porn, compared to 98.5% of straight guys and 88.3% of bi guys. This study is discussed in *Cosmopolitan* (MacMillen, 2016).

My experience in working with straight men who watch gay porn is that they are interested in elements of the porn but not necessarily attracted to the men in the porn. They enjoy watching anal sex and maybe imagining being one of the guys, but they are more interested in the sex act than the men. Many gay men tell me they watch straight porn because they enjoy watching a more "alpha" man, and these gay men have often fetishized straight guys as more "masculine" than gay guys.

I discuss lesbians who enjoy watching gay male porn in Chapter 9. They say they enjoy it not because they are attracted to the men in the video but more because the sexuality between the men is visually overt, erotic, and balanced in terms of power between the two actors. A scene in the movie *The Kids Are All Right* has Julianne Moore's lesbian character explaining to her son why she watches gay male porn with her female partner. She tells him that good lesbian porn just isn't available. In fact, lesbians still complain about this today, although there are growing numbers of women making porn for women.

Is It Sexual Fluidity or Bisexuality?

Bisexuality is an orientation; fluidity is not. How can we tell the difference? In particular, how can a therapist guide a client who is concerned about bisexuality?

This will generally require considering the client's lifetime sexual, romantic, and social patterns. Once we understand that people can be sexually fluid and to different degrees of fluidity, we won't overreact to isolated sexual or romantic incidents. Even long-term relationships with both genders may not indicate that a person is bisexual. We carefully consider the evidence for bisexuality or other orientations and allow for fluidity without letting it distract us from the more persistent patterns.

Being fluid means occasionally "straying" outside of the boundaries of a sexual orientation. What, then, does it mean for a bisexual person to be fluid (or not be fluid)? Everybody has a sexual realm, usually consistent with their orientation and identity, which limits their choices of sexual and romantic partners and determines their patterns of engagement in sexual situations. A bisexual person will have a sexual realm, which they may be consciously aware of or not. For example, a bisexual man may have sex with men and women but fall in love only with women. If this person "suddenly and unexpectedly" falls in love with a man, this might be considered fluid behavior for him because he has gone outside of the realm that defined his bisexuality.

We have already considered in Chapter 15 a woman who self-identified as lesbian, then fell in love with a man, married him, and thereafter claimed a bisexual identity. Although she accepted a bisexual identity, she might also have considered herself a sexually fluid lesbian. A key clinical consideration to delineate the difference would be whether she is sexually attracted to men in general or just the man she fell in love with.

Some people do not want to be labeled gay, straight, bisexual, or anything else. Some choose the pseudolabel "nonheterosexual." I always honor a client's right to self-identify, including avoiding an identity.

However, some people become very upset because they want a label and can't find one. Men, especially, seem to worry about this. In my experience, many women can be happy without a clear sexual identity; the men I've treated feel like they need to know. I think it's a matter of community. If you're not gay, not straight, and not bi, then where is your sexual-identity home? Some very fluid individuals seem to be haunted by not being able to pin down their identities. I sympathize, but I tell them they have to decide for themselves.

In the 19th century, men would have open "romantic friendships" that were everything but sexual. They slept together, cuddled, and kissed but drew the line at genital involvement. It may be that men today have such friendships but don't talk about them. Such a friendship would not be an example of sexual fluidity, because it isn't a sexual connection. There is discussion on the Internet of straight men engaging in these types of cuddling male friendships these days; however, I have not yet met any of these men.

Why do we need sexual labels, anyway? In history and politics, sexual labels have been pivotal in denying certain "outcasts" their human rights. Is the main use of sexual labels exclusionary? Do they do more harm than good? Some activists think so. On the other hand, having labels to self-identify has been useful for those mobilizing and establishing global networks to be able to claim legal rights (Sexuality and Social Justice: A Toolkit, 2016). And these efforts at advocacy can help in treating the psychological consequences societal homophobia has had on LGBTQ people.

Special Situations

Our model for "ordinary" sexual fluidity is spontaneous sexual attraction that takes individuals beyond their "expected" sexual orientation. You make eye contact or are engaging in conversation with someone of the "wrong" gender, and "suddenly" you just want to have sex with him or her. But there are other situations in which people will be drawn out of their expected sexual realm. Here, I've collected a list. Some cases have already come up above. Some are clearly special. Some are perhaps not properly sexual fluidity. I list them here not as a final judgment that they are sexual fluidity but merely to note that they might be.

- *Sex for a reward* that has nothing to do with attraction between the parties: sex for money, sex to make a porn movie, two girls having sex because their boyfriends want to watch (or the guys in the fraternity want to watch). Here, the question would be: Is behavior sexually fluid if the motivation is not sexual or romantic desire?
- *Sexual play* that is strongly desired but not strongly linked to the gender of the participants. Straight (or gay) people with a BDSM orientation will play with people of the same (or other) gender for the sake of the BDSM experience. Straight men involved in threesomes, say in cuckolding, may have sex with men even though they are straight.
- *Sex as a part of hazing or initiation* sometimes has straight men engaging in sexual behaviors with one another. A great book on this is Jane Ward's *Not Gay: Sex Between Straight White Men* (2015).
- *Availability and opportunity.* If no women are available, men may accept sex with each other. For example, in prison, isolated outposts, temporary situations, communities without women. This is by definition "out-of-gender" sexual behavior, but the degree of "unexpectedness" might vary.
- *High-sex-drive individuals.* Some of my clients have sought sex with anyone of any gender who would have them.

- *The voluntary heterosexual.* For example, a gay man who knows he's gay chooses to marry a woman (a mixed-orientation marriage). He might do this so that he can fit in society and have a family.
- *The involuntary heterosexual.* A gay man who doesn't know he's gay falls in love with and marries a woman.
- *Sex while drunk or high.* For example, two straight guys are drinking. At some point they fall in bed together and have sex.
- *Father hunger (and mother hunger)* and other behavior caused by a lonely or otherwise difficult childhood (deprivation, abandonment, neglect). For example, a man discovers to his surprise that he's sexually (or romantically) drawn to a man who unconsciously reminds him in some way of this father.
- *The influence of childhood.* For example, a gay man meets a woman at a party who resembles his mother. He is totally drawn to her for unconscious reasons. She responds sexually, and he can't resist.
- *Narcissism.* A straight man loves the attention he gets from gay men. He works out and has a great body, and the men admire and worship him in a way he never experiences with women. He's willing to have sex with these men to get this positive attention.
- *A first sexual experience.* A virgin might be surprised to encounter someone and have sex with him or her, and later discover a different orientation.
- *Trauma reenactment leading to trauma play.* A typical case: A straight man (who has repressed the fact that he was abused by an adult when he was a child) surprises himself by compulsively seeking sex with men. I would hesitate to call this an example of sexual fluidity, because he's responding to a compulsion. However, if he gets therapy and is no longer compulsive, he might still enjoy sexual encounters with men. Perhaps he doesn't plan them; they "just happen." Or perhaps he does plan them. It's a form of fluidity because these men *even after the trauma heals* continue to enjoy the fantasy, continue to enjoy the sex. So trauma reenactment leads to trauma play, which is a form of sexual fluidity. The case of Scott below illustrates this process.

The Case of Scott

Scott was caught by his wife looking at gay porn and watching men masturbate on a webcam.

She was shaken and angry. "You must be gay," she told him.

He was embarrassed and scared. He tried to brush it off. No big deal. He wasn't gay.

"Then why are you doing it?" she demanded, and he realized he didn't know.

They came to see me and raised those questions: Is Scott gay, and if not, why does he like to watch men masturbate?

When I met with Scott privately, he confirmed he'd been watching gay porn and camming for many years. It went further than his wife knew. He masturbated on cam for other men to see, and a few times he had met men for oral sex. I asked him what kind of guys he was attracted to.

"I'm not attracted to the guys," he told me. "I'm only attracted to giving oral sex."

"When you do that, or imagine doing that," I asked him, "what do you imagine the guy is thinking about you?"

"There is no guy," he insisted. "It's just a body part. I like being submissive by orally pleasing a penis, and there's no encounter with another person."

So this alerted me immediately that he might not be gay, because most gay men who are into oral sex are thinking about looking up while they're doing it and seeing a hot guy.

Scott: Clinical Interpretation and Treatment

I went through the guidelines listed at the beginning of this chapter. I asked him which genders he noticed on the beach. It was all women. He couldn't recall any youthful noticing of other boys. He wanted to wake up next to a woman. He'd never fallen in love with a man or had any romantic feelings toward a man. He didn't think gay sex was degrading. He wasn't homophobic at all.

Scott told me that even though he'd performed oral sex on men, he hadn't enjoyed it. (There are some straight men who do, but he didn't.) Since this suggested a compulsive behavior, and perhaps trauma reenactment, I reviewed his history carefully with him for incidents of sexual abuse.

I should note here that such desires can (apparently) come from nowhere. Some straight guys enjoy performing fellatio and that's it. Years of therapy reveals no abuse or other plausible cause. In Scott's case, however, we discovered a single abusive incident that apparently had set him on a course of compulsive acting out. With other clients, I've found a different situation that leads to compulsive trauma reenactment: a history of repeated sexual abuse. But, as in Scott's case, a single traumatic incident can be enough.

When he was 10 years old, he was walking with his brother and a male cousin, both of whom were 15. They were chewing gum, and Scott wanted some. He wanted to feel like one of the guys.

He said, "Can I have a piece?"

They said, "If you want a piece, you've got to suck our dicks."

"I don't want to do that," he told them.

They said, "Then no gum."

He thought about it. He was 10 years old. He really wanted to belong, which is what sharing the gum meant to him. He said, "Okay, I'll do it."

His male cousin unzipped his pants and pulled out his penis. Scott went to put his mouth on it, and the two older boys threw him to the ground. They laughed at him, called him "a fucking faggot," and threw a piece of chewed-up gum at him. "There's your gum, faggot. We always knew you were gay." And then they left him in the dirt, crying.

He had never told this story to a soul until he told me. It was a deeply destructive event that he had carried into his adulthood, and it was motivating his compulsive interest in oral sex with men. This pattern is a classic case of "trauma reenactment." It was compulsive and unconscious.

I worked with him to get him to understand that he was not attracted to men. He wasn't gay. He wasn't bisexual. He was reenacting an early childhood trauma. We did psychotherapy. We did some EMDR. I did some couples work with him and his wife to help them reclaim their trust and understand that his compulsive sexual activity came from trauma, not from sexual desire.

Sexual trauma reenactment is not an example of sexual fluidity because it is compulsive. However, after therapy, the compulsivity may be lifted, but the fantasy might still be sexually exciting. Scott continued to look at gay porn (but not web camming), and his wife agreed he could do this with some negotiated limits. And he should stop and seek help if it began to feel compulsive again.

I call this fantasizing after therapy "trauma play" to distinguish it from "trauma reenactment." That is, it's no longer compulsive, but it is still pleasurable.

This kind of sexually fluid trauma play is common even after therapy, and I do not believe it is necessarily harmful. Like all sexual behaviors, it should not be allowed to interfere with other activities or relationships (as compulsions inevitably do). I do not believe that abstinence is necessary after a compulsion has been overcome, although abstinence is of course one approach to setting limits on dysfunctional behaviors. The individual and the individual's loved ones have to decide what the best path will be on a case-by-case basis.

Although behaviors can be monitored and moderated, the fact that a particular sexual fantasy is erotic for an individual usually can't be changed. Clients have often asked me to help them stop being turned on by a fantasy that they have been turned on by all their lives. Often, I have to help them understand that this is impossible.

Summary

Every year our understanding of sexual orientation expands and becomes more sophisticated. Only a few decades ago, many gay advocates would not admit the reality of bisexuality. Political considerations still warp our willingness to embrace the true complexity of desire, but we must, especially we therapists must, move forward to engage with what is real rather than what is convenient or even what is safe.

Sexual fluidity is real. It exists, and it is different from sexual orientation. Everybody has a natural sexual realm that aligns (more or less) with their sexual orientation. Some people hold to sexual behaviors and interests that remain rigidly within their sexual realm, while others are so fluid it can be difficult to discover what their sexual realm really is.

As therapists, we must keep as a cardinal rule that while we help clients attain clarity and reduce grief, depression, and self-destructive tendencies, we do not assign anyone a sexual orientation. People self-identify or choose not to self-identify, but no one else has the right to tell them "what" they are. This doesn't mean that a sexual orientation is chosen. It isn't. It is biologically determined and unchangeable. But there are no gatekeepers here. No one has the right to look in another person's pants or spy on their bedroom behavior or decide what communities they should be allowed to join.

Fluidity can happen to anyone—gay, straight, bi, or other. It can be relational or just sexual objectification. If you are helping clients who are struggling with their sexual orientation, move slowly. Use the Klein Sexual Orientation Grid and consider its nuances. Too many therapists move to "You must be gay" too quickly and lead the client in the wrong direction. Don't jump to conclusions. Let the client lead.

Glossary

SOPHIA (*to Blanche*): Jean is a lesbian.
BLANCHE: I've never known one personally,
but isn't Danny Thomas one?
DOROTHY: Not *Lebanese*, Blanche. Lesbian!
—Transcript from an Emmy-winning
episode of *The Golden Girls*

The following is a set of terms and their meanings used by, and in reference to, those who are LGBTQ. Please understand that such a list cannot be definitive because the meanings of the terms change over time, and at any one time different people give the same terms different meanings. One individual will find a term offensive; another person will not. Some of the terms are used by older people, but not by younger people, and the meanings and implications change with the generations, too. (Some younger gay men are using the term *homosexual*, while older gays generally find it offensive.) Terms become obsolete; new terms come into usage.

I jokingly say when I provide my trainings that it is 8 a.m. right now and by the end of the day, things will be different. I have emphasized throughout this book that the best therapeutic stance to take with clients is to ask what *they* mean by the terms they use.

Why do you need to have a basic understanding of LGBTQ terms? Consider the following scenarios.

Your lesbian client comes in and says:

I'm looking for a relationship with a lipstick lesbian, not a chapstick one. I don't want some militant dyke who's all butch and is attracted to me for political reasons! I'm not into that butch/femme thing. I just want a normal relationship with an effeminate woman like me.

I once dated this woman I met at Womyn's Fest who turned out to be a granola dyke. On our first date she was packing, and I was horrified. I told her I was not into that. But I was actually very sexually attracted to her, and that was a plus because in my last relationship, we experienced lesbian bed death, and I don't want to go there again. Unfortunately, though, I found out later that she was married to a man, using him as her beard, so I broke up with her.

My best friend—my ex, that is—tells me I'm too picky about the type of woman I look for in a partner. But what does she know? She lived for a while as an ex-gay. That reparative therapy stuff is awful, and it's what caused our breakup. I'm looking through the entire LGBTQ community for the perfect woman, who is not questioning, isn't from Dykes on Bikes and isn't doing an Anne Heche on me.

Your gay male client tells you:

I went barebacking last night with a poz leather daddy I've seen at the baths and on Grindr and Scruff. I got sick of the circuit party I was at, so I went to a leather bar. I did some crystal meth along with some poppers. The guy's partner was there, but they are monogamish, so my hookup with his BF wasn't an issue. The leather daddy was not a bit nellie, and he was a great alpha top, especially because I am an oral bottom. I have been with too many queeny guys who just want to bottom. I really want a straight-acting guy.

I told my fag hag friend Michelle about this, but she just doesn't understand. Michelle is not lesbian, but I consider her family even though she's a breeder. Michelle is more like a drag queen than anything else. She has the best gaydar and has helped find me boyfriends as a result.

A bisexual client might say:

I am so sick of bi-erasure. I am tired of being alienated by the queer community and by the straight community, and I feel isolated and alone. I do exist. I can commit to either gender, but people feel I am "bi now, gay later." I am also tired of monosexual people defining me. All this talk about sexual fluidity adds to the confusion about who I am as a bisexual. Everyone should know the Klein Grid, so they can understand all the different ways we express our bisexuality. These days I am just going with the term *queer* so that I don't continuously get left out.

A transgender client could start out like this:

Please don't call me by my dead name. I want to be called by my real name. I don't identify as gender-fluid or genderqueer. My pronouns are they/them/theirs, and my pronouns are not "preferred pronouns." I am the gender I tell you I am. I also hate it when the LGBTQIA community tries to fit intersex folks into being transgender, because I don't think they are. I do believe that most lesbians and gays are truly transgender. They just don't know it yet. I used to think I was nonbinary, but now I know I am trans female. I got upset with my last therapist because she kept asking me about my brothers and sisters and not my "siblings." My new partner is cisgender, and I tend to be attracted to those who are. And don't say I have "gender dysphoria." I experience "gender oppression."

When working with LGBTQ clients, it's imperative to get the terms correct. Just as when working with any minority—religious, ethnic, or otherwise—making sure your vocabulary is medically accurate and politically correct creates a safe, supportive space for your clients.

The LGBTQ communities use different terminologies and jargon. Of course, there's some overlap, but each group has its own unique slang, "code" words, and euphemisms. Also, the same terms may have different connotations for each community.

Over the years, other minority groups have changed how they want to be referred to in an attempt to change how they're treated. For example, African Americans went from being called "Negro" and "colored" to "black" and "people of color" and finally to the current politically correct term "African American." Today, the word *queer*, once a pejorative term, is often used in a positive way. Dozens of books and articles are published with *queer* in their titles, and the term has come into common, affirmative usage by LGBTQ people.

It is always best to ask how your clients self-identify and use the same terms they use, even if you feel uncomfortable with the terms on a personal level. (See the next paragraph for exceptions.) For example, I don't personally like to use the term *homosexual*. But when my clients identify themselves as "homosexual" and dislike the terms *gay* or *lesbian*, then that's the word I use. The word *gay* is affirmative and refers to a life of being out and open about one's sexual and romantic orientation. However, many people in the beginning stages of coming out feel uncomfortable with the term. Similarly, some lesbians prefer to be called "gay" rather than "lesbian," whereas others find the term offensive when used to describe women. And many gay men, lesbians, and bisexuals—and even some straight people—are now self-identifying as queer.

It is also important to understand, as a therapist, that some "reclaimed" terms used by LGBTQ people to refer to themselves are considered offensive when used by straight people. For example, some lesbians call themselves "dykes" and some gay men call themselves "fags," and some transgender folks call each other "trannies," but these same LGBTQ individuals would take offense if a straight person called them that. And some take offense if anyone outside of their community uses the terms—

for example, a gay or lesbian calling a transgender person a "tranny." (In fact, there is some disagreement in the LGBTQ community itself about these terms, with some LGBTQ individuals finding them offensive regardless of who uses them.) In these cases, therapists should *not* use the same terminology the client uses, just as a Caucasian person should never use the N-word to refer to African Americans, even if some African Americans use the word themselves. If you are unsure about whether you are using a term that might be considered offensive, it is best to not use it until you have established a rapport and can ask the client how he or she feels about you using it.

I don't pretend to know everything that's current in the LGBTQ community or to cover it all in this book. But I can give you, as a practitioner, some good basic information. When clients enter your office, you'll be equipped with the basics of what you need to know. I've heard numerous clients say they didn't want to have to teach their therapists about the LGBTQ community—or were tired of having to do so. If they hear basic errors in your language, they will be quick to assume you are uninformed or misinformed, patronizing, or—even worse—that you'll try to change them.

Pay particular attention to terms related to sexuality. The number one reason LGBTQ clients will leave a therapist is their judgment that the therapist is uneducated and lacks training in sex education and sex therapy.

As you grow familiar with the following terms, check in with your own countertransference. What are your feelings about these words and their connotations? Then, consider how you will feel responding to an LGBTQ client using them. Better you use this chapter for checking your own judgments and feelings than waiting to do so in real time with a client.

Mainstream Terminology

The following terms are used by the mainstream population to describe things pertinent not only to LGBTQ individuals but also to heterosexuals.

homoerotic—Usually, sexual arousal or desire for a member of the same gender on a subtle level. Also can be used to describe the enjoyment of watching or participating in same-gender sexual activity.
sexual behavior—The acts that one regularly performs when aroused.
sexual fantasy—Imagining or playacting various sexual acts and behaviors, either to facilitate masturbation or to jump-start arousal with a partner.
sexual orientation—The innate, main focus of one's sexuality, often with the under-

standing that a sexual "orientation" is also affectionate, spiritual, emotional, relational, and psychological. It is enduring, lasting, and unchanging.

sexual preference—What makes up one's core erotic scripts and brings one sexual stimulation and fulfillment; not necessarily limited to orientation, but often includes preferred sex acts and a personal affinity for certain body or personality types. See also sexual preference in the glossary section on derogatory and offensive terms.

sexual fluidity—The capacity to be spontaneously and erratically attracted to sexual relationships and behaviors with a person whose gender is outside one's sexual orientation.

Terms of "Enqueerment"

These terms are used within LGBTQ community and by heterosexuals who are gay affirmative.

allies—Heterosexuals who confront heterosexism, homophobia, microaggressions, and heterosexual privilege in themselves and others out of a concern for the well-being of lesbian, gay, bisexual, and transgender people.

ex-gay—Someone who does not want to be homosexual and believes he or she has "changed" his or her sexual and romantic orientation to heterosexuality; a popular term in reparative therapies.

unwanted same-sex attraction (USSA)—These are predominately males who recognize they have attraction sexually or romantically to men but do not see themselves as gay or even homosexual. This is often seen in religious communities.

LGBTQIA—An umbrella acronym to include everyone within the community (lesbian, gay, bisexual, transgender, queer/questioning, intersex, ally/asexual).

PrideFest—A yearly local gathering of LGBTQ individuals where businesses and organizations can share information. Often, but not always, held the same weekend as an LGBTQ pride march.

queer—Originally a verbally abusive word to put down LGBT people, now a largely political term to describe gay, lesbian, bisexual, and transgender persons. It is an umbrella term for the LGB community and has been growing in popularity. Usually it is used solely in a political context to refer to people who strive to subvert the heterosexual paradigm; for example, you might refer to an activist or very openly gay man, bisexual, or lesbian as "queer," or you might use the term to describe the community as a whole (the "queer community"), but you probably wouldn't use it to describe an individual who is still closeted. Unlike the terms *dyke* and *fag*, *queer* is generally considered acceptable for use by gay-friendly heterosexuals (although not all lesbians and gay men feel this way). There are even straight individuals who have decided to self-describe as queer.

Self-Identification

bisexual—A term used to describe someone who forms emotional, romantic, or erotic attraction to members of either gender, or who has the potential to form it. Many of these individuals prefer to call themselves simply "bi," as it reflects their romantic interests in members of the same gender, whereas *bisexual* emphasizes the sexual aspect.

bi-curious—A term used to describe heterosexual individuals who wonder what it's like to be sexual with a member of the same gender.

cisgender—People with no incongruence between their experienced/expressed gender and assigned gender (and presumably their anatomy). *Cis* is Latin for "on the side of."

gay—An affirmative word to describe men who form their primary romantic and sexual relationships exclusively with other men, including affectional, psychological, spiritual, and erotic attraction to their own gender. Some women prefer to be identified as "gay" as well.

hetero-emotional—Emotionally attracted to the other gender but sexually attracted to the same gender.

heteroflexible—This is used mostly to designate straight males or females who find themselves randomly attracted sexually to members of their own gender.

homoflexible—This is used mostly to designate gay males or lesbians who find themselves randomly attracted sexually to members of other gender.

heterosexual—Having an enduring affectional, psychological, spiritual, and romantic, erotic attraction to the other gender exclusively.

homo-emotional—Emotionally attracted to the same gender but (possibly) sexually attracted to the opposite gender.

homosexual—A mostly outdated and offensive term historically referring to a lesbian or gay male. Because of the clinical history of the word's being used in the "disease" model of homosexuality, it has become offensive, just as *Negro* and *colored* have for African Americans. Though still in use as a clinical and technical term (and used by antigay reparative therapists and religious organizations), it's not generally used by LGBTQ individuals, except those in the early stages of coming out.

lesbian—An affirmative word for women who form their primary romantic and sexual relationships with other women and have an enduring affectional, psychological, spiritual, and erotic attraction to someone of their own sex. The word derives from the Greek island of Lesbos, where the poet Sappho lived, circa 600 B.C.E., and wrote many love poems to other women. It's not clear when the word *lesbian* was first used to describe women who love other women, but it can be traced back to the 1800s and came into popular use during the feminist era of the 1960s and '70s. Some lesbians prefer to be identified as "gay" rather than "lesbian."

monosexual—Someone who practices exclusive heterosexuality or exclusive homosexuality. A monosexual person may identify as straight or gay.

MSM—An umbrella term for gay, straight, or bisexual men who have sex with other men. It does not involve romance and often is used to describe men on the "down low."

natal gender—gender assigned at birth, usually congruent with anatomical sex.

pansexual—This is considered a sexual orientation of an individual who is gender blind and has the potential to be sexually, romantically, or emotionally attracted to people of all gender identities and sexual orientations.

questioning—Being undecided or confused about one's sexual or romantic orientation; often used by gays and lesbians in the early stages of coming out. Also used by some bisexuals who are beginning to explore bisexuality.

transgender—Used to designate a person who experiences incongruence between their gender identity and their natal gender. *Trans* is a Latin term meaning "across from" or "on the other side of." This is gender identity, not sexual identity. Transgender individuals may be heterosexual, gay, lesbian, or bisexual.

WSW—An umbrella term for lesbian, straight, or bisexual women who have sex with other women. It can involve romance or just sexual behavior.

Terms of Endearment

Heterosexual couples describe themselves in standard and simple terms—"husband and wife," "boyfriend and girlfriend," and "fiancé and fiancée." There's no standard governing which terms of endearment are best for LGBTQ individuals and couples. Now that marriage equality is legal, more lesbian and gay couples are using "husband" and "wife" and fiancé are used more and more.

boyfriend or girlfriend—A term that many gay and lesbian couples use even when they've been together for many years.

husband or wife—Terms being used now that gay marriage is allowed in some areas. Some couples use these terms regardless of whether there are legal sanctions or whether they've had a formal wedding ceremony—religious or otherwise. Other couples may reject these terms on the grounds that they feed into a heterosexist marriage model.

life partner—A term used by people who feel that *partner* is too ambiguous and that the addition of the word *life* better reflects the relational part of their relationship.

lover—A term more commonly used in the 1960s, '70s, and '80s by both gays and lesbians. Many now feel it refers only to the sexual side of the relationship.

LTR—Acronym for long-term relationship.

partner—A term that originated when gays and lesbians began legalizing their relationships, creating wills and power of attorney. The then-popular word, *lover*, did not work for legal documents. Now *partner* has become common outside of legalese as well.

significant other—This term, commonly used by unmarried heterosexual couples living together, has been adopted by many lesbian and gay couples who want to recognize the true nature of their unmarried relationship.

Terminology Specific to Gay Men

Gay men organize their lives around sexual expression more than lesbians tend to do. Thus, the words and expressions specific to gay men often involve sexuality.

From the 1960s to the 1980s, before the Internet, gays used nonverbal signals to indicate their sexual preferences. For example, a man wearing a tattoo, band, earring, or other jewelry on his right side was a bottom. If these things were on the left, the man was a top. Gay men also wore handkerchiefs whose colors signified certain sexual practices. Wearing these colors in the left or right hip pocket would alert potential partners if the wearer was a top or bottom. The system finally grew so complex that some enterprising soul issued an informative poster, often seen in gay bars, headlined "The Ultimate Hankie Code"! These nonverbal signs are rarely used today due to gay men's ability to communicate in less pressured environments, such as Internet chat rooms.

alpha top—A gay man who enjoys anally penetrating a partner and receiving oral sex but often never receiving anal sex or giving oral sex himself. See also top.

barebacking—Having anal sex without a condom. Gay men state that there are benefits to barebacking, which include increased sensation to the penis, a greater feeling of closeness to their partner, and more spontaneity. The sex seems "unplanned." The danger, of course, is an increased risk of STIs.

bathhouses/baths/tubs—Buildings designed for gay male sexual contact. Bathhouses frequently have swimming pools, saunas, a weight room, lockers, and individual rooms. Men walk the halls wearing towels or nothing. They "cruise" each other, enjoy sexual contact and release, and then leave. Group sex or one-on-one hookups can occur anywhere, but usually in a room or steam room. Often, gay pornography is shown on multiple televisions. Though gay men commonly frequent bathhouses, a stigma exists against it. Gay men who go to the baths are looked down on and judged harshly for being promiscuous by other gay men, even those who have frequented the baths themselves.

bear—A gay man who is "beefy," if not overweight, and usually hairy as well.

bottom—A term often used to describe the partner who is penetrated during anal sex, but it can also describe the passive partner in a relationship. There is much negative social stigma attached to being a bottom. It's often equated with effeminacy, even though it inherently has nothing to do with mannerisms or gender expression. There is an awful joke in the gay male community: "Who pays for the wedding? The father of the bottom."

bug chasing—Purposely seeking to be infected with HIV. There are so-called bug-chasing or gift-giving parties which men attend with the intention of getting infected or infecting others.

bug juice—A term used by bug chasers to talk about HIV-infected sperm.

circuit parties—Highly organized parties attended by thousands of gay men from all over the world. A block of events is scheduled throughout the weekend, with numerous parties and one main party on Saturday night. These parties feature many recreational drugs along with promiscuous barebacking sex, but they can otherwise be an entertaining way for gay men to literally dance all night and have fun.

closed-loop groups—Underground clubs frequented by heterosexually married men who want a boyfriend (also heterosexually married) on the side. The men remain "monogamous" to both their wives and their boyfriends. Each man knows of the other's secret life, but their wives don't.

cruising—Seeking contact in a public place such as a park, rest area, bathroom, or bathhouse to hook up with another gay man for sex and nothing more. This promiscuous behavior, very businesslike and genitally focused, is the opposite of flirting; it is not relational and there is no emotion involved. Today, most cruising is done online. Many younger gay men consider cruising to be something of the past that older gay men and closeted gay men on the down low did, which is predominately true.

drag queen—A gay man who likes to dress in women's clothing, often in public or as part of a theatrical performance.

gift giving—See bug chasing.

leather daddy—An older gay man who wears leather and often, though not always, practices bondage/dominance (B/D) or sadomasochism (S/M). Leather daddies like to take care of their "boys." This is all about role-playing and leather drag.

nellie—A gay man who is thought to be innately effeminate.

oral bottom—A gay man who enjoys being anally penetrated and providing oral sex but not giving anal penetration nor receiving oral sex. See bottom.

otter—Gay men within the bear community who are slim and hairy.

queeny—A gay man who is judged to be innately effeminate; can also be used to describe behavior that is catty and stereotypically female in a negative sense.

rent boy—A man over 18 who is paid for sex by other men; otherwise known as a hustler, male prostitute, or sex worker.

rice queen—A gay man interested primarily, if not exclusively, in Asian men.

rimming—A common sexual practice, also known as analingus, wherein a partner gives or receives oral stimulation to the anus. Although some straight men do this to women (as popularized on the show *Sex and the City*), it's more common among gay men.

size queen—A gay man primarily attracted to genitally well-endowed men.

tea dance—Gay male parties that involve drinking and dancing and usually begin at 4 p.m.; considered pre-parties before the bigger parties at the clubs later in the evening. The term is derived from what historically were called "tearooms"— restrooms where men met for hookups (Humphreys, 1970).

top—A term often used to describe the penetrating partner during anal sex. Usually the top is also the one who is orally fellated and may not reciprocate. Can also describe the dominant partner in a gay relationship. This dynamic is agreed upon in the relationship and not imposed, as in many heterosexual relationships.

versatile—Men who enjoy being either a top or a bottom. In a gay relationships, versatile men enjoy shared dominance. They're comfortable being dominant, passive, or both. Some versatile men let the nature of each relationship dictate which role (or roles) they assume.

Terminology Specific to Lesbians

Many of these terms have to do with relational issues or self-identification.

bottom—The partner who passively allows her partner to direct the sexual acts, which usually consist of the bottom being pleasured; often (though not always) the "femme" in "butch/femme" relationships. In terms of power dynamics, the top is generally considered to be in control because she directs the sex; however, the bottom can also be seen as in control because she is the one being pleasured (like a gay male top being orally fellated).

butch—A woman masculine in her dress and behavior; usually is sexually and romantically attracted to femmes.

butch/femme—Role-playing that replicates the "old" pattern of heterosexual behavior, with one partner being masculine and the other feminine.

chapstick lesbian—One who is unaffected, natural, and forgoes makeup and dressing in feminine clothes.

drag king—A lesbian who likes to dress in male clothing.

Dykes on Bikes—A group of lesbians who enjoy riding motorcycles and often appear in gay pride marches.

femme—A feminine woman; usually is sexually and romantically attracted to butches.

granola dyke—A lesbian of the Birkenstocks-wearing, tofu-eating, folk-music-loving, "earthy crunchy" hippie variety. Often she has unshaven legs and armpits and prefers a more natural look.

herstory—The experiences and accomplishments of women as seen from a historical perspective; also, the composite of experiences making up a woman's life.

lesbian bed death—A controversial expression describing the slow decline of sexual interaction between lesbian partners in a couple. See Chapter 9.

lipstick lesbian—A feminine woman who wears makeup and enjoys the stereotypically feminine role. She can be attracted to other lipstick lesbians or more masculine lesbians.

packing—Wearing a strap-on dildo or phallus object either for sex or hidden under clothing while out in public. Usually women do this during sexual intercourse. Trans men (natal female to male) wear this to give the impression they have a penis or have a bulge in their pants as some cisgender men have.

power dyke—A lesbian who has gained a position of power professionally or politically, either in the LGBTQ community or in the world at large.

sapphist—A lesbian of culture and refinement.

stone butch—Historically, a lesbian who gets pleasure from pleasing her partner but does not like to be touched sexually. Now it is understood that many stone butches are trans males, which helps to understand why they do not like to be touched.

top—The partner who assertively directs the sexual acts, which mostly consist of pleasuring the bottom; often (though not always) the "butch" in "butch/femme" relationships.

womyn—A variation of the word *woman* that is purposely misspelled by feminists and lesbians who find it offensive to have the suffix "man" in *woman*. Not all feminists and lesbians like this term, but it's been claimed as a subtle empowerment tool by both groups. Some lesbians go through a developmental stage during their identify formation of being anti-male and use this spelling to correct the sexism and patriarchy they have suffered.

WomynFest—An all-women's festival, primarily lesbian.

Other Expressions

beard—A gay man or lesbian's straight spouse.

closeted—A term used to describe lesbians, gays, or bisexuals who hide their identity.

fag hag—A straight woman who prefers to socialize primarily with gay men. This term was popularized by the television show *Will & Grace*, in which the title character Grace creates a life around her gay friend Will. Often such women suffer low self-esteem and have issues with heterosexual men.

fisting—Slowly inserting the hand and forearm into the anus or vagina by keeping the fingers straight and close together and then typically (though not always) clenching into a fist.

fresh off the boat—Someone just coming out who is considered undateable because they are in the adolescent stage of coming out and are engaging in multiple hookups and relationships.

gaydar—The ability to intuit whether a person is gay or lesbian; a takeoff on the word *radar*.

gay friendly—A term used to describe nongays who are allies and supporters of LGBTQ individuals.

on the down low (or "on the DL")—A term used to describe men who do not self-identify as gay but who enjoy homoerotic and homosexual sex and secretively seek it out.

out of the closet (or just "out")—Being open or public about one's orientation. Some people are "out" in some settings (for example, with friends) but not in others (at work or with family).

passing—Pretending to be straight by presenting physically, behaviorally, and verbally as if one were heterosexual. Also used by trans individuals referring to their ability to be seen as either a cisgender man or a cisgender woman.

straight acting—A term popularly used by gay men to refer to an alpha masculine, gay, "macho, macho men"; sometimes used by lesbians as well to describe effeminate lesbians. Actually, it is an internalized homophobic word that equates male heterosexuality with masculinity and being gay with effeminacy.

straight but not narrow—A term used to describe gay-friendly heterosexuals who are supportive of gays and lesbians.

Code Words and Symbols

Over the years, gays and lesbians coined words and expressions to let them speak openly in public settings where they weren't out.

family—Someone who is part of the gay or lesbian community, though usually closeted. Often, a gay person will say "he's family" about someone he knows to be gay.

friend of Dorothy—A takeoff on "friends of Bill," a euphemism that members of Alcoholics Anonymous use to "pass" in the presence of ordinary social drinkers, still used by older LGB individuals. "Friend of Dorothy" is usually used by gay men as a way of identifying themselves or someone else as gay. On the daily calendar of cruise ships (both gay and straight), "friends of Dorothy" is used to identify a gay AA meeting.

black triangle—Lesbians began wearing black triangles in remembrance of lesbians killed by the Nazis during World War II. The Nazis not only targeted Jews but also rounded up millions of homosexuals, gypsies, prostitutes, and "antisocials." Although they assigned lesbians no specific color patch, some believe that lesbians were grouped with other "antisocials," who wore a black triangle. Lesbians today sometimes wear black-triangle buttons or jewelry as a symbol of pride and as a covert way to identify themselves.

pink triangle—The Nazis forced men of homosexual orientation to wear pink triangles on their clothing. Gay men today have reclaimed the pink triangle, along with other former badges of shame such as the term *queer*, and turned it into as a symbol of strength and solidarity.

rainbow flag—In 1978, Gilbert Baker of San Francisco designed a flag with six stripes, each in a different color of the rainbow, as a symbol of gay and lesbian community and pride. It quickly replaced the pink-triangle symbol, which until then had been the most popular symbol of gay pride. You'll now see it used in gay pride marches, on bumper stickers and decals, as well as in storefronts to indicate that a business is gay owned or gay friendly.

Drug Terms

The following drugs are popular at gay male circuit parties and bathhouses. Although some lesbians also use such drugs, especially while clubbing with gay male friends, they don't play a role in the lesbian community.

crank/crystal meth/ice/tina—Considered a "party drug," crystal methamphetamine is one of the fastest-growing drugs in the gay community. It provides a quick sexual arousal and the ability to stay up and aroused all night or even for days. Long-term, it inhibits penile erection, causing users to go from tops to bottoms, requiring Viagra or other erectile medications; and it carries a risk of HIV infection through unsafe sex due to impaired judgment. Crystal meth is highly addictive and harder to kick than most other drugs, even crack cocaine.

ecstasy—A party drug widely used at circuit parties. Originally prescribed for physical and mental pain relief and as an adjunct to psychotherapy, it quickly became a street drug that was abused at rave parties and by gay men. It is now illegal.

poppers—Amyl nitrite, an inhaled stimulant commonly used by gay men to enhance sexual arousal. Once a party drug used at tea dances and gay clubs, it is now used only as a sex drug in the bedroom and while cruising. Thought to contribute to HIV infection in 1989, it was banned for sale at all locations such as porn shops and bathhouses. However, urban gay male culture continued selling it, and it is widely available on the Internet, where websites use coded words such as "leather cleaner" or "liquid incense" to market it. Although it does not cause HIV infection, it does impair reasoning, putting users at risk for unsafe sexual practices. Poppers in their present form are little brown bottles containing a liquid mixture of volatile nitrites. When inhaled during arousal and before orgasm, poppers seem to enhance and prolong the sensation. Poppers facilitate anal intercourse by relaxing the muscles in the rectum and deadening any sense of discomfort.

PrEP—Pre-exposure prophylaxis. Anti-HIV medication that keeps HIV-negative people from becoming infected.

PEP—Short for "post-exposure prophylaxis," PEP is an HIV-prevention strategy in which HIV-negative people take anti-HIV medications *after* coming into contact with HIV to reduce their risk of HIV infection.

tweaker—Someone who is heavily under the influence of crystal meth. The expression is: "He is tweaked" or "He is tweaking."

Derogatory and Offensive Words

When I was a boy, degrading, humiliating names like "faggot" and "queer" were hurled at me repeatedly. Today, younger kids and teenagers still use "gay" to degrade and humiliate others. You can hear "That is so gay!" in school corridors and at the mall. Like slang expressions such as "I was gypped" (derived from gypsies being thieves), these slurs have become so commonplace that people use them without even knowing where they originated or how they might offend.

alternative lifestyle—refers to the lives of LGBTQ people. Implies that being gay is a choice. For LGBTQ individuals, heterosexuality is the "alternative lifestyle." The only community using "alternative lifestyle" in a nonderogatory term is the kink and fetish community.

breeder—What some LGBTQ people derogatively call heterosexuals.

dyke—A term sometimes reclaimed and used with positive connotations in the gay and lesbian community to describe lesbians but considered offensive when used by heterosexuals.

fag—Commonly believed to be derived from the word *faggot*, a term sometimes reclaimed and used with positive connotations in the LGBTQ community to describe gay men but considered offensive when used by heterosexuals.

LGBTQ lifestyle—Most gays and lesbians say they have a "life," not a "lifestyle." As a gay comic once said, "It is like my dog. He doesn't have a lifestyle—he just has a life!" Like the term *sexual preference*, *lifestyle* implies that being gay is a choice.

sexual preference—An offensive term when used to describe a person's sexual orientation, as it implies that homosexuality is consciously chosen or "preferred" rather than innate. Used correctly, *sexual preference* refers to what makes up one's arousal template and brings one sexual stimulation and fulfillment. For example, one's sexual preferences might include oral stimulation but not penetration.

References

Aarons, L. (1996). *Prayers for Bobby: A mother's coming to terms with the suicide of her gay son.* New York, NY: HarperCollins.

Ainsworth, M., Blehar, M., Waters, E., & Wall, S. (1978). *Patterns of attachment: A psychological study of the strange situation.* Hillsdale, NJ: Erlbaum.

Alexander, C. J., & Nunno, V. (1996). Narcissism and egocentricity in gay men. In C. J. Alexander (Ed.), *Gay and lesbian mental health: A sourcebook for practitioners* (pp. 1–13). New York, NY: Haworth Press.

Allred, J. D. (2016, February 24). Utah senate declares porn a public health crisis. *Deseret News.* Retrieved from www.deseretnews.com

Amazon. (2014). *Transparent* [Web TV series].

American Psychiatric Association. (1980). *Diagnostic and Statistical Manual of Mental Disorders* (3rd ed.). Washington, DC: Author.

American Psychiatric Association. (1987). *Diagnostic and Statistical Manual of Mental Disorders* (3rd ed., rev.). Washington, DC: Author.

American Psychiatric Association. (1994). *Diagnostic and Statistical Manual of Mental Disorders* (4th ed.). Washington, DC: Author.

American Psychiatric Association. (2013). *Diagnostic and Statistical Manual of Mental Disorders* (5th ed.). Washington, DC: Author.

Amico, J. (2003). Healing from spiritual abuse: Assisting gay and lesbian clients. *Addiction Professional, 1*(9), 18–20.

Anderson, J. R., & Barret, R. L. (2001). *Ethics in HIV-related psychotherapy: Clinical decision making in complex cases.* Washington, DC: American Psychological Association.

Avnet, J., Bates, K., Masterson, M. S., Parker, M.-L., Tandy, J., Flagg, F., & Universal Pictures (Firm). (2006). *Fried green tomatoes.* Universal City, CA: Universal Pictures.

Baker, J. M. (2002). *How homophobia hurts children.* Binghamton, NY: Haworth.

Ball, A. L. (2004, December). When gay men happen to straight women. *O, The Oprah Magazine*, pp. 236–265.

Barron, N. (1998). Living into my body. In D. Atkins (Ed.), *Looking queer: Body image and identity in lesbian, bisexual, gay and transgender communities* (pp. 5–15). Binghamton, NY: Harrington Park.

Bartholomew, K., & Horowitz, L. (1991). Attachment styles among young adults. *Journal of Personality and Social Psychology, 61*, 226–244.

Beemyn, G., & Rankin, S. (2011). *The lives of transgender people*. New York, NY: Columbia University Press.

Bernstein, J. (2010, July 18). The lesbians who love male gay porn. *The Daily Beast*.

Berzon, B. (2001). *Positively gay* (3rd ed.). Berkeley, CA: Celestial Arts.

Berzon, B. (2004). *Permanent partners: Building gay and lesbian relationships that last* (Rev. ed.). New York, NY: Plume.

Besen, W. R. (2003). *Anything but straight: Unmasking the scandals and lies behind the ex-gay myth*. Binghamton, NY: Harrington Park.

Biaggio, M., Coan, S., & Adams, W. (2002). Couple's therapy for lesbians: Understanding merger and the impact of homophobia. *The Journal of Lesbian Studies, 6*(1), 129–138.

Bieber, I., Dain, H. J., Dince, P. R., Drellich, M. G., Grand, H. G., Gundlach, R. H., . . . Bieber, T. B. (1962). *Homosexuality: A psychoanalytic study*. New York, NY: Basic Books.

Bilodeau, B., & Renn, K. A. (2005). Analysis of LGBT identity development models and implications for practice. *New Directions for Student Services, 111*, 25–39.

Bisexual.org. (2016, August 4). Revealing research on why many bisexual men don't come out.

Blumstein, P., & Schwartz, P. (1983). *American couples*. New York, NY: William Morrow.

Bowlby, J. (1988). *A secure base: Parent-child attachment and healthy human development*. London, England: Routledge.

Boyd, H. (2003). *My husband Betty: Love, sex, and life with a crossdresser*. Berkeley, CA: Seal Press.

Boyd, H. (2007). *She's not the man I married: My life with a transgender husband*. Berkeley, CA: Seal Press.

Boykin, K. (2005). *Beyond the down low: Sex, lies, and denial in black America*. New York, NY: Carroll & Graf.

Braun-Harvey, D., & Vigorito, M. (2015). *Treating out of control sexual behavior: Rethinking sex addiction*. New York, NY: Springer.

Brown, L. S. (1989). Lesbians, gay men and their families: Common clinical issues. *Journal of Gay and Lesbian Psychotherapy, 1*(1), 65–77.

Brown, T. (2002). A proposed model of bisexual identity development that elaborates on experiential differences of women and men. *Journal of Bisexuality, 2–4.* Retrieved from www.tandfonline.com/doi/abs/10.1300/J159v02n04_05

Bruno, F. (2017, February 25). Two consonants walk into a bar. *The New York Times.* Retrieved from www.nytimes.com

Budnick, J. (2016, November 1). Straight girls do kiss on campus, but what about those who don't go to college? *The Conversation.* Retrived from theconversation.com/straight-girls-do-kiss-on-campus-but-what-about-those-who-dont-go-to-college-65227

Buloff, B., & Osterman, M. (1995). Queer reflections: Mirroring and the lesbian experience of self. In J. M. Glassgold & S. Iasenza (Eds.), *Lesbians and psychoanalysis: Revolutions in theory and practice* (pp. 93–106). New York, NY: Free Press.

Buxton, A. P. (1994). *The other side of the closet: The coming-out crisis for straight spouses.* New York, NY: John Wiley and Sons.

Campbell, R. J. (2004). *Campbell's psychiatric dictionary* (8th ed.). New York, NY: Oxford University Press.

Cass, V. (1979). Homosexual identity formation: A theoretical model. *Journal of Homosexuality, 4*(3), 219–235.

Center for Disease Control, 2010 https://www.cdc.gov/hiv/risk/prep/index.html

Chernin, J. N., & Johnson, M. R. (2003). *Affirmative psychotherapy and counseling for lesbians and gay men.* Thousand Oaks, CA: Sage.

Clark, D. (2004). *Loving someone gay* (4th ed.). Berkeley, CA: Celestial Arts.

Coleman, E. (1981/1982). Developmental stages of the coming-out process. *Journal of Homosexuality, 7*(2–3), 31–43.

Corley, D., & Kort, J. (2006). The sex addicted mixed-orientation marriage: Examining attachment styles, internalized homophobia and viability of marriage after disclosure. *Journal of Sexual Addiction & Compulsivity, 13*(2–3), 167–193.

Dahir, M. (2001, February 21). A gay thing. *Windy City Times..*

Dalbey, B. (2016, November 30). Detroit mom accused of beating gay daughter due to her sexual orientation. *Detroit Patch.*

Diamond, L. M. (2003). What does sexual orientation orient? *Psychological Review, 110*(1), 173–192.

Diamond, L. M. (2004). Emerging perspectives on distinctions between romantic love and sexual desire. *Current Directions in Psychological Science, 13,* 116–119.

Diamond, L. M. (2009). *Sexual fluidity: Understanding women's love and desire.* Cambridge, MA: Harvard University Press.

Downing, M. J., Schrimshaw, E., Scheinmann, R., Antebi-Gruszka, N., & Hirshfield, S. (2016). Sexually explicit media use by sexual identity: A comparative analysis of gay, bisexual, and heterosexual men in the United States. *Archives of Sexual Behavior.* doi:10.1007/s10508-016-0837-9

Downs, Alan (2006) *Velvet Rage. Cambridge, MA: Da Capo Press*

Dr. Phil. (2009). https://www.youtube.com/watch?v=bXue5IknI2U&t=18s

Drescher, J. (1996). Psychoanalytic subjectivity and male homosexuality. In R. P. Cabaj & T. S. Stein (Eds.), *Textbook of homosexuality and mental health* (pp. 173–187). Washington, DC: American Psychiatric Press.

Drescher, J. (1998). *Psychoanalytic therapy and the gay man.* Hillsdale, NJ: The Analytic Press.

Drescher, J., & Merlino, J. P. (2007). *American psychiatry and homosexuality: An oral history.* Binghamton, NY: Harrington Park.

Duberman, M. (1991). *Cures: A gay man's odyssey.* New York, NY: Dutton.

Duberman, M. (1993). *Stonewall.* New York, NY: Plume.

Erikson, E. H. (1997). *The life cycle completed.* New York, NY: Norton.

Exner, J. E., Jr. (1969). Rorschach responses as an index of narcissism. *Journal of Projective Techniques and Personality Assessment, 33,* 324–330.

Falco, K. (1991). *Psychotherapy with lesbian clients: Theory into practice.* New York, NY: Brunner/Mazel.

Falco, K. (1996). Psychotherapy with women who love women. In R. Cabaj & T. Stein (Eds.), *Textbook of homosexuality and mental health* (pp. 397–412). Washington, DC: American Psychiatric Association.

Fisher, H. (2004). *Why we love.* New York, NY: Henry Holt.

Friedman, R. C., & Downey, J. I. (2002). *Sexual orientation and psychoanalysis: Sexual science and clinical practice.* New York, NY: Columbia University Press.

Fugere, M.A. (2016, November 4). 3 of the strangest rules of sexual attraction. *Psychology Today.* Retrieved from www.psychologytoday.com

Gartner, R. B. (1999). *Betrayed as boys: Psychodynamic treatment of sexually abused men.* New York, NY: Guilford Press.

Genderfluid (n.d.) Nonbinary wiki. Retrieved from https://nonbinary.miraheze.org/wiki/Genderfluid.

Gideonse, T. (1997, June 24). Sexual blur. *The Advocate.*

Gonsiorek, J. C. (1982). The use of diagnostic concepts in working with gay and lesbian populations. *Journal of Homosexuality, 7*(2–3), 9–20.

Gottman, J. (2004). What we've learned: What makes same-sex relationships succeed or fail? Retrieved from www.gottman.com

Gould, D. (1995). A critical examination of the notion of pathology in psychoanalysis. In J. M. Glassgold & S. Iasenza (Eds.), *Lesbians and psychoanalysis: Revolutions in theory and practice* (pp. 3–17). New York, NY: Free Press.

Green, R. (1987). *The sissy boy syndrome and the development of homosexuality.* New Haven, CT: Yale University Press.

Greenan, D. E., & Tunnell, G. (2003). *Couple therapy with gay men.* New York, NY: Guilford.

Grever, C. (2012). *My husband is gay: A woman's guide to surviving the crisis.* Berkeley, CA: Crossing Press.

Greytak, E. A., Kosciw, J. G., & Diaz, E. M. (2009). *Harsh realities, the experiences of transgender youth in our nation's schools.* Gay, Lesbian and Straight Education Network. Retrieved from www.glsen.org

Haas, A. P., Rodgers, P. L., & Herman, J. L. (2014). *Suicide attempts among transgender and gender non-conforming adults: Findings of the national transgender discrimination survey.* UCLA School of Law.

Hall, M. (1987). Sex therapy with lesbian couples: A four stage approach. In E. Coleman (Ed.), *Psychotherapy with homosexual men and women: Integrated identity approaches for clinical practice* (pp. 137–156). Binghamton, NY: Haworth.

Hamadock, S. (1996). Reinventing your erotic relationship: A couples group approach to lesbian bed death. *In the Family Magazine, 2*(2), 6.

Hanley-Hackenbruck, P. (1989). Psychotherapy and the coming-out process. *Journal of Gay and Lesbian Psychotherapy, 1*(1), 21–39.

Hardin, K. N., & Hall, M. (2001). *Queer blues: The lesbian and gay guide to overcoming depression.* Oakland, CA: New Harbinger.

Helminiak, D. A. (2000). *What the Bible really says about homosexuality* (Millennium ed.). San Francisco, CA: Alamo Square Distributors.

Hendrix, H. (2001). *Getting the love you want: A guide for couples.* New York, NY: Owl Books.

Herbert, S. (1996). Lesbian sexuality. In R. P. Cabaj & T. S. Stein (Eds.), *Textbook of homosexuality and mental health* (pp. 23–742). Washington, DC: American Psychiatric Press.

Herek, G. M. (2006a). *Facts about homosexuality and mental health.* Retrieved from electronic resource psychology.ucdavis.edu/rainbow/html/facts_mental_health.html

Herek, G. M. (2006b). *Facts about homosexuality and child molestation.* Retrieved from psychology.ucdavis.edu/rainbow/html/facts_molestation.html

Herman, J. L. (1992). *Trauma and recovery.* New York, NY: HarperCollins.

Hooker, E. A. (1957). The adjustment of the male overt homosexual. *Journal of Projective Techniques, 21,* 18–31.

Human Rights Campaign, 2012 www.hrc.org

Humphreys, L. (1970). *Tearoom trade: Impersonal sex in public places.* New York, NY: Aldine de Gruyter.

Iasenza, S. (1999). The big lie: Debunking lesbian bed death. *In the Family Magazine, 4*(4), 8.

Isay, R. (1994). *Being homosexual: Gay men and their development.* Northvale, NJ: Jason Aronson.

Isay, R. (1996). *Becoming gay: The journey to self-acceptance.* New York, NY: Pantheon.

"It Gets Better Project - YouTube". *YouTube.* 2016-11-26.

Jones, E. (1957). *Sigmund Freud: Life and work* (Vol. 3). London, England: Hogarth.

Kaufman, G., & Raphael, L. (1996). *Coming out of shame: Transforming gay and lesbian lives.* New York, NY: Doubleday.

King, J. L. (2004). *On the down low: A journey into the lives of "straight" black men who sleep with men.* New York, NY: Broadway Books.

Kinsey, A. C., Pomeroy, W. B., & Martin, C. E. (1948). *Sexual behavior in the human male.* Philadelphia, PA: Saunders.

Kinsey, A. C., Pomeroy, W. B., Martin, C. E., & Gebhard, P. H. (1953). *Sexual behavior in the human female.* Philadelphia, PA: Saunders.

Klein, F. (1993). *The bisexual option.* Philadelphia, PA: The Haworth Press.

Klein, M. (2016). *His porn, her pain: Confronting America's porn panic with honest talk about sex.* Santa Barbara, CA: Praeger.

Kleinberg, S., & Zorn, P. (1998). Multiple mirroring with lesbian and gay couples: From Peoria to P-town. In W. Luquet & M. T. Hannah (Eds.), *Healing in the relational paradigm: The imago relationship therapy casebook* (2nd ed., pp. 135–150). Washington, DC: Brunner-Routledge.

Kort, J. (2002). Gay men and their porn. *In the Family, 8*(1), 8–12.

Kort, J. (2003). *10 smart things gay men can do to improve their lives.* New York, NY: Alyson Books.

Kort, J. (2004, May/June). Queer eye for the straight therapist. *Psychotherapy Networker,* pp. 56–61.

Kort, J. (2005a, September/October). The new mixed marriage: Working with a couple when one partner is gay. *Psychotherapy Networker,* pp. 83–89.

Kort, J. (2005b). Covert cultural sexual abuse of gay male teenagers contributing to etiology of sexual addiction. *Journal of Sexual Addiction and Compulsivity, 11*(4), 287–300.

Kort, J. (2006). *10 smart things gay men can do to find real love.* New York, NY: Alyson Books.

Kort, J. (2013, April 16). Guys on the 'side': Looking beyond gay tops and bottoms. *Huffington Post.*

Kort, J. (2016, February 2). Going with the flow: male and female sexual fluidity. *Huffington Post.*

Kort, J., & Morgan, A. P. (2014). *Is my husband gay, straight, or bi? A guide for women concerned about their men.* Lanham, Maryland: Rowman & Littlefield.

Krakauer, I. D., & Rose, S. M. (2002). The impact of group membership on lesbians' physical appearance. *The Journal of Lesbian Studies, 6*(1), 31–43.

Kubler-Ross, E. (2003). *On death and dying.* New York, NY: Scribner.

Laird, J. (1998). Invisible ties: Lesbians and their families of origin. In C. J. Patterson & A. R. D'Augelli (Eds.), *Lesbian, gay, and bisexual identities in families: Psychological perspectives* (pp. 197–228). New York, NY: Oxford University Press.

LaSala, M. C. (2000). Monogamous or not: Understanding and counseling gay male couples. *Families in Society, 82*(6).

LaSala, M. C. (2010). *Coming out, coming home: Helping families adjust to a gay or lesbian child.* New York, NY: Columbia University Press.

Lee, J.A. (2016, January 12). Do transgender individuals who used hormones during their transition have observations about how hormones affect behavior, cognition and emotions? [Online forum comment]. Retrieved from www.quora.com/Do-transgender-individuals-who-used-hormones-during-their-transition-have-observations-about-how-hormones-affect-behavior-cognition-and-emotions

Lev, A. (2004). *Transgender emergence: Therapeutic guidelines for working with gender-variant people and their families.* New York, NY: Haworth Clinical Practice Press.

Levine, P. (2006). *Waking the tiger: Healing trauma.* Berkeley, CA: North Atlantic Books.

Lew, M. (2004). *Victims no longer: The classic guide for men recovering from sexual child abuse* (2nd ed.). New York, NY: Perennial Currents.

Lewes, K. (1988). *The psychoanalytic theory of male homosexuality.* New York, NY: Jason Aronson.

Ley, D. (2016). *Ethical porn for dicks: A man's guide to responsible viewing pleasure.* Berkeley, CA: ThreeL Media.

Lorde, A. (1984). *Sister outsider.* Freedom, CA: Crossing Press.

Loulan, J. (1987). *Lesbian passion.* Minneapolis, MN: Spinsters Ink.

Loving v. Virginia (1967). www.law.cornell.edu/supremecourt/text/388/1

Lowen, L., & Spears, B. (2016a). The couples study. Retrieved from www.thecouplesstudy.com/128-2/

Lowen, L., & Spears, B. (2016b, November 2). New trends in gay male relationships: The choices study. Retrieved from www.etr.org/blog/my-take-choices-study/

Lowen, L., & Spears, B. (2016c). *Choices: Perspectives of gay men on monogamy, non-monogamy, and marriage.* CreateSpace Independent Publishing Platform.

Luscombe, B. (2016, March 30). Porn and the threat to virility. *Time Magazine.* Retrieved from www.time.com

MacMillen, H. (2016, October 11). The percentage of straight men who watch gay porn may surprise you. *Cosmopolitan.*

Maltz, W. (2001). *The sexual healing journey: A guide for survivors of sexual abuse* (Rev. ed.). New York, NY: HarperCollins.

Maniaci, T., & Rzeznik, F. (Directors). (2004). *One Nation Under God* [DVD]. New York, NY: First Run Features.

Massachusetts Youth Risk Behavior Survey Results. (1999). Malden, MA: Massachusetts Department of Education.

Malyon, A. K. (1982). Psychotherapeutic implications of internalized homophobia in gay men. In J. C. Gonsiorek (Ed.), *Homosexuality and psychotherapy: A practitioner's handbook of affirmative models* (pp. 59–70). New York, NY: Haworth Press.

Maza, C., & Krehely, J. (2010). How to improve mental health care for LGBT youth. *Center for American Progress.* Retrieved from www.americanprogress.org/issues/lgbt/reports/2010/12/09/8787/how-to-improve-mental-health-care-for-lgbt-youth/

McNaught, B. (1993). *Homophobia in the Workplace* [Video]. Retrieved from www.brian-mcnaught.com

McNaught, B. (1997). *Now that I'm out, what do I do?* New York, NY: St. Martin's Press.

McWhirter, D. P., & Mattison, A. M. (1984). *The male couple: How relationships develop.* Upper Saddle River, NJ: Prentice Hall.

Milrod, C. (2013, May 13). My brother is a cross dresser – help! Retrieved from sexandlifecoaching.com/site/2013/05/my-brother-is-a-cross-dresser-help/

Mizock, L., & Hopwood, R. (2016). Conflation and interdependence in the intersection of gender and sexuality among transgender individuals. *Psychology of Sexual Orientation and Gender Diversity, 3*(1), 93–103.

Mohr, J. J., & Fassinger, R. E. (1998). *Individual differences in lesbian/gay identity: An attachment perspective.* Manuscript submitted for publication.

Money, J. (1988). *Gay, straight, and in-between.* New York, NY: Oxford University Press.

Morin, J. (1996). *The erotic mind: Unlocking the inner sources of sexual passion and fulfillment.* New York, NY: Harper Perennial.

Morrow, S. L. (2000). First do no harm: Therapist issues in psychotherapy with lesbian, gay, and bisexual clients. In R. M. Perez, K. A. DeBord, & K. Bieschke (Eds.), *Handbook of counseling and psychotherapy with lesbian, gay, and bisexual clients* (pp. 137–156). Washington, DC: American Psychological Association.

Moser, C. (2016). Defining sexual orientation. *Archives of Sexual Behavior, 45*(3), 505-508.

Mustanski, B. (2013, September 18). What does it mean to be 'mostly heterosexual? *Psychology Today*. Retrieved from www.psychologytoday.com

Myers, A., Taub, J., Morris, J. F., & Rothblum, E. D. (1998). Beauty mandates and the appearance obsession: Are lesbians better off? In D. Atkins (Ed.), *Looking queer: Body image and identity in lesbian, bisexual, gay and transgender communities* (pp. 17–25). Binghamton, NY: Harrington Park.

Nadal, K. L. (2013). *That's so gay!: Microaggressions and the lesbian, gay, bisexual and transgender community.* Washington, DC: American Psychological Association.

National Institute of Mental Health. (1987). *National lesbian health care survey.* (Contract N. 86MO19832201D). Washington, DC: DHHS Publication.

Neisen, J. H. (1993). Healing from cultural victimization: Recovery from shame due to heterosexism. *Journal of Gay and Lesbian Psychotherapy, 2*(1), 49–63.

Newman, F. (2004). *The whole lesbian sex book: A passionate guide for all of us* (2nd ed.). San Francisco, CA: Cleis.

Nichols, M. (2014). Therapy with LGBTQ clients: Working with sex and gender variance from a queer theory model. In Y. Binik and K. S. Hall (Eds.), *Principles and practices of sex therapy* (5th ed.). New York, NY: Guilford.

Nicolosi, J. (1997). *Reparative therapy of male homosexuality: A new clinical approach.* Northvale, NJ: Jason Aronson.

Nicolosi, J., & Nicolosi, L. A. (2002). *A parent's guide to preventing homosexuality.* Downers Grove, IL: InterVarsity Press.

Nimmons, D. (2002). *The soul beneath the skin: The unseen hearts and habits of gay men.* New York, NY: St. Martin's.

Noelle, M. (2002). The psychological and social effects of antibisexual, antigay, and antilesbian violence and harassment. In P. Iganski (Ed.), *Hate crimes: The consequences of hate crime* (Vol. 2). Westport, CT: Praeger.

Nutt, A. E. (2016). *Becoming Nicole: The transformation of an American family* (Reprint ed.). New York, NY: Random House Trade Paperbacks.

Ochs, Robin Retrieved from https://robynochs.com/quotes/

Ogas, O., & Gaddam, S. (2011). *A billion wicked thoughts*, New York, NY: Plume.

Olson, K., & Durwood, L. (2016). Are parents rushing to turn their boys into girls? *Slate*. Retrieved from www.slate.com/blogs/outward/2016/01/14/what_alarmist_articles_about_transgender_children_get_wrong.html

Parsons, J. T., Starks, T. J., DuBois, S., Grov, C., & Golub, S. A. (2013). Alternatives to monogamy among gay male couples in a community survey: Implications for mental health and sexual risk. *Archives of Sexual Behavior, 42*(2), 303–312.

Pedophiles About Pedophilia (2015). Retrieved from medium.com/pedophiles-about-pedophilia/setting-the-stage-the-non-offending-pedophile-c26c78b49fd#.os11fevm8

Perel, E. (2006). *Mating in captivity: Reconciling the erotic and the domestic.* New York, NY: HarperCollins.

Pre-Exposure Prophylaxis. (n.d.). Centers for Disease Control and Prevention. Retrieved from https://www.cdc.gov/hiv/risk/prep/index.html.

Prause, N., & Pfaus, J. (2015). Viewing sexual stimuli associated with greater sexual responsiveness, not erectile dysfunction. *Sexual Medicine.* doi:10.1002/sm2.58 [Epub ahead of print]

Prause, N., & Fong, T. (2015). The science and politics of addiction research. In L. Comella & S. Tarrant, *New views on pornography: Sexuality, pornography, and the law.* Santa Barbara, CA: Praeger.

Raychaudhuri, M., & Mukerji, K. (1971). Homosexual and narcissistic reflections in the Rorschach: An examination of Exner's diagnostic Rorschach signs. *Rorschachiana Japonica, 12,* 119–126.

Real, T. (1997). *I don't want to talk about it: Overcoming the secret legacy of male depression.* New York, NY: Scribner.

Reiss, B. F. (1980). Psychological tests in homosexuality. In J. Marmor (Ed.), *Homosexual behavior: A modern reappraisal* (pp. 296–311). New York, NY: Basic Books.

Rich, A. (1980). Compulsory heterosexuality and lesbian existence. *Signs, 5,* 631–660.

Richards Fink, P. (2014, December 14). Bisexual identity development: Perspectives, similarities, and contrasts. *Queerer Theory: Notes and Reflections from a Male-Identified Bisexual.* Kindle Firsts. Retrieved from fliponymous.wordpress.com/2014/12/14/bisexual-identity-development-perspectives-similarities-and-contrasts/

Ritter, K. Y., & Terndrup, A. I. (2002). *Handbook of affirmative psychotherapy with lesbians and gay men.* New York, NY: Guilford.

Rothblum, E. D. (1994). Lesbians and physical appearance: Which model applies? In B. Greene & G. M. Herek (Eds.), *Lesbian and gay psychology: Vol. 1. Theory, research, and clinical applications, psychological perspectives on lesbian and gay issues* (pp. 85–97). Thousand Oaks, CA: Sage.

Ryan, C., Russell, S. T., Huebner, D., Diaz, R., & Sanchez, J. (2010). Family acceptance in adolescence and the health of LGBT young adults. *Journal of Child and Adolescent Psychiatric Nursing, 4,* 205–213.

Salon. (2015). I'm a pedophile but not a monster. Retrieved from www.salon.com/2015/09/21/im_a_pedophile_but_not_a_monster/

Salter, A. C. (2004). *Predators, pedophiles, rapists and other sex offenders.* New York, NY: Basic Books.

Savin-Williams, R. (2005). *The new gay teenager.* Cambridge, MA: Harvard University Press.

Schmider, A. (2017, January 9). GLAAD Calls for increased and accurate media coverage of transgender murders. Retrieved from www.glaad.org/blog/glaad-calls-increased-and-accurate-media-coverage-transgender-murders

Schwartz, P. (1994). *Peer marriage: How love between equals works.* New York, NY: Free Press.

Selterman, D. (2014). Debunking myths about sexual fluidity. *Science of Relationships.* Retrieved from www.scienceofrelationships.com/home/2014/10/13/debunking-myths-about-sexual-fluidity.html

Selva, K. (2016). Puberty blockers and puberty inhibitors. Retrieved from www.transactiveonline.org/resources/youth/puberty-blockers.php

Sexuality and Social Justice: A Toolkit (2016). *Sexuality, Poverty and Law.* Retrieved from spl.ids.ac.uk/sexuality-and-social-justice-toolkit

Siegel, D. (1999). *The developing mind: How relationships and the brain interact to shape who we are.* New York, NY: Guilford.

Signorile, M. (1996). *Outing yourself.* New York, NY: Fireside.

Silverstein, C. (1991). Psychotherapy and psychotherapists: A history. In C. Silverstein (Ed.), *Gays, lesbians, and their therapists* (pp. 1–14). New York, NY: Norton.

Silverstein, C., & Picano, F. (2004). *The joy of gay sex: Revised and expanded* (3rd ed.). New York, NY: HarperCollins.

Slater, S. (1995). *The lesbian family life cycle.* New York, NY: Free Press.

Snow, J. (2013, June 20). "Ex-gay" ministry apologizes to LGBT community, shuts down. *MetroWeekly.*

Socarides, C. (1968). *The overt homosexual.* New York, NY: Grune and Stratton.

Solomon, M., & Siegel, D. (2003). *Healing trauma: Attachment, mind, body, and brain.* New York, NY: Norton.

Stacey, J., & Biblarz, T. J. (2001). (How) does the sexual orientation of parents matter? *American Sociological Review, 66,* 159–183.

Stewart, E. F. (2002, Summer). Hot man on man action (and the lesbians who love watching it). *In the Family,* 13–14.

Straight Spouse Network (www.ssnetwk.org)

Sue, Derald Wing (2010). *Microaggressions in Everyday Life: Race, Gender, and Sexual Orientation.* Wiley. pp. xvi.

Take Our Renewed Pledge. (n.d.) It Gets Better Project. Retrieved from http://www.itgetsbetter.org/page/s/pledge/.

Tando, D. (2016. *Gender blog.* Retrieved from darlenetandogenderblog.com/2015/01/19/persistent-consistent-insistent/

Taormino, T. (2008). *Opening up: A guide to creating and sustaining open relationships*. Berkeley, CA: Cleis Press.

van der Kolk, B. (1996). The complexity of adaptation to trauma: Self-regulation, stimulus discrimination, and characterological development. In B. van der Kolk, A. C. McFarlane, & L. Weisaeth (Eds.), *Traumatic stress: The effects of overwhelming experience on mind, body and society* (pp. 182–213). New York, NY: Guilford.

Vanderbilt University School of Medicine (2017). Key transgender health concerns. Retrieved from medschool.vanderbilt.edu/lgbti/key-transgender-health-concerns

Vencill, J. A., & Wiljamaa, S. J. (2016, March). From MOM to MORE: Emerging research on mixed orientation relationships. *Current Sex Health Reports*.

Ward, J. (2015). *Not gay: Sex between straight white men*. New York, NY: NYU Press.

Weinberg, G. (1983). *Society and the healthy homosexual*. New York, NY: St. Martins.

Weinrich, J. D., Klein, F., McCutchan, A., Grant, I., & the HNRC Group (2014). Cluster analysis of the Klein sexual orientation grid in clinical and nonclinical samples: When bisexuality is not bisexuality. *Journal of Bisexuality, 14*(3–4), 349–372. doi:10.1080/15299716.2014.938398, www.ncbi.nlm.nih.gov/pmc/articles/PMC4267693/

Welcome to the Family Acceptance Project (n.d.) Family Acceptance Project. Retrieved from https://familyproject.sfsu.edu/.

Wilson, G., & Rahman, Q. (2005). *Born gay: The psychobiology of sex orientation*. London, England: Peter Owen.

WPATH SOC (2001). World Professional Association for Transgender Health, standards of care, version 7. Retrieved from www.wpath.org/

Wright, D. (2000). Illusions of intimacy. In J. Cassese (Ed.), *Gay men and childhood sexual trauma: Integrating the shattered self* (pp. 117–126). Binghamton, NY: Harrington Park.

Zur, O. (2007). *Boundaries in psychotherapy: Ethical and clinical explorations*. Washington, DC: American Psychological Association.

Index

avoidance, chronic trauma and, 75
avoidant attachment style, 105
avoidant personality disorder, effects of
  covert cultural sexual abuse resem-
  bling, 273, 278

Baker, G., 407
Baker, J. M., 39, 103
barebacking, 396
  circuit parties and, 110
  cutting behavior and, 92
  defined, 403
bargaining
  family reaction after child comes out
  and, 161, 168
  loss of heterosexual privilege and, 141
Barr, R., 114
Barret, R. L., 185
Barron, N., 112
bathhouses
  defined, 403
  drugs popular at, 408–9
  gay, 212
BDSM, sexual play and, 298, 390
beach test
  men deciding if they are straight or
  not, 376
  women deciding if they are straight
  or not, 378
bear, defined, 403
beard, 396
  defined, 406
Becoming Gay (Isay), 11, 36
Beemyn, G., 332
behavior
  difference between sexual orientation,
  fantasy, and, 132
  sexual abuse and influence on, 69
  sexual. *see* sexual behaviors
Being Homosexual (Isay), 11
being "outed," intense fear of, 82

belonging
  LGBTQ teens and sense of, 294, 320
  self-worth and sense of, 117–18
Berzon, B, 21
Berzon, B., 216
Besen, W., 14, 15
betrayal bonds, teaching clients about,
  115
Beyond Acceptance, 174
biases, knowing your own, 179–85
biattractional tendencies, core sexual
  identity and, 132
bi-curious, defined, 400
Bieber, I., 6, 7, 11
"Big Lie, The: Debunking Lesbian Bed
  Death" (Iasenza), 196
bigotry
  trans children and, 352
  transgender people and, 330
*Billion Wicked Thoughts, A: What the
  Internet Tells Us About Sexual Relationships* (Ogas & Gaddam), 191
Bilodeau, B., 372
biology, sexual orientation and, 3
biphobia, 364
  within gay and lesbian community,
  361, 365
  internalized, 372
  sex addiction treatment and, 202
  see also homophobia; transphobia
bipolar disorder, behavior of individuals
  in Stage 5 of coming out and, 143
bipolar/hypomanic disorders, effects of
  covert cultural sexual abuse resem-
  bling, 273, 280–82
"bisexual adolescence," 262, 372–73
bisexual client, 359–74
  internalized biphobia and, 372
  questions for, regarding self-identification, 359–60, 363, 369
  range of issues to talk about with, 373

Lowen, L., 239
LTR, as term of endearment, 402

magnified family dynamics
    after child comes out, 164, 168
    case studies, 164–69
Mailman School of Public Health
    (Columbia University), 293
male bonding, constraints on, 382
male escorts, 100, 101
male/female roles, gay and lesbian rela-
    tionships and, 215
male privilege, 362
males, punishing for nontraditional
    male behavior, 43. *see also* men
male sexual fluidity, female sexual flu-
    idity *vs.*, 382–88
male to female transition, difficulties
    in, 332
Maltz, W., 54
Malyon, A., 20, 21
man crush, 387
Manilow, B., 212
marital therapy, 172
masculine lesbians, internalized
    homophobia about, 126–27
masturbation
    "compulsive," 206
    gay men and, 187
Mating in Captivity (Perel), 196
McCutchan, A., 368
McNaught, B., 36, 71, 78
"meat rack," in gay bars, 138
medical insurance companies,
    gender-variant adult clients, and
    letters for, 334–36
men
    bisexuality and, 367
    fetishes and, 208
    gay, bisexual, and straight, sexual
        behaviors and, 188

hetero-emotional, homosexual, 251,
    252
porn practices and, 189, 190, 191
stereotypical behaviors of, 214
understanding sexual orientation of,
    guidelines for, 376–77
see also bisexual men; gay men; hetero-
    sexual men; straight men; trans men
men who have sex with men (MSM)
    gay men *vs.*, 133
    renaming behaviors and feelings, 256
    ruling out, identity confusion and,
        132–33
merging, in lesbian relationships,
    229–31
microaggressions, 53, 85
    "a couple is a couple" belief and, 214
    anti-LGBTQ, 319
    in asking questions about lesbian and
        gay sexual behaviors, 187
    coining of term, 31
    as inherent to covert cultural sexual
        abuse, 54, 55
    LGBTQ children and, 44
    screening yourself for, 37
    toward African Americans, examples
        of, 31–32
    toward LGBTQ individuals, exam-
        ples of, 32
    transphobia and, 329–30
Midler, B., 212
millennials, sexual fluidity and, 178
minority families, as united minority,
    153–54
"minority stress," LGBTQ teens and,
    292, 293, 295
misandry, lesbians and, 114–15
misdiagnosis, 273
misogyny
    gay men and, 110–11
    as gender-neutral, 114

puberty
    discovering if you are gay, lesbian, or
        trans during, 351–52
    hormone-induced, second adoles-
        cence, and, 345–46
    trans men and onset of, 333
    trans women and onset of, 333
puberty blockers, parents' dilemma
    around, 352–53
puberty suppressors, trans women and,
    332
purging, 342

queeny, defined, 404
queer
    defined, 399–400
    use of term, 397
*Queer Blues: The Lesbian and Gay Guide
    to Overcoming Depression* (Hardin
    & Hull), 280
questioning, defined, 401

racial identity, coming-out discrepancy
    and, 224
rainbow flag, defined, 407–8
Rankin, S., 332
rape, 54
    male victims of, 82–83
Raphael, L., 35
reactive depression (adjustment disor-
    ders), 274
Real, T., 43, 234
"reclaimed" terms, 397–98
Reddit, 353
reframing, coming-out discrepancy
    and, 226
"refrigerator moms," 4
relational integrity, coming-out discrep-
    ancy and, 225
relationship satisfaction, in gay and
    lesbian couples *vs.* in heterosexual
    couples, 216–17

religion, reparative therapies and, 15
religious and spiritual abuse, 45–48
religious beliefs, homosexuality and,
    135, 258, 260
religious families, becoming more reli-
    gious, after child comes out, 162
religious groups, LGBTQ-friendly, 46
religious identity, coming-out discrep-
    ancy and, 224
renaming behaviors and feelings, mar-
    rying heterosexually and, 256
Renn, K. A., 372
rental properties, discrimination against
    gays and, 89
rent boy, 101
    defined, 404
reparative therapy, 1, 2, 4, 8, 13, 15,
    135, 202, 307
    client vulnerability to, 134
    common concepts in, 15
    development of, 14
    gender confusion causes homosexual-
        ity belief in, 61
    parentm s wanting to send child
        into, 162
    transference and harmful practices of,
        62
    trauma associated with, 17
repressed memories, coming-out pro-
    cess and, 150
repression, as dysfunctional coping
    mechanism, 94–96
resistance, coming-out discrepancy and,
    224
resources for clients, not offering, 26
responsibility, 122–24
responsible nonmonogamy, 269, 270
restrictive socialization messages,
    LGBTQ children and, 49
restrooms at school, very young trans
    child and, 350, 351
rice queen, defined, 404